16,00

BAD, MAD OR GOD?

JOHN REDFORD

Bad, Mad or God?

Proving the Divinity of Christ from St John's Gospel

"For surely, if he were not God,
he would be no good man either, since he
plainly said he was God."

Thomas More, *Dialogue of Comfort Against Tribulation*, 1535

ST PAULS

Nihil Obstat:
Rev. John Henry, M.Th., L.S.S.
Imprimatur:
The Most Rev. Kevin McDonald,
Archbishop of Southwark. B.A., S.T.L., S.T.D.

The Nihil Obstat and Imprimatur are official declarations that a
book or pamphlet is free of doctrinal or moral error. No implication
is contained therein that those who have granted the Nihil Obstat
of Imprimatur agree with the contents, opinions or statements
expressed.

ST PAULS Publishing
187 Battersea Bridge Road, London SW11 3AS, UK
www.stpauls.ie

Copyright © ST PAULS UK 2004

ISBN 085439 694 2

First published 2004. Reprinted 2005.

Set by Tukan DTP, Fareham, UK
Printed by Interprint Ltd., Marsa, Malta

ST PAULS is an activity of the priests and brothers
of the Society of St Paul who proclaim the Gospel
through the media of social communication.

CONTENTS

ACKNOWLEDGEMENTS

To acknowledge all the help I have been given in writing this book would necessitate writing the story of my life, at least since I first studied the Greek text of St John's Gospel in 1959, using the admirable commentary by C.K. Barrett which has been a lifelong companion, and even further back when as a teenager I was first convinced by the Bad, Mad or God apologetic so ably expressed by C.S. Lewis.

But I must especially thank my Ordinary for more than a quarter of a century, the Most Rev. Michael Bowen, Archbishop *Emeritus* of Southwark. When I finished my term as lecturer at St John's Seminary, Wonersh, he gave me a sabbatical year in 1982 to pursue my initial ideas about the *Quest of the Historical Jesus*. Then, in 2000, when I had been given new impetus in my researches by reading N.T. Wright's *Jesus and the Victory of God*, he supported the then President of the Maryvale Institute Archbishop Maurice Couve de Murville and its then Director Mgr. Daniel McHugh in their kindness in giving me a six-month sabbatical in Paris at L'Institut Catholique. He continued to believe that my work was worth pursuing, even when many others, I am sure, were convinced that it was yet another wreck on the shore of abandoned theses.

I must also thank Jack Scarisbrick, Professor *Emeritus* of History, Warwick University, who spent many months working through the initial edition with me, which was more than twice the length of the present book, and giving invaluable advice. I would like also to thank all those eminent scholars of diverse biblical, historical, philosophical and theological disciplines who have encouraged me in this project; Fr Paul Watson, Director of the Maryvale Institute, Terry Tekippe,

Michael Mullins, Bishop Martin Drennan, Francis Clark, John Henry, Caroline Farey, Cardinal Avery Dulles, Bill Redmond, Michael Hodgetts, Maurice Hogan, John McDade, Petroc Willey, Richard Conrad, Aidan Nichols, Daniel Rees, Henry Wansbrough, Michael Green, Robert Ignatius Letellier, John Orme Mills, Stratford Caldecott, Ulrika Yeomans; and especially my colleague Andrew Beards and his wife Tina, who read the text as I wrote it chapter by chapter.

I would like to thak the many students of the B.A. (Divinity) programme here at Maryvale, who for the past ten years have patiently endured my lectures on the historical Jesus at residential weeks and weekends. Without their perceptive questions and views, and stimulating interest, this book would not have carried through its argument.

I also thank especially, Maria Yatsiv and Dzvenyslawa Soviak, Maryvale theology graduates, who gave me the beautiful book of Ukrainian icons from which the front cover picture was taken: and I thank the author of that book for kindly allowing its reproduction.

Finally, I would like to thank St Pauls Publishing staff, especially Fr Andrew Pudussery and Annabel Robson, Teresa Rees who typeset the work, Mary Bull my assistant who worked so hard on the index and proofreading, and the B.A. Secretary Ann Weston, who helped with the large correspondence connected with this work.

I must acknowledge many peoples' help; but my work must be judged on its own merits. Whatever the limitations of this book, I have striven to follow the advice of my late scripture Professor at Wonersh, Peter Giffin, S.T.L., L.S.S. He gave two commandments for sound biblical exegesis: "Read the text", and "Use your common sense". That, I submit, I have done.

To my mother Kathleen, R.I.P.,
who first taught me to believe the Gospel

Part One
The State of the Question

INTRODUCTION:
THE FAITH OF CHRISTIANS

A notice on the Baptist Church in Stafford, Christmas 2001, proclaimed "There is one Church, and One Lord Jesus Christ. Come and worship him."

As a Roman Catholic, I would have some theological disagreements with Baptist Christians. Those disagreements are not minimal. But they pale into insignificance in comparison with what we have in common. The Baptist invites me to worship One Lord Jesus Christ. I could accept that invitation together with all the main line Christian denominations.[1] The most distinctive Christian doctrine is that a Jewish male called Jesus of Nazareth, who lived in the Roman Province of Syria, in present-day Israel or Palestine, and who was crucified by the Roman Governor Pontius Pilate some time between 26 and 36 AD, was none other than God the Son Incarnate come to bring a final message of salvation to the human race.

This is not only the most clearly distinctive doctrine of Christianity, together with the parallel and implicit faith that God is in nature Father, Son, and Spirit, Jesus of Nazareth being truly the "second person of the blessed Trinity". It is also the most astounding thought possible, that the Creator of the universe should for any reason wish to become a creature in his own creation, and share human life as a baby, as a growing boy, and as an adult man, even accepting a criminal's death.

The story

In a crowded Jerusalem Temple courtyard, a prophet was preaching his last sermon, on the Feast of Tabernacles. He was summoning his own people, the Jews, to fulfil their destiny as God's people, to lead the world in understanding the Torah, God's ways. But they first would have to follow him, become his disciples, and join that motley group of Galileans, fishermen, tax collectors, even women of easy virtue, who had followed him around the north; encouraged by that rebel preacher and ascetic John the Baptist (eventually executed by King Herod) who had proclaimed the One to Come, and to baptise with the Spirit and with fire. They had been taken in by this prophet's miracles of healing, even stories about his walking on the Sea of Galilee and feeding five thousand people with five loaves and two fish! These spectacular activities combined with his powerful preaching, which pandered to the popular taste by berating the Pharisees, scribes, and wealthy Sadducees.

But the people in the Temple courtyard for the feast were not taken in. They thought he was blaspheming, taking the place of God. He was shouting out "I am the Light of the World". Who was he to say that *he himself* was the Torah, the Law? He was saying "Before Abraham was, I AM". Who was he to say that he existed before their father Abraham? He was saying "I and the Father are One". Who was he to say that he was One with God? After all, the creed of Israel, the *Sh'mah* said "Hear, O Israel: The LORD is our God, the Lord is One". Who was he to say that he shared in the unity of the one God? That was sheer blasphemy, uttered in God's own holy place.

That prophet himself knew that he would die for saying this. They had tried to stone him to death for blasphemy before. He had forbidden his disciples to take up arms in his cause, but on previous occasions he had escaped his punishment without any skirmish.

Jesus knew that he had to make a last appeal. They would understand when they had, as he himself had said, "lifted him up", after he was crucified and God had vindicated him by raising him from the dead, that he truly was the One come to save his people. But it was not possible for them to believe all this yet. Now he faced a terrible death by crucifixion, because the high priestly party probably would no longer be content with stoning him This would be an unofficial exercise of Sanhedrin authority while Pilate, the Roman Prefect, looked the other way. Normally, what would it matter to Pilate if one more miserable Jew died anyway? But in this case, to avoid possible riot by these Galileans and an increasing number of gullible Judeans (after the man Lazarus, dead for three days, walked out of his tomb alive, with Jesus shouting out "Come out, Lazarus!"), it would have to be an official Roman execution.

Forty years later, in 70 AD, those same Romans marched into that very temple courtyard, killing, raping and pillaging, to crush a Jewish revolt. They went into the temple itself, the holy of holies, carrying off the seven-branch candlestick mentioned in the Torah to join the triumphal procession in Rome together with captured Jews. The temple itself would never be used again for sacrifice, even to this day. Jesus himself had prophesied that the temple would be destroyed, but for him and for God that would not matter. The whole history of the Jewish people was of temples and holy places being destroyed and rebuilt. He, Jesus, would raise a new one. Saying that was also close to blasphemy, for who could build a new temple without a specific mandate from God himself?

The same day that the Romans entered Jerusalem to destroy the temple, forty years after his death by crucifixion, Jesus' own temple was itself rising up out of the ashes. The new Christian community had already spread throughout the Roman Empire like wildfire, largely thanks to the dynamic preaching and church-founding of a Pharisaic Jew, Paul of Tarsus. Those Christians believed that Jesus was truly God the Son as he had claimed in that temple courtyard. They believed that his tomb had been found empty on that first Sunday after his crucifixion, that Jesus himself had appeared to his disciples bodily, and now was ruling in heaven with God his Father. They needed no temple building. They could celebrate their services in their own houses, making memorial of that one sacrifice for them made by Jesus to God his Father and in the Spirit he had left them.

According to Christian tradition handed on by Irenaeus a second-century church father, this story was recorded by one of Jesus' closest disciples, a Galileean Jew called Johanan Ben Zebedee. Christians call him John the Evangelist. He wanted future generations to share his faith.

What I have just narrated is the most amazing story in the history of the human race. But since 1778, thanks to an Enlightenment philosopher-playwright and a philologist from Hamburg, it has also become a thesis needing to be proved. Hence this book.

CHAPTER 1

A NEW LOOK AT AN OLD ARGUMENT

The thesis to be proved:

- **Jesus of Nazareth claimed to be God.**
- **He therefore could not have just been a "good man".**
- **If he was not God, he would have been either bad or mad.**
- **He was demonstrably neither bad, nor was he mad.**
- **Therefore he must have been whom he claimed to be, God the Son sent to save us and give us the life of God;**
- **as demonstrated by his life, his teaching, his miracles, and above all by his bodily Resurrection from the dead.**
- **He is therefore worthy of our faith and worship.**

Can we "prove" the Incarnation?

Many Christians today, whether scholar or lay, would consider that trying to "prove" the divinity of the historical Jesus is at best a tendentious and at worst a blasphemous enterprise. After all, does not Paul assert "no one can say 'Jesus is Lord' except by the Holy Spirit." [1 Corinthians12:3]? Only by faith, surely, can we say with doubting Thomas who saw the risen Jesus "My Lord and my God" [John 20:28]. How can we prove what we can only believe?

However, while faith in Jesus is indeed a gift of God, this in no way dispenses with the need for historical proof, since such faith is in the Word who became flesh [John 1:14] in a particular time and a particular place. The Acts of the Apostles, sometimes called the "Gospel of the Holy Spirit", while emphasising the descent of that Spirit on the apostles at Pentecost, Chapter 2, yet states "After his (Jesus') suffering he presented himself alive to them by many convincing proofs,[2] appearing to them during forty days and speaking about the kingdom of God." [Acts 1:3]. An intelligent adult questioning that faith in a sceptical age will naturally feel the need to test the validity of these "proofs" from a position many generations after those first Christians.

The First Vatican Council met in 1870 to counter what the Bishops saw as the errors of growing materialism and secularism. Having already stated that faith is a supernatural gift and is beyond reason, their Lordships then balance this statement by insisting that there is an investigative process, with the assistance of the Holy Spirit, whereby the human mind attains reasonable certainty of the fact that divine revelation has occurred:

> Nevertheless, in order that the submission of our faith should be in accordance with reason, it was God's will that there should be linked to the internal assistance of the holy Spirit outward indications of his revelation, that is to say divine facts (*facta divina*), and first and foremost miracles and prophecies, which clearly demonstrating as they do the omnipotence and infinite knowledge of God, are the most certain signs of revelation and are suited to the understanding of all.[3]

It is such an investigative process with which we are engaged in this book. The *Concise Oxford Dictionary* defines "prove" as to "demonstrate the truth of by evidence or argument".[4] That is precisely what I intend to do in this book; to attempt to demonstrate the truth of Christian belief that Jesus is truly God become man for our salvation, using the evidence from the four Gospels, but most of all from the Fourth. Some will naturally also question whether the Fourth Gospel has the value of historical evidence. Thus at the same time my task will be to indicate how and in what sense a document of faith written nearly two millenia ago can be valid historical evidence, and indeed is so.

Bad, Mad or God? The proof set out

That, as Gerald O'Collins explains, was the standard apologetic argument of the twentieth century for the doctrine of the Incarnation:

In the twentieth century, G.K. Chesterton (d.1936) and, even more clearly C.S. Lewis (d.1963)[5] developed a 'bad', 'mad' or '(Son of) God' argument. The claims Jesus made to an authority that has to be acknowledged as divine, leaves us with three possibilities: he was morally and religiously wicked; or he was out of his mind; or his claims were true and he genuinely was the Son of God come among us. At the end of the first century AD, John's Gospel presents a similar choice in Jesus' controversy with his critics; either Jesus is a 'liar', or he is unbalanced and 'has a demon', or else he is truly the divine 'Light of the world'. (John 8:13-52)[6]

This argument, of course, was not only used in modern times. We have quoted in our title page St Thomas More "For surely, if he were not God, he would be no good man either, since he plainly said he was God". [7] More wrote this book during his final imprisonment in the Tower of London, before his execution by Henry VIII in 1535 for refusing to accept the King as the Head of the Church of England. More shows that the "bad, mad or God" argument could be developed from any intelligent reading of the Gospel of John, assuming its essentially historical character.

- Jesus of Nazareth claimed to be God.

First, this old apologetic stated that Jesus claimed to be God, and was not just a good man. Jesus said things like "before Abraham was, I AM" [John 8:58] and "I and the Father are one" [John 10:30].

- He therefore could not have just been a "good man".

The argument continues: a good man could not claim to be God if he was not actually God. He would either be a liar, in which case he was bad. Or he was deceiving himself, in which case he would be mad. This was the reaction in St John's Gospel to Jesus' extraordinary teaching "The Jews answered him, 'Are we not right in saying that you are a Samaritan and

19

have a demon?'" [John 8:48] So also "Many of them were saying, 'He has a demon and is out of his mind. Why listen to him?'" [John 10:20]

• He was demonstrably neither bad, nor was he mad.

In Jesus' own time, there were those who said that he could not have been either bad or mad, because of his extraordinary gifts. "Others were saying, "These are not the words of one who has a demon. Can a demon open the eyes of the blind?" [John 10:21] Nor does he appear in the Gospels to have been a man lacking integrity or sense.[8]

• Therefore he must have been whom he claimed to be, God the Son sent to save us and give us the life of God.

Most recently, Stephen T. Davis has revisited the argument "Was Jesus Bad, Mad or God?" (which he abbreviates to BMG), and tested out its logic.[9] He finds that, if Jesus did either explicitly or implicitly claim divinity, BMG stands up logically. We must, on the other hand, be clear as to where the strength of this argument lies. It would be hardly credible to put it this way: "Jesus claimed to be God. He was neither bad, nor was he mad. Therefore he must have been God". However logical that might seem to be, it would not be convincing to present only *a negative proof* for that man's divinity, that he was neither bad nor mad. Note that Thomas More puts it the other way round: "For surely, if he were not god, he would be no good man either, since he plainly said he was God". Jesus would clearly *not* have been God if he were proven to be either bad or mad, and by the same token, he would not have been a good man either. Certainly, if Jesus had claimed to be God, and was demonstrably neither bad nor mad, then there would be a clear *prima facie* case for investigating whether or not his extraordinary claims had any substance. It might even be difficult to imagine any other possibility, granted that he was neither bad nor mad, but that he was in some sense or other divine. But to prove himself beyond any doubt to be what he claimed to be, God, he would surely have to produce some more positive reasons to back up his claims; as, in the account of the Gospel of John, he does.

• as demonstrated by his life, his teaching, his miracles, and above all by his bodily Resurrection from the dead.

For John, the miracles of Jesus are "works" (*erga*), linking with the creative activity of God, which demonstrate that "the Father Himself may be said to perform Jesus' works".[10] It is because Jesus works the works of the Father that his hearers see this as a claim to be "equal with God" [John 5:18].[11] This claim of Jesus to do the works of the Father is seen itself as blasphemy by Jesus' Jewish hearers. In the Fourth Gospel account, Jesus says "'The Father and I are one.' The Jews took up stones again to stone him. Jesus replied, 'I have shown you many good works from the Father. For which of these are you going to stone me?' The Jews answered, 'It is not for a good work that we are going to stone you, but for blasphemy, because you, though only a human being, are making yourself God.'" [John 10:32-33]

Even more, Jesus' resurrection appearance bodily to doubting Thomas through the closed doors of the room in Jerusalem where the apostles were huddling in fear after his death, leads to Thomas' famous confession of faith "My Lord and my God". [John 20:28] R.E. Brown, the author of perhaps the best and certainly the most serviceable twentieth-century commentary on John, quotes the scholarly consensus that the evangelist intends us to see Thomas' confession as "a reference to Jesus and not merely an exclamation in honour of God the Father".[12]

• He is therefore worthy of our faith and worship.

The writer of St John's Gospel clearly intends the reader of his work to share the same faith as Thomas, and put away any doubts. In response to Thomas' confession of Jesus' divinity, the Lord replies:

> "Have you believed because you have seen me? Blessed are those who have not seen and yet have come to believe."
> Now Jesus did many other signs in the presence of his

21

disciples, which are not written in this book. But these are written so that you may come to believe that Jesus is the Messiah, the Son of God, and that through believing you may have life in his name. [John 20:29-31]

It is the almost unanimous conclusion of the scholars that this represents the original conclusion of the Fourth Gospel, and that Chapter 21 was added by the hand of a later editor (called "redactor" in academic biblical terminology[13]), or at least possibly added later by the same author as the rest of the Gospel. In any case, the summons to faith by the author of the Fourth Gospel after the confession of the apostle Thomas in the divinity of Christ gives us a powerful climax to his story, and an even more powerful challenge to all subsequent generations to believe that this Jesus is truly worthy of our faith and worship, in order to receive the gift of eternal life.

The Myth of God Incarnate and The Jesus Seminar

If we are to attempt to "prove" the Incarnation, quite obviously many difficulties will present themselves, for instance whether the idea of God becoming human is logically coherent, and whether it is possible to demonstrate that miracles occur. But first, an even more fundamental problem presents itself, particularly since the rise of the biblical critical movement. How reliable is the evidence we have from the Gospel of John that Jesus did in fact claim to be divine? As O'Collins explains, the validity of the bad, mad or God argument depends first and foremost essentially upon the historical character of the Gospel account:

> The most controversial element in this 'mad, bad or Son of God' argument is undoubtedly its point of departure. Can we verify that Jesus, at least by implication, claimed an authority and identity that were truly divine?[14]

During the last quarter of the twentieth century, some theologians and biblical scholars both in Britain and in the

United States of America challenged the traditional Christian doctrine that Jesus Christ was truly God become Man for our salvation. Their principal reason was that the historical Jesus never made such divine claims for himself. Their scepticism was based largely upon their negative historical assessment of the Gospel of John, attributed traditionally to one of the disciples of Jesus, John the Son of Zebedee, where the full divinity of Christ is most clearly expressed.

This way precisely was taken by John Hick, the editor of the British symposium *The Myth of God Incarnate*, published in 1977. Hick, in the leading article of that symposium, raises the whole question as to whether in this day and age the concept of God becoming incarnate in Jesus is still intelligible, and perhaps whether Christianity itself needs the doctrine of the Incarnation any more.[15] For him, the key question is that of the historical reliability of the Fourth Gospel:

> ...the later stages of that development (i.e. the early Christian development of the doctrine of the Incarnation) were greatly influenced by the evidence of the Fourth Gospel understood in a straightforwardly historical way. How else could one interpret a Jesus who said 'Before Abraham was, I am' and 'I and my Father are one'? As I was still being taught in my confirmation class, such a Jesus must be either 'mad, bad or God'. But if the Fourth Gospel is understood in a less straightforwardly historical way (as on general critical grounds I believe it has to be) then its implications for doctrine may prove to be somewhat different from what they appeared to earlier ages to be.[16]

A similar link between scepticism regarding the Incarnation and scepticism concerning the historicity of the Fourth Gospel was made by a group of American scholars who led what they call the *Jesus Seminar* in the United States, which also attracted some media attention.[17] In 1985, thirty scholars accepted an invitation to lead a Seminar together with "more than 200 professionally trained specialists".[18] The Seminar then took a poll of views on which words attributed to Jesus had actually been said by him, and what had been added later by the

Church. The participants dropped coloured beads into a box to signify whether they considered this or that saying consisted of Jesus' own words, or were probably more or less his or expressed ideas close to his.

The verdict of the *Jesus Seminar* on the historical Jesus in the Gospel of John was less than favourable. Not only the Jesus saying in John 8:58 "Before Abraham was, I AM" would be judged inauthentic. Virtually all the words attributed to Jesus in the Fourth Gospel were black coded;[19] that is to say, came under the heading, "Jesus did not say this; it represents the perspective or content of a later or different tradition."[20]

According to the *Jesus Seminar*, therefore, the Fourth Gospel contains virtually nothing which even approximates to what Jesus said. It is not just that John's Gospel re-wrote the words of Jesus in the evangelist's own words while nonetheless faithfully recording Jesus' teaching, but according to the meaning that Jesus originally gave them. That would maintain the substantial accuracy of John; a position which we will attempt to maintain in this book. According to the *Jesus Seminar*, that would be either pink or grey beads. No; according to the *Jesus Seminar*, St John's Gospel deliberately misleads us about the historical Jesus, i.e. what he really said and did during his life on earth. John's Gospel, the *Jesus Seminar* claims, is patently untrue. It replaces the historical Jesus with the mythical Jesus of the Christian Creed:

> *I believe in God the Father almighty.*
> *Creator of heaven and earth,*
> *I believe in Jesus Christ, God's only Son, our Lord,*
> *who was conceived by the Holy Spirit, born of the*
> *Virgin Mary.*
> *suffered under Pontius Pilate, was crucified, died,*
> *and was buried; he descended to the dead.*
> *On the third day he rose again;*
> *he ascended into heaven, he is seated at the right hand*
> *of the Father, and he will come again to judge the living*
> *and the dead.*[21]

How can we continue to believe this mythology about Jesus, say the *Jesus Seminar*, when the historical Jesus never said anything like this? We have an equally radical point made by Maurice Casey, invited to give the Cadbury Lectures in Birmingham in the autumn of 1985. He entitled his lectures *From Jewish Prophet to Gentile God.*[22] For Casey, "The Gospel attributed to John is the only New Testament document in which the deity and incarnation of Jesus are unequivocally proclaimed".[23] In this, Casey insists, the Fourth Gospel is entirely fictional. This Incarnational faith in John, for Casey, corresponds in no way to what the historical Jesus believed about himself. For Casey also, as for Hick, this has serious implications for Christian faith itself:

> "If the standard picture of Jesus as incarnate and divine is too much a part of the churches' identity to be shifted, official Christianity will become increasingly a matter of belief in the impossible, as its evangelical and catholic wings may already be thought to be."

For these scholars, therefore, the reliable historical information which we can actually glean about Jesus does not justify our faith in Jesus as God become man. The historical Jesus was a Jewish prophet, they would claim. Christianity mythologised Jesus into making him the Son of God. To this extent, therefore, these scholars would maintain that they have disproved the Incarnation historically; or at least, that traditional proofs regarding the Incarnation have been undermined by the historical evidence. Pope John Paul II's confidence, therefore, in that "there is no doubt that already in his historical existence Jesus was aware of his identity as the Son of God"[24] is, according to these scholars, without historical justification. Jesus was in fact a Jewish prophet divinised by Christian faith.

Is John to be trusted?

Such scepticism regarding the Incarnation among academics, many of them in prestigious posts in Christian theology departments in Britain and in the USA, must cause some anxiety among orthodox Christians. It will not take long for faith in the divinity of Christ among lay Christians to be undermined, if it has not already begun to be so.

As we have seen, the main reason for such a challenge to the traditional doctrine of the Incarnation has been doubts regarding the historical reliability of the Fourth Gospel. Such doubts do seem to be general in the world of scholarship, even among those who would themselves fully accept the traditional Christian belief that Jesus of Nazareth was truly God become Man.

On the one hand, modern biblical scholars are by no means entirely negative concerning the historical worth of the Fourth Gospel. Theissen and Merz insist that although the Gospel of John "is the most stylised on the basis of theological premises... Nevertheless, the Gospel of John, which is independent of the Synoptics, is not worthless. At some usually quite emphatic places it hands down data which diverge from the Synoptics, and can go back to old traditions."[25] One example given of this early reliable and independent historical tradition given by Theissen and Merz is that the disciples of Jesus were formerly disciples of John the Baptist [John 1:35]. We may add the famous example that Jesus only goes up to Jerusalem once in the Synoptic tradition cf. Matthew, Mark, and Luke; [cf. Matthew 16:21] while in John, Jesus goes up to Jerusalem three times: [John 2:13, 5:1,7:10]. Many scholars think that in this matter at least John is more likely to be correct.

But modern criticism, as we will see more clearly as this book takes its course, will not in general accept the historicity of the Fourth Gospel where John presents a Jesus conscious of himself as divine. Theissen and Merz present the consensus of criticism in their "Evaluation of the Sources", where they refer to "The unhistorical Johannine picture of Christ". They proclaim that "There are irresolvable contradictions between the Synoptic picture of Jesus and the Johannine Christ", one of those "irresolvable contradictions" being the fact that "in the Gospel of John Jesus is a divine being walking over the earth, the creator of all things who is even aware of his pre-existence. By contrast the Synoptics do not know the idea of pre-existence."[26] Theissen and Merz see this idea of Christ as "the result of a special development which is limited to the Johannine circle..."[27] This "picture of Christ in the Gospel of John" therefore has minimal reference to the historical Jesus for them. Rather, it results from theological development within the Johannine community.

Apologetics without John

This caution regarding the historicity of John's "high" view of Jesus' own awareness of himself as divine has meant that even eminent Christian theologians defending the divinity of Christ have not used the Fourth Gospel as evidence. Typical of such argumentation for the Incarnation is in C.F.D. Moule's approach. Moule does not attempt in *The Origin of Christology* to prove what the historical Jesus actually said and did; or rather, this is not the main point of his argument. He is mainly concerned with showing that the faith of the early Christians, as expressed in the Gospels and in the letters of Paul, was in a Jesus who was clearly unique. For instance, the earliest Christians called Jesus *Kurios*, Lord [Philippians 2:11].

Moule argues that, contrary to Bultmann, the early Christians did not call Jesus *Kurios* only as a result of Hellenisation, moving to consider Jesus as a Greek type mythical god. Rather, use of the Aramaic *mar*, Lord, for Jesus, reveals that early on in Christian thinking, "Our Lord" and comparable phrases "had already been applied in Semitic-speaking regions to a more than human being".[28] After all, claims Moule, "you do not call upon a dead Rabbi to 'come'; and, since it is demonstrably possible for *mar* to signify also a divine or transcendent being, it appears that in this context it must have done so."[29]

Moule therefore is not arguing so much from what Jesus

himself said during his life on earth. He is discussing the implications of what Jesus said and did during his life and on how the earliest Christians reacted by stating their faith in Jesus:

> It is notoriously questionable whether Jesus made any explicit claims for himself. The claims of earliest Christianity were based not, primarily at least, on claims explicitly made by Jesus, but rather on the implications of his life, his actions, his teaching, his death, and, most notably, its extraordinary sequel. And if it was all these factors that led to the Christian estimate of Jesus, then I submit that it is not just a chain of spoken and unverifiable claims that lies behind the claims of earliest Christianity, but historical events demanding evaluation, if not explanation.

> Certainly there is idealisation, if by this is meant the interpretation of historical events in terms of what transcends history and therefore cannot be historically verified, and is not accepted by all alike. The conceptual chain, 'Jesus – Israel – Man', is certainly not accepted by all, and is not self-evident. But it was reached, none the less, not by arbitrary theologising, but by observing, in Jesus, all that is implied in a right relation to God, and finding this clinched by the absolute and irreversible aliveness which (as his disciples believed) belonged to him.[30]

A similar "developmental" approach mapping the progress of Christian faith in the Resurrection of Jesus to faith in his being divine Son of God is to be found in the complex but convincing argumentation of James D.G. Dunn in his *Christology in the Making; An Inquiry into the Origins of the Doctrine of the Incarnation.*[31] But all of these scholars steer clear from any evidence presented in the Fourth Gospel of Jesus' own self-consciousness. Thus they do not use in any shape or form the "Bad, Mad or God?" argument in their apologetic for the Incarnation.

The "development" argument: is it sufficient?

The argument for the divinity of Christ from the developing faith of the early Christians is by no means to be belittled. On the contrary, it must become an essential part of any apologetic for the Incarnation. Most of all, it makes redundant the old critical opinion, prevalent from the nineteenth century onwards, that the concept of the divinity of Christ entered into early Christian thinking from Greek philosophical influence.

This view was first outlined by Willhelm Bousset (1865-1920),[32] of the "history of religion" school, who attempted to apply scientific principles to the study of Christian origins. Bousset was convinced that the worship of Jesus as Lord originated not with the early Palestinian Christian community, but with the Hellenistic converts to Christianity, chief among whom was St Paul. For Bousset, Paul's use of *kurios* in Philippians 2:9-10 would be prime evidence of early Hellenistic Christianity's Kurios worship.

This view is questionable in the extreme. We have already seen C.F.D. Moule[33] question it. The problem with Bousset's claim that Kurios was rooted in Hellenistic soil is, as Michael Green says, that we have its original Aramaic in *Maranatha* [1 Corinthians 16:22]. "The Old Testament was, of course, written in Hebrew not Aramaic (apart from a section of the book of Daniel), but *mara* is a title for God in the Aramaic intertestamental documents that have come to light at Qumran (Aramaic Enoch 9:6; 89:31, 33 and 36 where the Greek has no *Kyrios*). The last plank of the supposed derivation of the deity of Jesus from pagan parallels has proved utterly untrustworthy."[34]

We are led therefore to conclude that the worship of Jesus as God goes back to the first Aramaic-speaking Christians, not to Greek Gentile converts, who began to come into the Christian community in numbers only two decades after the death of Jesus. St Paul, therefore, was only expressing in Hellenistic terms a faith which was already affirmed in very Semitic language prior to his Gentile mission. Bousset's view, which continued to dominate New Testament scholarship in the twentieth century, that the first Christians only viewed Jesus as a Rabbi, the Gentile converts making Jesus into a God, is now well past its sell-by date.

Why give up our best lines?

But this now leads us back to a further question. From whence did those first Aramaic Christians derive their idea that Jesus was *mar*, divine Lord? Those espousing the "developmental" view see the Resurrection of Jesus as the catalyst among the early Christians leading to their worship of him as divine. But the Resurrection in itself would not necessarily lead to faith in Jesus as God, but only in Jesus as vindicated Messiah. And if this apologetic insists that this certainty in the Resurrection of Jesus is combined with the early Christian *experience* of Jesus as God, then this still begs the question as to why such an experience can be rationally justified and is not an illusion, particularly if we cannot demonstrate that Jesus understood himself as divine.

By the same token, many apologetes down the centuries have seen the phenomenal growth of the early Church throughout the hostile Roman Empire as a powerful argument for the truth of its message. No religious movement has grown so rapidly in its early years without military support, indeed, where Christianity is concerned, under fierce persecution. But whereas the success of the early church could be seen as one supporting argument of a convincing apologetic, it cannot so convince without an authentication of the truth of its message. Otherwise, the cause of its early success might be simply attributed to its providing a refuge for unhappy slaves, who made up a considerable portion of its numbers.

Christian apologetics, therefore, cannot avoid the question of Jesus' own consciousness of himself. Brockmuehl has convincingly argued that "the emergence of Christology can be seen as an authentic and consequential expression of the Apostolic faith in the risen Jesus."[35] But is it also a *necessary* development, but rather is it only one of many possible? And if it is only one of many possible interpretations, must we revert to the *Jesus Seminar* and *Myth of God Incarnate* questions, and ask whether it is still a necessary article of faith for orthodox Christians? I submit that doubts as to whether the historical Jesus either knew or proclaimed himself to be fully divine will tend to lead to the question as to whether Christians are still committed to believing in his full divinity.

All admit, therefore, that there must be some foundation for this development in the early church towards a high Christology rooted in the life of the historical Jesus himself. Otherwise, how can we discern those significant events which were interpreted after his Resurrection, and, according to Moule, interpreted rightly by the earliest Christians as reason for calling him Lord, *Kurios*? Obviously, it must be something remarkable. Raymond Brown summarised the post Second World War consensus of New Testament criticism thus; "it seems that an irreducible historical minimum in the Gospel presentation of Jesus is that he claimed to be the unique agent in the process of establishing God's kingship over men."[36] Critical scholars generally agreed that the following text in Luke is authentically from Jesus. (The *Jesus Seminar* gives Luke 11:17-22 the pink bead, "Jesus probably said something like this")[37]:

> Now if I cast out the demons by Beelzebul, by whom do your exorcists cast them out? Therefore they will be your judges. But if it is by the finger of God that I cast out the demons, then the kingdom of God has come to you. [Luke 11:19-20]

But if the historical Jesus can be demonstrated to be only "the unique agent in the process of establishing God's kingship over men", called by some an "eschatological prophet", then the 'baby' is not the same being as the developed post-Resurrection 'man'. The eschatological prophet (the historical Jesus) has become in Christian consciousness God made man. Is this not more like a new species than development?[38] How is this great gap between the human historical Jesus and the divine God of the Christian community to be bridged, and even more to be justified? Such a gap will always reveal

31

itself if the historical Jesus did not actually reveal his divinity during his lifetime.

Why, it will be asked, did Jesus not proclaim this full divinity explicitly during his lifetime if he really was divine? If it is replied that Jewish monotheism would have made such a claim scandalous, then would not the same scandal apply after the death and resurrection of Christ as before it? If it is affirmed that Jesus did not proclaim his divinity during his lifetime because his disciples would have not have been able to accept it, then the objector would reply that he could have revealed his divinity during his lifetime, for his disciples to accept it in faith only after his resurrection. It is not at all inconceivable that some things Jesus revealed during his lifetime, but realised that they would not be understood until after his Resurrection. The Fourth Gospel itself tells us that it was only after the Resurrection that the disciples came to understand what Jesus said during his lifetime about the Temple [John 2:19-21].

This apologetic becomes even more complicated when faced with the fact that the Fourth Gospel tells us that Jesus *did* make such claims during his lifetime; and that document, as we shall see, was written not later than the turn of the second century AD, only two or three generations after the historical Jesus' life. Such an apologetic would then have to say "The Fourth Gospel is fiction. But Jesus was truly what the Fourth Gospel proclaimed him to be, even if the historical Jesus never actually made such a claim." The objector would then in frustration be tempted to say, "If God did reveal himself through this man Jesus his divine Son, he indeed chose a bizarre way to do it."

Surely, at least at first sight, the most obvious and reasonable *apologia* for the Incarnation must be rooted in the historical Jesus himself. If he himself thought he was divine, then this would be the most logical starting point for the development of the idea of the Incarnation in the early church, and the most convincing reason for such an idea to take root. And, as we shall see in what follows, the only early Christian document which sets out unambiguously the claims of Jesus to be fully divine is the Fourth Gospel.

32

The Second Vatican Council professes to speak for Christian tradition in this matter. It says more than that there was an implicit revelation in the life of the historical Jesus. Rather, it seems to affirm that Jesus made an explicit revelation of himself during his lifetime:

> 4. After God had spoken in many and various ways by the prophets, "in these last days he has spoken to us by a Son" (Heb 1, 1-2). He sent his Son, the eternal Word who enlightens all humankind, to live among them and to tell them about the inner life of God (see Jn 1:1-18). Thus it is that Jesus Christ, the Word made flesh, sent as a human being among humans, "speaks the words of God" (Jn 3,34) and accomplishes the work of salvation which the Father gave him to do (see Jn 5,36; 17,4). To see Jesus is to see also his Father (see Jn 14,9). This is why Jesus completes the work of revelation and confirms it by divine testimony. He did this by the total reality of his presence and self-manifestation (*tota suipsius presentia ac manifestatione*)– by his words and works, his symbolic acts and miracles, but above all by his death and his glorious resurrection from the dead, crowned by his sending the Spirit of truth. His message is that God is with us, to deliver us from the darkness of sin and death, and to raise us up to eternal life.[39]

This statement seems to imply, even explicitly to affirm, that Jesus of Nazareth revealed himself and his message *while on this earth*. The Second Vatican Council insists that Jesus as the Incarnate Word revealed himself "by the total reality of his presence and self-manifestation". His miracles, even his resurrection, which was the supreme part of his revelation, was only one aspect of that complete revelation of the incarnate *person* Jesus Christ. But was that manifestation complete if he did not explicitly reveal his divinity by his words as well as by his implicit presence?

I am quoting this text from Vatican II not as an authority (although that document has an authority which I accept as a member of the Roman Catholic communion). Rather, I am offering it to the reader of any persuasion as a statement of what may be described as the unanimous Christian tradition;

that Jesus of Nazareth declared who he was during his life on earth, and confirmed who he was by his miracles, and above all by his Resurrection. His self-revelation was more than implicit, it was explicit. I would suggest that this self-revelation is the best foundation of an incarnational apologetic, a self-revelation which is expressed most clearly in the Fourth Gospel.

That is why, in order to counter the *Myth of God Incarnate* and the *Jesus Seminar* objections to the Incarnation, I would suggest that we might look at more direct arguments than that provided by implicit Christology. Rather, we should look again to see whether the Fourth Gospel, which seems to state so clearly that Jesus saw himself as fully divine, is as devoid of reliable information about the historical Jesus as some would insist.

The way forward – did Jesus say it?

If it could be demonstrated that the Fourth Gospel is historically reliable in reporting that Jesus claimed to be God the Son, that he performed miracles to justify this claim, and that he was put to death because his contemporaries thought him blasphemous in making this claim, then this would be a most powerful historical argument for the Incarnation.

We propose to examine the criteria by which a saying of Jesus is consigned to being that of the primitive Christian community rather than from the historical Jesus. We will contend that, if the possibility of the Incarnation is not denied *a priori*, and if the criteria elaborated in the past two centuries of Gospel criticism are fairly applied, a much more positive estimate regarding the historicity of the Fourth Gospel will result.

There are echoes of this exalted Jesus in the Synoptic tradition. The contrast between the Synoptic tradition and the Johannine is not as great as Theissen and Merz suggest. This book, therefore, will not draw its argument from St John's Gospel alone, but from the totality of the evidence from all four Gospels.

In fact, one could produce at least the beginnings of a bad-mad-or God? argument from Matthew, Mark, and Luke. For example, when some in his own time claimed that he was indeed bad, and that Jesus cast out devils by Beelzebub, the Prince of Devils. Jesus reacted strongly against this accusation [Matthew 12:27]. He was not just a wonder-worker, but demonstrated his goodness in many ways, e.g. by treating outcasts with kindness and by forgiving his persecutors when put to excruciating death on the cross. The Gospels state the truth with the centurion, that the man hanging on the cross behaved not like a bad man at all. [Luke 23:47] "When the centurion saw what had taken place, he praised God and said, 'Certainly this man was innocent'." Likewise, Jesus was not mad. Some, including even his relatives (Mark 3:21), thought that Jesus was "out of his mind". But his teaching as recorded in the Gospels does not show us a madman, but a rational and intelligent man, indeed a sage by any criterion of religious leadership.

But when the Synoptic texts present an exalted Jesus, more than a Jewish prophet, historical Jesus criticism will bring out the black beads, and insist that the historical Jesus never actually made such high claims for himself, but rather the early Christian community put such claims into his mouth unhistorically, for example:

• At the trial of Jesus before the Sanhedrin, according to Mark, the High Priest challenged him a second time after Jesus had been originally silent. The High Priest demands "Are you the Christ, the Son of the Blessed?" (14:61), to which Jesus replies:

> Jesus said, "I am; and 'you will see the Son of Man seated at the right hand of the Power,' and 'coming with the clouds of heaven.'" Then the high priest tore his clothes and said, "Why do we still need witnesses? You have heard his blasphemy! What is your decision?" All of them condemned him as deserving death. [Mark 14:62-64]

But Schillebeeckx[40] is convinced that 'I am; and you will see the Son of man seated at the right hand of the Power, and coming with the clouds of heaven" (Mark14:62) is 'what the post-Easter Church put into Jesus' mouth later on', and not the words of the historical Jesus. For Schillebeeckx, Jesus was condemned for his silence, not for claiming divine power. For him, and for the majority following the post-Bultmannian tradition, Christ's identification of himself as the Son of Man coming with divine power is much too high a Christology to be the words of Jesus himself when he lived on earth.

• Likewise, Bultmann, in treating the miracle story of the man cured from his paralysis after having been let down a hole in the roof of a house, comes to a similar conclusion about Jesus' pronouncement of the forgiveness of the sick man's sins:

> When Jesus saw their faith, he said to the paralytic, "Son, your sins are forgiven." Now some of the scribes were sitting there, questioning in their hearts, "Why does this fellow speak in this way? It is blasphemy! Who can forgive sins but God alone?" [Mark 2:5-7]

Bultmann is certain that "Mk.2.5b-10 has manifestly been given its place because the Church wanted to trace back to Jesus *its* own right to forgive sins."[41] For him, therefore, the whole of 2:5b-10 is a later insertion by the Tradition.

Therefore, wherever a text even comes close to supporting the doctrine of the Incarnation in the words or deeds of the historical Jesus, the critical tradition immediately makes a negative judgement regarding its historicity. Such a saying cannot be the authentic word of the historical Jesus, modern criticism claims, it must be the early Church expressing its faith in the risen Lord.

But how do we know this? How do we know that the historical Jesus was not conscious of himself as divine, and that he revealed this to others during his lifetime on earth? Schweitzer at the end of his *Quest of the Historical Jesus* posed this most radical question of all: "For, after all, why should not Jesus think in terms of doctrine, and make history in action just as well as a poor Evangelist can do it on paper, under the pressure of the theological interests of the primitive community?"[42]

Why not indeed! In our examination of the history of the Quest of the Historical Jesus since Reimarus in 1778, we shall show how German criticism in particular has been driven by an anti-supernaturalist bias, combined with a subjectivist and idealist philosophy. These philosophical tendencies have led to a reduction of the historical Jesus to proportions manageable by rationalism, but not, we will attempt to demonstrate, adequate to what we can actually discover by using historical criteria about what Jesus actually said and did. We shall then attempt to demonstrate that a correct use of these historical criteria leads us to very different conclusions.

NOTES – CHAPTER 1

1   The self-definition of the World Council of Churches, the primary ecumenical association of Christian churches worldwide, states that it is a "fellowship of churches which confess the Lord Jesus as God and Saviour according to the Scriptures and therefore seek to fulfil together their common calling to the glory of the one God, Father, Son, and Holy Spirit". Cf. ODCC, 1499. The WCC consists of representatives of all the major Christian denominations except the Roman Catholic, who nevertheless have a permanent liaison with the WCC, and who are full members of the Faith and Order Commission of the WCC.

2   Greek *tekmériois*, Translated "infallible proofs" by the King James Authorised Version. Cf. ALGT, "a sign, indubitable token, clear proof". Moulton and Milligan, VGT, 628, notes that in classical Greek literature outside of the New Testament, *tekmérion* refers explicitly in medical terms to demonstrative evidence, whereas *sémeion* ("sign") refers to a less scientific form of proof.

3   Tanner, II, *807, Vatican I, Dogmatic Constitution on the Catholic Faith, Chapter III, *de Fide.*

4   COD 962.

5   C.S. Lewis expounded this argument in *Mere Christianity*, New York, Macmillan, 1960, 40-41. Cf. Davis., 221.

6   INC, 2002, 130-131.

7   *Dialogue of Comfort Against Tribulation.* Transl. Monica Stevens, London, Sheed and Ward, 1951, 191

8   Davis, 226.

9   Davis, 221-245.

10 Brown I, 527.

11   Barrett, 256.

12   Brown, II, 1026.

13   In biblical scholarship, the German word *Redakteur* ("Editor") or *Redaktion* ("Edition") is used in an anglicised form *redactor, redaction*, to describe the work of an editor or an editorial process in the writing of a biblical book.

14   INC, 131.

15   There was a rapid and competent reply from the viewpoint of orthodox Christology in the symposium *The Truth of God Incarnate*, edited by Michael Green (TGI).

16   MGI, 4.

17   There is a fierce and sustained attack on the *Jesus Seminar* in Timothy Luke Johnson, *The Real Jesus: The Misguided Quest fot the Historical Jesus and the Truth of the Traditional Gospels*. Harper Collins, San Francisco, 1997, 1-27.

18   FG, 34.

19   Cf. FG 401-470. Only John 4:43b (pink: "Jesus probably said something like this") and 12:24-5 (grey: "Jesus probably did not say this, but the ideas contained in it are close to his own").

20   FG, 36.

21   FG, 7.

22   JPGG, 178.

23   JPGG, 23.

24   As expressed in his encyclical Apostolic Letter *Novo Millenio Ineunte* of His Holiness Pope John Paul II to the Bishops Clergy and Lay Faithful at the Close of the great Jubilee of the Year 2000, para 24b. Vatican, 6 January, 2001.

25   HGCG, 36.

26   HJCG, 96.

27   HJCG, 97.

28   OC, 37.

29   OC, 149.

30   OC, 163.

31   CM.

32   NTHIP, 270.

33   Cf. p. 27.

34   TGI, 39.

35   MLM, 166.

36   CBQ, 1967, 341.

37   FG, 329.

38   OC, 2.

39   DV4. Tanner II, 972-3.

40   JEC, 315.

41   HST.*15-*16.

42   QHJ, 348.

CHAPTER 2

THE BLINKERED *QUEST*

> Critical judgement against the historicity of the Fourth Gospel since the post-eighteenth-century Quest of the Historical Jesus has been influenced by bias against the Incarnation and bias against the possibility of the miraculous.

The Quest begins

It is a common myth of the media that modern historical studies have "proved" the factual unreliability of the Gospels. But the briefest of studies of what has come to be called the "Quest of the Historical Jesus" demonstrates rather that, from its beginning, the Quest assumed what it purported to prove.

The great Albert Schweitzer, from inside the critical movement, admits freely the anti-dogmatic presuppositions of the new Enlightenment Historical Jesus school of Gospel research, in his masterly book *Von Reimarus zu Wrede* (1906), given the English title in its first English edition of 1910 *The Quest of the Historical Jesus: A Critical Study of its Progress from Reimarus to Wrede.* Indeed, Schweitzer is quite prepared to insist that a truly 'historical' investigation into the life of Jesus could not even take place until those who began it had divested themselves of the traditional Christian faith in Jesus Christ as true God become true Man:

> This dogma had to be shattered before men could once more go out in quest of the historical Jesus, before they could even grasp the thought of his existence. That the historic Jesus is something different from the Jesus Christ of the doctrine of the Two Natures seems to us now self-evident.[1]

This systematic opposition to Incarnation and the miraculous began with the eighteenth-century Enlightenment, which

aimed at enthroning reason above all the allegedly superstitious
claptrap of the centuries, liberating the human race from the
bondage of outdated creeds, and, so it claimed, setting it free
for a life of rational virtue.

The religion of the Enlightenment was either Deism,[2]
whose God, remote from his creation, had set the world order
going and then left it to its own devices; or Pantheism,[3]
which identified God with those natural forces. The most
influential early Questers, who both had a huge influence on
modern critical studies, were Reimarus a Deist and Strauss a
Pantheist. It is absurd to think of them as unbiased scientific
researchers. As Schweitzer freely admits, they both wrote
their Lives of Jesus with hate:

> It was not so much hate of the Person of Jesus as of the
> supernatural nimbus with which it was so easy to surround
> Him, and with which He had in fact been surrounded.
> They were eager to picture Him as truly and purely
> human, to strip from Him the robes of splendour with
> which he had been apparelled, and clothe Him once
> more with the coarse garments in which He had walked
> in Galilee.[4]

Schweitzer insists that "their hate sharpened their historical
insight". But, as we shall insist equally strongly, that hatred
has led subsequent New Testament research to become
unjustifiably sceptical concerning the Gospels, and in particular
the Gospel of John.

The Wolfenbüttel bombshell

Herbert Samuel Reimarus was the first Enlightenment scholar
to strip Jesus of his supernatural robes. A professor of Oriental
Languages in Hamburg, Reimarus died in 1768, but not
before he had written a series of Deist works, including a
work denying the possibility "of a Revelation which all
men should have good grounds for believing."[5] The last
volume, after a work denying the supernatural character of

the Resurrection, was entitled *The Aims of Jesus and His disciples.*

Reimarus was too terrified to publish these explosive works himself during his lifetime. But, in 1774, the rationalist philosopher Lessing[6] began to publish his volumes anonymously. By 1778, the seven Wolfenbüttel Fragments, as they came to be called, were published, to the alarm and anger of the Chief Pastor of Hamburg.

Jesus, in this new construction of Reimarus, was a Jewish prophet who believed that he was the Messiah. He did not claim to be the universal Son of God, but only to "establish an earthly kingdom and deliver the people from political oppression. But he failed to perform the miracles necessary to convince all the people." The people deserted him, and he was put to death on the cross as a revolutionary.

How, then, was the Christian religion founded and the Gospels eventually written? For Reimarus, this was the work of the disciples of Jesus. After the ignominious death of Jesus, where their hero had said "My God, my God, why have you forsaken me?" they were not minded to return to fishing. Reimarus claimed: "They did not take kindly to the idea of returning to their old haunts; on their journeyings the companions of the Messiah had forgotten how to work."[7]

The disciples of Jesus therefore fell back on the Jewish belief that the Messiah would return a second time. They invented the myth that Jesus had risen from the dead. They stole the body of Jesus and hid it, proclaiming that He would soon return. This preaching was much more successful than the life of Jesus himself had been. The Christian religion was born, and flourished through this mythical preaching of the disciples.

The alarm of the orthodox Lutheran Pastor of Hamburg is understandable. Reimarus was thereby destroying faith in the central tenet of Christianity. But we have to be clear as to his premises. Reimarus has *a priori* rejected even the possibility that Jesus might genuinely have worked miracles, that he was truly the Incarnate Son of God, and that he rose from the dead. His Deism made this axiomatic. Reimarus did not "prove" that Jesus did not perform miracles, or that he was not the Word become flesh. Reimarus had assumed it from the outset.

No doubt Reimarus would have considered that he had adequately disposed of an orthodox approach to the Gospels since his former book had rejected the possibility "of a Revelation which all men should have good grounds for believing". We shall attempt, on the contrary, to show that such a credible revelation is not only possible, but has actually occurred, as we find is the expressed agenda of the Fourth Gospel. But even if we accept for the sake of argument that Reimarus has proved his point, he did not prove it by New Testament exegesis, but by coming into the study of the historical Jesus with the presupposition that supernatural revelation, and miracles and Incarnation, were impossible, and so must be rejected *a priori* to any examination of the biblical evidence. We find exactly the same *a priori* rejection of the Incarnation and of the miraculous in the tragic genius of David Friedrich Strauss.

Strauss' *Leben Jesu:* from rationalism to myth

Before Strauss and after Reimarus, critical scholars accepted the Gospel accounts as historical but gave them a naturalistic explanation. Thus Karl Heinrich Venturini (1800), in order to give a rationalistic explanation for the healing miracles, claimed that Jesus always carried a portable medicine chest with him.[8] And for Paulus (1828), belief in miracles simply follows from ignorance of secondary causes. Thus he explained the feeding of the five thousand by saying that Jesus persuaded the rich people to share their food with the poor, following his own example.[9] And he explains the Transfiguration by claiming that Jesus actually met two venerable strangers on a high mountain, and the three disciples, only half awake, saw the early morning sun shining through clouds, and thought they had seen a glorified Jesus together with Moses and Elijah.[10]

Strauss was entirely one with these early Rationalists in dogmatically rejecting the possibility of direct divine intervention in accounts of miraculous events.[11] But he went one stage further in rejecting such reconstructions of the naturalistic explanations as contrived nonsense. He proposed that the Gospels would be better understood rather as myths: stories with no historical basis, based upon creative reflection on Old Testament texts. This for Strauss is particularly true regarding the birth narratives, which "are woven on the pattern of Old Testament prototypes, with modifications due to Messianic or messianically interpreted passages".[12] The clearest example for Strauss was the "legend" of the virginal conception of Jesus. This has no historical basis whatsoever, Jesus in reality being the natural son of Joseph and Mary; but, in Strauss' view, Matthew's reflections on the Old Testament prophecies concerning the Messiah and meditating on the text "Behold a virgin shall conceive and bear a son, and his name shall be called Emmanuel (which means God is with us)" (Matthew 1:23, cf. Isaiah 7:14) led the first evangelist to write the mythical legend of the virgin birth of Christ.[13]

Strauss' new radicalism now turned towards the Fourth Gospel, and he thought that he found in it the most fruitful ground for the mythical view. Post-Enlightenment German criticism after Reimarus and before Strauss was generally prepared to look favourably upon the Fourth Gospel. There were points, after all, where John seems to be historically more credible . It seems likely that Jesus made more than one visit to Jerusalem, as the Fourth Gospel states [John 2:23, 5:1, 7:14] rather than the one visit recorded by the Synoptics [Matthew 21:1\\]. It is at least likely that Jesus cleansed the Temple early in his public ministry as John states [John 2:13-22], rather than later as stated in the Synoptics [Matthew 21:12-13\\]. And it is at least as possible that John [John 19:31] has the date of the Last Supper as right as the Synoptics, who make the celebration of the Last Supper a Passover meal [Matthew 26:18\\].

True, Bretschneider, the famous General Superintendent at Gotha (1776-1848) had listed a collection of *loci* in the Gospels where John seems to be historically unreliable compared with the Synoptics. But the great Friedrich Schleiermacher had thrown his full weight behind the Fourth

Gospel as the most reliable because it contained fewer miracles than the other three Gospels; and Bretschneider declared himself convinced by the arguments of the prestigious Berlin professor.[14]

But for Strauss, it was the *intention* of the writer of the Fourth Gospel which made his work the most mythical of all four Gospels. John is clearest of all about the divinity of Christ, the constant theme of the whole Gospel narrative. The smaller number of miracles for Strauss means nothing. In the evangelist's intention, these miracles are given a much more loaded meaning than in the Synoptics. From the very first miracle at Cana of Galilee, the turning of water into wine, where according to John Jesus "manifested his glory; and his disciples believed in him" [John 2:11], "it is entirely in the spirit of the Fourth Gospel, to place in relief the exaltation of Jesus as the divine logos."[15]

For Strauss, the fundamental myth was the Incarnation itself. As a radical Hegelian, he could not accept that a human individual could be the divine Son of God and remain so for all eternity. This is consistent with the Hegelian view that only the Absolute Idea survives the historical process of thesis, antithesis, and synthesis. Strauss demythologises the Incarnation by turning the God-man into the ideal of humanity.[16]

Strauss had always intended that his apparent work of destruction of the faith of Christians should lead only to the formation of a new and more adequate faith for the modern generation. That was the aim of his "concluding dissertation: the dogmatic import of the life of Jesus."[17] But the Christian reader will hardly be encouraged by Strauss' new faith, a mixture of Hegelian myth and emerging Darwinism. If a nineteenth-century intellectual accepted Strauss' radical scepticism concerning the Gospels, and particularly concerning the Fourth Gospel, Strauss' re-constructed Hegelian spirituality would seem to his contemporaries scarcely distinguishable from a more thoroughgoing atheism or agnosticism. Strauss was honest enough to recognise that he was no longer a Christian, although he claimed to be religious. His final plaintive poem is without consolation of a future life, and is addressed to a human friend, not to God.[18]

A myth too far

We must all pity Strauss in his unremitting gloom. But must we share Strauss' misery, his *angst* incarnate? However much he demonstrated genius as a ruthlessly systematic exegete, Schweitzer is quite right in saying that we do not have necessarily to agree with him. Schweitzer, even while speaking from his own radically critical position, insists that Strauss has extended the boundaries of myth too far:

> For one thing, he overestimates the important of the Old Testament motives in reference to the creative activity of the legend. He does not see that while in many cases he has shown clearly enough the source of the *form* of the narrative in question, this does not suffice to explain its *origin*.[19]

Schweitzer gives as an example of his over-use of myth the Strauss interpretation of the feeding of the multitude. Schweitzer insists that this cannot simply be dismissed as a myth based upon the manna in the desert, or the miraculous feeding of a multitude by Elisha. "The story in the Gospel has far too much individuality for that, and stands, moreover, in much too closely articulated an historical connection. It must have as its basis some historical fact..."[20] We could ask a similar question of the account of the virginal conception in Matthew 1:18-24. Did the evangelist, or the tradition on whom he might be dependent, create the myth of the virginal conception of Jesus from the text in Isaiah 7:14 "A virgin shall conceive and bear a son"? Or was there an actual event, the virginal conception of Jesus, for which the author of Matthew searched for an Old Testament proof text?

This Schweitzerian distinction between the *form* of the narrative and its *origin* is a vital one, to which we shall frequently be returning. Merely because an account in the New Testament echoes in its form an Old Testament parallel is not proof that the latter is the source of the New Testament story, and therefore has no historical value, but is Straussian myth. Strauss considered that he could almost in a mechanistic

45

way determine whether a narrative was myth simply, or at least predominantly, by consideration of its form. We find the same methodology in Bultmann, and in Form Criticism, itself so much a child, or a grandchild, of Strauss.

But even more radical questions must be asked of Strauss. What if his main presupposition is questionable, that "the absolute cause never disturbs the chain of secondary causes by single arbitrary acts of interposition, but rather manifests itself in the production of the aggregate of finite causalities, and of their reciprocal action"[21] that therefore any story involving divine intervention without secondary cause must be without historical value? What if his fundamental presupposition, that the Incarnation is philosophically impossible, is itself questioned, and we begin with at least the possibility that Jesus was and is what Christian faith asserts he was and is? What kind of study of the Fourth Gospel would ensue if again we admitted at least the possibility that miracles can happen, and even more that they can happen at the hands of one who actually claimed during his life on earth to be the eternal Son of God? Potentially at least more positive judgements about the historical Jesus in the Gospel of John become feasible.

Many more scholars are now beginning to recognise the anti-supernaturalist bias of the early German critics.[22] That at least is gratifying. But what some are slower to recognise is that, if we begin with a different set of presuppositions, based upon at least the possibility that Christian orthodox faith in Jesus might be right, this could radically alter both the method and the conclusions in studying that most problematic of all New Testament books, the Gospel of John. This possibility becomes even more obvious when we look at the remarkable but fundamentally blinkered studies of Rudolf Bultmann, and at twentieth-century historical Jesus research in general, so much influenced by him. But first, to understand Bultmann, we need also to grasp what had happened in the last quarter of the nineteenth century to historical Jesus research, while Bultmann was yet in his early formative years.

The liberal protestant compromise

Strauss' influence on nineteenth-century German criticism, and indeed on growing European scepticism regarding the Christian faith, was huge. The English translator of Strauss' *Life of Jesus* was none other than Miss George Eliot, who is justly more famous for her novels, e.g. *Middlemarch*. George Eliot undertook the monumental task of translating *Das Leben Jesu Kritisch Bearbeitet* out of her philosophical interest in Rationalism, Deism and science. Even she eventually grew impatient with Strauss' ruthless belabouring of the miracle stories and his minute dissection of the passion narratives. She was said to be "Strauss-sick" at his treatment of the crucifixion scene. At the end she wrote "I do really like reading our Strauss – he is so *klar und ideenvoll* – but I do not know *one* person who is likely to read the book through, do you?"[23] But Strauss' scepticism had increasing influence on those who did not even read a word of his massive book.

Nineteenth-century criticism came to reject the historical value of the Fourth Gospel on the grounds which caused Strauss himself to reject John: above all, the Greek logos language of that Gospel, which for him made it a mythical presentation of the life of Jesus influenced by Gentile Christians who had elevated Christ to being fully God to be worshipped.

This led to an even more radical stance regarding historicity of all four Gospels taken up by the Tübingen school,[24] which even denied that Jesus existed,[25] and placed the writing of the Gospels back into the second half of the second century. For Bruno Bauer, not only John's Jesus was mythical. Jesus himself was a myth.

As we shall see later, the grounds for the existence of the historical Jesus are incontrovertible, even if they have been on occasion controverted. Late nineteenth-century German criticism recoiled from the extreme Tübingen view, and thought it had found a solid historical source for the life of Jesus based upon the priority of Mark's Gospel.[26] Mark became viewed as the main historical source for the life of the historical Jesus, first written within two generations of the crucifixion.

Heinrich Holtzmann used the theory of Marcan priority

to form the basis of a liberal Protestant theology of the life of Jesus. Mark had no infancy narratives or stories of the virginal conception of Jesus to embarrass the sceptic. His account therefore could be accepted as a basically reliable presentation of the Messiahship of a Jesus intent on founding a kingdom of justice and peace.[27] It accommodated Christianity to an increasingly sceptical Europe, without throwing away the entire Christian corpus as a myth.

Even Strauss himself, perhaps punch-drunk after the storm of criticism over his original *Leben Jesu*, modified his radical approach somewhat, to the disgust of Albert Schweitzer. "Everywhere feeble compromises,"[28] complained Schweitzer of Strauss' Revised Edition. Strauss was trying, obviously unsuccessfully, to make a belated return to his own version of the Jesus of German Liberalism.

German criticism heaved a sigh of relief that Jesus really existed, and that Mark gives us an essentially historical account, save what it considered to be one or two inconsequential miracles.[29] To let the human spirit go too free is dangerous, as the evolution of Nazism and Communism demonstrates; and a philosopher or theologian who cannot accept divine revelation will often eventually return to the only process which apparently can keep that roaming spirit in check, reason. That is why Liberal Christianity remains an option, indeed a refuge, for a modern Christian who sees orthodoxy as fundamentalism, and cannot accept that Christianity is based upon a direct revelation from God, above, although not incompatible with, reason.[30]

It also helped to establish what came to be called the "critical minimum": a basic assembly of facts about Jesus which were historically acceptable, namely that he was a Jewish prophet from Nazareth in Galilee, that he was renowned as a miracle worker and as a popular teacher, that he was crucified during the procuratorship of Pontius Pilate 26-36 AD, and that it was his disciples who after his death preached his resurrection and his divinity. By the turn of the century, however, what was not acceptable in German critical scholarship was a return to orthodox incarnational doctrine, and to belief in the historicity of the miracles which were used by Christian apologetics to defend the doctrine of the incarnation, such as the walking on the water, the feeding of the multitude, and, above all, the appearances of the risen Jesus in bodily form to his disciples and chosen witnesses. These "supernatural" events were rejected for the same reasons as Reimarus and Strauss had rejected them, because they were unacceptable to post-Enlightenment "scientific" thinking.

The Messianic secret

Late-nineteenth-century criticism did not allow liberalism to stay for long in its contented position regarding the historical trustworthiness of Mark. William Wrede (1859-1906) shattered its simple faith by the turn of the century.[31]

The importance of Wrede's *Messianic Secret*, published in Göttingen in 1901, in the history of New Testament criticism can scarcely be over-stated. Holtzmann thought that having found that Mark's was the earliest Gospel, he could reconstruct a reliable life of the historical Jesus from the beginning of his public ministry to the end of his life by using that Gospel. Wrede contested that presumption with ruthless analysis. Why, asked Wrede, in Mark's Gospel is Jesus' "Messiahship a secret and yet no secret, since it is known, not only to the disciples, but to the demoniacs, the blind man at Jericho, the multitude at Jerusalem – which must, as Bruno Bauer expresses it, 'have fallen from heaven' – and to the High Priest?"[32] Because says Wrede, in fact Jesus did not claim Messiahship at all. That was Mark's "dogmatic idea", which expressed his own faith in Jesus as Messiah.

What, then, was the real history of Jesus? In fact, claimed Wrede, Jesus was a Jewish prophet who caused a stir because of his miracles. He preached regarding the Law an attitude of some freedom, which led to the opposition of the Pharisees and the Jewish authorities, for which he was condemned to death.[33]

Regarding the so-called Messianic secret, Wrede separates out with his critical scalpel those sayings of Jesus which state explicitly his Messiahship, and concludes that these must be additions of the primitive church, or of Mark the Gospel writer with his faith in Jesus as the Messiah. But is this necessarily so? Is Wrede's scepticism justified? Mark portrays Jesus as attempting to stop people revealing his Messiahship. But why should this not be actual fact? In St John's Gospel, people attempt to make him king, and Jesus has to withdraw [John 6:15]. And we read in Mark, "Whenever the unclean spirits saw him, they fell down before him and shouted, 'You are the Son of God!' [Mark 3:12]. But he sternly ordered them not to make him known" [Mark 3:11-12]. There is historical credibility in the Gospel account, granted that, as Wrede himself admits, Jesus was renowned as a miracle worker.

New Testament scholars in general no longer accept Wrede's view, that Mark's Messianic Secret is the invention of the early church to explain why the historical Jesus did not in fact claim to be the Messiah. Trocmé [34] goes so far as to say that Wrede's explanation of the Messianic Secret is "absurd, namely that in Mark, wherever Jesus enjoins silence on anybody (demon, sick person, disciple) about any subject, whenever he teaches his disciples in private, whenever his disciples fail to understand, is an indication of the author's own literary work, designed to impose on rebellious sources the strict theory that Jesus concealed throughout his life that he was the Messiah. In fact, all these cases are very different from one another; in some places the passages are drawn from tradition, in others they are editorial notes…" [35] And Vincent Taylor claims that the historical Jesus himself taught his own Messianic secrecy. "This (Mark's) view of the Messianic Secret is in line with the Markan Christology and soteriology. The agreement is too astonishing to be the work of art; it is the reflection of historical reality." [36]

But New Testament scholars still follow Wrede in rejecting statements of Jesus in the Gospels which imply a high Christology as emanating rather from the faith of the primitive community. That this position became general in twentieth century Gospel criticism is largely due to the decisive influence of Rudolf Bultmann (1884-1976) [37] who strides twentieth century New Testament studies like a colossus. But Bultmann himself acknowledged that, in pursuing Redaction – and Form – Criticism, he was indebted to his critical predecessors.

The birth of form – and redaction criticism

From Wrede onwards, it became the task of criticism to identify the theological tendencies of the second evangelist, which became generally accepted as the first Gospel written, just as Strauss had identified the logos theological tendency of the fourth evangelist. First, Johannes Weiss (1863-1914)[38] tried to isolate the apostle Peter's historical reminiscences in Mark. He strongly believed that Peter was the source behind Mark's account.[39] Then the celebrated Old Testament scholar Julius Wellhausen (1844-1918)[40] now applied his critical genius to the New Testament, working his source analysis on Mark. As Bultmann says, "His work is more comprehensive than Wrede's for he has shown how the theology of the early Church has influenced the traditional material, not only in Mark, but also in Matthew and Luke, and therefore in Q, which, like Mark, lies behind them."[41] Wellhausen finds the work of a redactor (editor) in Mark:

> "Wellhausen stated very clearly the fundamental assumption that the tradition consists of individual stories or groups of stories joined together in the Gospels by the work of the editors; and he also showed how pieces of primitive tradition alternated with secondary material…"[42]

By now, therefore, there were descending levels of scepticism in preparation for the Form-Criticism of Bultmann and Dibelius:

Level One:
Strauss rejects the historicity of the Fourth Gospel.

↓

Level Two:
Acceptance of Marcan Priority lessens the historical worth of Matthew and Luke, according to the Two Source theory dependent on Mark.

↓

Level Three:
Wrede, Weisse and Wellhausen detect theological
overlay in Mark, and see the need for
source analysis to uncover the historical Jesus in
Mark, Q, M and L.

Like archaeologists, the scholars are hoping by this source analysis to dig deeper into the soil of history to find the Jesus who really preached the Gospel two thousand years ago, and whom history they thought concealed with layers of dogma and myth. Note that by now the question as to which Gospel was first is becoming of less importance than the source analysis itself. Wellhausen is quite prepared to find original traditions not only in Mark but in those texts which are peculiar to Matthew or Luke (e.g. the Infancy Narratives, Matthew 1-2 and Luke 1-3); and the material in the hypothetical document 'Q', common to Matthew and Luke but not in Mark (e.g. The Lord's Prayer, Matthew 5:9-13, Luke 11:2-4).

There is pretty well universal agreement with Wellhausen also that the Synoptic Gospels consist "of individual stories or groups of stories joined together in the Gospels by the work of the editors". In Synoptic studies, therefore, while most accept Marcan priority, most are now prepared to find the earliest historical traditions not only in Mark, but also in the other completed documents Matthew, Luke, and Q.

Bultmann's decisive contribution, together with the lesser celebrated Martin Dibelius (1883-1947),[43] was to attempt to organise the history of the various traditions in the Synoptic Gospels according to the "history of forms", (German *Formgeschichte*, somewhat inaccurately translated into English "Form Criticism") to uncover the way in which the Christian community shaped the earliest traditions about Jesus for its own needs.[44]

Critique of *formgeschichte*

Bultmann's form-critical methodology dominated twentieth century study of the Synoptic Gospels. What is surprising is how little it has been radically questioned. What is even more surprising is that, when it was questioned in a devastating critique, by Pierre Benoit, in 1946, his criticisms largely have not even been considered by either exegetes or theologians.[45] That is still more surprising, since Benoit enjoyed the highest international reputation as both exegete and theologian.

We will bypass the fact that the Two Document Hypothesis, which is the foundation of the Form-Critical approach, is itself questionable. For instance, if the traditional view, that Matthew's Gospel was first, is accepted, as it is by an important minority of New Testament scholars,[46] then Redaction Criticism, and thus consequently Form Criticism, would have an entirely different methodology.

We may accept the majority solution to the Synoptic Problem for the purposes of argument as at least a tenable hypothesis. But even on these terms we must question the procedures and the proposed solutions of Form-Criticism. This question is so important that it is worth setting out Benoit's critique in detail. He begins by insisting that all is not bad with *La Formgeschichtliche Methode*. He announces his aim, to separate the "chaff from the good grain". He has no problem when those using the *Formgeschichtliche Methode* indicate that the evangelists have worked on the material, which means that often we cannot be sure of historical details in a narrative; e.g. Mark 16:5, has one angel at the tomb of Jesus, while Luke 24:4 has two.

But, as Benoit says, "the new critics wish to go much further and presuppose something entirely different. We would speak of 'souvenirs'; they speak to us of 'creations'. The Tradition has not only been received and selected; it has been most frequently invented."[47]

This, for Benoit, is the "anti-historical" thesis of the Form Critics, e.g.

> This healing of a leper, this raising of the young man of Nain, has nothing actually to do with Jesus. These are

the Christians of Damascus or of Antioch who have attributed them to him, to make a comparison with the gods of paganism.[48]

What remains therefore of the historical, one must ask, when one has eliminated from the tradition all the creations of the community? Something very little; a most inoffensive residue: Jesus of Galilee, who believed himself to be a prophet, who had to speak and act in this sense, without being able to say either just, what or how, finally who was put to death in a lamentable way. All the rest, his divine origin, his mission of salvation, the proofs which he gave them by his words and his miracles, finally the Resurrection which has sanctioned his work, all that is pure fiction, issue of the faith and of the worship, and invested with a legendary tradition, which has been formed at the whim of the preaching and of the struggles of the primitive community.[49]

On what principle is this scepticism, asks Benoit? On three principles. Benoit finds that none of these principles are solidly based rationally, and simply stem from philosophical presuppositions.[50]

1. **The first Presupposition is that the First Christians did not wish to write history.** As we shall ourselves demonstrate later in more detail, Benoit responds that:

> Perhaps the first Christians did not have a concern for "history"; but they did have a concern for the "historical". The preachers of the new faith did not wish to recount *everything* about Jesus, but they did only wish to recount what was sound.[51]

2. **The Second Presupposition is that the Gospel Narratives are to be Compared with Jewish and Hellenistic contemporary sources.** But, we cannot conclude from this that the Gospel stories are fiction, says Benoit. He insists that the value of the veracity depends on the milieu from whence

these forms come, not from the forms themselves.[52] Benoit agrees that the Rabbis wrote fictional stories; but that was an entirely different context. Here, we have to do with one sole Master, Jesus: where, in place of a tradition which has persisted orally over many centuries and was only fixed much later, one has memories which go back no more than thirty or forty years.[53] Regarding the Rabbinic stories, Benoit thinks there is more history in them than Bultmann seems to admit. Regarding the miracles of paganism, he agrees with Bultmann, that their fiction is more manifest. But, Benoit asks, what right has one to conclude that those of the Gospel are equally fictitious, *because they resemble them in their mode of narration?*

3. **The Third Presupposition is that it is the community which has invented these myths.** The historical Jesus tradition, for Bultmann, is transmitted to the pagan world, and after being divinised by Paul, Jesus is transformed into the divine man. This is the motivation for the creation of the Gospel myths. But this tradition was created only thirty or forty years after the death of the historical Jesus. Is one to say that no one at the time of the writing of the Gospels knew Jesus when on earth?[54] We have evidence that during the sixties, apostles were living. Did they not communicate a true tradition regarding Jesus? Is it conceivable, asks Benoit, that a social group, an amorphous mass of anonymous number, would be capable of creating a doctrinal and literary tradition, above all a tradition as original as the Christian tradition?[55] A crowd is a sociological phenomenon, which could amplify impulses received, but could not create them.[56] The great movements of history come not from a crowd, but from an individual person. Benoit continues: the Christian religion in its early days provoked the hostility of Judaism, the hatred of paganism, the persecutions of the Roman empire, and yet conquered the world. How can one explain this formidable movement, if one does not put at its origin Jesus, or his direct testimonies, but posits an anonymous and indefinable collectivity, which had constructed little by little its legend from the impact of inventions and creations? Such a genesis of Christianity, insists Benoit, would be a nonsense.[57]

The principle reason for this creativity of the *Form-geschichliche Schule* is not sociological. Rather, for Benoit, it is the demand of confirming the radical anti-supernatural scepticism of German criticism, while not wishing to portray the apostles themselves as deceivers. The answer is the anonymous primitive Christian community, full of mythical imagination.[58]

The History of the Synoptic Tradition
How much can Jones swallow?

Benoit's critique is surely telling. Bultmann's epoch-making work *The History of the Synoptic Tradition* puts to use in a masterly way the most sophisticated exegetical tools in sketching the history of the Jesus tradition in Matthew, Mark, and Luke.

But, in deciding what is unhistorical, Bultmann allows his straightforward historical scepticism to have the final say. We have already seen how Bultmann saw Jesus' claim to forgive sins [Mark 2:5-7] as the reflection of the primitive church's faith rather than a historical reminiscence.[59] Even more decisively, Bultmann dismisses Peter's Confession in Mark 8:27-30 saying that the passage is to be "characterised as legend". Where Peter says to Jesus in response to a question as to who Jesus is, [Mark 8:29] "You are the Messiah."

> This then is a legend of faith: faith in the Messiahship of Jesus is traced back to a story of the first Messianic confession which Peter made before Jesus. The historical Peter would indeed have had to confess Jesus as the future Messiah! And it would then be necessary to suppose, according to Reitzenstein's precedent, that Jesus understood himself in terms of the myth of the archetypal man, and that Peter had seized on this understanding too.[60]

This clearly is not so much an exercise in form or literary criticism[61] as, in Ronald Knox's terms, a test of how much Jones can swallow. Bultmann rejects Mark 8:27-30, the

Confession of Peter, not because of criticism of forms, or of literary criticism. It is because to him it is *historically incredible* that the historical Jesus was either professed by his disciples, or professed himself, to be the Messiah. But what if Peter's confession of Jesus as Messiah was rooted in Jewish thinking, and not in Reitzenstein's archetypal man? We shall be looking later at some "high" Jewish concepts of Messiahship contemporary with the historical Jesus.[62] No longer then would Peter's confession be incredible historically; even though his concept of Messiahship during the life of the historical Jesus might well have fallen short of the confession of the full divinity of Christ, that full insight coming only after the Resurrection.

But nothing could prevent Bultmann proceeding apace with his radical literary and Form-Critical method combined with the historical scepticism learnt from nineteenth-century German criticism. Bultmann made the biblical opinion common in the twentieth century that primitive Christianity developed from a "low" view of Jesus very much in Jewish terms to an essentially Greek and Gentile view of Jesus' metaphysical status, as did Reimarus early in the Historical Jesus Quest. As Bultmann said, "Greek Christianity soon represented Jesus as Son of God in the sense of ascribing a divine 'nature' to him, and thus introduced a view of his person as far removed as possible from his own."[63]

Once again, therefore, as with Reimarus and Strauss, with Bultmann what is often presented as "proven" we see clearly is simply presumed. In the same way Bultmann sees the miracle as such as outside the area of investigation of the historian *qua* historian.[64] For Strauss, miracles are simply philosophically impossible. For Bultmann, they might happen; but they cannot be scientifically investigated. For him,

> "The historical method includes the presupposition that history is a unity in the sense of a closed continuum of effects in which individual events are connected by the succession of cause and effect... This closedness means that the continuum of historical happenings cannot be rent by the interference of supernatural, transcendent

powers and that therefore there is no miracle" in this sense of the word.[65]

What we might call epistemological positivism came to dominate New Testament scholarship during the twentieth century. It enabled New Testament scholars to do exegesis without scepticism becoming as rampant as it was during the nineteenth century. Whether miracles actually happened became increasingly a no-go area of exegesis. Whether a miracle has occurred became a matter of the personal decision of the believer and could not be an historical question.

But the effect on theological and exegetical investigation is the same for Bultmann's epistemological positivism as for the more ontological positivism of the Deist and the Pantheist. All held dogmatically to a closed system of reality open to scientific research. God could not directly act in his own world, or at least could not have been discerned to have done so.

But is it obvious that "It is in accordance with such a method as this that the science of history goes to work on all historical documents"? The investigations of miraculous cures at Lourdes may or may not have been successful in detecting miracles. But no one could deny that those who conducted these investigations were distinguished medical scientists who were attempting to demonstrate that this or that cure could not be explained by the known laws of science, and that a special divine intervention was the best explanation.[66] It is the same for those who investigate paranormal phenomena. They attempt to judge whether those phenomena occurred. Who is therefore to say that an historian, *qua* historian, may not make judgements as to the authenticity of a miraculous account?

Twentieth century scepticism set on its way

In the twentieth century, Bultmann's view concerning miracle prevailed. But was he simply running away from the problem of faith and granting an easy concession to Strauss? Schweitzer, before he went off into the primeval jungle to practise surgery as a Lutheran missionary, showed his contempt for a biblical scholarship which he saw already developing at the beginning of the twentieth century which ducked the question of miracle, stating that this was simply continuing the reign of Strauss.[67]

We do not think that Strauss is unshakeable. We intend to attempt to shake him, by looking once more at the real possibility of miracle as a sign of revelation, and verifiable as such. To demonstrate that there is another way in which we might look at history and historical investigation is part of the purpose of this book. But we must even at this point observe that with Bultmann exegesis and philosophy are never separated. His positivistic view of miracle is an integral part of his exegesis. Furthermore, as also with Strauss, Bultmann's view of the Fourth Gospel is as much philosophical as exegetical, and his philosophy has influenced, indeed dominated, his exegesis. In the twentieth century, with miracle as with the Fourth Gospel, where Bultmann went, New Testament exegesis tended to follow.

Bultmann traced in detail the evolution of primitive Christology, somewhat analogously to a biologist setting out successively the evolution of species. The stages reconstructed by Gospel criticism, as assumed in Bultmann's *History of the Synoptic Tradition*, are as follows:

A.	First Stage	The Teaching of the Historical Jesus.
B.	Second Stage	The Palestinian Christian Community (Acts 2).
C.	Third Stage	The Hellenistic Jewish Christian Community.
D.	Fourth Stage	The Gentile Christian Community (Antioch, Paul).
E.	Fifth Stage	Developing Gospel Oral Tradition.
F.	Sixth Stage	Pre-Gospel written traditions (e.g. Q, Ur Marcus[68]).
G.	Seventh Stage	Mark's Gospel.
H.	Eighth Stage	Matthew's and Luke's Gospel.
I.	Ninth Stage	John's Gospel. Not a source for the teaching of Jesus.

The first four stages can be directly taken from New Testament evidence. Bultmann's view of stages E and F,[69] oral tradition and pre-Gospel written traditions, has won general acceptance. Those who accept the Marcan or Two Document Hypothesis (and the majority do today) would agree with stages F to H.

The stages themselves are not really the problem. The problem is the historical judgement which Bultmann makes; that each stage, from early Palestinian to Hellenistic, is increasingly unreliable historically, with the Gospel of John the end point of the stage of development away from any real contact with the teaching of the historical Jesus.[70] From the Bultmann viewpoint, therefore, the Gospel of John must be viewed as entirely theological fiction, without value as a source for the historical Jesus.

Thus, essentially, the situation remained during the twentieth century. In one sense, therefore, the challenge of the *Jesus Seminar* in the United States and the *Myth of God Incarnate* in Britain was hardly surprising. If Bultmann's view is accepted, that John's Gospel is devoid of historical worth, at least where the claims of Jesus to be God the Son and the miracles which vindicated those divine claims is concerned, is it surprising that intelligent academics asked questions about the validity of Christian faith in the Incarnation, most strongly advocated in that Gospel which had been judged critically to be unhistorical?

In the 1960s, the world of New Testament scholarship was stirred by what was called the "New Quest", stimulated by the monograph of James M. Robinson *A New Quest of the Historical Jesus.*[71] Bultmann's pupils, some of whom became distinguished biblical scholars themselves, were not happy with the complete radicalism of their professor.[72] But the New Quest never threatened any of the principles held by Bultmann as the *Vorverständnis* of his work. The New Quest did not raise the question of miracle in all seriousness, nor did it consider admitting sayings of high Christology as being possibly from the historical Jesus.[73]

As we shall see later, it was not until the last decade of the twentieth century, in particular with the work of N.T. Wright, Margaret Barker, and Marcus Brockmuehl, that a radically new look at the Gospel evidence for the historical Jesus has really begun. This book hopefully takes its place in that post-Bultmannian era, its particular contribution being to challenge the assumption that the Fourth Gospel is unhistorical, and so to find a path to a new apologetic for the Incarnation, or at least to a hopefully convincing restating of an old one.

But first, we must look at the Gospel evidence in general, indeed methodologically ignoring the Fourth Gospel, in our Part Two. We intend first to demonstrate that the Synoptic Gospels, often in our opinion erroneously represented as in conflict with John's Gospel from the historical viewpoint, on the contrary presents us with a Jesus implicitly at least claiming divinity, and paying the ultimate price for this claim in his condemnation to death for blasphemy. This will provide us with a credible taking-off point to look at the Fourth Gospel itself, to demonstrate its coherence with the Synoptic account.

NOTES – CHAPTER 2

1   QHJ, 3-4.
2   ODCC, 388.
3   GEAT, 65, ODCC 1300.
4   QHJ, 4-5.
5   QHJ, 14.
6   Gotthold Ephraim Lessing, 1729-81. ODCC, 816.
7   QHJ, 21.
8   QHJ, 44.
9   QHJ, 52.
10 QHJ, 52-3.
11 LJCE, 88.
12 QHJ, 81.
13 LJCE, 126-133.
14 QHJ, 85.
15 LJCE, 526.
16 LJCE, 780.
17 LJCE, 757.
18 QHJ, 76-77.
19 QHJ, 84.

20 QHJ, 84.
21 LJCE, 88.
22 E.g. it is well recognised by JR, 28.
23 LJCE xlviii.
24 ODCC 1398.
25 E.g. for Bruno Bauer, 1809-82, QHJ, 156.
26 NJBC, **40:13,** 590.
27 NTHIP, 151-2.
28 QHJ, 119.
29 NTHIP, 146-155.
30 "Not only can faith and reason never be at odds with one another..."
    Tanner, II, *809, Vatican I On Faith and Reason.
31 HST, 1.
32 QHJ, 332.
33 QHJ, 336.
34 TROC, 124, n.1.
35 TROC, 123-4.
36 Taylor, 122-4.
37 ODCC, 209-2.
38 NTHIP, 494.
39 HST, 1-2.
40 ODCC 1465. Cf. GEAT, 258.
41 HST, 2.
42 HST, 2.
43 ODCC 400.
44 HST, 2-*3.
45 One who does radically question Form-Critical method is Erhaardt
    Güttgemanns in his *Candid Questions Concerning Gospel Form Criticism:
    A Methodological Sketch of the Fundamental Problematics of Form and
    Redaction Criticism,* 1979.
46 Orchard, Longstaff, ed. 1978, 51 NJBC, art. *The Synoptic Problem,*
    by Frans Neirynck. **40,** 587-595.
47 ET, 43.
48 ET, 44.
49 ET, 46.
50 ET, 46.
51 ET, 47-48.
52 ET, 48.
53 ET, 49.
54 ET, 52.
55 ET, 52.
56 ET, 53.
57 ET, 53.
58 ET, 54.
59 Cf. p.36.
60 HST, 257*-8*.

61 Bultmann says, "the fact that Jesus takes the initiative with his question suggests that this narrative is secondary." But why? Once again, we have Schweitzer's strictures in mind where he warns against assuming too quickly that the *form* of the narrative in question is sufficient to explain its *origin*. QHJ, 84, cf. p.45. Much more significant is its *content,* we would suggest.

62 Cf. pp.149-50.

63 JW, 152.

64 Malevez, 1958 133.

65 EF, 345.

66 Cf. pp.223-7.

67 QHJ, 111.

68 Bultmann recognises the possibility of an *Ur-Marcus*, HST, 6*. For consideration of the various views, cf. Neirynck, NJBC **40:1-36**, 587-595.

69 Cf. HST Introduction, 6*.

70 JW, 17.

71 Robinson, J.M. *A New Quest of the Historical Jesus*. London, SCM, 1959.

72 JVG, 114.

73 For different options as to the identity of the historical Jesus since Bultmann, cf. JR, 78-97.

Part Two
Building up the case from the Synoptic Gospels

CHAPTER 3

THE GOSPELS: SOURCES OF HISTORY?

> **We submit that the first three Gospels, Matthew, Mark, and Luke, are potentially reliable sources for the historical Jesus.**

Christian tradition

Albert Schweitzer, writing after a century of the Quest, might have spoken of "the absolute indifference of early Christianity towards the life of the historical Jesus".[1] In keeping with his eschatology, Schweitzer claimed that primitive Christianity lived "wholly in the future with the Christ who was to come, and to preserve of the historic Jesus only detached sayings, a few miracles, His death and resurrection."[2]

But Christian tradition down the centuries had a different view of the four Gospels. However short and selective they are, for Christians those Gospels were precious accounts of the history of the earthly Jesus; and by "historical" they meant "fact". In this we accept for the moment the common-sense definition of the Concise Oxford Dictionary, of 'historical' as "1. Of or concerning history (*historical evidence*). 2. Belonging to history, not to prehistory or legend."[3]

Belief that the Gospels recounted fact arose first from belief in the inspiration of Holy Scripture. Before the Enlightenment it was assumed that the whole Bible (including, e.g. the Creation account in Genesis) was factual unless it was obvious from the context that an account was fictional, e.g. a parable of Jesus. But this belief in the historical reliability of the Gospels was reinforced by the doctrine of the Incarnation, that in Jesus of Nazareth the Word became flesh, that is, entered our history. The Gospels, as our only possibly reliable documentation of the life of Jesus of Nazareth, were to Christian tradition the actual historical life of the Incarnate Word, who lived died and rose again for our salvation in time and place.

If proof were needed of this Christian tradition of treating the four Gospels as factual, the Rationalist lives of Jesus at the beginning of the Quest of the Historical Jesus would provide it, coming as they did from Lutheran Germany. Thus Paulus explained the feeding of the five thousand in that Jesus persuaded the rich people to share their food with the poor, following his own example.[4] Then, after what Schweitzer considered to be Paulus' relatively simple natural explanation of the Feeding of the Multitude, he goes on to give a detailed description of the Heidelberg professor's[5] "scientific" interpretation of the Transfiguration:

> The explanation of the *transfiguration is* somewhat more complicated. While Jesus was lingering with a few followers in this mountainous district He had an interview upon a high mountain at night with two dignified looking men whom His three companions took for Moses and Elias. These unknown persons, as we learn from Luke ix.31, informed Him of the fate which awaited Him at Jerusalem. In the early morning, as the sun was rising, the three disciples, only half awake, looked upwards from the hollow in which they had been sleeping and saw Jesus with the two strangers upon the higher part of the mountain, illuminated by the beams of the rising sun, and heard them speak, now of the fate which threatened Him in the capital, now of the duty of steadfastness and the hopes attached thereto, and finally heard an exhortation addressed to themselves, bidding them ever to hold Jesus to be the beloved Son of the Deity, whom they must obey... Their drowsiness, and the clouds which in an autumnal sunrise float to and fro over those mountains, left them no clear recollection of what had happened. This only added to the wonder of the vague undefined impression of having been in contact with apparitions from a higher sphere. The three who had been with Him on the mount never arrived at any more definite knowledge of the facts, because Jesus forbade them to speak of what they had seen until the end should come.[6]

What is fascinating here is how Paulus accepts every detail of the account of the Transfiguration in the Synoptic Gospels [Matthew 17:1-9, Mark 9:2-9, Luke 9:28-36] as strictly factual. Although he admits that the disciples had a "vague and undefined impression of having been in contact with apparitions from a higher sphere", they still recounted what they had actually seen and heard on the mount of Transfiguration, and this was relayed to us in the Gospel account. In his belief in the facticity of the Gospel story Paulus is in line with Christian thinking down the centuries regarding the Gospels. What caused the scandal at the end of the eighteenth century and the beginning of the nineteenth century with the Rationalist lives of Jesus was not that they considered the Gospels fiction. They considered them fact. Rather, the Rationalists gave a natural *interpretation* according to the new science of what Christian traditional understanding of the Gospels saw as supernatural happenings in the life of Jesus. In this somewhat curious way, therefore, they are testimony to that Christian tradition, in which they themselves were immersed, of treating the Gospels as historical and factual.

Strauss and Bultmann: from history to myth

As in much regarding Gospel criticism, it was David Friedrich Strauss who was the true and complete revolutionary. He took scepticism to a further stage. He rejected the Rationalist presupposition that the miracle stories in the Gospels were factual accounts, albeit to be interpreted according to natural laws rather than to special divine intervention. Strauss introduced to criticism systematically the concept of myth: that the miraculous accounts were themselves only creations of the evangelist, based upon an imaginative reading of the Old Testament accounts of wonders.[7]

Strauss directed the subsequent history of criticism towards rejection of the historicity of the Fourth Gospel. But, we have also seen, this negative judgement was in the first instance due to Strauss' presuppositions against the miraculous and against the orthodox doctrine of the Incarnation.[8] Strauss had rejected the historicity of the Gospels prior to any actual investigation of individual texts.

We saw that,[9] in the German critical movement, the adoption of priority of Mark's Gospel may have solved the Synoptic Problem, but it did not solve the problem of the historical Jesus. It was followed by scepticism at a deeper and deeper level, leading to Form Criticism, where any reference to the post-Easter proclamation of Jesus as the incarnate Lord must be referred to the primitive community rather than to Jesus himself.

Regarding the Synoptic Gospels, Bultmann realises that his own methodology in *The History of the Synoptic Tradition* takes off with a negative assessment of the Gospels from the viewpoint of their historicity. It is because of that negative presupposition that he has to dig deeper and deeper into the traditions to find a core of historical data. If the documents were assessed to be historically trustworthy, then a presumption in their favour would be a necessary implication of that favourable judgement.

But Bultmann does not pay us the compliment of giving us any lengthy reasons why he considers that the Synoptic Gospels are to be assessed negatively regarding their historicity. We have to be content with a dismissive footnote, which one will print for the reader at least in readable type:

> I have no wish to deal with my much-criticised scepticism in detail. I need only refer to M. Kähler and his book *Der sogenannte historische Jesus und der geschichtliche biblische Christus* (1896). He saw quite clearly that of the life of Jesus 'we have reports, but none that demonstrably are assessable as original sources in the strict sense of these words.' (p. 22), and that it was essential to see that 'there is no comprehensibly clear distinction between oral tradition and the saga; not even with full certainty and unexceptionably even if the generation following the eye and ear-witnesses is concerned' (p. 36.1: cp. p. 88). Many are ready to admit that, though thereafter, thinking they have paid enough service to criticism in such a general concession, struggle against criticism where it is applied in particular cases.[10]

Bultmann here is not only being cavalier with his critics, of whom he admits there are many. In refusing to answer the more general question of the historicity of the Synoptic Gospels before embarking on taking them apart, Bultmann has not provided adequate foundations for his own methodology. Does he not have to provide his own defence of Kähler's assertion that of the life of Jesus 'we have reports, but none that demonstrably are assessable as original sources in the strict sense of these words.'[11] Surely he must explain in his Introduction why he requires "full certainty" regarding the historicity of the Gospels, while he is quite prepared to accept much less than certainty regarding every process of the form critical method.[12]

Bultmann's *History of the Synoptic Tradition* would have been a much different book had he accepted in principle the serious possibility that the Synoptic Gospels go back substantially to eye-witness sources. Does he not need to justify his refusal to do so?

Contrary evidence? Memory and manuscript

The predominant view since Bultmann has been that oral tradition operated in the early days of Christianity, which primarily shaped the Gospel format. This oral tradition operated freely, without real concern for historical veracity. But in fact, we have no evidence for this, only surmise. There is an important minority view expressed by Birger Gerhardsson. He is of the opinion that, "he (Jesus) used a method similar to that of Jewish-and Hellenistic-teachers: the scheme of text and interpretation. He must have made his disciples learn certain sayings off by heart; if he taught, he must have required his disciples to memorise. This statement is not intended to be dogmatic or apologetic but is a consideration based on a comparison with the contemporary situation."[13]

We cannot be certain that Jesus taught his disciples this way. He just might have been different from the "contemporary situation". Against Gerhardsson, the fact that there are differences in wording between Matthew, Mark and Luke even regarding the same teaching of Jesus (e.g. the Lord's Prayer in Matthew 6:9, cf. Luke 11:2-4) might be an indication that the copiers and memorisers were not always that accurate.

But Gerharddson's view is a timely reminder that there is another way of looking at Gospel formation, which is at the very least no more gratuitous than Bultmann's scepticism. Luke, in most scholars' estimation, was the last written of the Synoptic Gospels, or at least was written after Mark,[14] in the last quarter of the first century AD. Luke [15] has a very precise view of his own agenda in writing the Gospel bearing his name:

> Since many have undertaken to set down an orderly account of the events that have been fulfilled among us, just as they were handed on to us by those who from the beginning were eye-witnesses and servants of the word, I too decided, after investigating everything carefully from the very first, to write an orderly account for you, most excellent Theophilus, so that you may know the truth concerning the things about which you have been instructed. [Luke 1:1-4]

Luke[16] is not claiming to be an eye-witness, but is dependent on the tradition *(paredosan)*[17] of those who were "eye-witnesses and servants of the word."[18] He is using his sources creatively; but he is writing history, not fiction, more in the style of the ancient historians than the other evangelists. In this statement of Luke, we are breathing the atmosphere of one who is writing serious history for the stated purpose of encouraging the readers of his Gospel; not a collection of myths and fairy tales concerning the wishful thinking of a creative faith community.

But is Luke entirely misleading or misled in this? Was he in fact only recording the legends of the faith community? Again, there are just one or two indicators which might show a contrary view, namely that the Synoptic Gospel writers were concerned to record and to transmit what the historical Jesus said and did; and not only those scraps which can be dug out from the primitive Palestinian community. Howard

Marshall's view of the historicity of Luke's Jesus tradition seems to me to deserve at least a preliminary hearing:

> Nevertheless, it is important to observe that in many cases the reasons often given for ascribing the origins of traditions to the early church rather than to Jesus himself are both speculative and unconvincing, and that the case for finding the origins of most of the Gospel tradition in the activity and teaching of Jesus is stronger than is sometimes allowed... It is clear that the basic tradition of the sayings of Jesus was *modified* both in the tradition and by the Evangelists in order to re-express its significance for new situations; it is by no means obvious that this basic tradition was *created* by the early church.[19]

Indeed, there is evidence from Paul's letters that the early Christians were concerned to preserve the authentic tradition of the historical Jesus.

Paul quotes the tradition accurately

St Paul never knew Jesus while on earth. Paul was converted on the Damascus Road on his way to put Christians in prison, well after the crucifixion of Jesus. [Acts 9:1-22, 22:1-18]. For Bultmann, that was an advantage, because Paul then did not have to found his faith on the historical Jesus; "and that means nothing other than 'Christ after the flesh'.[20] However, we must be cautious before we conclude that Paul was not interested in the historical Jesus, as does Bultmann. It seems more than likely from his quotation from "the Lord's" words on divorce, [1 Corinthians 7:10-12] that he knew of a body of the sayings of Jesus.

We have a very interesting instance where Paul apparently quotes the words of Jesus about divorce; and he apparently gets it right:

1 Corinthians 7:10-12	Matthew 19:7-9	Mark 10:4-5, 10-12
[1 Cor 7:10] To the married I give this command – not I but the Lord – that the wife should not separate from her husband	They said to him, "Why then did Moses command us to give a certificate of dismissal and to divorce her?"	[Mk 10:4] They said, "Moses allowed a man to write a certificate of dismissal and to divorce her."
[1 Cor 7:11] (but if she does separate, let her remain unmarried or else be reconciled to her husband), and that the husband should not divorce his wife.	He said to them, "It was because you were so hard-hearted that Moses allowed you to divorce your wives, but from the beginning it was not so.	[Mk 10:5] But Jesus said to them, "Because of your hardness of heart he wrote this commandment for you.
[1 Cor 7:12] To the rest I say – I and not the Lord – that if any believer has a wife who is an unbeliever, and she consents to live with him, he should not divorce her.	[Mt 19:9] And I say to you, whoever divorces his wife, except for unchastity, and marries another commits adultery."	[Mk 10:6] But from the beginning of creation, 'God made them male and female.'
[1 Cor 7:15] But if the unbelieving partner separates, let it be so; in such a case the brother or sister is not bound. It is to peace that God has called you.		[Mk 10:11] He said to them, "Whoever divorces his wife and marries another commits adultery against her;
		[Mk 10:12] and if she divorces her husband and marries another, she commits adultery."

Paul wrote his letter to the Corinthians about AD 57. Some have suggested that when Paul speaks of "not from me but from the Lord", he is referring to a charismatic experience he has had of the risen Lord. If he was speaking from a charismatic experience, Paul was much more likely to refer to the Spirit which was guiding him, rather than the risen *Kurios*. Barrett is right in not even questioning that it is from the tradition of the Lord's sayings:

On 7:11. "and the husband is not to divorce his wife." "Not even the higher evaluation of the celibate life should lead to the dissolution of a marriage once it has been contracted; an *a fortiori* argument will lead to the conclusion that no other ground will suffice. This *charge* Paul gives not on his own authority, but on that of the Lord himself; see Mark 10:2-12 and the parallels. Since 1 Corinthians is earlier in date than any of the gospels this passage gives additional support to the claim of Mark 10 (rather than the Matthean parallel) to give the original form of Jesus' saying on divorce. Paul's specific references to the teaching of Jesus are notoriously few…[21]

They may be notoriously few. But why does everyone seem to miss the fact that Paul is completely accurate when he states the actual teaching of Jesus as expressed in Matthew and Mark? As Barrett says, 1 Corinthians pre-dates the earliest Gospel, Mark, since according to the scholars, it was written in 57 AD. Incidentally, on the principle that the earliest Gospel does not necessarily contain the earliest tradition, it is likely that Matthew, although finally published later, is closest to the *ipsissima verba Jesu*, since Jesus would most likely have followed the Jewish practice of allowing only husbands to divorce their wives. Mark, and Paul, are following the more Greek practice of wives being allowed to divorce their husbands.

What is even more significant is that Paul knows when he is *not* quoting the Lord. A professor is always much more impressed with a student who can tell him "that is not a quotation from X the theologian", because that indicates a substantial knowledge of the text in question; more than a student who throws in the hat and guesses one quotation that he knows, and only one, from a given text. Paul knows what is *not* in the corpus of the sayings of the Lord; and he knows it accurately, as far as we can tell, because there is not anything about relationships between believing and unbelieving partners in the Synoptic Gospels. Paul has it right. Following the Jesus tradition, it seems accurately, he allows separation, not condemned in the Gospels, but not divorce and remarriage, which are.[22]

That is only one straw in favour of some historical reliability regarding the Jesus tradition; but indeed it should make us think twice before we assume gratuitously that Paul is not interested in the historical Jesus, or that the Jesus tradition on which he was drawing was not faithfully presented in the Gospels.

The other straw is the question of circumcision. In the Acts of the Apostles Chapter 15, Peter claims the benefit of a revelation from God to the effect that convert Gentiles did not have to be circumcised. This caused great friction in the early church, because more conservative Jewish Christians would wish to continue the law of circumcision for all Christians, Jew and Gentile.

In all, the fierce debate which ensued, as recounted in Acts, Galatians, and Romans, no one ever suggested that Jesus ever said anything about changing the law of circumcision. His message was for the Jews only, and therefore the question of circumcision never came up. Peter gave as his authority the Spirit, and the vision which he had received concerning the house of Cornelius. Now, if the early Christians so freely adapted the words of Jesus to their own convictions, is it not strange that they put no words into the mouth of Jesus saying something like "After my Resurrection, there is to be no more circumcision", or some such law. Again, the early Christians seem to preserve sobriety, not attributing words to the historical Jesus which they had just invented, even when it might appear to their advantage to do so.

This contact with eye-witness tradition is even more possible when we consider that our New Testament manuscripts are reliable, which is the unanimous conclusion of biblical scholarship.

Our manuscripts are reliable

This only confirms the results of successful labours of textual critics on the Greek New Testament manuscripts. Many who write about the historical Jesus do not see it necessary to demonstrate the reliability of the manuscripts of the four

Gospels which we have to hand. But anyone who has spoken to those coming for the first time to an interest in the Gospels will find that this is one of the first questions asked,[23] and, gratifyingly, has the surest and most positive answer.

The reader who knows nothing of New Testament palaeography might be initially concerned that the earliest complete manuscripts are three hundred years later than the first edition of St John's Gospel; although the reader might also be surprised to hear that the earliest complete Hebrew manuscripts of the Old Testament are often more than a thousand years later than the original, as are, for instance, the works of the Greek philosopher Plato.

However, scholars have no doubt that the Greek editions we possess are to all intents and purposes the original text,[24] granted thousands of minor variants, nearly all without significance in interpretation, and concerning which there is endless discussion. This is due to the painstaking work of such as Tischendorf[25] and Westcott and Hort,[26] who compared thousands of disparate manuscripts of the New Testament from the fourth to the tenth century AD, eradicating the work of mistaken copyists, to provide as reliable a text as we have for any work of ancient times.

It is important to emphasise that nearly all the myriad variations in the Greek text which we possess have no relevance to its theological import.[27] To all intents and purposes, we have the text as originally written by the authors of the entire New Testament, including all four Gospels. This is agreed by all scholars of whatever persuasion.[28] Sir Frederick Kenyon summarises the present agreement:

> We must be content to know that the general authenticity of the New Testament text has been remarkably supported by the modern discoveries which have so greatly reduced the interval between the original autographs and our earliest extant manuscripts, and that the differences of reading, interesting as they are, do not affect the fundamental doctrines of the Christian faith.[29]

How is Kenyon able to come to this conclusion, and for this conclusion to remain unchallenged in that most critical field of scholarship, the New Testament? This is because of two facts, at first sight somewhat paradoxical, relating to the history of New Testament manuscripts:

1. Manuscript scholars such as Westcott and Hort attempted to trace the lineage of manuscripts, some as late as 1,000 AD, back to dependence on a parent manuscript, thus creating "families" of manuscripts. They were then able to eliminate all but the parent manuscript as worthless, since those dependent manuscripts were only copies of the parent. But they could not find a common parent manuscript from which all these manuscripts descended. Rather, they could only group the manuscripts into different families (Western, Alexandrian, etc.) which were not dependent upon each other. This worked in favour of the reliability of the manuscripts; since if, for example, textual critics had discovered that the common manuscript was a third century one, it might be argued that a scribe in the third century had radically altered the Gospel of John in copying earlier editions. But because no such original parent had been proven, the scholars had to reckon with the fact that there was an unknown manuscript X, much earlier than those extant, on which all depended, the first edition of John. Granted the existence of early second and third century papyri, this original parent manuscript X could not be posited much later than the beginning of the second century AD.

2. The second important fact has already been noted, that very few of the thousands of differences in the manuscripts were of any theological significance. With the invention of printing in the fifteenth century, Stephanus of Paris printed the Greek New Testament using uncritically manuscripts many of which were very late. This early Greek Testament became known as the accepted edition, the *Textus Receptus*,[30] on which the late Renaissance translations of the Bible, such as the Douay and the King James Authorised Versions, were based. More modern versions, such as the New Revised Standard Version of the Bible which we are using for this book, use much more sophisticated critical apparatus to

discover the best Greek text following Tischendorf and Westcott/Hort. But the reader of the New Testament will not notice many significant differences between the *Textus Receptus* and the more recent translations. Variations are indeed many, but tiny in significance.

Thus we have an interesting paradox. Because the Christian scribes made mistakes in their transmission of the text (unlike the Jewish Massoretic scribes who were meticulous copyists[31]), and thus produced families of texts based upon common scribal errors or glosses, we cannot go back to a single original later than the beginning of the second century AD. *And because the variations between those early manuscripts are generally speaking minute, we can be certain that the unknown original manuscript on which all depended did not differ significantly from the manuscripts we have before us.*

Once we have traced New Testament manuscripts back to the end of the first century AD, or the beginning of the second century AD, the debate ceases concerning the reliability of the manuscripts. It focuses instead on the original formation of the Gospels before their first publication substantially as we have them now, two or at the most three generations after the death of Jesus c. AD 30.

The Synoptic Gospels: eye-witness testimony?

Likewise, scholars all agree that Matthew and Mark must also have been published in their first edition before the close of the first century AD. That is because we have the testimony of Papias, Bishop of Hieropalis, c.60-130,[32] that Matthew wrote the first Gospel, and that Mark was the "interpreter of Peter the apostle, and the author of Mark's Gospel." This statement of Papias, quoted in Eusebius' fourth century *Ecclesiastical History*, the authenticity of whose reference to Papias is unquestioned, demonstrates at the very least that Papias knew of the existence of the Gospels of Matthew and Mark prior to 130 AD, and possibly much earlier.[33]

Regarding the Gospel of Luke, we have a later first patristic reference, the evidence of the Muratorian Canon,[34] an ancient list of scriptural works accepted as canonical, dating back to 80-200 in its original form. This canonical list mentions "the physician Luke" as the author of the Third Gospel.[35] Since the date of Luke from external evidence could be pushed back to the latter half of the second century, this has generated a wider range of dating than that proposed by the critical minimum.

At the end of the day, as an *historian* one could be satisfied with at least two of the three Synoptic Gospels having been written in the first century, if the arguments for Luke's final edition being published well into the second century were convincing, particularly because all agree that Luke has some well authenticated Jesus traditions. The *Jesus Seminar* treats Luke quite favourably.[36] But in reality, we should surely, with Karris,[37] agree with the traditional ascription of authorship of Luke and of Acts as being authentic. If the Muratorian Canon, written only a century and a half after the events recorded, attests that the author was Luke, and there are no arguments against Lucan authorship except that of methodological scepticism, then the tradition should stand.

We may conclude, therefore, that all four Gospels were written no later than the end of the first century AD and the beginning of the second. *Per se*, therefore, there is no objection to their having been written by eye-witnesses, or at least by those who had personal knowledge of eye-witnesses to the Jesus tradition, and could rely upon their testimony. It is no objection that one of the three Gospel writers copied another. Who has not been present at a meeting, an eye-witness of the proceedings, and asked for someone else's written account?

However, the problem for New Testament criticism, as we have seen, is that historical Jesus scholarship has rejected as unhistorical those passages in the Gospels which seem to promote a high Christology. To discover whether the historical Jesus made those claims which the Fourth Gospel says he made, therefore, we have to go to rock bottom in our investigation, and begin from zero, even methodologically doubting the very existence of Jesus. This will enable us to build upwards from firm historical foundations, hopefully in order to validate the more unique picture of Jesus presented in the Fourth Gospel as the Incarnate Word.

The way forward

We have only just had a preliminary look at the Synoptic Gospels, to see whether there is any possibility that they might be sources of authentic history for the earthly life of Jesus of Nazareth. But, clearly there is a possibility. All three Gospels emanate at the latest from the end of the first century and the beginning of the second, thus clearly within the lifetime of those who were the first apostolic witnesses of Jesus. Secondly, we have also shown that the scepticism of the Form Critical school is not necessarily to be accepted without question. We have found straws of evidence which at least might lead us to think that the Gospels might be more reliable as a source of the history of Jesus than has been the predominant view in the twentieth century.

We will now proceed to make a new start to the investigation, beginning by attempting to establish, in no more than a common-sense way, a methodology for judging the veracity of an "historical event", particularly as testified in a document ancient in origin.

NOTES – CHAPTER 3

1   QHJ, 2.
2   QHJ, 3.
3   COD, 558. The Concise Oxford Dictionary has other meanings for "historical", e.g. '4, belonging to the past, not the present'. But here, regarding Christian tradition's concept of the four Gospels, we take the prime meaning as relating to history, and so to fact.
4   QHJ, 52.
5   Heinrich Eberhard Gottlob Paulus, after a stormy academic career at Jena and later Würzberg, was appointed a member of the Bavarian educational council (*schulrat*), and eventually in 1811 was appointed

Professor of Philosophy at Heidelberg University where he stayed until his death in 1851, at the age of ninety. QHJ, 49.

6 QHJ, 52-3.

7 Cf. pp. 42-3.

8 LJCE, 88.

9 Cf. pp. 48-9.

10 HST, n.3, *5.

11 NTHIP, 222 ff.For Kähler, "the real Christ [is]... the Christ who is preached." But Kümmel, who, while respecting Kähler's concern for proclamation, chides Kähler for failing "to appreciate the inescapability of historical research in the Gospels...". NTHIP, 225.

12 HST, *50.

13 SHJ, 33-4.

14 I. Howard Marshall, *The Gospel of Luke: A Commentary on the Greek Text*, Exeter, Paternoster Press, 1978, 30: "The view that Luke used Mark substantially as we have it seems to me to be beyond reasonable doubt."

15 Marshall, ibid. 34, "As for the date of composition, this is closely bound up with the date of Mark and Acts. There are two serious possibilities, a date in the early sixties or a date in the later decades of the first century."

16 "One should accept the tradition that Luke composed the Gospel" NJBC, **43:2**, 675.

17 PCB, 824, 719a. "Delivered" *(paredosan) denotes* an authoritative transmission, as from teachers to pupils, and covers both oral and written records."

18 PCB, 824. 719a. "Lk probably intends us to understand the original apostles as the source of the authoritative tradition."

19 Marshall, ibid. 33.

20 FU, 132.

21 Barrett, C.K., *A Commentary on the First Epistle to the Corinthians*, 2nd edition, London, Adam and Charles Black, 1971, 166.

22 Murphy O'Connor has introduced a lively debate on this logion, cf. *The Divorced Woman in I Cor 7:10-11.* JBL 100/4 [1981] 601-666. But Fee, G.D. *The First Epistle to the Corinthians.* Grand Rapids, Michigan, Eerdmans, 1987. For our purposes here, Paul has the Lord's teaching right, both as to what the Lord says and what he does not.

23 This question of the reliability of the Gospel manuscripts is obviously pressing even to those who are academics, but in a different discipline to that of theology and biblical exegesis. A case in point is Professor Brian Thomas, who wrote a letter to *The Daily Telegraph*, published on October 11, 2002. He doubted whether Jesus was ever confronted by Pontius Pilate, because the manuscripts of the Gospels had been tampered with subsequently. Bishop Henry Richmond replied, *Daily Telegraph* letters, p. 23, October 15, 2002: "Sir, Professor Thomas attacks the reliability of the Gospel narrative by claiming that 'the

documents which later became the Gospels were heavily and repeatedly revised when Christianity became the official religion of the Roman Empire' (i.e. some time after AD 312). The very Gospel narrative that provoked his letter, the conversation between Jesus and Pilate [letters, October 5 and 14], is to be found, word for word, in the earliest known fragment of John's Gospel, discovered in the sands of Egypt, now in the John Rylands University Library, Manchester, and dated by scholars some time before AD 150." Bishop Richmond's point is well made. But the effectiveness of the argument in general for the reliability of the Gospel manuscripts does not depend only upon one discovery, however, important, but upon the convincing studies of Westcott and Hort, and Tischendorf, of which we take full account in this section.

24 Kenyon, F., *Our Bible and the Ancient Manuscripts*. London, Eyre and Spottiswoode, 1958.
25 ENTM, 63.
26 ENTM, 64.
27 ODCC, 1356.
28 Kenyon, Ibid, 179.
29 Kenyon, Ibid, 179.
30 Kenyon, Ibid, 104.
31 Kenyon, Ibid, 37-8.
32 ODCC, 1028.
33 Klijn, INT 1967, 197-200.
34 ODCC, 950.
35 Klijn, INT, 218.
36 FG, 271-400.
37 NJBC, **43:2-3,** 675-6. Kümmel himself opts for 70-90. Kümmel, INT, 115-135.

CHAPTER 4

DID IT REALLY HAPPEN?

> For an event to be accurately described as a 'proven historical fact':
> - its credibility must have been satisfactorily tested in such a way that the events to which testimony was given were *per se* credible or credible as to circumstances;
> - the witnesses to that event were not deceiving nor were they deceived;
> - the witness' intent in describing that event has not been misunderstood;
> - the document or documents relating to that event are not demonstrably false.

X tells me that Y really happened. I believe X.

The fragility of historical evidence is well illustrated in Orwell's novel *1984*:

> O'Brien smiled faintly. "You are no metaphysician, Winston", he said. "Until this moment you had never considered what is meant by existence. I will put it more precisely. Does the past exist concretely in space? Is there somewhere or other a place, a world of solid objects, where the past is still happening?"
>
> "No."
> "Then where does the past exist, if at all?"
> "In records. It is written down."
> "In records. And…?"
> "In the mind. In human memories."
> "In memory. Very well, then. We, the Party, control all records, and we control all memories. Then we control the past, do we not?"[1]

George Orwell wrote a classic novel in the 1930s called *1984*. He had become increasingly disillusioned with Communism, and wrote his novel to portray in graphic fashion an imaginary future living in the horrors of a totalitarian regime. *1984* told of a state ruled by a Big Brother, who controlled peoples' lives completely. There was a television screen in everyone's room, which not only communicated propaganda from Big Brother, but spied on every single individual every day of their lives. In the communication of propaganda including "history", events were simply fabricated. Thus a "war" was going on with a rival State which was entirely fictional. It was shown in order to build up the morale of the people in obedience to Big Brother. Books too were written in order to concoct a history which never happened, again in order to serve a particular line of thought at the time. Myth is not essentially limited to stories of gods in the ancient world. Big Brother was projecting mythical wars. Even though the pictures of those wars may have been real, in their false contexts they were myth.

Poor Winston is a rebel in the state. He is eventually caught, not realising that all his actions have been monitored for months. He is taken for interrogation and his final torment leading to his breaking down being a visit to Room 101, where he confronts that in life which he most fears; in his case, rats. He is given a brain-washing lecture by O'Brien, his interrogator on the nature of history.

This horror situation only goes to emphasise what the nature of history really is. History depends upon records. So-called "historical science" is the attempt to verify history writing. But really we are asking about the veracity of a human person or persons. The knowledge of an historical event which is not personal to our own experience has to be communicated to us by a third party. Since the person or persons communicating such knowledge might conceivably be deceiving us or be deceived, this introduces us to the concept of the human witness to such historical events.

We might put it into a formula:

X TELLS ME THAT Y REALLY HAPPENED. I BELIEVE X.

X may be equivalent to thousands of witnesses, like the events in the Second World War. Y may be a whole sequence of events, like a flood, or a whole human life requiring thousands of witnesses. But still the formula is the same. To talk about an "historical event" is nothing other than to speak of an event witnessed by someone else, whose testimony we accept in faith. And we accept the reality, the facticity, of what has been communicated to us in historical writing.

In the communication of knowledge of an historical fact, apart from those facts to which I am party in my own experience, there is a threefold dimension:

Factual Event

Witness

Believer

An "historical fact" is therefore nothing more than an event testified as having really happened by a person or persons whose testimony we accept. "Scientific history" means nothing more than an account of an event testified by a person or persons to be factual whose testimony has been subject to a process of verification before being accepted.

Criteria of verifying an historical event

For the purposes of this book, it is reasonable to accept three notions as given, as pre-conditions of any valid knowledge; (a) the existence of ourselves, (b) the existence of a world external to ourselves, i.e. a "real world", and (c) the existence of an order of nature whereby things in the real world generally operate according to predictable laws, which we call laws of "cause and effect". To accept these three pre-conditions of knowledge is not to propose any particular philosophical answer to the problems posed in post-Cartesian[2] philosophy, which problems have dominated modern Western philosophical thought. But it is to insist that we cannot even live a normal human life unless we do accept these pre-conditions of scientific knowledge; and certainly human knowledge can make no progress without such presuppositions. Finally, these three presuppositions cannot be themselves scientifically demonstrated. Rather, they are truth-statements of "pre-physics" or (dare one say it?) metaphysics.

Usually, therefore, verification of our own direct experience is unnecessary. But when events have been recounted by others, then such verification is necessary to remove possible doubt, particularly if the events are to be recorded in writing. We wish to be sure of our 'historical facts'? How do we verify them? Again, without attempting a deep philosophical analysis, we use the following criteria as commonsense guides to checking the veracity of an account:

A. Is the Event *Per Se* Credible?

The first criterion is that of the credibility of the event *per se*. We might have been told that our maternal grandmother died years before we were born. People do die, particularly those who tend to be advanced in age, like grandmothers. We also have no reason to doubt the veracity of those who told us that she did die. We would tend to believe it as *per se* credible. If, however, we were told that our great grandmother was still alive, we would tend to disbelieve that story, because she would most likely be over 120 years old. It is *per se* difficult to believe that someone should live beyond 120 years, even if it is not impossible; therefore I should tend to disbelieve it, unless strong evidence to the contrary was offered, such as a photograph, or a letter from her.

B. Are the Circumstances Credible?

The circumstances of an event, when it happened, to whom it happened, and why it happened, make a great difference regarding its credibility:

1. *Who*

If we were told that a world-famous snooker player scored 150 points, potting all the snooker balls, and that he performed this feat three frames successively, then we would tend to believe it. If, however, we were told that our best friend Charlie, with whom we play snooker every Saturday evening, performed this same feat, we would be amused, and would demand much more strict proof of the veracity of this claim. Either Charlie must be a snooker genius with a great future hitherto unrealised, or he must have been incredibly lucky on that one occasion, or someone was telling me a tall story about Charlie. The *who* of an event to a very large extent determines its credibility.

2. *When*

If we were told that a man flew like a bird in the year 1520, we would tend to dismiss this report as legend. But if we heard the same story today, we would perhaps think that modern technology had now advanced to such an extent that individuals could use their arms as part of a flying device. *When* is important in this case, because it was only in the twentieth century that flying machines began actually to fly.

3. *Where*

The alleged place of an event will affect its credibility. If we were told that in a given place the temperature reached 45 degrees centigrade, we would be much more likely to believe it if the place where this high temperature was recorded was tropical Africa rather than northern Siberia during the winter.

4. *How*

The alleged cause of an event will also affect its credibility. Generally speaking, I would tend not to believe an account given that a man's heart stopped beating for three days, and then started again. If, however, I was informed by reliable scientific opinion that a technique had been developed whereby a man could be frozen after the heart stopped beating, and then he could be resuscitated by using sophisticated medical equipment, I would tend to believe such an account, because a new causal factor, that of a new technique of heart resuscitation, made such an account credible.

C. Is the Witness Credible?

Clearly, the credibility of the witness or witnesses, those handing on the historical information, must be established in order for us to be certain that X is an historical fact. Even if that witness or witnesses are proven unreliable in every other instance of the recounting of historical information, the very fact that we accept their reliability in transmitting Historical Fact X makes that witness or witnesses at least credible in recounting Historical Fact X. On the other hand, as we have seen earlier, it will also begin to create a presumption in our minds that our witness is credible. Perhaps our witness is having a conversion, and beginning to tell the truth.

If the witness is not credible, it will be for one of four reasons:

1. *The Witness is Deceiving*

We may conclude after our historical investigation that the witness recounting this so-called historical information is deliberately trying to deceive us. In a court of law, the cross-examination of a hostile witness by a barrister often has a single aim, that of breaking down the witness' testimony, to demonstrate that that witness is attempting to deceive the court.

2. *The Witness is Deceived*

We may conclude after our historical investigation that the witness, however sincere, has recounted false information because one factor or another caused that witness to be deceived. Bernadette Soubirous was interrogated rigorously by church and state authorities after she recounted the vision she had for many days of the Lady she identified as Mary the Mother of Jesus. Some originally thought that Bernadette was deliberately deceiving everyone, either to achieve publicity for herself, or to acquire some money for her bankrupt father. Then, when Bernadette's sincerity became obvious to all, even to sceptics, many considered that her so-called vision of

Mary was the product of her sick mind. Bernadette, many felt, was deceived, and thus her testimony was valueless; and she had to try to prove them wrong.

3. *The Witness has been Misunderstood*

The danger that a witness' account of an event may be misunderstood is particularly great when that testimony is only available in writing. Documents may be easily mis-interpreted.

Biblical scholars have in recent years claimed that the inspired biblical writers have been misunderstood, in that they have been taken as we say 'too literally'. Apart from Fundamentalists, most would interpret the Book of Revelation not as a work which makes solid historical predictions, but as a piece of apocalyptic writing which must be interpreted symbolically.[3]

When, therefore, the writer of the Book of Revelation tells us that the heavens opened and he was told in his vision that the faithful saints in heaven who did not have the mark of the beast 'lived and reigned with Christ for a thousand years' (Revelation 20:4), he is speaking symbolically of the reign of Christ. We are not, as some fundamentalist groups of Christians claim, to wait for Christ to come down from heaven to reign in modern Jerusalem for a thousand years. Most modern Christians would follow Augustine and Origen, "who understood the passage spiritually rather than historically. Augustine associated the binding of Satan with the life of Jesus and the thousand-year reign with the time of the church. His view was dominant until millenarianism was revived in different ways by Joachim of Fiore and the radical reformers."[4] We can therefore see what a complicated business it can be to discover the witness' true meaning, and not to be misled by the literary *genre* that witness is using.

4. *The Document may be False*

A historical document which purports to be factual, or which is considered to be factual by some, may not in fact be so.

The document may describe a witness' testimony to an historical fact, but in reality the witness in question never made this testimony. An example of this was the 'Donation of Constantine', a document purporting to be from the Emperor Constantine the Great, in which he was supposed to have donated his Western Empire to succeeding Roman Pontiffs. In the fifteenth century, however, this document was proven to be false by Nicholas of Cusa, one of the "morning stars" of the Renaissance.[5]

Absolute incredibility and positivism

Is there such a thing as an event which is absolutely incredible? We think of course, immediately of miracles, Jesus walking on the water, appearing through closed doors to his disciples. The distinguished molecular scientist Denis Alexander, in his excellent study on science and faith *Rebuilding the Matrix: Science and Faith in the twenty-first century*, summarises Anthony Flew's objections to miracles, and answers them.

Alexander agrees with Flew that a miracle is a "highly improbable" event. We might even agree that a miracle is a "practically impossible" event, in the sense that, *in normal circumstances*, we would exclude the possibility as a principle of action that a miracle has occurred. In normal circumstances, a fisherman would not assume that his colleague would be able to walk on the water in crossing from one boat to another.

But, in accounts of miracles, we are not dealing with normal circumstances. The question is not whether a miracle is highly improbable, but as to whether it is ever possible, or must be excluded absolutely as a possibility in any particular circumstance. We have seen how the credibility of an alleged historical event can be affected by who performed that act. If the *who* happens to be a man claiming to be God, who could say that such a man could not walk on the water?

As Alexander responds in answer to Flew, "historical possibility or impossibility ought to be defined in terms of historical evidence, not in terms of prior metaphysical commitments".[6] Alexander proposes that the courtroom is a better analogy for this type of investigation into events purporting to happen in the past, than a scientific laboratory.[7] Alexander says, criteria of credibility as tested out in a court of law "are particularly relevant for investigating claimed miracles – since miraculous claims depend on the reliability (or otherwise) of witnesses, they involve claims about what in fact took place, and so specialise in the weighing of evidence, and they also include consideration of the counter-claims that the purported events did not occur."[8]

As we have already seen, Reimarus, Strauss and those who embarked early on the Quest of the Historical Jesus, saw the world as a closed system of laws where miracles are just impossible. That we would call a position of *ontological positivism*; namely that the closed system of secondary causality will not, or even cannot, ever be broken. Scientists are less and less inclined to be so dogmatic about what can or cannot occur in the world in which we live.

We noted Strauss as saying that "the absolute cause never disturbs the chain of secondary causes by single arbitrary acts of interposition, but rather manifests itself in the production of the aggregate of finite causalities, and of their reciprocal action".[9] Strauss is therefore denying that God can work directly without using the secondary causes of nature. By the use of this principle, Strauss thereby will dismiss any report as "unhistorical" which claims such direct divine intervention.

Perhaps Strauss himself paused to consider that this kind of restriction might be a strange limitation on the God who had created the world in the first place. He says that "in general, the intermingling of the spiritual world with the human is found only in inauthentic records". But need this always be so? Need the records always be inauthentic? Which criteria does Strauss operate to demonstrate that they *must be* inauthentic? There seem to be no criteria operating at all, only presupposition, even post-Enlightenment prejudice.

Miracles can be the subject of historical investigation

Less and less people would say today that miracles are impossible. Many however would say that we cannot know whether or not a miracle has occurred, particularly if we are dealing with ancient documents. Or, if they accept even that we could know that miracles have occurred, they would say that this is outside the field of modern historical investigation. This includes Christian scholars whose orthodoxy could never be questioned. They would say that it can only be a matter of pure faith whether or not a miracle occurred. This we would designate as a position of *epistemological positivism.*

Thus George Eldon Ladd has no doubt, with us, that "Bultmann's view of history is such that he cannot conceive of God acting objectively in history, but only in human existence."[10] Ladd wants to make clear that he, from within the Conservative Evangelical tradition, believes very clearly in such divine interventions objectively. "Christian theology must realise that the critical-historical method is a child of rationalism and as such is based on a naturalistic world view... Therefore, the Christian theologian must insist that there is a dimension of the actual, past, objective events which occurred in history which goes beyond the presuppositions of modern critical historiography."[11]

But then, Ladd outlines his problem:

> The question at stake is how the modern Christian is to relate his theological formulation and communicate with those who do not share his Christian convictions. Is the Christian theologian to construct his own definition of history and ask the secular world to accept it? Or is the theologian to accept the basic validity of the modern secular understanding of history, and attempt to interpret his faith in terms which at least communicate with those who do not share his faith? If the theologian is to demand that the secular world accept his definition of history, he is faced with a forbidding task; for the Christian insists that in redemptive history, events occurred which are truly unique and without historical analogy. Furthermore,

regularity, continuity, and causality in human history are facts universally recognised and assumed, even by theologians, in the study of world history. Indeed, without such regularity and continuity, there could be no history, and elements of discontinuity could not be recognised. Therefore, it would appear to be a better methodology to admit basic validity of the prevailing scientific historical method, but to insist on its limitations at the point of redemptive history where God has entered history in self-revelation and redemption.[12]

But why could not discontinuity be part of the historian's study as well as continuity? Which group of historians have canonised this "prevailing scientific method" of studying and writing history? We have seen above that a believing scientist, Denis Alexander, is quite prepared to consider historical evidence for miracles, just as much as what we would call "natural events". He does not seem to be bound by the "prevailing scientific method", but seems on the contrary open to treating miracles as potential subjects of scientific investigation.

If modern historiography presupposes a closed chain of secondary causes which preclude direct intervention from the Almighty, and we admit this fact, then have we not effectively and practically reduced ourselves to accepting the rationalist position? It seems here that, quite unnecessarily, Ladd is moving towards a position of epistemological positivism. But if Ladd believes that divine interventions are really possibly *in reality*, and *in history*, as indeed he does, then why cannot the historian's study include redemptive history?

The historical Jesus is the real Jesus

During the last decade, a most important study has appeared, *A Marginal Jew: Rethinking the Historical Jesus*, by a Catholic priest and Professor of the New Testament in Indiana, Father John P. Meier. Like Ladd, Meier's orthodox faith in Christ cannot be doubted. "In my own case, I must candidly confess that I work out of a Catholic context. My greatest temptation, therefore, will be to read back anachronistically the expanded universe of later Church teaching into the 'big bang' moment of Jesus' earthly ministry. In what follows I will try my best to bracket what I hold by faith and examine only what can be shown to be certain or probable by historical research and logical argumentation."[13]

This is indeed a laudable aim. Meier wrote that he "would be delighted if systematic theologians would pick up where this book leaves off and pursue the line of thought further."[14] Meier's labours are therefore most relevant to our purpose, of attempting to write a post-critical apologetic. However, Roch Kereszty, Avery Dulles,[15] and other Catholic exegetes and theologians of repute[16] have expressed severe reservations as to Meier's methodology. To summarise their objections, they would accuse Meier of what N.T. Wright calls "split-level writing about Jesus", a charge which Wright lays before the massive work of Edward Schillebeeckx.[17] In his methodology, these theologians would submit, Meier has set up an unbridgeable chasm between Incarnational faith and historical investigation which *by definition* can never be bridged.

The fundamental problem is that Meier makes an unjustified distinction between the "historical Jesus" and the "real Jesus". Meier claims that we can never know the "real" Jesus. First of all, "obviously we cannot mean the total reality of that person, everything he or she ever thought, felt, experienced, did, and said."[18] That would be more like "comprehensive knowledge", which we can have of no one; presumably not even of ourselves.

But the distinction between "real" and "historical" has nothing whatever to do with the completeness or incompleteness of the account. We know very little indeed about Philo of Alexandria, the Jewish thinker and exegete.[19] Little is known of Philo, except that he lived in Alexandria, and in 39 AD he took part in a delegation to Rome to plead the Jewish cause.[20] Now that is all we know of the "historical Philo". Far from being complete, or near complete, our historical knowledge of Philo is miniscule. But we do know two facts about the "real Philo", presuming that the records are reliable, which we have no reason to doubt. That is our knowledge of the "historical Philo", plus the fact that he wrote a great deal, *which is the same as our knowledge of the "real Philo"*. If there was a spurious legend that he swam the Atlantic and founded a philosophical school in the Americas, then we would not only have "the historical/the real Philo". We would also have "the mythical Philo".

We may indeed admit with Meier that there is more to the "real" Jesus than that which can be determined by historical investigation. Presumably, there always will be, since no account of a person's life, however voluminous and reliable, could be absolutely complete. But we would insist that, at the end of the day, anything which we discover about the "historical Jesus" has also been discovered about the "real Jesus", and that therefore the terms "real" and "historical" are interchangeable.

That, as we saw in our second chapter, was certainly the terms of the enquiry of the Quest of the Historical Jesus from Reimarus onwards. In searching for the historical Jesus, Reimarus was searching for the real Jesus as opposed what he saw as the legendary Jesus of Christian faith. This was also the agenda of the *Jesus Seminar*, which, as we saw right at the beginning of this book, denied that the historical Jesus (= the real Jesus) ever claimed that he was God. We must perforce ourselves accept this same agenda, to attempt to demonstrate that the historical/the real Jesus was not bad or mad, and did in fact claim to be God, vindicating those claims by his miracles and above all by his Resurrection. For us too the historical Jesus must be identical with the real Jesus, since we wish to demonstrate that the Word in reality became flesh in Jesus.[21]

Modern historiography can be inconclusive

Meier claims that we can have concerning modern figures a "reasonably complete" picture, e.g. of a public figure such as Nixon. That, he says, is not true of ancient figures such as Socrates or Pythagoras, apart from "in Marcus Aurelius (reigned 161-80) we have the rare case of a Roman emperor who wrote down his innermost musings in a book called *The Meditations*. This, plus large amounts of correspondence, official records, ancient histories, coins and archaeology, allow the noted historian Anthony Birley to write a fairly clear biography. Yet even here there are certain years in which it is unclear where Marcus was or what he was doing."[22] Thus, Meier argues, an ancient Marcus Aurelius manifests his defects as an ancient historian.

But again this distinction Meier makes between ancient and modern documents as sources of history cannot bear investigation. Recently, I read a book called *The Assassination of Marilyn Monroe*,[23] consisting of tapes and reported conversations by which means the author was attempting to put together the last weeks of the film star's life. Was she assassinated, did she commit suicide, or was her death an accident? Was the Kennedy family involved? Here was a famous woman who lived towards the end of the last century. But how did the "historical Marilyn Monroe" die? However recently she lived, it is still a mystery how and why she died.

Thus whether the document is ancient or modern is irrelevant. We are not certain as to why Marilyn Monroe died, even if her death occurred only a few decades ago. We are much more certain regarding the death of the historical Jesus. We know, as we shall see later, that he was put to death some time during the Procuratorship of Pontius Pilate 26-36 AD. We know that he did not commit suicide, and that he did not die of old age. He was put to death by crucifixion as a common criminal. That we know from documents nearly two thousand years old; but *in this case*, they are more reliable as historical records, and as records of what happened in reality, than books and television documentaries which theorise as to the cause of death of Marilyn Monroe, who died within our lifetime.

We return, therefore, to our primary definition of historicity: X told me that Y happened, and I believe X. Whether the document is ancient or modern is irrelevant. And whether a group of academics agree to it is also irrelevant, except as giving some weight to a particular argument.[24] What is relevant is as to whether a document whether ancient or modern is credible in this or that statement of what actually occurred in the past. And the discipline of "historical science" consists only of the application of criteria of credibility which we have earlier outlined. Is what happened *per se* credible? Are the circumstances credible? Are the documents false? Have we understood the writer's intention? It may be that ancient documents are often less credible than more modern ones, although George Orwell's *1984* warns us of the possibility of modern myths. But in principle, there is no distinction.

Writers knew "myth" from "reality"

It is sometimes suggested that ancient authors were so credulous that their histories are without value. But this is surely to indulge in prejudice against the common-sense of our pre-scientific forebears. Any individual of any age must find stories of feeding five thousand people with five leaves and two fishes somewhat difficult to believe. So the author of II Peter, writing no later than the first half of the Second Century,[25] assumes that the story of the Transfiguration might be difficult to believe, and insists that it actually happened:

> It was not any cleverly invented myths (*muthois*) that we were repeating when we brought you the knowledge of the power and the coming of our Lord Jesus Christ; we had seen his majesty for ourselves. He was honoured and glorified by God the Father, when the Sublime Glory itself spoke to him and said, 'This is my Son, the Beloved; he enjoys my favour. We heard this ourselves, spoken from heaven, when we were with him on the holy mountain. [II Peter 1:16-18]

There can be no doubt that the writer of II Peter, even if not himself the apostle Peter,[26] is claiming to be a part of an eye-witness apostolic tradition testifying to the Transfiguration, which, he says, actually occurred, and is not a *myth*.[27] *Muthos* in the Greek world of the New Testament means a "fable", "fanciful story" which in later Greek was "opposed to *logos* (a true narrative).[28] Christianity was concerned to insist that, at the end of the first century when II Peter was written, their faith was not a *mythos*. The early Christians knew well the distinction between fact and fairy story.

In this connection, Raymond E. Brown notes the conclusion of D.E. Nineham[29] to the effect that "while dependence on eye-witness testimony for the appearance of the risen Jesus is attested in early New Testament writings [I Corinthians 15:5-8], the claim to have eye-witness backing for an account of the ministry of Jesus appears only in later works, like Luke, Acts, John, and II Peter. A question naturally arises, then, as to what extent the claim to eye-witness testimony has been exaggerated at this later period in order to bolster apologetics."[30]

A post-critical reading of New Testament literature must indeed, as Brown says, take account of the *possibility* that eye-witness testimony has been exaggerated in order to bolster apologetics. We have already admitted that the Gospels are faith documents. But does that necessarily mean that they *created* stories in order to bolster their faith? We submit, certainly not necessarily.

It is equally possible that the Christians of the late first century and early second century had good grounds in emphasising the *truth* and *historical reliability* of eye-witness testimony of the apostolic age. This was in order that the post-apostolic Christians of the second century did not come to the false conclusion that the amazing events in the life of Jesus, to which the apostles gave testimony, were myth. This would have discredited Christianity as it began the post-apostolic age. And here precisely, contrary to Nineham, we see in our reference to II Peter that an early Christian writer is insisting that they are not creating stories to bolster the truth claims of Christianity, but rather the opposite, ensuring that the stories which were transmitted to future generations were not myth, but fact.

We come to this enquiry with conditional faith

Kereszty commends Paul Ricoeur's concept of *conditional faith*, and insists that this is necessary for any fruitful historical investigation.[31] It is clear that Reimarus and his successors in the historical Jesus movement did not accept the possibility either of incarnation or of the miraculous actually occurring, as we have seen. This for them they took as a presupposition prior to the investigation. We do accept this possibility.

Our position is equivalent to that of Pierre Benoit:

> All our philosophy is built upon the idea of a personal God, distinct from the world, transcending it by the whole distance of his 'supernatural' Being, but being able to intervene in this world which he has created. And all our theology nourishes itself by the *fact* that he has really and personally intervened. We presuppose, philosophically and theologically, the possibility of the existence of facts which are *supernatural-historical* such as miracles, of a supernatural objective Word such as the Revelation of the Sacred Scriptures. These facts and this word are not for us the creation of the human spirit; they result from an initiative of God who intervenes in the plan of the world.[32]

We have not yet demonstrated the fact of such a supernatural revelation. We only do not exclude its possibility at the outset of the investigation. This therefore implies:

- Belief at least that the existence of a personal God is possible.
- belief in the possibility that this God can reveal himself to the human race through direct intervention in history.
- belief that this man Jesus of Nazareth might possibly be the Son of God as Christian faith claims him to be.

The Christian believer's faith, if it is correct, as we believe it is, will more than survive historical investigation. Part of faith, therefore, is unconditionally committing oneself to that historical investigation while not believing that one will cease to believe in the Christian faith as a result, but only find that faith confirmed. If this seems bizarre, then one might ask a similar question of a scientist. Would a committed Darwinist ever believe that a scientific investigation would change his or her view concerning the mutations of species? Absolutely, intellectual honesty would demand that such a view would change; yet in reality, the Darwinist does not really believe that investigation will change such a fundamental set of convictions as belief in the origin of species by mutations from one species to another. In the same way, the Christian theologian is convinced that no historical investigation will change his or her fundamental beliefs, but rather will confirm them; even if that faith is differently perceived after the investigation. Like every other aspect of human knowledge, faith develops in each individual.

Part of the problem, as we have already seen, is that since the Enlightenment all legitimate forms of knowledge and of attaining certainty have tended to be linked with the laboratory; hence the expression "scientific history writing". But, as we have seen in this chapter, a better model for historical investigation is not the laboratory, but rather the courtroom, where bias is accepted.

A judge, a jury, even a counsel for the defence or the prosecution, could begin an investigation into a crime convinced one way or the other, of the accused's guilt. The evidence may seem to be pointing in one direction, so much so that the person investigating could not imagine that the verdict could go any other way than "guilty". But this does not mean that a fair trial is impossible. Such bias would only be unfair if it led to contrary evidence being ignored, or misused. No court of law requires that those participating be without bias or inclination to believe one party or another. It only requires that all the evidence be fairly considered in order for a just decision to be reached.

Thus a Christian coming to the investigation of the historical Jesus may well come with faith in Jesus as Son of God, and expecting that historical investigation will only confirm that faith. But that does not mean that such investigation will be less objective than that of a person coming from a position of neutrality, provided that all the evidence is fairly considered. This will lead us hopefully to the final judgement of credibility, accepting the claims of Jesus of Nazareth's disciples, who came to believe that he was indeed "The Way, the Truth, and the Life" [John 14:6][33]:

X SAYS Y IS THE REVELATION OF GOD. I BELIEVE X.

1 Orwell, G. *1984*, London, Penguin Books, 1954, 199.
2 For a summary of the life and philosophy of René Descartes, 1596-1650, an explanation of his *Cogito, ergo sum*, "I think, therefore I am", cf. ODCC 394-5, and standard Philosophy introductions.
3 NJBC, **63:3,** 996.
4 ODCC, 739.
5 ODCC, 419, 971.
6 RM, 449.
7 We have earlier employed the analogy of the courtroom in our discussion of the verification of an historical event, p. 88.
8 RM, 450.
9 Cf. LJCE, 88.
10 Ladd, G.E., *The New Testament and Criticism*, London, Hodder & Soughton, 1967, 189.
11 Ibid, 190.
12 Ibid, 190-1.
13 MJ1, 6.
14 MJ1, 6.
15 Dulles, *First Things*, December 1992. 20-25.
16 James F.Keating: "If Meier expected to be roundly applauded for his finely tuned Catholic sensibilities, he must be quite disappointed. He has been attacked from all sides." ITQ, 66(2001), 218.
17 JVG, 7-9.
18 MJ1, 21.
19 ODCC, 1083-4.
20 ODCC, 1083.
21 This understanding of "real" is also in the popular mind, in Britain at least. *The Sunday Telegraph*, a British broadsheet, in its Review of December 19, 1999, carried the banner headline **Who was the real Jesus?** It is clear that A.N. Wilson, the author of the article preparing us for a Christmas with our faith challenged, meant by "the real Jesus" the Jesus of historical fact, i.e. the historical Jesus, rather than the Christ of Christian faith, which he saw as the mythical Jesus.
22 MJ1, 23.
23 Donald H.Wolfe, *The Assassination of Mailyn Monroe*. London, Little, Brown and Company, 1998.
24 MJ1, 2.
25 Brown, INT, 767.
26 It is the unanimous critical opinion that 2 Peter was not written by the apostle Peter, but is an anonymous testimony to the Christian faith in the first half of the Second Century AD. For a summary of reasons, cf. NJBC, **64:2,** 1017,
27 NJBC, **64:12,** 1019.

28 VGT 418. Cf. AS 297. Also I Timothy 1:1, 4:7, II Timothy 4:4, Titus 1: 14.

29 Nineham, D.E. *Eye-Witness Testimony and the Gospel Tradition, III.* JTS 11 (1960), 254-264.

30 Brown, II, 1127.

31 Kereszty, Communio. Kereszty, R. Historical Research, theological inquiry, and the reality of Jesus: Reflections on the method of J.P. Meier. Communio 19 (Winter 1992), 598-9.

32 ET, 59.

33 "If Jesus is the way in the sense that he is the truth and enables men to know their goal, he is also the way in the sense that he is the LIFE" (*zóé*). Cf. Brown, II, 630.

CHAPTER 5

JESUS EXISTED

We demonstrate the historical existence of Jesus of Nazareth from extra-canonical sources such as Josephus, Tacitus, the Talmud, and Mara Bar Sarapion. These demonstrate that Jesus was a prophet who was put to death during the prefecture of Pontius Pilate some time between 26-36 AD. It is surely highly significant that none of these sources questioned the existence of Jesus, when they would surely have known if Jesus had not existed from their contemporaries.

There was a well-known joke about Bultmann that someone telephoned him to inform him that the bones of Jesus of Nazareth had been found in Jerusalem. Without doubt, therefore, the bodily Resurrection was a myth. The one providing the information thought that Bultmann would have been pleased that his scepticism about the Resurrection accounts was finally vindicated. Instead, the distinguished professor replied, "You mean to tell me that he really existed?"

But in fact, the joke itself is a case of a mythical legend developing about Bultmann himself. The historical Bultmann had no doubt that Jesus existed:

Of course, the doubt as to whether Jesus really existed is unfounded and not worth refutation. No sane person can doubt that Jesus stands as founder behind the historical movement whose first distinctive stage is represented by the oldest Palestinian community.[1]

In fact, we could say that the existence of Jesus of Nazareth is as secure a historical fact as the existence of Julius Caesar or Shakespeare. However, it cannot be dismissed as a "non-question", because the question is still asked. It is important to find out why it is affirmed that Jesus did actually exist, at least as a historical foundation on which to build more specific data about the Jesus of history.

Josephus

The first important source is Joseph ben Matthias AD 37-100, known as Flavius Josephus[2] by his patrons the Flavian emperors Vespasian, Titus and Domitian. Josephus, son of a priest and from a well to do family, was first of all a commander in Galilee during the Jewish war of 67-70. But he turned to the Romans as the Jews inevitably were being defeated, and Josephus successfully prophesied that Vespasian would become emperor. When this happened, Josephus was pensioned in Rome by the Emperor and wrote his historical and apologetic works. Josephus wrote an account of the *Jewish War*, where he does not mention Jesus at all. As Meier states, "This simply reminds us that Jesus was a marginal Jew leading a marginal movement in a marginal province of a vast Roman Empire."[3]

There are two texts from Josephus which are particularly worthy of consideration. The first is a reference to James as the brother of Jesus – to his death by stoning at the instigation of the high priest Ananus. (Catholic tradition, which has affirmed the perpetual virginity of Mary, interpreted "brother" to mean that James was either "cousin" or "half-brother" of Jesus[4]):

> Being therefore this kind of person [i.e. a heartless Sadducee], Ananus, thinking that he had a favourable opportunity because Festus had died and Albinus was still on his way, called a meeting [literally, "sanhedrin"] of judges and brought into it the brother of Jesus-who-is-called-Messiah [*ton adelphon Iēsou tou legonenou Christou*], James by name, and some others. He made the accusation that they had transgressed the law, and he handed them over to be stoned.[5]

Scholars are quite convinced that this text is authentic, i.e. it is not a Christian interpolation.[6] Many reasons are given for this authenticity, particularly in Meier, to whom the reader is referred.[7] Even the slightly less than respectful "brother of Jesus" is a pointer. Would not a Christian scribe have put "brother of the Lord Jesus" or some much more deferential appellation? And Jesus "who is called Christ" (*ho legomenos christos*) is likewise impersonal and an unenthusiastic way for a Christian scribe to designate Christ. (Cf. Colossians 4:11, *Iésous ho legomenos Ioustos*, Jesus with the surname Justus, equally neutral as a designation).[8]

If this text of Josephus is authentic, which it certainly seems to be, we have a non-Christian testimony to the existence of Jesus of Nazareth clearly identified in the last quarter of the first century AD, less than half a century after the death of Jesus. That is impressive in itself. This also makes more than possible the authenticity of the most famous text of all from Josephus:

> At this time there appeared Jesus, a wise man, **if indeed one should call him a man.** For he was a doer of startling deeds, a teacher of people who receive the truth with pleasure. And he gained a following both among many Jews and among many of Greek origin. **He was the Messiah.** And when Pilate, because of an accusation made by the leading men among us, condemned him to the cross, those who had loved him previously did not cease to do so. **For he appeared to them on the third day, living again, just as the divine prophets had spoken of these and countless other wondrous things about him.** And up until this very day the tribe of Christians, named after him, has not died out.[9]

The three bolded texts are the obvious Christian interpolations admitted both by Meier[10] and Theissen/Merz.[11] But is what remains, the unbolded text, authentic? Meier thinks so, but cautiously, estimating that at least "some reference to Jesus stood here in the authentic text of *The Antiquities*."[12] If so, this would be at least a confirmation by a first century Jewish writer that Jesus existed. This is a complicated discussion, which still has no firm resolution either way.[13] This text has been worked over, and for that reason revision theories abound.

In conclusion regarding Josephus, the reference to James seems the best authenticated, and is all we need to confirm the existence of Jesus. Could Josephus be mistaken about the *historical existence* of one whom he describes as a well known prophet in his own country living only half a century before the time when he wrote his books, and indeed *during his own lifetime?* The thought is surely bizarre.

Jesus existed: Tacitus

The most important Roman witness to Jesus' existence is the historian Tacitus, (AD 55-120) who, writing his Roman annals between AD 115 and 117, mentions the Great Fire of Rome in AD 64 and Nero's attempt to fasten the blame for it on the Christians. This was a ruse on Nero's part because the populace of Rome were beginning to think that he, Nero, had in fact himself started the fire:

> Therefore, to squelch the rumour, Nero created scapegoats and subjected to the most refined tortures those whom the common people called "Christians" [a group] hated for their abominable crimes. Their name comes from Christ, who, during the reign of Tiberius, had been executed by the procurator Pontius Pilate. Suppressed for the moment, the deadly superstition broke out again, not only in Judea, the land which originated this evil, but also in the city of Rome, where all sorts of horrendous and shameful practices from every part of the world converge and are fervently cultivated.[14]

This is obviously very important evidence of the existence of Jesus, since clearly Tacitus is not biased in favour of Christianity, and wrote his annals as an historical account less than a hundred years after the death of Jesus.

If we accept Tacitus' testimony, as is most reasonable, we would have knowledge of the following as historical facts about Jesus of Nazareth:

• That he lived in "Judaea" the area, equivalent to the southern region of Israel and Jordan today) some time during the procuratorship of Pontius Pilate, who held office in Judaea from 26-36 AD.

- That he was put to death by sentence of Pontius Pilate, during the imperatorship of Tiberius, who was emperor from 14-37 AD.

- That he was, wittingly or unwittingly, the founder of a religion which came to bear his name, called by the unflattering title of "a pernicious superstition" (*exitiabilis superstitio*[15]) by the cynical Tacitus.

If Tacitus is a genuine independent historical source for the existence of Jesus, then, it appears that the case is closed. Jesus existed; he was put to death by the Roman procurator Pontius Pilate some time between 26-36 AD, and he was the founder of the sect known as Christians.

For those, therefore, who still doubt the historical existence of Jesus of Nazareth, it is essential somehow to break down this testimony of Tacitus. The question of the sources of Tacitus becomes the main point of attack. Is Tacitus any value as a testimony, if he is only relaying information from Christians themselves, who may be preaching a mythical and not an historical Jesus?

Firstly, negatively, it cannot be argued that Tacitus has his information from official Roman sources. Otherwise, why does he name Pontius Pilate as the *procurator* of Judaea, whereas in fact he was the *prefect* of Judaea? This has been proved by the Pilate inscription found in Caesarea in 1961.[16] If Tacitus was dependent on official records, surely he would not make a mistake like that?

Equally undemonstrable is whether Tacitus depended on Josephus for his information. This was Harnack's view; but Josephus knows "Christus" as a messianic title, whereas Tacitus "regards the surname 'Christus' as Jesus' own name."[17] Thus Harnack's opinion does not have wide currency now.

It is most likely that Tacitus received his information simply from common knowledge about Jesus. If Christianity was proving a problem, as it obviously was towards the end of the first century and the beginning of the second, it would hardly be surprising that an intelligent Roman, particularly an historian, would find out some basic facts about the foundation of that troublesome sect. Furthermore, if Jesus had not existed at all, would not that have been a point where Tacitus could have further ridiculed Christianity, since he was looking for such areas of attack? Tacitus may have made a mistake over a relatively minor matter, as to whether Pilate was procurator or prefect; but the events of the death of Jesus of Nazareth were near enough to his own time, less than a century, for him to have known that the existence of such a prophet, supposedly with some fame in first-century Judaea, was itself a myth, if indeed it were. Tacitus' testimony, from whatever source, must surely stand.

Jesus existed: Mara Bar Sarapion

"Remarkably, what is probably the earliest pagan testimony to Jesus is little known."[18] Our thanks are due to Theissen and Merz in *The Historical Jesus: A Comprehensive Guide* for drawing it to our attention. Mara bar Sarapion was a Syrian Stoic, who came from Samosata, to which he wrote to his son Sarapion from a Roman prison concerning whose location we are unaware. Mara is giving fatherly advice to his son with the possibility of his own execution in mind. Above all, he commends his son to be wise:

> What good did it do the Athenians to kill Socrates, for which deed they were punished with famine and pestilence? What did it avail the Samians to burn Pythagoras, since their country was entirely buried under sand in one moment? Or what did it avail the Jews to kill their wise king, since their kingdom was taken away from them from that time on?

> God justly avenged these three wise men. The Athenians died of famine, the Samians were flooded by the sea, the Jews were slaughtered and driven from their kingdom, everywhere living in the dispersion.

Socrates is not dead, thanks to Plato; nor Pythagoras, because of Hera's statue. Nor is the wise king, because of the new law which he has given.[19]

It is indeed remarkable that more reference is not made to this text. Its date seems to be very early indeed, "Probably it was composed soon after 73 CE"[20] Mara mentions the Jewish war of 66-74, and so it was written after that. "But in that case we must assume that the author does not know of the renewed clashes in Palestine which broke out in 132 CE"[21] Thus a date from the late first century AD and the early second century seems most likely.

This Syrian Stoic, therefore, living in a region which had already seen its first converts to Christianity just north of from where Jesus himself came only a few decades before, compares Jesus with the wise men Socrates and Pythagoras. He does not mention the Resurrection, but simply equates Jesus with the great philosophers he knows about. Jesus lives on in the laws he has left. He knows too that Jesus has been put to death unjustly. Again, although this gives us little information about Jesus we cannot read about in the Gospels, Mara gaining his information no doubt from early Syrian Christianity, what a strong testimony Mara is to the *existence* of Jesus. He knows about a wise man put to death in his own region very recently. How is it possible that this wise man did not exist, along with Socrates and Pythagoras who lived many centuries before Jesus?

Jesus existed: Jewish sources

The existence of Jesus is testified in the Talmud (i.e. "teaching"), a collection of teachings from different periods in Jewish history. Meier points out that Jewish scholars themselves are sceptical about references in the Jewish literature to the historical Jesus.[22] One Jewish scholar, Johann Maier in fact, concludes that "all such references to Jesus are later interpolations inserted in the Middle Ages".[23] However, there is general acceptance at least of the possibility that one text, the Babylonian Talmud's tractate *Sanhedrin* 43a, does make a genuine reference to Jesus,[24] and can be dated early, in the second century:

> On the Sabbath of the Passover festival Jesus (Yeshu) the Nazarene was hanged. For forty days before execution took place, a herald went forth and cried: 'Here is Jesus the Nazarene, who is going forth to be stoned because he has practised sorcery and enticed Israel to apostasy. Anyone who can say anything in his favour, let him come forth and plead on his behalf.' But since nothing was brought forth in his favour, he was hanged on the eve of the Passover.[25]

We can accept for the moment at least Klausner's view that this text is genuine. It seems to me that the view of Maier in his *Jesus of Nazareth* "that the name Jesus was inserted only secondarily into the account of the execution of some magician and deviant teacher who by chance had been killed on the eve of the Passover"[26] is a little far-fetched. The text does not mention the role of the Roman authorities, since the Talmud wishes to take responsibility for putting to death one who led Israel astray. Interestingly, saying that Jesus was hanged on the "eve of the Passover" contradicts the Synoptic account, but goes with the Fourth Gospel chronology, where Jesus was crucified on the "Day of Preparation" for the Passover [John 19:31, 42].[27]

It is impossible to demonstrate one way or the other whether or not the Talmud had a distinct source of historical information for the trial and execution of Jesus which is relayed in the text above, or whether the Talmud here is relying on Christian sources such as the Gospels for its information. What is important, however, as with the information supplied by Tacitus above, is that the Talmud *never contests the existence of Jesus.* Surely, the Judaean Jews of the first century would have known whether or not a famous prophet actually existed or not? And, if he had not existed, would not this have been the strongest of arguments against Christianity, in the early stages of the Christian movement when friction was already in evidence [e.g. Acts 13:45]? Yet never was Jesus' historical existence ever questioned. As Theissen/Merz say, "both opponents and neutral or sympathetic observers of Christianity presuppose the historicity of Jesus and do not indicate a shadow of doubt about it."[28]

Neither should we doubt it. The existence of Jesus is well proven by the criterion of historical coherence, which we shall discuss in our next chapter. It coheres with all the other facts of history we know contemporary with the time when Jesus was presumed to be alive. Plenty of people in the first century would have known that one reputed to be a famous man in their own time did not exist. The idea of a famous man not existing is incongruous. If he was reputedly famous, then those who lived contemporary with him or a generation or two after him, would have questioned whether he ever existed if they had known of his fame, but had never heard of him. "Jesus a famous man in Judea, put to death by Pontius Pilate? I lived in the country at the time, but I never heard of him." The idea is really quite absurd. If the existence of Jesus was never questioned by those living during or just after his time, and Jesus was reputedly famous, then Jesus must have existed.

However, there is a final reason which is less tangible, but perhaps even more convincing, why Jesus actually existed. Why has the idea never gained currency, even among sceptics concerning the claims of Jesus and his followers that he never existed? First and foremost, one would suggest, because Jesus is such an extraordinary figure as he appears in the Gospels, that it would have been more difficult to have invented him, than for him actually to have existed. As a person, he appears so unique to us, even to those who do not believe, that he is beyond the power of human invention.

NOTES – CHAPTER 5

1   JW, 17.
2   MJ1, 56. ODCC, 759. HJCG, 64-74.
3   MJ1, 56.

4   Cf. McHugh, J., *The Mother of Jesus in the New Testament*, London, Darton, Longman & Todd, 200-254.

5   MJ1, 57. HJ, 64-65. Cf. complete text in HJ 470, *Antt.* 20, 199-203.

6   "The *authenticity* of the text may be taken as certain; it is improbable that it is a Christian interpolation." HJCG, 65.

7   MJ1, 57-58.

8   MJ1, 65.

9   MJ1, 60.

10 MJ1, 60-61.

11 HJCG, 69.

12 MJ1, 62.

13 Cf. HJCG, 71-74.

14 MJ1, 90-91. We are grateful to Meier for the translations from ancient sources on the existence of Jesus.

15 HJ, 82. Tacitus *Ann.* 15.44.3.

16 HJCG, 83.

17 HJCG, 83, n.58.

18 HJCG, 76.

19 HJCG, 77. We are indebted to Theissen/Merz for this translation.

20 HJCG, 77.

21 HJCG, 77.

22 MJ1, 93-98.

23 MJ1, 95.

24 MJ1, 96. Meier names this as the view of Klausner, cf.107, n.49.

25 Our translation on this occasion is from HJCG 75.

26 HJCG, 75, n.38.

27 HJCG, 75. "Here perhaps we can see an apologetic answer to the Christian charge that Jesus had been tried over-hastily."

28 HJCG, 85.

THE CRITICAL MINIMUM

- Jesus was a Jewish prophet and teacher.
- He was renowned as a miracle worker.
- His teaching caused religious offence to the Judaism of his day.
- He was arrested and put to death by crucifixion by Pontius Pilate, the prefect of Judaea, some time between 26–36 AD.

How do we decide what comes from Jesus?

This is the title of John P. Meier's chapter 6, volume 1 of *A Marginal Jew: Rethinking the Historical Jesus.* Various criteria have been developed particularly by the post-Bultmannians to separate out the words and deeds of Jesus in the Gospels from the "theological overlay" of the primitive Christian community; e.g. the criterion of embarrassment, sayings which are likely to be from the historical Jesus because they would embarrass the Christian community, and thus are unlikely to be invented by them.

As with so many areas of the subject matter we are treating, the bibliography is enormous. Meier gives an extensive list, as does Schillebeeckx.[1] We must first acknowledge with Meier that all such criteria "are only more or less probable; certainty is rarely to be had."[2] If we go back to our analogy of the witness,[3] it is as if we were examining an untrustworthy witness who nevertheless will reveal some facts whether that witness intends to or not. Such cross-examination will always be problematic. Either the witness might be bullied by counsel into admitting less than what really happened, or the court might be duped by a clever witness into accepting as credible what is less so.

Recently, J.G. Dunn has expressed severe reservations about these criteria, similar to those expressed by Timothy Luke Johnson, who calls the criteria "slippery and subjective":[4]

Few, however, are wholly satisfied with these criteria. If the criterion of dissimilarity is applied consistently, and only that material is added which coheres with the limited findings of the first trawl through the Jesus tradition, then the historical Jesus who emerges is bound to be a strange creature, with anything which links him to the religion of his people or to the teaching of his followers automatically ruled out of court, "a unique Jesus in a vacuum."[5]

We are attempting to understand a *human mind*, that of Jesus of Nazareth. To reject dogmatically sayings of Jesus either because they are too strongly rooted in his past, or on the other hand because there seem to be no roots in other thinkers, could simply be an example of the narrowness of our minds, not an indication that the primitive church has invented this or that saying. Schweitzer recognised this, as we have seen,[6] a hundred years ago.

These criteria, therefore, do not provide us with a knockdown certainty of what Jesus said and did *taken in isolation*. But cumulatively, the application of these criteria can have some use in helping us to build up a credible picture of Jesus' life and ministry. And if, as we can see it does, this leads to a scholarly consensus, a "critical minimum",[7] this can be a starting-point for a consideration of more disputed questions.

The criteria

A. *The Criterion of Embarrassment; a saying in the Gospels by Jesus is likely to be historically authentic if it would seem to cause embarrassment to the primitive church.*

The point of the criterion is that the early Church would hardly have gone out of its way to create material that only embarrassed its creator or weakened its position in arguments with opponents."[8] The example given is the baptism of the supposedly superior and sinless Jesus by his supposed inferior

John the Baptist [Mark 1:4-11]. As Goulder says, "So Mark quite often tells us things about Jesus and the apostles which Matthew and Luke omit or colour."[9]

B. *The Criterion of Double Discontinuity. A saying in the Gospels by Jesus is likely to be authentic if it could not have been derived from Judaism at the time of Jesus or from the early Church after him.*

"Closely allied to the criterion of embarrassment, the criterion of discontinuity (also labelled dissimilarity, originality, or dual irreducibility) focuses on words or deeds of Jesus that cannot be derived either from Judaism at the time of Jesus or from the early Church after him."[10] Thus Jesus' rejection of voluntary fasting for his disciples [Mark 2:18-22\\], does not seem to have any place in Judaism at the time of Christ or in the primitive Christian community.[11]

C. *The Criterion of Multiple Attestation. A saying of Jesus in the Gospels is likely to be historically authentic if it is attested in more than one independent literary source (e.g. Mark, Q, Paul, John), and/or in more than one literary form or genre.*

"The criterion of multiple attestation (or "the cross section") focuses on those sayings or deeds of Jesus that are attested in more than one independent literary source (e.g. Mark, Q, Paul, John) and/or in more than one literary form or genre (e.g. parable, dispute story, miracle story, prophecy, aphorism). The force of this criterion is increased if a given motif or theme is found in both different literary sources and different literary forms. One reason that critics so readily affirm that Jesus did speak in some sense of the kingdom of God (or kingdom of heaven) is that the phrase is found in Mark, Q, special Matthean tradition, special Lucan tradition, and John, with echoes in Paul, despite the fact that "kingdom of God" is not Paul's preferred way of speaking. At the same time, the phrase is found in various literary genres (e.g. parable, beatitude, prayer, aphorism, miracle story). Granted this *wide* sweep of witnesses in different sources and genres, coming largely from the first Christian generation, it becomes extremely difficult to claim that such material is simply the creation of the Church."[12]

D. *The Criterion of Coherence. A saying of Jesus in the Gospels is likely to be historically authentic if it coheres with other sayings and deeds of Jesus.*

"The criterion of coherence holds that other sayings and deeds of Jesus that fit in well with the preliminary 'data base' established by using our first three criteria have a good chance of being historical (e.g. sayings concerning the coming of the kingdom of God, or disputes with adversaries over legal observance). As can already be seen, this criterion, by its very nature, is less probative that the three on which it depends."[13] Schillebeeckx sees, however, a legitimate extension of this criterion in forming "a total and historical picture of Jesus"[14] giving rise to what Schillebeeckx calls "sub-criteria".

E. *The Criterion of Sufficient Reason. A saying in the Gospels is likely to be from the historical Jesus if it explains what would otherwise be inexplicable.*

Meier says "If a sizeable collection of facts or data requiring a coherent and sufficient explanation are given an explanation that clarifies and harmoniously combines all those elements (which would otherwise remain puzzling), then we may conclude that we are in the presence of an authentic datum (a deed, action, attitude, or statement of Jesus)."[15] Thus, as we shall later demonstrate, a most adequate sufficient reason for Jesus' being arrested and handed over to Pilate for execution was his own divine claims for himself and his mission[16].

F. *The Criterion of Economy ("Occam's razor"). A saying in the Gospels is most likely from the historical Jesus if alternative explanations of its origin involve hypothesis without concrete evidence, and/or unnecessarily convoluted argument.*

This as a criterion[17] has a good philosophical basis, namely that, in William of Occam's terms, *entia non multiplicabuntur praeter necessitatem.* Beings are not to be multiplied without necessity. In historical investigation, evidence must have precedence over unsubstantiated hypothesis. We shall see later that Jesus' claim to be the transcendent Son of Man is usually assigned by historical Jesus researchers to the primitive community rather than to the historical Jesus. However, since we have no knowledge of any Christian community which explicitly professed Jesus as the transcendent Son of Man (second-century Christians did not express their faith in the exalted Christ in terms of his being the Son of Man, but used Greek expressions such as *Kurios*), such a primitive Jewish Christian community has to be invented by the scholar, a "transcendent Son of Man" community. Surely, the criterion of economy would suggest that the historical Jesus is preferable as the origin of such an idea expressed by Jesus, since that is what the text says.

G. *The Criterion of Historical Presumption. This criterion states that a saying of Jesus in the Gospel is presumed to be from the historical Jesus unless proved otherwise.*

Meier comments "This criterion brings us squarely into the debate about where the "burden of proof" lies: on the side of the critic who denies historicity or on the side of the critic who affirms it?"[18] Meier insists on the former. "However, common sense and the rules of logical argument seem to be on the side of critics like Willi Marxsen and Ben Meyer, who state the obvious: the burden of proof is simply on anyone who tries to prove anything."[19] We must agree that, at least in a work which is an apologetic for the divinity of Christ as is this book, we cannot presume what we are attempting to prove; even if, as we saw earlier, those such as Reimarus and Strauss who initiated the Quest of the Historical Jesus most certainly did![20]

However, the criterion of historical presumption comes very much into play *as we build up a cumulative case* for the historical authenticity of the Gospels. We recall our formula for an historical event "X tells me Y happened and I believe

X". As more and more events as recounted in the Gospels are authenticated by these (admittedly rough and ready) criteria, we are led more and more to trust the veracity of the Gospels. If, as we have argued, the analogy of a law court is useful for considering the authenticating of historical records, then trust in a given witness will breed more trust if once or twice proven, just as a couple of cracks in a criminal's testimony in court will throw doubt on his whole story.

Also, we have already generated some credibility when considering our witness, the writers of the four Gospels. Our consideration of the manuscripts of our Gospels, and consideration of their authorship, at the very least gives us initial confidence that the documents are not false.[21] Our consideration of the *genre* of Synoptic Gospels has led to the conclusion that they are not to be dismissed *a priori* as fiction.[22] Thus we may justifiably anticipate some historical fact to be contained in their records, granted that they are documents of faith and in the "form of preaching".[23]

Finally, we have already tested the evidence external to the Gospels and discovered that Jesus existed, and that he was put to death as a criminal by Pontius Pilate sometime between 26-36 AD. This confirms the Gospel account. Thus we are justified in having some optimism that more genuine historical information will be contained in those documents as we proceed in our investigations.

The Critical Minimum described

By the use of the above criteria, we can conclude with reasonable historical certainty the critical minimum as described above regarding the life, ministry and death of Jesus:

- *Jesus came from Nazareth in Galilee.*

Christ came from Nazareth, since there seems no theological reason why the Christian community should have invented this. Nazareth was not highly regarded from a religious point of view. The question of a potential disciple of Jesus when told that he came from Nazareth in Galilee was "can anything good come out of Nazareth?" [John 1:46]. That statement itself has historical credibility by virtue of the criterion of embarrassment.[24]

• *Jesus was linked with the preaching of John the Baptist, a popular prophet who preached in the desert of Judea, and who baptised his followers as a sign of repentance and of preparation for the coming of God.*

Christ submitting himself to the baptism of John would seem to be to the disadvantage or even embarrassment of the early Christian community, therefore is historically admissible [Matthew 3:13[25]].

• *Around 30 AD, Jesus emerged as a prophet himself, preaching the kingdom of God which he believed was near, and whose coming was related to his own ministry.*

That Jesus preached the kingdom of God through his own acts of power has no parallels in Judaism: "But if it is by the Spirit of God that I cast out demons, then the kingdom of God has come (*ephthasen*) to you." [Matthew 12:28, Luke 11:20], nor is the "kingdom of God" a characteristic expression of the early Christian community about Jesus' ministry. The scholars accept this as part of the critical minimum using the principle of double discontinuity.[26] That Jesus began his ministry at approximately 30 AD is calculated from the date of his execution by Pilate 26–36 AD.

• *He became renowned as a worker of healing miracles, and of exorcisms. Many people acknowledged him as a prophet.*

The fact that Jesus had a reputation as a miracle worker is itself good grounds for the historicity of this particular tradition. Not every prophet had a reputation as a miracle worker, e.g. John the Baptist did not. And the reaction to miracles was not necessarily Christological, betraying theological interest. Reaction to the earlier miracles was praise of God, not necessarily faith in Jesus. Matthew 15:31. The criterion of multiple attestation,[27] a tradition manifested in different contexts and in different traditions, would seal the place of Jesus as a reputed miracle worker in the critical minimum.

• *Jesus became unpopular with the Jewish religious authorities, because he healed on the Sabbath day, and seemed to make light of some Rabbinic and Old Testament regulations. He also associated himself with outcasts and sinners in society, which was against some Pharisaic thinking of the time.*

Critical scholars are prepared to admit to the critical minimum that Jesus was a rebel against the strict Rabbinic laws. [Mark 2:25-28, Jesus approving of his disciples rubbing the corn between their hands on the Sabbath]. It is debatable how much of Jesus' conduct which appears to provide tension with his Jewish contemporaries was in fact against Jewish law. E.P. Sanders "above all has put Jesus' ethics and conduct in the tradition of Jewish expectation of the Torah. Thus neither the breaches of the Sabbath nor the antitheses leave the Jewish Torah behind."[28] The modern tendency is to emphasis Jesus' Jewish roots. Thus we might not have here the principle of discontinuity, but rather of multiple attestation. Jesus appears in all contexts as adopting a liberal attitude to Sabbath law, and as involving himself with "sinners", those unacceptable within Pharisaism [Luke 7:37]. The Christian community itself would also have found Christ's ethics a challenge, and would hardly have wanted to have invented them.

• *Jesus went up to Jerusalem to celebrate the Passover. He was arrested at night, being betrayed by Judas one of his disciples, in order to avoid a possible rebellion and insurrection. The Roman Prefect Pontius Pilate condemned him to death by crucifixion.*

We have independent evidence from Tacitus, or at least confirmation by him, that Jesus was put to death by Pontius

Pilate some time between 26-36 AD. All four Gospels implicate Pilate in finally sending Jesus to his death by crucifixion, even if he washed his hands of it [Matthew 27:24]. It does seem that Pilate was frightened of possible revolution, and saw Jesus as a possible threat. Jesus' opponents played on this fact at Jesus' trial before Pilate: "They began to accuse him, saying, "We found this man perverting our nation, forbidding us to pay taxes to the emperor, and saying that he himself is the Messiah, a king." [Luke 23:2]. The critical minimum, therefore, based upon the criterion of coherence[29] will allow that Pilate condemned Jesus to death probably for sedition.

Questions remaining

We have just outlined the "agreed minimum", called often "the critical minimum", of historical facts about Jesus of Nazareth which are accepted by the broad consensus of contemporary New Testament scholarship.[30] But before we become too excited about the critical minimum, it is worth noting that Wrede and Schweitzer[31] a hundred years ago, and even Reimarus two hundred years ago, as well as the *Jesus Seminar* only a decade ago, would also have been happy to agree substantially with that critical minimum, while of course disagreeing about individual points of the assessment of historical data about Jesus in the Synoptic Gospels.

In harsh reality, the critical minimum is only a confirmation of historical Jesus studies from Reimarus onwards, which studies seem to have all concluded, whatever the variations on the theme, that a historical Jewish prophet or sage called Jesus became a Gentile God in the view of the first-century Christians.

We now suggest that there are three problems, three unanswered questions in critical scholarship, which we propose to answer by the simple method of demonstrating the trustworthiness of the Gospels, and in particular the Gospel of John, in their account:

The Enigma of Jesus – The critical minimum accepted Jesus as a prophet renowned for working miracles and preaching the kingdom of God. But how did the early Christians come to see him as the divine Son of God, the Lord, in the twenty years after his death? What we may call the "Bousset" solution, that the Christian community applied Greek deifying categories to one who was essentially a Jewish prophet, is the standard critical answer, which, as we have seen, is now increasingly discredited.

How could the first Christians have believed in his resurrection if Jesus had not lived a life in some way or other which made them think he *had* risen from the dead? This is precisely the argument used by Peter in his speech to the Jewish nation in Acts 2:22, that Jesus was "a man attested to you by God with deeds of power, wonders, and signs that God did through him among you, as you yourselves know", and that the Resurrection was the *vindication of the life of the just man* Jesus. Somehow, then, they must have thought that his life on earth was at least an important factor in their coming to see him as divine.

The Enigma of his Death – The critical minimum accepts that Jesus was put to death at the command of Pontius Pilate the Roman Prefect. But Pilate would not have put Jesus to death if there had not been some reason for it in Jesus' own message and life. Even he was not that indifferent to human life. Critical scholarship has no united answer to this question; but is this critical confusion not generated by the simple fact that historical Jesus scholarship will not accept that, as the Gospels state, Jesus was thought to be a blasphemer by his enemies because of his divine claims?

The Enigma of his Resurrection – The third problem is the strangest of all, the phenomenon of the Christian faith in the Resurrection of Jesus bodily from the dead. We saw earlier[32] that Reimarus considered that the disciples of Jesus, not willing to return to their fishing and viewing the attractive prospect of a clerical career, went back to an early idea that the Messiah would rise from the dead. But this begs an important question, as we will discuss more in detail later in the chapter on the Resurrection. There is no Jewish tradition for the Messiah to come back *bodily* from the dead as Jesus did, after his death. What then actually happened after his death, so that the early Christians believed that he had risen in physical form from the dead? Sanders asks pertinently "Without the Resurrection, would [Jesus'] disciples have endured longer than did John the Baptist's? We can only guess, but I would guess not."[33] But why did they believe in his Resurrection? *What actually happened* to make them do so?

From Reimarus onwards, these have been the three main questions still to be answered by all those who accept the critical minimum as described above, but cannot accept the answer given by a straight reading of the Gospels; namely:

- That Jesus did himself claim during his lifetime to be the divine Son of God, and substantiated this claim by his life, teaching, and by his miracles.
- That this claim led to his being handed over for blasphemy to Pilate, and led to his death by crucifixion.
- That the first Christians found his tomb empty and he appeared bodily to them. This was the cause of their faith in him.

We shall now proceed to attempt to demonstrate that it is most reasonable to accept that this Gospel account is authentic historically.

NOTES – CHAPTER 6

1 MJ1, 186,n.7. Schillebeeckx, 88-90.
2 MJ1, 168.
3 Cf. pp. 90-1.
4 Johnson, L.T., *The Real Jesus: The Misguided Quest for the Historical Jesus and the Truths of the Traditional Gospels*, Harper, San Francisco 1997, 129, "We can observe in Meier's careful consideration of individual sayings, or specific actions, just how slippery and subjective the so-called criteria for historicity really are."
5 JR, 82. Dunn quotes JEC, 1974, 94.
6 QHJ, 348. Cf. p. 36.

7 Here we see value in Meier's "formula of concord" reached at by his hypothetically imprisoned academics of different persuasions when charged to reach a consensus as to what the historical Jesus said and did. MJ1, 2.

8 MJ1, 168.

9 MGI, 50.

10 MJ1, 171.

11 MJ1, 173. cf. JEC, 94.

12 MJ1, 174-5.

13 MJ1, 176.

14 JEC, 96.

15 In this I agree with Meier, MJ2, 1035, n.315.

16 Chapter 8, "You Have Heard the Blasphemy".

17 I am most grateful to Professor J.J. Scarisbrick, the historian, who suggested this criterion to me when reading the draft manuscript of this book. I have not seen this criterion expressed in print anywhere else, but it seems to me not only eminently reasonable, but most useful in Jesus research.

18 MJ1, 183.

19 MJ1, 183.

20 Chapter 2, "The Blinkered Quest".

21 Cf. pp. 89-90, "The document may be false".

22 Cf. p. 89, "The witness has been misunderstood".

23 DV 19.

24 Cf. p. 114.

25 Hughes, J.J., *John the Baptist: Forerunner of God Himself. Novum Testamentum,* 14 (1972), pp.190-218, argues that John the Baptist was looking forward not so much to the Messiah, as to the coming of God Himself.

26 Cf. p. 115.

27 Cf. p. 115.

28 HJ, 352.

29 Cf. p. 116.

30 HJCG 569-572, *Retrospect: A Short Life of Jesus* presents a typical Critical Minimum in narrative form.

31 Indeed, Schweitzer did not think much of this critical minimum at all: "Those who are fond of talking about negative theology can find their account here. There is nothing more negative than the result of the critical life of Jesus" QHJ, 396.

32 Cf. p.41.

33 Sanders, E.P., *Jesus and Judaism*, London, SCM, 1985, 240.

CHAPTER 7

BUILDING UP A PROFILE
THE WRIGHT WAY

We opt to follow a methodology forged by N.T. Wright in his *Jesus and the Victory of God*. It consists of using all the criteria, but particularly that of historical consistency, in order to build up a coherent picture of the historical Jesus from the Gospels.

The Wright way

N.T. Wright's *Jesus and the Victory of God* is one of the most important books on the historical Jesus since Schweitzer's *Quest*. Perhaps it is the most important book, since it maps a method which breaks the post-Wrede and post-Bultmann mould of Cartesian scepticism and Kantian subjectivism, and indicates the way forward to a fruitful Quest of the historical Jesus. Jesus research will never be the same again.

To use McDade's extension of Wright's own terminology, Wright goes up the "Schweitzer Street" (*Schweitzerstrasse*) rather than the "Wrede Way" (*Wredebahn*).[1] That is to say, he opts for the eschatological Jesus, the Jesus looking for the breaking-in Kingdom of God, rather than the Jesus of the sceptical critical minimum of Wrede.[2] Schweitzer opens up the possibility that we will see Jesus as he really was, not just as a post-Enlightenment reconstruct. Wright follows up this more imaginative path, and continues on from it. "What is more, this argument advances across the swamp of historical scepticism not by means of the tightrope of isolated sayings, but on the broad and well-built causeway formed out of praxis, stories and sayings taken as a whole."[3]

This use of the criteria outlined in the last chapter therefore avoids the strictures of those such as Timothy Luke Johnson and J.D.G. Dunn, who, as we have seen, are sceptical of their use.[4] Wright uses these criteria not as individual proofs of what the historical Jesus said or did taken in isolation, but forming together an increasingly coherent and convincing profile of the historical Jesus built upon historical/critical methodology, but not bound necessarily to post-Enlightenment scientific dogmatism.[5]

Jesus saw himself as a Prophet

Jesus was a Prophet both in his own understanding of himself, and in people's understanding of him. This is Wright's starting point for our understanding of the historical Jesus.[6] Jesus emerged in Galilee, and said about himself that a prophet is not without honour except in his own country [Matthew 16:14, Mark 8:28]. When Jesus entered eventually into Jerusalem, the crowds said, "This is the prophet Jesus from Nazareth in Galilee" [Matthew 21:11]. People wanted to arrest Jesus, but they feared the crowds "because they held him to be a prophet" [Matthew 21:46]. When the sinful woman washes Jesus' feet with her tears, the Pharisee says to himself "if this man were a prophet, he would have known…" [Luke 7:39-50]. Thus, for the Pharisee, Jesus is claiming to be a prophet. And, when warned about Herod's threats, Jesus replies to "that fox" that it is impossible for a prophet to perish outside Jerusalem. He accepts the role, and the fate, of a prophet. [Luke 13:33].

Wright uses the standard criteria such as multiple attestation, discontinuity, coherence, and rejection and execution to justify the historicity of these texts above.[7] Of course, Wright wishes eventually to argue that Jesus understood himself to be much more than a prophet. But he is surely correct in making Jesus' prophetic status as his starting point, rather than that Jesus saw himself just as a Rabbi, because in the Israelite tradition, the prophet was the direct vehicle of the Word of God.

Jesus' miracles, return from exile

For Wright, Jesus preached the kingdom of God having come with himself; that is to say, he was announcing a "new

126

deal" for Israel where a renewed heart would replace the Temple as the centre of Israel's worship. This would be a new Return, as the people of Israel returned from exile in Babylon in the sixth century BC.

The miracles of Jesus for Wright must be also seen in this context of prophetic challenge.[8] "The warnings were... balanced by the welcome to those who heeded the message."[9] Criticism has always accepted Jesus as renowned as a miracle worker, even if it refused to accept the supernatural cause of his miracles.[10] Jesus performed miracles welcoming back those who otherwise were not full members of the community into the fellowship of God's renewed people led by himself: the lame, the deaf, the dumb, the ostracised like the woman with an issue of blood.[11]

Jesus announced a "new deal" for Israel

For Schweitzer, when Jesus announced the kingdom of God, he was announcing the end of the world, about which Jesus was mistaken. But Wright contends that in announcing the kingdom of God, Jesus was not first and foremost announcing the end of the world, the "end of the space-time universe", but rather "the climax of Israel's history, involving events for which the end-of-the-world language is the only set of metaphors adequate to express the significance of what will happen, but resulting in a new and quite different phase *within* space-time history."[12]

Thus Wright would contend that as an exegete he is as "eschatological" as Schweitzer; but for him "eschatology" is the action of God in history here and now, or at least very soon. "The time of restoration was at hand, and people of all sorts were summoned to share and enjoy it; but Israel was warned that her present ways of going about advancing the kingdom were thoroughly counter-productive, and would result in a great national disaster."[13]

Jesus preached the destruction of the temple

Jesus preached the destruction of the Temple in Jerusalem, due to the religious leaders of Jerusalem having the wrong set of religious values. This would bring in his own vision of a restored Israel.

Wright claims that in his cleansing of the Temple, Jesus was predicting the downfall of the Temple. [Mark 11:15\\].[14] Again, a "Schweitzerian" interpretation of the Gospels would see all Jesus' predictions as referring to the end of the world. But, for Wright, the prophecy about the Temple was of the more immediate future. Amos, in about 747, predicted the end of the northern kingdom of Israel and its ten tribes [Amos 3:12[15]]. The end of the northern kingdom in fact happened in 721 BC, twenty-five years later. Jesus predicted the destruction of the Temple in 30 AD, which occurred in fact in 70 AD. Wright insists that the historical Jesus predicted the destruction of the Temple, because it was for him an integral part of his exile-restoration message. The Temple had to be destroyed in order that the new order centred on the kingdom programme of Jesus be put in place:

> As he came out of the temple, one of his disciples said to him, "Look, Teacher, what large stones and what large buildings!" Then Jesus asked him, "Do you see these great buildings? Not one stone will be left here upon another; all will be thrown down." [Mark 13:1-2]

Vincent Taylor states "There is no good reason for regarding the saying as a *vaticinium ex eventu* (a prophecy after the event). In prophesying the destruction of the Temple Jesus stands in line with the prophets: cf. Micah 3:12 and Jeremiah 26:6, 18."[16]

Wright argues that since the time of the Maccabees in the second century BC, the Jews had fought and died for four particular aspects of their faith and, even more importantly, its practice: Temple [1 Maccabees 2:24- 8], Sabbath [2 Maccabees 6:10], Circumcision [2 Maccabees 6:11], and Purity of Food [2 Maccabees 6:19-20[17]].

It is worth pointing out these examples of biblical accounts of Maccabeean martyrs in order to understand the mentality of pious Jews at the time of Christ, who lived less than two hundred years later. Far from the early Christians despising the Maccabeean martyrs for dying for the Jewish laws, the Letter to the Hebrews brings them forward as a heroic example of living faith, together with the Old Testament heroes such as Noah, Abraham, Jacob, and David (Hebrews 11:35 probably refers to the Maccabeean martyrs). They would have been the saints and martyrs of Jesus' own time.

We can therefore more easily understand why Jesus' so-called "liberal" attitude to the Jewish Sabbath was unpopular with stricter Jews of his own day. [Mark 2:23, 3:2]; why his apparently liberal attitude to the purity laws caused offence [Matthew 15:2] and why his cleansing of the Temple seemed also to threaten the whole structure of the Judaism of his day. As Wright points out, "As in Jeremiah's day, the Temple had become the focal point of the hope of national liberation, and hence was regarded as a guarantee of security against the pagans."[18] It was not just a case of individual freedom against legalism. That is entirely to misunderstand the issue in Jesus' own day, as Wright correctly observes. By his teaching, Jesus was seeming to undermine the very structure of the identity of God's own people, for which their martyrs and freedom fighters had only in recent history suffered and died.

Jesus intended to found a church

Did Jesus intend to found a church? As Wright replies, "Put baldly like that, it is bound to seem as out of place as the attempt to discover what sort of computer Paul used to write his letters."[19]

What seems clear from Wright, and from any sensible discussion of the question, is that unless Jesus thought the end of the world was coming when he went to Jerusalem for the last time, which according to Wright he certainly did not, he *must* have envisaged some kind of community forming with him. Even more, if there was a programme in Jesus' mind of a renewed Return of his people, and people were to make decisions about effecting that renewal, then there must have been some kind of community with Jesus, and Jesus must have intended that. Even more, if, as Wright contends, Jesus foresaw the destruction of Jerusalem, and that destruction would be the beginning of a renewal of Israel, he would have seen his own community as leading that renewal.

Jesus saw himself as Son of God

Who was Jesus? What was his own self-understanding? Obviously, for Wright, Jesus is more than simply a prophet, even though he began by claiming to be one, and was seen as one by the people. "The one who is least in the kingdom of heaven is greater than John (the Baptist)" [Matthew 11:11]. In other words, Jesus himself, the kingdom-bringer, is no mere prophet. He is the one for whom John, and with him the true hopes of Israel, had been waiting."[20]

Wright has already proposed that the historical Jesus' view of himself was Messianic.[21] But what kind of Messiah, and with what kind of status? For Wright, and in this again he is surely correct, the answer is almost entirely found in the parable of the wicked husbandmen:

> "Listen to another parable. There was a landowner who planted a vineyard, put a fence around it, dug a wine press in it, and built a watchtower. Then he leased it to tenants and went to another country. When the harvest time had come, he sent his slaves to the tenants to collect his produce. But the tenants seized his slaves and beat one, killed another, and stoned another. Again he sent other slaves, more than the first; and they treated them in the same way. Finally he sent his son to them, saying, 'They will respect my son. 'But when the tenants saw the son, they said to themselves, 'This is the heir; come, let us kill him and get his inheritance. "So they seized him, threw him out of the vineyard, and killed him. [Matthew 21:33-39 \\]

Here is the key to Jesus' authority. The prophets are the "servants" (perhaps "slaves" is a little exaggerated, they were hired servants) who give the message to Israel, and, like Amos, Hosea, Jeremiah, are not particularly popular with the people. That is the story of Israel's history. But Jesus is the Son of God. That is his authority. In this parable, he is more than the "eschatological prophet" mentioned in Deuteronomy 18:15. And his calling God Abba, his Father, is not just an indication of his claimed intimate relationship with God, although of course that is implied. It tells us that Jesus saw himself as the Son claiming his inheritance on behalf of his Father.

Many scholars think that this parable of the Wicked Husbandmen is "an allegory constructed in the early Church with reference to the death of Jesus."[22] Vincent Taylor lists the following who believe it was the product of the early Church: Bousset, Bultmann, Klostermann, Branscomb, Loisy, and Montefiore. But Taylor himself, while admitting allegorical additions to the parable, considers that the core of the parable is authentic. Meier, with Wright,[23] also accepts the parable of the Wicked Husbandmen through his very tight net. Meier says "discernible under heavy redaction are the outlines of a parable that ended simply with the death of the son, with no note of reversal, vindication, or resurrection.[24] ... Such a parable would be a strange invention of the post-Easter church, but perfectly understandable in the mouth of Jesus as he clashed with his opponents for the last time in Jerusalem."[25]

The decisive objection for many is that this parable implies that Jesus claimed to be the Son of God, and refers to his death. But this objection depends upon a circular argument, that all sayings of Jesus where he claims to be the Son of God have their origin post-Easter, without any reason being given for this assertion. The possibility that some might be from the historical Jesus is simply not allowed.[26] But, as Wright says, this simply "begs the question".[27] Here we have an outstanding example of Jesus' originality of thought, which is historically most credible.

Dunn, while accepting the authenticity of the Parable of

the Wicked Husbandmen, cautions that "one should not read too much Christological weight into Jesus' possible use of the motif."[28] Indeed, we are a long way from demonstrating that, in the Gospels, the historical Jesus saw himself as God from God, light from light. But Dunn adds, "Even so, it cannot but be significant that Jesus was remembered as likening his mission to that of a son, and both in continuity with and in distinction from the earlier missions of the prophets as servants. The same sense of eschatological climax is evident."[29] Indeed, it is. The parable looks to the death of the son, and disaster for those entrusted with looking after the vineyard, which Jesus described as the future destruction of the Temple and all they held so dear.

NOTES – CHAPTER 7

1   JRR, 1998, 497.
2   We are by no means entirely happy with every aspect of Schweitzer's historical Jesus, because he was just as dismissive as Wrede about the incarnation and the miraculous. Cf. p. 39, QHJ, 3-4.
3   JVG, 533.
4   Cf. p. 113.
5   Cf. JR, 121.
6   JVG. 164-5. I am using Wright's translation of the Gospels when quoting his biblical references directly.
7   JVG, 166-7.
8   JVG, 182. Wright gives a series of "judgement" texts, 183-4.
9   JVG, 185.
10 JVG, 187. Cf. chapter 11, "Miracles in John".
11 JVG, 192.
12 JVG, 208.
13 JVG, 201. Cf. summary in McDade, *The Month*, December 1998, 501.
14 JVG, 417.
15 NJBC, **13:12**, 212.
16 Taylor, 501.
17 JVG, 387.
18 JVG, 420.

19 JVG, 222-3.
20 JVG, 496.
21 This is also the view of MLM, 164.
22 Taylor, 472.
23 JVG, 566..
24 NJBC **78:36,** 1324. Meier quotes (so Jeremias, *The Parables of Jesus,* London, 1963, 72-73)
25 NJBC, **78:36,** 1324.
26 Bultmann ascribes any statement in the Gospels which states that Jesus is the Son of God to Hellenistic Christianity. JW, 152
27 JVG, 566
28 JR, 722.
29 Ibid. Indeed, we can go further. What is the difference between Jesus being "like a son" and being actually son of God? He was never projected as "like a prophet", but he was seen as actually a prophet, even if more than a prophet. Does not Jesus then present himself in the Parable of the Wicked Husbandman as actually the Son of God? This is for our consideration in what follows.

CHAPTER 8

"YOU HAVE HEARD THE BLASPHEMY"

> We argue for the historical authenticity of Mark 14:57-65.
> We propose that, in this text, Jesus was making a claim to be
> divine, and this is seen as blasphemy by the High Priest.

Why did Jesus die?

We must not underestimate the importance of what we have
discovered so far. Our first Enigma was the *Enigma of Jesus*.
How did the early Christians come to see him as the eternal
Son of God only decades after his death? The "Bousset"
solution, that in reality the early Christians took a Jewish
prophet and turned him after his death into a Hellenistic
divine man, we have already seen contradicted by the fact
that the early Aramaic Christians developed on the contrary a
very Semitic view of Jesus, yet calling him *Mara,* the Aramaic
word for God.[1]

But we can now go back even further, to the life and
teaching of the historical Jesus to find our origin for the early
Christians calling Jesus Son of God in a high Christological
sense. Far from using Hellenistic categories, Jesus expressed
his understanding of himself in the Semitic form of a parable,
a *mashal.* As Dunn says, "Typically it (a parable) denoted
proverbial wisdom, as in Ben Sira. But in wider usage it often
referred to an obscure or puzzling saying... If Jesus referred to
his teaching (in whole or in part) as *meshallim,* then the
double entendre lay close to hand. He could hardly have been
unaware that his teaching, while bringing light to some, came
across to others as obscure and puzzling."[2]

Thus the *mashal* of the Wicked Husbandmen, where
Jesus claims to be the son inspecting his father's inheritance,
may in itself be a simple concept. But there is no reason in
itself why it should not be able to express in the deepest
language the uniqueness of the relationship between Jesus

and his Father, and above all his authority as Son. Just as Jesus compares himself with the prophets as son, so later the Letter to the Hebrews compares the Son of God with the prophets, saying that Jesus is, in contrast, "the reflection of God's glory, and the exact imprint of God's very being, and sustains all things by his powerful word" [Hebrews 1:3]. Hebrews, as an early product of Hellenistic Jewish Christianity, is using language far from the Semitic parable. But Hebrews could easily be seen as a more sophisticated expression of what is expressed simply in the parable.

That the parable could bear that meaning in Jesus' own thinking all depends upon the context of meaning in his general teaching. But the "higher" meaning can in no way be excluded *a priori*.

This is why at this point we must go even further than Wright, while continuing to use his method, and acknowledging our debt to him. The second of our three Enigmas was "Why did Jesus die?"[3] Wright gives a reason at first convincing, fully in line with the biblical and historical evidence, why Jesus should not only accept his death, but even encourage it: his death would presage the destruction of the Temple and usher in a new renewed Israel community, a new Temple with himself as head and his community as members. This explains the dark shadows in Jesus' own mind; his prophecy of his own death after Peter has confessed him as Messiah in Matthew 16:21.

But the Gospels themselves go further than this. There is only one reason given in all four Gospels why Jesus' religious enemies wanted him dead. They thought he was blaspheming.

Jesus the blasphemer

It is worth initially to list all the occurrences of the verb "blaspheme" (both the verb *blasphémeó* "I blaspheme", and the noun *blasphémia*, "Blasphemy") which occur in the Gospels as a reaction of Jesus' hearers.

[Matthew 9:2-3] And just then some people were carrying a paralysed man lying on a bed. When Jesus saw their faith, he said to the paralytic, "Take heart, son; your sins are forgiven." Then some of the scribes said to themselves, "This man is blaspheming"(*blasphēmei*).

[Matthew 26:64-6] Jesus said to him, "You have said so. But I tell you, From now on you will see the Son of Man seated at the right hand of Power and coming on the clouds of heaven." Then the high priest tore his clothes and said, "He has blasphemed (*eblasphēmēsen*)! Why do we still need witnesses? You have now heard his blasphemy (*blasphēmian*). What is your verdict?" They answered, "He deserves death."

[Mark 2:5-7] When Jesus saw their faith, he said to the paralytic, "Son, your sins are forgiven." Now some of the scribes were sitting there, questioning in their hearts, "Why does this fellow speak in this way? It is blasphemy (*blasphēmei*)! Who can forgive sins but God alone?"

[Mark 14:62-4] Jesus said, "I am; and 'you will see the Son of Man seated at the right hand of the Power,' and 'coming with the clouds of heaven.'" Then the high priest tore his clothes and said, "Why do we still need witnesses? You have heard his blasphemy (*blasphēmias*)! What is your decision?" All of them condemned him as deserving death.

[Luke 5:20-21] When he saw their faith, he said, "Friend, your sins are forgiven you." Then the scribes and the Pharisees began to question, "Who is this speaking blasphemy (*lalei blasphēmias*)? Who can forgive sins but God alone?"

[John 10:33] The Jews answered, "It is not for a good work that we are going to stone you, but for blasphemy (*peri blasphēmias*), because you, though only a human being, are making yourself God."

[John 10:36] Can you say that the one whom the Father has sanctified and sent into the world is blaspheming (*hoti blasphēmei*) because I said, 'I am God's Son'?[4]

The above instances noted by all four evangelists, Matthew, Mark, Luke, and John, where Jesus is accused of *blasphémia*, or to blaspheme *(blasphemei)* are not especially frequent, But they are all highly significant. The occurrence of the accusation of blasphemy against Jesus fulfils all the criteria of multiple attestation. The word, either the verb or the noun, occurs in Matthew/Mark (presuming Matthean dependence on Mark), Luke and in John. Furthermore, in Matthew/Mark it occurs in two different contexts: in Matthew/Mark during the life of Jesus after he has performed a miracle [Matthew 9:2-3\\], and then during his trial [Matthew 26:66\\].

They share one thought in common, remembering the criterion of multiple attestation, occurring as they do in different contexts. They all refer to an *arrogation of authority* on the part of Jesus. His accusers level the accusation of arrogating to himself activity which is in Jewish minds the prerogative of God alone This claim to divine authority is a unique characteristic of Jesus in the Synoptic Gospels, and is characterised by the fact that Jesus never refers to another person, even to God's authority, in justification for his actions. This is in plain contrast to the Old Testament prophets, who justify the truth of their message by the fact that it is the Word of YHWH. (e.g. Jeremiah 1:2, etc.) coming to them. This apparent arrogation of authority is universal throughout the Synoptic Gospels, as J.A.T. Robinson exhaustively argues.[5]

Indeed, we willingly concur with Dulles, in affirming that the Synoptic Gospels present Jesus as revealing his identity by implication during his life on earth. The Synoptic Gospels surely present Jesus as more than an "eschatological prophet."[6] Rather, as Dulles perceptively remarks, "Historical research can show with great verisimilitude that Jesus in His earthly life gave numerous hints that He was more than an ordinary man, and that the secret of His personality was wrapped in an aura of mystery."[7]

What was "blasphemy" in Jewish law?

Haim Cohn, in his book *The Trial and Death of Jesus*,[8] claims that Jesus, in claiming to be the Messiah, and in claiming divine authority for his actions, would not have been counted as blaspheming.[9] Furthermore, Cohn claims, in order to be guilty of the capital crime of blasphemy:

> There is, as well as this problem of evidence, the question of substantive law. It is not oral but scriptural law that "Whosoever curses his God shall bear his sin" (Lev. 24:15), but he that pronounces[33] the name Yahweh shall be put to death and all the congregation shall stone him (24:16). A clear distinction is drawn between cursing God, which is an offence not punishable with death, and blaspheming God by pronouncing His ineffable Name, which is a capital offence; the distinction is scriptural, and hence part of the Sadducean law. To get around this, it has been said that Jesus' offence was not blasphemy by pronouncing God's name, but "doing presumptuously" and thus "reproaching the Lord" (Num. 15:50); but it seems to have been overlooked that this alternative offence is not a capital one either, but earns only divine punishment (*ibid*) or flogging.[10]

But was the Jewish legal definition as narrow as Cohn and others maintain during the first century AD? According to the unanimous testimony of the New Testament, and not only as far as the Fourth Gospel was concerned, it was not. The word "blasphemy" is used in a much wider sense Acts 6:11, and on the lips of Stephen, just before he was stoned [Acts 7:56-57] for the same blasphemy as was uttered by Jesus concerning seeing the Son of Man at the right hand of God.

How reliable is the New Testament in this? Again, our knowledge of Jewish practice in the first century AD is limited. But A.E. Harvey in his fine little study *Jesus on Trial: a Study in the Fourth Gospel*,[11] draws upon some very interesting relevant information. He begins by saying that there seems some ground for thinking that for a formal charge of blasphemy, naming the name was necessary, quoting the Septuagint translation of Leviticus 24:16 in support. In such a case an ordinary cursing of God earns a lighter punishment than naming the name, which was punishable by death. As

Harvey says, this view was taken up by the Rabbis after the first century AD.

But, in the previous century, the first century AD, Harvey insists, "it is highly significant that both Philo and Josephus – who furnish us with evidence for views held in the first century AD. in widely different cultural environments – take a quite different view." For Josephus, "naming the Name" "means any 'unseasonable' uttering of God's name – the kind of thing which is regarded as relatively trivial… Yet even this is punishable by death."[12]

Harvey is worth quoting in full, since the significant witnesses Philo and Josephus are not always brought into play in the discussion about blasphemy. It needs emphasising that Judaism after the Council of Jamnia, which to some extent at least defined post-Christian Judaism,[13] does not always reflect pre-Jamnia practice. Harvey's point about the difficulty of defining what blasphemy is precisely, is also well worth noting. The British law on blasphemy is notoriously difficult to apply. In any case, to arrogate to oneself divine authority surely would come within anyone's definition of "blasphemy", unless one believed that that person actually was divine. One might almost say that for a loyal monotheist, if a blasphemy law did not exist against such a claim, it would have to be invented.[14]

Jesus Son of God in Mark

We saw earlier that, in the history of historical Jesus criticism, the priority of Mark formed the basis of Holtzmann's Liberal Protestantism.[15] Jesus, according to Holtzmann, preached a message of the kingdom of God, an ethical ideal, which the later Gospel writers Matthew and Luke "supernaturalised" by legends of the miraculous birth of Jesus and of his bodily appearance to his disciples after his death.

But, as we also saw earlier.[16] William Wrede soon exposed the fallacy of Holtzmann's interpretation of Mark. Wrede insisted that Mark's Gospel is soaked throughout with the Church's faith. Indeed, Mark's Jesus is just as "supernatural" as the other three Gospels. The miracles performed by Jesus appear even more starkly prominent in Mark, since they are not accompanied by any lengthy presentation of the teaching of Jesus, as they are in Matthew and Luke. And Mark's Gospel, even if we admit that the account of the appearances 16:9-20 is a later insertion,[17] ends with the discovery of the tomb of Jesus being empty, and with everyone reduced to silence because they were all afraid [Mark 16:8]. An "ethical Jesus" would surely have ended Mark's Gospel with an exhortation to good works rather than leaving his readership with a terrified group of women contemplating the mystery of the empty tomb.

Even more, a straightforward look at the story line[18] of Mark's Gospel is an indication that the "supernatural" is integral to his whole message about Jesus. Mark announces "the beginning of the good news about Jesus, Son of God."[19] As Vincent Taylor says, "The idea (Son of God) is not simply Messianic. A supernatural being is described, but not with the precision of Philippians 2:6 or Luke 1:35."[20]

Precisely described or not, this "supernatural being" is declared to be Son of God by the divine voice at his baptism by John [Mark 1:11]; he begins by calling disciples and then performing miracles, declaring to the paralytic that his sins are forgiven [Mark 2:5]; the unclean spirits scream out "You are the Son of God" [Mark 3:11]; as does the poor man possessed by unclean spirits "What have you to do with me, Jesus the Son of the Most High God?" [Mark 5:7]; the disciples are terrified to find out that even the winds and the sea obey Jesus [Mark 4:41]. Jesus is declared by the heavenly voice once again at the Transfiguration "This is my Son the Beloved, listen to him" [Mark 9:7]; Jesus tells the Parable of the Wicked Husbandmen, the son being sent by the owner of the vineyard only to be killed by the tenants [Mark 12:1-12]; Jesus denies that the Messiah is the Son of David, surely implying that he is rather the Son of God [Mark 12:35-37];[21] finally, Jesus admits before the Sanhedrin that he is the Son of the living God [Mark 14:61-62]; and at his crucifixion, the centurion at the foot of the cross says "Truly that man was God's Son"[22] [Mark 15:39].

Furthermore, just as the theme of Jesus as Son of God is a thread throughout the narrative, its north pole as it were, so the shadow of his impending arrest is the south pole of the story. When Jesus cures the paralytic, and claims authority to forgive sins, he is accused of blasphemy by the scribes [Mark 2:7]; when he cures the man with the withered hand on the Sabbath, "The Pharisees went out and immediately conspired with the Herodians against him, how to destroy him." [Mark 3:6] Jesus prophesied his own suffering and death at the hands of the authorities [Mark 8:31]; and finally, the high priest tears his garments when Jesus finally declares himself openly to be the Son of God [Mark 14:64].

Is Mark fact or fiction?

Read this way, as I am sure Mark intends us to read it, straight through, the meaning of Mark's Gospel is almost embarrassingly simple. Jesus is declared by God to be his Son. He speaks and acts throughout with the authority of the Son of God. The religious leaders in Jerusalem think he is blaspheming. Eventually, at his trial, Jesus admits that he is the Son of God. This is the reason for the "Messianic Secret". Jesus knows that as soon as he admits publicly that he *is* the Son of God, he will die. So he waits until he has finished his mission on earth before he makes a public statement of his divinity. He is handed over to Pilate for execution as a blasphemer. But he is declared truly to be the Son of God by the centurion, and the story ends with his tomb being found empty by the frightened women.

But is Mark recounting history here, or legend? Bultmann's *History of the Synoptic Tradition* has accustomed scholarship to view Mark as a collection of imaginative legends handed on by a credulous Christian community,[23] finally put in preaching form by Mark. But we have seen how flimsy and hypothetical Benoit demonstrates Bultmann's principles of interpretation are. Perhaps Birger Gerhardsson[24] overplays the accuracy of memory in the Christian tradition. Yet we cannot exclude *a priori* the possibility that Mark is recounting

141

substantially what is history, even if memory was not by rote. Of course, Mark's Gospel was a document of faith from start to finish. In this at least Wrede was correct.[25] But that in no way implies necessarily that it was fiction. On the contrary, Mark's faith may have made him even more concerned to preserve the facticity of his account, in order to be faithful to the apostolic tradition.

How are we to decide? Who bears the onus of proof, the sceptic or the believer? One thing is clear; with a date given by criticism as 64 AD, Mark is the earliest testimony we have to the life and teaching of Jesus of Nazareth if we accept the majority solution to the Synoptic Problem. Furthermore, according to Trocmé, who accepts with the majority the priority of Mark, "And so there is no document extant that can be said to be the source of Mark."[26] Thus Mark could have written his Gospel straight, no doubt using sources no longer detectable even with relative certainty, but with the intention as we have seen, of stating that Jesus was Son of God put to death for blasphemy, claiming eventually to be Son of God, but who rose again from the dead to vindicate his message. If on the other hand we accepted the minority and traditional view, that Mark's Gospel depended on Matthew, then the case is even clearer. Mark has selected out of the tradition elements to make a story which emphasises Jesus as Son of God.

Regarding the miracle stories so prominent in Mark, Trocmé has to admit their eye-witness source is possible; "it might have been thanks to stories told by the apostle or another of the disciples either in the presence of the Evangelist or even expressly for his benefit... It does not seem very probable, however, so sharp is the contrast between the accounts of the miracles, with their rather crude theology and their sensational rather than edifying character and the 'sayings of Jesus' which formed the basis of the church tradition handed on and authenticated by the disciples."[27]

Needless to say, Trocmé's reasons for the rejection of the eye-witness source of the miracle stories in Mark are subjective, and the miracle stories, as indeed the whole of the Second Gospel, can be heard in an entirely different way. The finished product, Mark's Gospel, makes a superb narrative, so that an actor was able to fill a London West End theatre for six months doing no more than reciting dramatically the whole of the Gospel, with only a table on stage and a pocket copy on it of the Gospel in the King James Authorised Version as his sole prompt.[28] On the contrary, one who heard such a reading would not have had the impression that the miracle stories were sensationalist, but were brief, soberly told, and achieved their effect solely by the wonder of what was being described, and even more by the amazing fact that the one performing these miracles and giving this sublime teaching was none other than the Son of God, moving inevitably to his tragic death.

Mark's story is surely authenticated historically by the criterion of sufficient reason.[29] Answering our first Enigma, it gives the only sufficient reason why the early Christians came to believe that Jesus was the eternal Son of God. It was no Greek mythical divine man which was the source of that belief. It was not the creative credulity of the early Christian community. It was not Mark's imagination. It was the historical Jesus himself, who claimed to be the divine Son of God, and whose authenticated story was handed on from the apostolic eye-witnesses, which was the source of that belief which conquered the world.

That the historical Jesus was thought of as a blasphemer is authenticated by the criterion of multiple attestation; since Jesus by implication throughout the Synoptics makes claims which imply divine authority for him. As we have seen, this claim to divine authority is a unique characteristic of Jesus in the Synoptic Gospels, and is shown by the fact that Jesus never refers to another person, even to God's authority, in justification for his actions. This, as we have seen, is in plain contrast to the Old Testament prophets, who justify the truth of their message by the fact that it is the Word of YHWH. (e.g. Jeremiah 1:2, etc.) coming to them. This is cogently argued by Robinson, even if he stops short at accepting that John's Gospel proclaims the full divinity of Christ.[30] As he says correctly, "the 'I' of this Gospel (John), which we will consider later in chapter 13, is already in principle that of the Synoptics":

It is the 'I' of the great 'I have come' *(élthon, elélutha)* which declare the purpose of his mission and are common to all the Gospels (Mark 2.17 and pars.; 10.45 and pars. (where Luke substitutes 'I am' for 'the Son of Man came'); Matthew. 5.17; 10:34f.; Luke 12.49; 19.10; John 5.43; 9.39; 10.10 12.46f.; 16.28; 18.37; etc.); the 'I' to whom everything is given by his Father in the most intimate personal union (Matthew 11:25 = Luke 10.21f.); in whose person God's rule is made present (Matthew 12.28 = Luke 11.20); who in the name of the divine Wisdom speaks the invitation of God (Matthew 11.28-30; cf. Ecclus. 51.23-7) and sends his emissaries (Matthew 23.34; cf. Luke 11.49); the 'I' of the Sermon on the Mount, who goes behind what was said not merely by them of old time (AV) but to them by God on Sinai (Matthew 5.21-48); the 'I' who says *'Amen,* I say to you' (nearly twice as often in the Synoptists as in John); who as the Son of Man on earth is Lord of the Sabbath (Mark 2.28), enjoying the same superiority, as John is to bring out (5.16f.), to the Sabbath-rest as the Creator himself; who pronounces the forgiveness of sins (Mark 2.1-12, cf. Luke 7.48f.), thereby stepping into the space reserved in the minds of his contemporaries for God (cf. John 5.18*);* who quells the powers of demons and of nature (Mark 1.23-27; 4.35-41; cf. the *egó* of 9.25), and exercises before the time the prerogatives of the last judgment, saying that men's attitude to him will decide God's attitude to them (Mark 8.38 and par.; Man. 10.33 = Luke 12.9 cf. John 14.21, 15.23); the 'I' too, as in John, who will dispense the Father's Spirit (Luke 21.15 in conjunction with Matthew 10.19f. 24.49; Acts 2.33; John 15.26) and promises his abiding presence (Matthew 18.20; 28.20; John 14.3, 18-20, 23, 28; etc).[31]

All of them condemned him as deserving death

Why Jesus was handed over to Pilate is much controverted.[32] Some have claimed that the whole story of a Jewish trial was a piece of Christian anti-Semitic fiction.[33] In fact, the historical

Jesus had only one trial, says this view, and that before the prefect Pontius Pilate. We will have to deal with this issue in more depth later. Sufficient it is to say here that the Gospels themselves are quite clear. They all say that Jesus was unpopular with the Jews because he had blasphemed, for which reason they thought he should be put to death [Matthew 26:65, Mark 14:64, John 10:36, Matthew 9:3, Mark 2:7]. The Gospels assume that, although the Jewish authorities wanted Jesus condemned to death for blasphemy, they were not allowed to put anyone to death [John 18:31]. Only the occupying power, represented by the Roman Prefect, had such power in Judaea. Therefore, having condemned Jesus to death for blasphemy, the Jewish authorities handed him over to Pilate and attempted to have him put to death for political sedition.[34]

It is only in the Fourth Gospel that the nature of the blasphemy is made clearer, when the Jews answered, "It is not for a good work that we are going to stone you, but for blasphemy, because you, though only a human being, are making yourself God." [John 10:33]. Again, we must analyse this verse much more in depth later,[35] along with other references in the Fourth Gospel with the same thrust of meaning, to test their historicity.

But even if we confined ourselves to the Synoptic record, the two verses we have listed already show that Jesus was making claims *for himself* that the Jews found blasphemous. After Jesus in the Marcan account had said to the paralytic "Your sins are forgiven", the Pharisees were angry: "Why does this fellow speak in this way? It is blasphemy! Who can forgive sins but God alone?" [Mark 2:7].[36]

Much more important, at Jesus' trial, both Mark 14:64 and Matthew 26:65 have the high priest rending his garments because of Jesus' blasphemy, while, in Luke 22:70-71, Jesus is considered to have condemned himself by his high claims for himself. In Mark, the accusation of blasphemy forms a kind of inclusion at the beginning 2:7, and at very nearly the end of the Gospel, with the climax at his trial:

Again the high priest asked him, "Are you the Messiah, the Son of the Blessed One? Jesus said, "I am; and 'you will see the Son of Man seated at the right hand of the Power,' and 'coming with the clouds of heaven.'" Then the high priest tore his clothes and said, "Why do we still need witnesses? You have heard his blasphemy! What is your decision?" All of them condemned him as deserving death. [Mark 14:61b-64\\]

Why does the high priest consider that Jesus' reply is blasphemous? The real point is immediately seen by Vincent Taylor. "Jesus not only claims to be the Messiah, but that He will sit at God's right hand and fulfil the visions of Daniel."[37] Claiming to be the Messiah would not itself have been blasphemous. Gamaliel the wise member of the Sanhedrin, speaking about Jesus to a nervous assembly, reminded them about two rebels: Theudas[38] [Acts 5:36], and Judas the Galilean[39] [Acts 5:37]. Presumably such men thought that they were specially called by God, even if not specifically Messiahs. There was no suggestion that the Sanhedrin thought Theudas and Judas were blaspheming simply because they felt called by God to lead his people to freedom.

However, claiming to be the Messiah *at the right hand of God*, says Vincent Taylor, would have been blasphemous. In fact, the real blasphemy was to combine two, indeed three, texts from the Old Testament and for Jesus to apply them to himself. These texts were Daniel 7:13-14; Psalm 110:1; and finally Isaiah 14:12-15.

The text in Daniel identifies the Son of Man as "a quite specific heavenly being".[40] Psalm 110:1 – The Lord sitting at the right hand of God is linked now with that Son of Man figure coming with the clouds of heaven. The symbolism is one of authority[41]; and finally, Isaiah 14:12-15[42] is part of a "Taunt Song against the King of Babylon,"[43] an unnamed king who seems to be a type of a wicked world ruler. Jesus, then, in speaking of "sitting at the right hand of God and coming in the clouds of heaven" was making what was a potentially blasphemous statement for a zealous and intelligent reader of the Old Testament. He was using the same language as the idolatrous pagan king of Babylon. No wonder, then that the high priest tore his garments, "All of them condemned him as deserving death".

Did the historical Jesus see himself as son of man?

For Bultmann, Jesus in referring to that transcendent Son of Man could not have been referring to himself, as he does in the text we are considering. Says Bultmann, "For it seems too fantastic to me to suppose that Jesus believed that he would one day become the 'Son of Man'."[44] For Bultmann, it is derisory that Albert Schweitzer should interpret Mark 12:35-37, where Jesus questions whether the Messiah is the Son of David since David calls him Lord, by positing that "the Messiah, who, quite unknown by the Scribes, was present in the person of Jesus first as a man of David's seed living in humility among men, afterwards being transformed into the transcendent Messiah, as which, although son of David, he would be David's Lord".[45] Bultmann comments on Schweitzer's newfound Christological mysticism, "Such fantasies and their consequences seem to me wholly unjustified by the tradition we have of the Lord's sayings."[46]

But what tradition of the Lord's sayings do we have, since Bultmann has himself written up that tradition according to his own theology? His own interpretation of the evolution of the attribution of the transcendent Son of Man sayings to the historical Jesus is itself by no means straightforward. It runs thus. At the first stage, in Palestinian Christianity, the Son of Man sayings refer to a future apocalyptic figure as in Daniel and the later apocalyptic literature. At the second stage, the primitive Christian community, under the influence of Hellenism, increasingly sees Jesus as the divine man, the *theios anér*. At the third stage, a *hypothetical* Semitic Christian community converts this concept of Jesus as Hellenistic divine man into Semitic terms, by putting on the lips of the historical Jesus his self-designation as the exalted Son of Man.

First of all, we could consider the criterion of double discontinuity.[47] As a matter of fact, Mark 14:64 is discontinuous with both Judaism and the beliefs of the early Church. There is nothing in Jewish theology like the statement Jesus made to the High Priest, and certainly not with any clear Messianic reference. It certainly did not come out of the stock of references within Judaism to the Messiah, or at least it appears in no such document available to us today.

Moreover, we have no evidence apart from the New Testament, or in post-New Testament Christian literature, that the early Church applied these words exalting the Son of Man to Jesus. There are 79 references in the four Gospels to the enigmatic figure "Son of Man".[48] In contrast, there are only three references in the rest of the New Testament to the "Son of Man". The only other occasion where a similar phrase is used is Stephen at his trial, saying "Look," he said, "I see the heavens opened and the Son of Man standing at the right hand of God!" [Acts 7:56]. But Stephen is in a parallel situation to Jesus at his trial, making a statement which is considered blasphemous.[49] Also, as Haenchen observes, it is remarkable that Acts has Stephen seeing that the Son of Man is *standing* at the right hand of God, not *sitting* as Jesus describes. "According to Bauernfeld, the departure from the normal vouches for the authenticity of the account of the vision." [50]

Have we not here a classic candidate for Occam's razor, a being invented without necessity, Scarisbrick's Criterion of Economy?[51] This hypothetical Semitic Christian community expressing its high Christology, influenced by Hellenistic Christianity, in Semitic terms, is a pure critical construct.[52] But what would prevent the historical Jesus himself from having the originality to identify himself in this way, as is expressed in the Marcan and Matthaean account of the trial of Jesus before the Sanhedrin, and which we have just analysed? In this view, no unnecessary being is created. The originality of Jesus was to express his own understanding of his being and nature in his own unique terms, by combining those Old Testament texts as we have seen above.

The self-designation "Son of Man" also helped the Messianic Secret, in that, as the great S.R. Driver[53] said a hundred years ago, "Christ's use of the term was *paedagogic.*

It veiled his Messiahship during the earlier part of His ministry, till the time was ripe for Him to avow it openly."[54] We are not saying that Jesus uttered Mark 14:62 necessarily at the Sanhedrin trial in precisely those words. We do not have necessarily his *ipsissima verba*. A process of *synthesis*[55] by the evangelist might well have been operative. But, we would propose, this synthesis was a reliable expression of what the historical Jesus understood about himself, and it was seen by his accusers as blasphemous, thus leading to his being handed over to Pilate.

The Barker runway

Earlier, we set out on what we called "the Wright way", following N.T. Wright's own analogy of the *Schweitzerstrasse* and the *Wredebahn*. Wright keeps the car steady on the road, building up the case for a Jesus who knew his own mission, who foresaw the destruction of the Temple and who believed that his own community which he began on earth would remain as his body after his death.

By the same analogy, however, Margaret Barker is not satisfied to keep on the ground, but wishes to take off exegetically. Margaret Barker strongly contends that Jesus, at his baptism, had the equivalent of what was known in Judaism as the *merkavah* mystical experience; an experience of being taken up to the throne of God and *becoming Son of God*. This experience, according to her, goes back in its thinking to pre-Christian Judaism. She mentions Metatron, a heavenly figure who appears in 3 Enoch, "an Enoch book which has survived in the Jewish community and is more correctly called the *Sepher Hekhalot*, the Book of Palaces."[56]

Now the idea that Jesus had a significant experience at his baptism which revealed to him his own vocation and mission is not alien to biblical scholarship. James D.G. Dunn, in his fascinating *Christology in the Making*, suggests that Jesus had a twofold consciousness regarding his mission; that he was aware of the loving care of God his Father and the startling power of the Spirit manifested in his work. "The most probable reason... is that Jesus underwent a significant experience – significant in terms of his consciousness of sonship and Spirit – on the occasion of his baptism by John."[57]

In favour of Dunn, it is difficult to see how, if this account by all four evangelists that a significant revelation of Jesus' Messiahship occurred at his baptism has, as we have argued, historical validity, that the baptism of Jesus had in its turn no effect on the human development of Jesus himself in terms of his own experience. In favour of Meier, on the other hand, who disputes Dunn's view of Jesus' "baptism experience", none of the four evangelists relates this revelation of Messiahship as the experience of Jesus himself, but rather as *a revelation of who Jesus is to others*. This would also count against the Merkavah interpretation of Barker. There is no implication that Jesus went up into heaven himself,[58] but rather the baptism narrative tells us how others were affected by the divine revelation of who Jesus truly was.[59]

But the contribution of Margaret Barker in this connection is still most important. She shows clearly that there is a different Jewish world view before us than is often presented, that is of unambiguous monotheism in the sense that "second gods" or "transcendent figures" are excluded; as also Melchizedek the high priest mentioned in Genesis 14, who is called in the Dead Sea Scrolls *Elóhim*, god.[60] It has been frequently argued that, when Jesus came on earth, the idea that he was in some sense divine was totally opposed to Jewish monotheism. That does not seem to have been the case, at least in some areas of Jewish theological speculation.[61]

This does not nullify the double discontinuity of Jesus claiming to be the heavenly Son of Man. There is no text in Judaism which identifies such a heavenly figure as *actually coming down to earth*. Nor are these ideas in any way reflected in the Christology of the early Church, which does not use apocalyptic language in its faith affirmations. But Margaret Barker enables us finally to escape from post-Bultmannian reductionism, and frees us to look at a Jesus with a truly unique view of his own person and mission.

1   Cf. p. 29. TGI, 39.
2   JR, 494.
3   JVG, Chapter 12, *The Reasons for Jesus' Crucifixion*. 540-611.
4   AS, 82.
5   PJ, 388-389.
6   Cf. p. 39.
7   APO, 87.
8   Cohn, Haim. *The Trial and Death of Jesus*. London, Weidenfeld and Nicolson, 1967. Cohn considers that the Sanhedrin trial was a Christian fiction. So also Flusser, "Thus, it would be safe to assume that the Sanhedrin was not mentioned in the Gospel sources." Flusser, D., *Judaism and the Origins of Christianity*, Jerusalem, Hebrew University, 1988, 625.
9   Cohn, 1967, 61. "No Pharisee would ever count as blasphemous or otherwise improper an assertion of divine authority." But surely they would count as blasphemous a person arrogating to himself what only God can do, i.e. forgive sins.
10 Cohn, ibid, 101.
11 Harvey, A.E. *Jesus on Trial: a Study in the Fourth Gospel*, London, SPCK, 1976, 78-9.
12 Harvey, ibid, 78-9.
13 ODCC, 726.
14 JVG, 551.
15 Cf. p. 48. NTHIP, 151-2.
16 Cf. p. 49. HST, 1.
17 NJBC, **41:109**, 629. This "longer ending, traditionally designated Mark 16:9-20, differs in vocabulary and style from the rest of the Gospel, is absent from the best and earliest manuscripts now available, and was absent from manuscripts in patristic times. It is most likely a second century compendium of appearance stories based primarily on Luke 24…"
18 I mean by "story-line" a straightforward reading of Mark's story, rather than attempting to discern the "plan" of Mark's Gospel, which is a more complex project, trying then to discern in detail how Mark has marshalled his sources to compose his work. For discussion of the plan, cf. TROC, 72-86. Taylor, 105-113.
19 "Son of God", *huiou theou*, is absent from some MSS, but inferior to those which include it, e.g. B, D, L,W. Cf. Taylor, 152.
20 Taylor, 152.
21 Taylor, 493, argues convincingly that the historical Jesus understood the Messiah as more than the Son of David.
22 NJB, Mark, 15g, 1685: "For the Roman officer, this admission would not have its Christian content, but Mark clearly sees in it an acknowledgement that Jesus was more than a man."

23 Cf. p. 53f.

24 Cf. p. 70.

25 Cf. p. 49.

26 TROC, 11.

27 TROC, 52.

28 Surely, that actor, and indeed the audience, would have disagreed with Trocmé's judgement that "The point is thus settled; the author of Mark was a clumsy writer unworthy of mention in any history of literature." TROC, 72.

29 Cf. p. 116.

30 PJ, 389. "In John this 'I' is portrayed and projected, backwards and forwards, in terms of the pre-existence and post-existence of a heavenly person. But that is the language of myth, picturing the other side, as Bultmann would put it, in terms of this side." Cf. our response to Bultmann's programme of demythologisation. Cf. our rebuttal of Robinson, chapter 13, pp. 240-3, "According to John did Jesus claim to be God?"

31 PJ, 388-389.

32 Brandon, Brandon, S.G.F. *Jesus and the Zealots,* Manchester 1967, believed that the historical Jesus was a Zealot, a political revolutionary HJCG, 143, but Theissen and Merz summarise the conclusions of scholarship "the evidence cited for this is insufficient". HJCG, 459.

33 So Cohn, 1967.

34 Brown II, 849.

35 Cf. chapter 14.

36 HST, 15-16. Bultmann is convinced that this accusation of blasphemy is a post-Easter formulation. So also Nineham. But cf. Taylor, 195.

37 Taylor, 569-70.

38 Haenchen, E. *The Acts of the Apostles.* Oxford, Basil Blackwell, 1971,252. "In reality Theudas promised his followers under the Procurator Fadus, between 44 and 46 AD – hence some ten years after the presumptive date of Gamaliel's speech-that he would lead them dry-shod across the Jordan, thus repeating Joshua's miracle."

39 In fact, says Haenchen, the revolt of Judas the Galilean "broke out on the death of Herod the Great." 252, n.7. Josephus mentions the temporary success of Judas, Ant.XX 102, but only temporary. "Moreover the sons of Judas the Galilean were killed. *R"mai"n apostésantos Kuriniou tés Ioudaiaas timéuontos.* Josephus says nothing about the end of Judas; the Zealot movement unleashed by him was not in fact suppressed but grew to greater dimensions…"

40 TJC, 17.

41 Fitzmyer, J. Essays on the Semitic Background of the New Testament. London, Chapman, 1971, 224.

42 I am grateful to A. Vanhoye, S.J., who convincingly established the link between this verse in Isaiah and Mark 14:64, in some unpublished lectures on the Passion Narratives at the Pontifical Biblical Institute, Rome, in 1970.

43 NJBC, **15:31**, 239. PCB, 500, 432h.

44 HST, *137.

45 HST, *137, n.2, quoting from Schweitzer's *The Mysticism of Paul the Apostle*, 1930, 83.

46 HST, *137, n.2.

47 Cf. p. 115.

48 Higgins, A.J.B., *The Son of Man in the Teaching of Jesus*, SNTS 39. Cambridge University Press, 1980.

49 "The writer presumes that those listening grasp the reference to Jesus and regard the exclamation as a blasphemy". Haenchen, E., *Acts of the Apostles*, Oxford, Basil Blackwell, 1971, 292.

50 Ibid, 292, n.4.

51 Cf. pp. 116-7.

52 TJC, 164.

53 Driver was one of the general editors of the famous *International Critical Commentary*, published by T and T. Clark in Edinburgh which, at the turn of the nineteenth and twentieth century did so much to introduce the best of critical scholarship into British biblical studies. Driver's own masterly commentary on *Deuteronomy*, 1895, enduring in its value, is one of the finest examples of the series.

54 HDB, IV, 586. Driver is by no means alone in his affirmation of the authenticity of at least some sayings about the exalted Son of Man. Higgins, ibid, 29, notes that Goppelt, Moule, Maddox, Marshall, Barrett, and Bruce all "find authentic words of Jesus in all three groups of sayings", including sayings about the exalted Son of Man.

55 DV, 19.

56 RL, 18.

57 Dunn, J.D.G. *Jesus and the Spirit*. Philadelphia, Westminster, 1975, 63. While having some sympathy with this view, however, Meier cannot agree with Dunn: MJ2, 108.

58 Barker says regarding the text from the Gospel of Philip which says that Jesus "first rose up and died" that "This could be a Gnostic fantasy but I think not". RL, 8. I cannot help thinking, however, that it is.

59 Taylor, 162, refers to the view of J. Weiss, who "suggests that the Markan version is secondary to that of the Western text of Luke iii.22 (cf. Psa.ii.7)."

60 Fitzmyer, J., *Essays on the semitic Background of the New Testament*, London, Chapman, 1971, 253-255.

61 CM, 80-1, refers to the "two powers heresy".

Part III
Clinching the argument from St John's Gospel

CHAPTER 9

THE ORIGINS OF THE FOURTH GOSPEL

- The Fourth Gospel is a Christian document written in its final form not later than very early in the second century AD. Its ideas are not demonstrably a product of Hellenistic philosophy. Rather its ideas are essentially Jewish. It is unique in seeing Jesus as the Word become flesh. Thus its author could be rooted in the earliest forms of Christianity, even in the historical Jesus.

- Both evidence from tradition (Irenaeus) and from investigation into the text of the Fourth Gospel leaves the possibility wide open, that John the Son of Zebedee was the author, or at least was the origin of its tradition.

- Furthermore, since there are no convincingly demonstrated Stages and Redactions out of touch with the historical Jesus, nothing prevents the Fourth Gospel in vital parts of its narrative being solidly rooted in the earliest Christianity, indeed in the life of the historical Jesus.

The authorship of John: varied views

At the beginning of the twentieth century, W. Sanday went to New York from Oxford to deliver eight lectures on The Criticism of the Fourth Gospel, at the Union Theological Seminary, New York. He began by surveying the state of Johannine studies at the beginning of the twentieth century. He found that there were, in his analysis, four different viewpoints concerning the Fourth Gospel, each radically different from each other, and with no immediate possibility of reconciliation:[1]

- Conservative opinion. This was represented by writers such as Westcott, and many continental authors, who maintained that the author of the Fourth Gospel was John the Son of Zebedee.

- Mediating theories which held that another disciple was the author, e.g. John the Elder.
- Partition Theories. Wendt 1886. These proposed that the author was John plus a Redactor.
- Uncompromising Rejection. These denied eye witness and apostolic authorship, e.g. Loisy, Jülicher.

It is quite remarkable that, reviewing the situation nearly one hundred years later, exactly the same apparently irreconcilable points of view are to be found, and maintained by scholars of high quality:

- Conservative opinion: Carson, Robinson.
- Mediating Theories: Hengel.
- Partition Theories: Brown.
- Uncompromising Rejection of apostolic authorship and of historicity: Bultmann, Fortna, Brodie.

These positions are widely different from each other, and cross at different points. Thus both Hengel and Brodie agree with the traditional view that the Fourth Gospel was fundamentally the work of a single author. But Hengel concludes that the author was an unknown Elder John, who, after a serious conflict in his church, as the head of the Johannine School "became his own 'redactor' in a critical situation, rewriting or redefining his own (unpublished) manuscript".[2] Brodie however, will have nothing of the historical Jesus nor of the Johannine Community, let alone John the Son of Zebedee.[3] Yet the Fourth Gospel was written by a single author nevertheless, who will for ever remain unknown to us. In this, Brodie opposes the critical viewpoint of Bultmann, rejecting any source or redaction theory, yet joining him in what Sanday called "uncompromising rejection" of authorship and of historicity. These positions can also be combined, as De Boer combines the Staged Composition Theory of Brown with redaction theories of Bultmann and Fortna.[4] The question of the authorship of the Fourth Gospel, as may easily be seen, is disputed.

Apostolic "origin" not necessarily "authorship"

We have to be clear from the outset what we need to prove in this investigation. In 1965, the Dogmatic Constitution on Divine Revelation of the Second Vatican Council affirmed that "the Church has always and everywhere affirmed the apostolic *origin* of the four gospels."[5] The word "apostolic origin" rather than "apostolic authorship" is used because two out of the four Gospels, Mark and Luke, have as their authors given to us in tradition men who were not members of Jesus' apostolic college of twelve. These the Council called "apostolic men" (*apostolici viri*). Authorship by such *apostolici viri* would be acceptable because they were in contact with eye-witnesses if they were not eye-witnesses themselves, and because they wrote their Gospels with apostolic authority.

The earliest evidence we have, towards the end of the second century, is that this Gospel was accepted in the early church as part of the canonical Scriptures, written by John the Son of Zebedee. This John was one of the three disciples closest to Jesus who, according to the first three Gospels, Matthew, Mark and Luke (the 'Synoptic Gospels'), accompanied Jesus up the Holy Mountain of Transfiguration [Matthew 17:1-8]. I consider myself here in total agreement with Raymond Brown's judgement concerning this ancient tradition, which still is difficult to refute:

> Thus it is fair to say that the only ancient tradition about the authorship of the Fourth Gospel for which any considerable body of evidence can be adduced is that it is the work of John son of Zebedee. There are some valid points in the objections raised to this tradition, but Irenaeus' statement is far from having been disproved.[6]

However, in Roman Catholic theology, the tradition handed down by the church regarding the authorship of biblical books is always to be respected. But it is not part of the church's dogmatic tradition, as are the doctrines of the Incarnation and the Trinity, and indeed the doctrine of the divine inspiration of all the biblical books. Thus traditions

158

regarding the human authorship of the biblical books can be tested historically by criticism, and judgements made which nuance that tradition. Thus, for instance, the traditional authorship by St Paul of the Letter to the Hebrews is no longer promoted even in liturgical books because sound historical criticism has disproved it. Readers in church will refer to the "First letter of *Paul* to the Corinthians", but simply to the "*Letter* to the Hebrews".

Thus it would be totally acceptable if we concluded, both in terms of Catholic theology and in terms of our argumentation, that John was not the actual author of the Fourth Gospel, but was the source of the ideas in the Fourth Gospel; or indeed that another author with contact with apostolic sources was in fact the author. That would maintain our thesis that the Fourth Gospel is a potentially valuable eye-witness source of the life, death, and Resurrection of the historical Jesus.

Only the fourth extreme opinion, that of "uncom-promising rejection" of apostolic origin, would be unacceptable to our position; or, a version of the third position which held that a proposed later editor of the Fourth Gospel has so overlaid the account of the life of Jesus in John with fictional glosses as to vitiate its historical worth. We shall argue that this case remains unproven, thus giving us the right, as we plan in this third part, to examine St John's Gospel using the same historical – critical criteria we have already applied with positive results to the Synoptic Gospels. In this chapter, our concern is at least to establish that the Fourth Gospel, just as we have shown regarding the first three Gospels, is potentially a reliable source for the history of Jesus of Nazareth.

Scholars agree on a date for John c. 90-106 AD

Unanimity is not common where Fourth Gospel scholars are concerned; but, as to the upper limit of the date of the Gospel, remarkable unanimity exists. Nineteenth-century theories dating the Gospel to the end of the second century, together with emerging second-century Gnosticism, have all been abandoned.[7] J.A.T. Robinson graphically presents the consensus in his *Redating the New Testament:*

> With marginal variation at each end (and even Bultmann goes down as far as 80 for the first composition), the span 90-100 is agreed by Catholic and Protestant, by conservative and radical, by those who defend apostolic authorship and those who reject it, by those who believe that John used the synoptists and those who do not.[8]

We can therefore safely put the upper limit, the *terminus ante quem*, at somewhere at the end of the first and beginning of the second century AD. But could the Fourth Gospel have been written even earlier? Robinson thinks so.

He produces weighty arguments to the effect that the writing of St John's Gospel reflects a period *before* the destruction of Jerusalem in AD 70 rather than before it. Not many scholars have accepted his view of an earlier possible date, although his reasoning is as always intriguing, reasons which are more relevant to our purposes later when we consider the involvement of "The Jews" or "The Judaeans" in the eventual death of Jesus by crucifixion.[9] But at least there is an increasing consensus among the scholars that, even if the final edition of the Gospel is as late as the nearly unanimous scholarly opinion, at least parts of John go back to an early pre-Gospel tradition of the life and teaching of Jesus. This is since the epoch-making studies of C.H. Dodd in *The Historical Tradition in the Fourth Gospel*, which we will discuss later in this chapter.[10]

But even if the entire Fourth Gospel was written only just before the second decade of the second century, the very latest date unanimously agreed by all critical scholars, the writing of the Gospel of John would still be close enough to the events recorded to be at least possibly an eye-witness account. As I am writing this book, I am living early in the first decade of the twenty-first century. Events in 1930 took place just before my own birth in 1936. This would be parallel to AD 30, the date approximately of the crucifixion, as compared with a person living in the first decade of the second century. Even without modern means of communication and modern medicine, people in the first century AD could live for eighty or ninety years, or at least could pass on their eye-witness testimony to the next generation.

This would be admitted as a possibility by critical scholarship itself. The proposed fictionality of the Fourth Gospel, as we have seen in the previous chapter, arises not from any incontrovertible historical evidence, but from the assumptions of post-Enlightenment Historical Jesus school, reinforced by the Form-Critical approach, that it was the end process of legend-building by the Christian community based upon its growing belief in Jesus as the Hellenistic divine man.

We intend to build our proposals in this book on more solid evidence. And the first foundations of such a building is to give the reasons why there is such scholarly unanimity on such early dating for the Fourth Gospel as certainly to have been written within the lifetime of those who witnessed the events narrated in it, or at least within the lifetime of those who knew personally those who witnessed the events narrated in it.

A precious fragment

How do scholars come to the date of 110 as the latest for the finished writing of the Fourth Gospel? The *terminus ante quem,* the fixing of the latest date for the writing of the Fourth Gospel, has been determined by the remarkable discovery of the papyrus P^{52}, a precious tiny fragment of the Gospel of John, our earliest New Testament manuscript, first published in 1935.

P^{52}, Papyrus Rylands Greek 457, is "a small piece of papyrus, 3.5 by 2.3 inches in size, with seven lines of writing on each side."[11] On one side is John 18:31-33, and on the other side is John 18:37-38, the account of the trial of Jesus in the Fourth Gospel. C.H. Roberts, who first studied and published his results in *An Unpublished Fragment of the Fourth Gospel* (Manchester: the Manchester University Press, 1935) concluded that P^{52} is to be dated between 94 and 127.[12] This dating is accepted without question in the demanding world of New Testament scholarship.

The fragment was discovered in Egypt, and, as we have seen, cannot be dated later than AD 127. It is clear that P^{52} was not a fragment of the first edition of John, and so the first edition of the Fourth Gospel was still earlier. As Brown says:

> The theory that John was composed in Egypt has had little support. If, as is generally supposed, it was composed its Asia Minor (or even Syria) we must allow time for it to have reached Egypt and to have passed into common circulation there. Moreover, the Bodmer Papyri reflect partially different textual traditions of the Gospel, that is, P^{66} is closer to the text we later find in Codex Sinaiticus; P^{75} is almost the same as the text of Codex Vaticanus. The development of such variation must have required time. To sum up, the positive arguments seem to point to 100-110 as the latest plausible date for the writing of the Gospel, with strong probability favouring the earlier limit of 100.[13]

John is first century Semitic

We have seen how the general view of nineteenth century criticism was that the Fourth Gospel had its roots in Greek thought. But this view must change after scrolls were discovered on the shores of the Dead Sea in 1947. At first, the media made sensationalist statements about the threat to Christianity which this discovery made. But now, a more sober assessment has reversed that judgement. The differences between Qumran and Christianity are indeed much greater than the similarities.[14] On the other hand, parallels are significant. Ideas which in the nineteenth century were said to prove the Hellenistic origin of John's ideas, such as his contrast between darkness and light [1:4-5,9], Jesus as the truth [14:6], and the Spirit of Truth [14:17,26], are present in the documents of the first century AD in Judea and are thoroughly Semitic.

Is it possible that John the Baptist, and indeed Jesus himself, were influenced by the Qumran Essenes? This is certainly a more fascinating and plausible influence than a Greek Gnosticism we only know from the second century. After all, the Qumran monastery was on the shores of the Dead Sea during the first century AD, by the Judaean desert where John the Baptist was preaching [Matthew 3:1]. We know also that Jesus followed John into the desert, and was baptised by him [Matthew 3:13 \\]. There are significant differences between Qumran and John. Qumran has no idea of the message of repentance central to John's proclamation, nor of the healing miracles as a sign of the coming kingdom, central to Jesus' original message. But their thought worlds were close.

A recent book by Paula Fredriksen, *Jesus of Nazareth King of the Jews: A Jewish Life and the Emergence of Christianity*, does not flinch from seeing the radical implications for Johannine study of the discovery of the Quman scrolls, implications which Fourth Gospel scholarship has yet fully to draw out:

> The Scrolls incontrovertibly show that early first century Jewish Jews spoke and thought in similar ways. And an earlier Jewish context of composition for John's Gospel then reopens the question of its historical value for reconstructing Jesus' life.[15]

It is precisely the purpose of this book to take Johannine scholarship forward as a result of discoveries such as at Qumran, and, as Fredriksen wishes, to reopen the question of the historical value of the Fourth Gospel for reconstructing Jesus' life.

Rabbinic Judaism is a sure background

One thing is clear. The author of the Fourth Gospel knew Rabbinic Judaism, and no doubt Rabbinic Judaism influenced his thought. The Fourth Gospel is aware not only of the Old Testament, but also of the Rabbinic interpretation of it. The

Rabbis of Jesus' time interpreted the Old Testament according to their living tradition, which, according to the Synoptic Gospels, Jesus respected, "The scribes and the Pharisees sit on Moses' seat" [Matthew 23:2]; even if he disagreed with their conclusions sometimes [e.g. Mark 2:25].

C.H. Dodd brings out strongly the influence of Rabbinic Judaism on the thought of the Fourth Gospel. For instance, in John chapter 7:22-24, Jesus defends his practice of healing on the Sabbath by saying that circumcision was allowed on the Sabbath. Dodd quotes more than one Jewish authority to the effect that "circumcision repels the Sabbath commandment"[16] The author of the Fourth Gospel seems here to be well acquainted with the Rabbinic interpretation of the Sabbath law.[17]

Furthermore, the idea in John of the pre-existence of the Logos is paralleled by the idea of the pre-existence of the Torah in Judaism. "Seven things were created before the world was created: the Torah, Repentance, Paradise, Gehenna, the Throne of Glory, the Sanctuary, and the Name of the Messiah."[18] We do not know when Rabbinic Judaism introduced these speculations about the Torah. Was it possibly influenced by Christianity? What is important, however, is that Judaism saw no problem in teaching the pre-existence of the Torah, just as the Fourth Gospel taught the pre-existence of Jesus as the Logos, and linked Jesus with the idea of the Torah, claiming that he himself claimed to be the Way [John 14:6] (the *halakah*, the moral interpretation of the Law). Here is evidence of an intra-Jewish debate, where the author of the Fourth Gospel is presenting very much a Jewish Jesus.

Likewise, there was Judaistic speculation about the Word of God, the *memra*. The Logos was the Son of God, just as the Torah was the daughter of God.[19] Westcott, well over a century ago, made the same connection as did Dodd much later:

In the Targum of Onkelos on the Pentateuch, which is the oldest in date, the action of God is constantly though not consistently referred to as "His Word" (Memra, *mymr*,

mymr'). Thus it is said that the Lord protected Noah by His word, when he entered the ark" (Genesis 7:16) that He "made a covenant between Abraham and His word" (Genesis 17:2); that the word of the Lord was with Ishmael in the wilderness (21:20)…[20]

Westcott was convinced that the Rabbinic tradition, which almost personified the Word, as it did the Torah, was early: "They [the Targums] were most probably not committed to writing in the shape in which we now have them, till some time after the Christian era; but all evidence goes to show that they embody the interpretations which had been orally current from a much earlier time."[21] Far from the Fourth Gospel idea of the Logos being fundamentally a Greek idea, therefore, we only have to search in the Rabbinic tradition for very clear echoes of its explicitation.

The author of the Fourth Gospel, according to C.H. Dodd, was likewise well acquainted with Jewish Messianic expectations. "The Messiah of the Jews is to be a descendant of David, He is to appear no one knows whence, He is to work signs and to reign as king, and He is to abide for ever"[22] [cf. John 7:27, 42, 12:34,]. For evidence of this Jewish background, Dodd draws not only upon the Targums, but upon late Jewish apocalyptic, such as the Similitudes of Enoch.[23]

Finally, the author of the Fourth Gospel, Dodd demonstrates, knows about Jewish Rabbinic reflection upon the Name of God. In the Jewish tradition, the Name of God YHWH (revealed first to Moses, cf. Exodus 3:13-15) was more and more withdrawn from public use, until eventually it was never used in the public reading of scripture. The name ADONAI ("My Lord") was substituted whenever YHWH appeared in the text of the Old Testament. This reverence for the divine name was linked in Rabbinic thought with the coming of the Messiah in the age to come: "In this age the prayer of the Israelites is not heard, because they do not know the *shem hammephorash* (i.e. "the mysterious name"); but in the age to come God will reveal it to them."[24] Dodd then argues that Jesus' own self-designation in John, I AM (*egó eimi*) "That you may know that *egó eimi*" [John 8:28] is in reality a translation of the Hebrew *'ani hu'* the divine name, "That you may know that *'ani hu'*, I AM" [Isaiah 43:10].

In John, therefore, Jesus is revealing himself precisely as the secret name of God.[25] Clearly, when we come to examine Jesus' own self-designation,[26] this text will be of vital importance. Suffice it is to say at this point that the origin of this Johannine thought is rooted solidly in Rabbinic Judaism, of which the writer of the Fourth Gospel shows ample knowledge. These Jewish roots are well established, in contrast to much less convincing speculations about Hellenistic and Gnostic influences. How much of this knowledge of Rabbinic Judiaism is a reflection of Jesus' own self-awareness we will of course have to leave until later discussion.

But how close is the Fourth Gospel to being an eye-witness account of the life, death, and Resurrection of Jesus? Was it so re-worked by later editors that it can no longer be called the product of any author or authors with possible eye-witness contact with the historical Jesus? We must therefore consider the question, again most complex, of the literary composition of the Gospel of John.

Theories of composition

We have already examined Bultmann's theological and philosophical presuppositions,[27] and will not be surprised to see them underpinning once more his literary-critical studies in his monumental commentary on John. Bultmann's approach is close to Wellhausen, who was the first to propose a theory of redaction in John.[28] For instance, Bultmann changes the order of Chapters 4, 5, 6, and 7 to what he considered to be the primitive order, 4, 6, 5, and 7:15-24. He likewise shifts the ordering of the Final Discourse, placing 14 after 15 and 17. Zumstein, who wrote a stimulating and original essay on redaction in John,[29] states: "The conclusion which the sage of Marburg draws from his study is that the traditional and canonical order of the gospel is the result of a final redaction, and not of the evangelist, a redaction which is expressed fully in Chapter 21."[30]

This redaction, subsequent editing, reveals itself also in dogmatic corrections and glosses. Bultmann finds 6:51-58, then 19:43b-35, which outline foundations of the sacraments, were the work of the ecclesiastical redactor, and are not part of the original Gospel. Likewise, references to future eschatology, Christ appearing again at the last times, 5:28-29, 6:39-40,44,54 and 12:48, must come from the ecclesiastical redactor, because, for Bultmann, the original writer of the Gospel did not believe in a futurist eschatology, but only in the Christ here and now. Bultmann was strongly of the opinion that the final editor was worried about ecclesiastical orthodoxy and saw it necessary to insert passages which emphasised the sacraments and the coming of Christ in the future.[31]

The same difficulty attends Bultmann's view as it does all radical redaction theories from Wellhausen onwards. Bultmann could be justly accused of imposing his own theological ideas on the Fourth Gospel. Why is it not possible for the same Gospel writer to believe both in a futurist and a realised eschatology? Has not Bultmann injected his own existentialist view of Christianity, emphasising the here and now decision of faith rather than a future heaven, to make it a principle of redaction criticism? In other words, have we not here *eisegesis* (reading a meaning into the text) rather than *exegesis* (reading out the meaning in the text)?

It is not possible to deal in detail with the large number of possible redaction theories which have abounded since Bultmann's commentary. Full consideration of each one would entail a book of this size devoted only to that subject.[32] The problems are real; the apparent strange ordering of Chapters 4, 5, 6, and 7, the strange transition from 14:31 to 15:1, and above all the fact that Chapter 21 seems to be an addition after the Gospel has come to a fitting conclusion in 20:31.

But do these breaks and evident unevenness in the narrative require us to believe that the Fourth Gospel is not the work of one author but a compilation by several hands? Still more, is there sufficient evidence for a *Signs Source* as proposed by Bultmann and Fortna?[33] The article by D.A. Carson, who has produced a fine commentary on John,[34] is to be commended, which has canvassed the major source theories produced in the twentieth century, and has shown that the methods used and the results obtained are inconsistent, and that at countless junctures evidence that is adduced to argue for the existence of a separate source is better understood a different way.[35]

It is difficult to disprove any complex redaction theory in dealing with ancient literature. But it is difficult also to see any hypothesis as more than purely speculative. The diversity of such theories in Johannine scholarship, and the inability to come to conclusions generally accepted, ensures that theories still persist that the work was written by one author, and that the so-called *aporias*, breaks and unevenness in the Fourth Gospel narrative, can be explained simply as the literary eccentricities of the author, or even as part of that author's genius.

My own view is that there are good historical grounds for considering that John the Son of Zebedee actually wrote the Fourth Gospel, and he wrote it as a unified literary composition, what Strauss called a "seamless robe". Martin Hengel indicates that there has always been a view in modern Johannine scholarship which has insisted on the stylistic and theological unity of the Fourth Gospel. Hengel notes the impressive literary criticism of the Fourth Gospel which has only demonstrated further its literary unity.[36]

This is based upon researches by Abbott in 1905/6, Schweizer in 1939, and most important of all Ruckstuhl in 1951.[37] Hengel insists that Ruckstuhl's conclusions "have been doubted, but they have never been refuted". As we have seen earlier, redaction theories proceed from breaks and apparent inconsistencies in the narrative of the Gospel, plus hypothetical theological tendencies. But Ruckstuhl's conclusions proceed from much more scientifically based literary-critical work. His conclusion is that the Fourth Gospel comes from one hand, and that the *aporias* are simply the characteristic of that single author's unique style.

Ruckstuhl considers that the fact that those proposing redactions from a different author have never produced literary-critical demonstrations is a strong argument from silence (*argumentum ex silentio*) that such more scientifically based criteria for redaction are lacking.[38]

Those who argue to the essential literary unity of the Fourth Gospel can explain the aporias and shifts in the narrative without recourse to anyone but to the work of a single author. This must make still more redaction theories unconvincing.

For our case, we do not need to prove that a single author wrote the whole of the Fourth Gospel throughout its process of composition. We may wish to interpret "wrote these things" (*ho grapsas tauta*) of John 21:24[39] to mean that John the Son of Zebedee wrote every word. This may be its most obvious meaning,[40] but is not necessarily its only possible meaning. It is not impossible *per se* that John the Son of Zebedee, albeit as the author of the Fourth Gospel, used written sources, or used a scribe or an editor. Or it is possible that John the Son of Zebedee similarly oversaw the writing of his Gospel by another author, such as John the Elder.[41] Even Moloney's view that *ho grapsas tauta* refers not to the Beloved Disciple as an author but rather as the source of the tradition underlying the Fourth Gospel, as its "authority"[42] would not be fatal to our argument. A later anonymous author or authors could have put together a work well in touch with the apostolic tradition, and substantially faithful to the historical Jesus. Too often the impression given (again, influenced by the post-Bultmannian tradition) is that any later redaction will take us away from the historical Jesus.[43] But this is by no means necessarily so.

For our purposes, we do not have to show that there is no evidence anywhere in the Fourth Gospel of later redactions or stages out of touch with the historical Jesus. What we have to prove is that, however and by whoever the Fourth Gospel was composed, in the events and in the words of Jesus recounted in John which are essential to our case, the Gospel author(s) and/or redactor(s) were in touch with the genuine and reliable historical tradition handed down by apostolic witnesses from Jesus of Nazareth.

Furthermore, as we have here demonstrated, there is no *convincing evidence* that the Fourth Gospel had a redactor or editor other than the author of the Fourth Gospel, though almost all theories are possible. We have already demonstrated that the Gospel as it stands could have been written by an eye-witness of the life, death, and Resurrection of Jesus. It therefore follows that speculative redaction theories cannot validly be used to undermine the substantial historicity of the Fourth Gospel account, if its historical reliability could be effectively demonstrated by other methods of argument

John's own independent historical tradition?

Did John know and use the Synoptic Gospels? It is at least *a priori* likely, or at least possible, that John knew of Matthew, Mark, and Luke, because those Gospels, it is generally assumed, were written earlier than, or at least published in their final form before, the Fourth Gospel. As we have already seen,[44] the most popular theory, usually called the Two Document Hypothesis,[45] is that Mark was written first, c.64 AD,[46] Matthew second (75-90),[47] and Luke third, both about (80-85).[48] Therefore, unless there was complete isolation between the various Christian communities, there is a fair chance that the author of the Fourth Gospel was at least acquainted in some way with one, two, or indeed all three of the other three Gospels. And even if he were an eye-witness, this would not prevent him using other accounts of the life and teaching of Jesus to help him write his own account.

Our concern in this book is with the historical trust-worthiness of the Fourth Gospel, in order to argue for the authenticity of John's presentation of the life, self-manifestation, death and Resurrection of Jesus. The question for us therefore is not whether or not John actually used the Synoptic Gospels, but whether in using those presumably earlier Gospels he was writing a fictional gloss on them without historical value. This was the general view, as we have seen, in nineteenth century critical studies post-Strauss, and continued into the twentieth century *via* Bultmann.

This view was challenged by C.H. Dodd. In 1963, he published *The Historical Tradition in the Fourth Gospel.*[49]

Dodd begins by outlining the way he intends to demonstrate what he calls an "historical tradition" behind the Fourth Gospel. He begins with the question "Can we in any measure recover and describe a strain of tradition lying behind the Fourth Gospel, distinctive of it, and independent of other strains of tradition known to us?"[50] He contrasts this with the other possibility, popular with criticism just before his own time, that John simply depends on the Synoptic Gospels. He then works out a careful methodology which he intends to apply throughout his book:

> The presumption, therefore, which lay behind much of the earlier criticism – that similarity of form and content between two documents points to the dependence of the later of these documents on the earlier – no longer holds good, since there is an alternative explanation of many such similarities, and one which corresponds to the conditions under which gospel writing began, so far as we can learn them: namely, the influence of a common tradition.[51]

Dodd gives many examples of what he calls this "historical tradition", independent of the Synoptic tradition and available to and used by he author of the Fourth Gospel.[52] For example, "the pre-Johannine tradition had a full and detailed account of the Passion and the events immediately preceding it."[53] All these examples, for Dodd, are manifestly John drawing upon his historical tradition, which tradition goes back before AD 66.[54]

This view has been recently contested by Thomas L. Brodie, who, in his fascinating study *The Quest for the Origin of John's Gospel*, is convinced that John is dependent on Mark for its literary structure.

> "But the historical tradition found in John is not independent. The reliance on the synoptics is pervasive. What is independent is John's reshaping of the tradition, his reworking of it in order to develop his theological vision. In his own way he was just as closely involved

with Matthew, Mark, and Luke as they were with one another. Thus the idea of an independent historical tradition is left without its foundation."[55]

But many Johannine scholars of note are convinced of an historical tradition in John independent of the Synoptics. Contrary to Brodie, Brown, for instance, looks at the differences in the respective Synoptic and Johannine accounts of the man born blind [John 9:1-7, cf. Mark 10:46-52\\], and finds the Fourth Gospel account of this miracle evidence of John's independent historical tradition:

> Actually, the similarities between the various Synoptic accounts and John's account are rather few. John is certainly not dependent on any single Synoptic account, nor is there any convincing evidence that John is dependent on any combination of detail from the various Synoptic scenes.[56]

The debate obviously remains open. But from our point of view, even if there is only a possibility that the Fourth Gospel has its own historical tradition, then we are legitimately free to examine John to see whether in his narrative there are sayings and stories which could authentically emanate from the historical Jesus, and that, in such an instance at least, John is not simply a fictional rewrite of the Synoptic account.

The same applies where the relationship between Paul's writings and the Gospel of John is concerned. Nothing prevents John being influenced by Pauline theology, yet containing within his Gospel authentic historical material from the life and teaching of the historical Jesus.

Reported speech of the historical Jesus

His high view of Jesus is not the only problem in John for critical scholarship. Particularly difficult regarding the historicity of the Fourth Gospel are the long homiletic discourses attributed to Jesus. Not only are these very different from those in the Synoptic Gospels. Granted the unity of style in John, as we have seen has been painstakingly argued by such as Ruckstuhl,[57] it is clear that the words of Jesus in John are themselves in the style of the evangelist rather than being the *ipsissima verba*, "the very words of Jesus himself".

However, it is easy to draw from this a critical conclusion which is a *non sequitur*, namely that because the voice of Jesus in the Fourth Gospel is not in the *ipsissima verba*, we must reject those words in John as having any historical reliability whatsoever. But in itself, this is no problem. No reasonable person would demand that the evangelist had actually to use the *ipsissima verba* of Jesus in order for the record of his words to be historically reliable. Daily in the newspapers, and indeed in minutes of meetings, we have before us the phenomenon of reported speech. A speech is recorded, not in the words of the actual speaker in question, but in the words of the reporter; although, very often, such a report will contain some of the *ipsissima verba* of the person whose words are being reported; particularly when a crucial point in the report is in question. "In response to this question, the Prime Minister said…" The report in this instance moves from being just reported speech to being *ipsissima verba*.

In this connection, the *Instruction of the Pontifical Biblical Commission Concerning the Historical Truth of the Gospels,* April 21, 1964, one would suggest, gives us a common-sense statement about the non-necessity of having the *ipsissima verba* of Jesus in order for their correspondence with facticity to be verified:

> For the truth of the story is not at all affected by the fact that the Evangelists relate the words and deeds of the Lord in a different order, and express His sayings not literally but differently, while preserving (their) sense. For, as St Augustine says, 'It is quite probable that each Evangelist in narrating a saying believed it to have been his duty to recount what he had to in that order in which it pleased God to suggest it to his memory – in those things at least in which the order, whether it be this or that, detracts in nothing from the truth and authority of the Gospel."[58]

Indeed, the *Jesus Seminar*, it seems, would be in perhaps surprising agreement with the Pontifical Commission in this respect. It gave four options, represented by four different colours of beads, by which each scholar taking part in the Seminar would determine the historical reliability, or lack of it, of any individual saying in the Gospels attributed to Jesus:

red: Jesus undoubtedly said this or something very like it.
pink: Jesus probably said something like this.
grey: Jesus did not say this, but the ideas contained in it are close to his own,
black: Jesus did not say this; it represents the perspective or content of a later or different tradition.[59]

The *Jesus Seminar* would appear to accept the first two colours, red and pink, as definitely to be included in their data-base of a genuine contribution towards our knowledge of the historical Jesus; that is, sayings which are indubitably to be attributed to Jesus, and sayings probably to be attributed to Jesus. Even regarding the red bead, the primary source, the *Jesus Seminar* would not require *ipsissima verba*, only that "Jesus undoubtedly said something very like it". And regarding the third bead, the grey, "Jesus did not say this, but the ideas contained in it are close to his own", the *Jesus Seminar* would not dismiss such statements attributed to the historical Jesus as valueless. Only the statement relegated to being represented by black beads, "Jesus did not say this; it represents the perspective or content of a later or different tradition" is cast into outer darkness where the *Jesus Seminar* is concerned:

red;   I would include this item unequivocally in the database for determining who Jesus was.
pink: I would include this item with reservations (or modi-fications) in the database.
grey: I would not include this item in the database. but I might make use at some of the content in determining who Jesus was.
black: I would not include this item in the primary database.[60]

In terms of our discussion up to now, it is clear that only a radical Bultmannian approach to the Fourth Gospel would lead logically to the conclusion which the *Jesus Seminar* reached regarding the historicity of the words of Jesus in John, namely, to virtually nothing but black beads dropped into the ballot box.[61] If we accept that the Fourth Gospel is a Mandaean document adapting the Redeemer myth to a Johannine Christianity towards the end of the first century and the beginning of the second, then the relationship which John has to the historical Jesus is nil. However, Dodd showed what singular lack of evidence there is for this theory.[62]

Schnackenburg's judgement seems perfectly reasonable for us as a working hypothesis to take through our investigation: "The deep faith of the writer moved him to clothe the thoughts and words of Jesus in their present dress, but his intention was to let the earthly Jesus speak and express his own thoughts."[63] In other words, we can begin by at least accepting the possibility that in John we have the reported speech of the historical Jesus by the evangelist. And, accepting Dodd's historical tradition in John,[64] we must also be open to the possibility that on occasions we have the *ipsissima verba* embedded in the discourses of the Fourth Gospel.

All our conclusions so far lead us towards the serious consideration that John is potentially based on eye-witness testimony. What we have to demonstrate is that in its singular clarity among the four Gospels concerning the claims of Jesus to be divine, and his validation of those claims by his miracles and by his Resurrection, the Fourth Gospel is not writing fiction, but is rooted in the authentic sources of the life and times of the historical Jesus.

The "Johannine Community": science fiction?

Towards the close of the twentieth century, speculation about the Johannine Community has tended to maintain traditional critical scepticism regarding the Fourth Gospel. It is commonly assumed now that the growth of a higher Christology was not the consequence of the teaching of Jesus himself, but of the evolution of a Christian community concerned to defend its new-found Christian faith against a similarly defensive

Judaism. We will be examining this view more closely when we deal with the whole question of "the Jews" in John.

Raymond Brown had a strong influence in the increased interest in the "Johannine Community" in the last quarter of the twentieth century. His view of the stages of the formation of the Gospel of John itself had a fascinating evolution. In his Anchor Bible commentary, the Five Stages appear simply as a hypothetical possibility.[65] But by the time Brown published his book *The Community of the Beloved Disciple: The Life, Loves and Hates of an Individual Church in New Testament Times* in 1979,[66] the stages have become staging posts for the evolution of the Johannine Community. Hypothesis (the Community's history) is based upon hypothesis (the stages), without any hard evidence for either.[67]

Timely indeed is the warning of J. Beutler against "science fiction" regarding the reconstructed history and sociology of the Johannine Community.[68] Thomas Brodie's stricture, after quoting the various opinions as to the identity, ideas and history of the Johannine Community, that "given the diversity of views, it is clear that the actual process of reconstructing is extremely hazardous",[69] is likewise most relevant.

The history of the Johannine Community can only be reconstructed from the Fourth Gospel (and to some extent from the Johannine Epistles and perhaps even from the Apocalypse). But was the Fourth Gospel written first and foremost as an expression of the psyche of the Johannine Community, or as an account of the life, teaching, claims, death, and Resurrection of the historical Jesus? If the latter, some of what is claimed to be evidence of "The Life, Loves and Hates of an Individual Church in New Testament Times" might turn out to be simply an account of what the historical Jesus said and did two or three generations back from the writing of the Fourth Gospel. This would be true even if it also reflects incidentally the faith and life-situation of the Johannine Community, which one would not in any way wish to deny.

The origin of the ideas of the Fourth Gospel, whether by an individual author or by "the Johannine Community", leads us now to consider why that author or authors wrote the

Gospel in the first place. This may in its turn lead us to consider to what extent that author or authors were concerned to relate, and were able to relate, what the historical Jesus actually said and did.

NOTES – CHAPTER 9

1 Sanday, W. *The Criticism of the Fourth Gospel*. Eight Lectures, Union Theological Seminary, New York, Nov 1904. Oxford, Clarenden Press, 1905, 22-3.

2 JQ, 94.

3 Brodie, 1993, 144-5.

4 De Boer, M.C., *Johannine Perspectives on the Death of Jesus. Contributions to Biblical Exegesis and Theology 17*, Kok Pharos Publishing House, Kampen, the Netherlands, 1996 88.

5 *Quattuor evangelia originem apostolicam habere ecclesia semper et ubique tenuit ac tenet.* DV 18. Tanner, II, 978, line 22.

6 Brown, I., XCII. Later, INT 368, Brown appears to be more exceptional. "As with the other Gospels it is doubted by most scholars that this Gospel was written by an eye-witness of the public ministry of Jesus." But at least, Brown leaves you the possibility that John, the Son of Zebedee was the *source* of the Gospel tradition.

7 Brown, I., LXXX11.

8 RNT, 261.

9 As for the final edition of the Gospel, Brown gives the earliest date at around 80. Brown argues that "There is a reasonably precise indication for the *terminus post quem* for the dating of John in the theme of excommunication from the synagogue which, as we saw in Part V;B, plays an important role in the Gospel. The problem does not seem to have been acute before 70; and the datable incidents like the formulation of the twelfth blessing in the *Shemoneh Esreh* and the use of formal excommunication at Jamnia belong to the period 80-90. This evidence makes unlikely a date before 80 for the final written composition of the Gospel, and indeed makes the 90s the probable era Brown, I, LXXXV. But Robinson is highly sceptical of Brown's, and others', interpretation of John's reference to excommunication here. The text concerns the reaction to the Jews when the man is born blind. His terrified parents were frightened even to admit their son had been healed because of the threat of excommunication:- "His [the man born blind's] parents said this because they were afraid of the Jews; for the Jews had already agreed that anyone who confessed Jesus to be the Messiah would be put out of the synagogue" [John 9:22].

The general critical opinion is that Jewish Christians were excommunicated after AD 70. Thus the date of the final edition of John is fixed at its lower limit at this year. But Robinson is sceptical of this argument. He argues first that the wording of the Benediction referred to by Brown was expressly intended "against Hebrew Christians of an extreme Judaizing kind, for whom the fourth gospel would have been anathema". RNT, 273. Secondly, Robinson argues that the idea of Christians being excommunicated is expressed in other words in the New Testament much earlier than a late John (e.g. Acts 13:45-50, 1 Thessalonians 2:14). We will be examining this argument in greater detail in chapter 15, "The Jews and the Death of Jesus".

10 HTFG. Cf. pp. 170-1.
11 ENTM, 85.
12 Finegan summarises Roberts' conclusions: "Paleographically, the way individual letters are formed has been compared (Roberts, *op.cit.* pp.13-16) most closely with papyri of the end of the first or beginning of the second century, among them ones bearing dates corresponding to AD 94 and AD 127. It is probable, therefore, that the present papyrus also belongs at the end of the first or beginning of the second century, at all events hardly later than AD 125. Since the text is of the Gospel according to John, the papyrus is evidence that that Gospel was circulating in Egypt already at this date. As a copy of such date of a portion of a New Testament text, the papyrus is our presently earliest known fragment of any part of the New Testament". ENTM, 86.
13 Brown, I, LXXXIII.
14 Brown, I, LXII-LXIV.
15 Fredriksen, P. *Jesus of Nazareth King of the Jews: A Jewish life and the Emergence of Christianity.* New York, Knopf, 1999, 5.
16 IFG, 79.
17 IFG, gives further examples as to how the author of the Fourth Gospel knew his Rabbinic theology, 79ff.
18 IFG, 85 (Pesahim 54a Bar.)
19 IFG, 86.
20 Westcott, 1880.
21 Westcott, 1880.
22 IFG, 92.
23 IFG, 91.
24 IFG, 93.
25 IFG, 95.
26 Cf. chapters 13 and 14.
27 Cf. pp. 56-8.
28 CJH, 209.
29 *La Redaction Finale de L'Évangile selon Jean (À L'Exemple du Chapitre 2),* in CJH, 207-230.
30 Kaestli, Poffet, CJH, 209.

31 RGG, col. 841.
32 For a much fuller treatment of source theories, together with an exposition of Ashton's own, cf. UFG.
33 In John, signs and discourses are woven together, which makes a separate Signs Source difficult to sustain. Brown, I, XXXI-II.
34 1991.
35 Carson, 1978. The source theory of Georg Richter, cf. CJH, 210-1.
36 JQ, 89-90.
37 E.A. Abbott, *Johannine Vocabulary* and *Johannine Grammar* (1905/6). "Then E. Schweizer in 1939 showed by means of thirty-three stylistic characteristics which he discovered that the earlier hypotheses suggesting divisions into sources could not in any way be supported 'on stylistic grounds'. E. Ruckstuhl refined Schweizer's method further in 1951 and also applied it to Bultmann's commentary which appeared in 1971." JQ, 89-90.
38 Ruckstuhl, E. *Die literarische Einheit des Johannesevangeliums.* NTOA 7, Göttingen, 1987, 9.
39 Brown, II, 1123-4, summarises the position.
40 "The most natural meaning of these words, and therefore the meaning to be adopted unless very strong reasons are brought against it, is that the disciple himself not only bore witness to but also wrote down *tauta.*" Barrett, 587.
41 "...we know that his testimony is true". This is a hotly disputed clause of 21:24. Brown, II, 1124-5.
42 Moloney, 7.
43 Cf. chapter 3, are the Gospels sources of history?
44 Cf. pp. 55, 60.
45 Cf. NJBC, **40:1-36**, 587-595.
46 NJBC, **41:2**, 596.
47 NJBC, **42:4**, 630.
48 NJBC, **43:3**, 675.
49 HTFG.
50 HTFG, 8.
51 HTFG, 8-9.
52 HTFG, 426.
53 HTFG, 430.
54 HTFG, 214.
55 Brodie, T.L., *The Quest for the Origin of John's Gospel: A Source-Oriented Approach*, Oxford University Press, 1993, 145.
56 Brown, I, 378-9
57 Cf. p. 168-9.
58 BI, 395, No. 930.
59 FG 36.
60 FG 36.
61 Cf. p. 24. FG 401-470.
62 IFG, 401-470.

63 Schnackenburg, I, 24.
64 Cf. pp. 170-1.
65 Brown, I, xlvii-li. Reprinted in SHJ, 103-108.
66 Brown, 1979.
67 Regarding Brown's stages, Carson says perceptively: "Brown of course prefers to talk about the development of 'traditions' rather than the delineation of 'sources'. Still, someone has to enter John's text with a literary scalpel and retrieve those traditions." Carson, 42.
68 CJH, 28. "*Tous ces travaux ont leur poids, mais ils restent souvent très spéculatifs. A ce propos, une mise en garde contre la "science fiction" historique n'est certainement pas inopportune.*"
69 Brodie, op.cit., 20.

CHAPTER 10

ST JOHN'S GOSPEL AS *APOLOGIA*

The Fourth Gospel was intended to proclaim and defend the truth that Jesus claimed to be God the Son, that he was neither bad nor was he mad, but demonstrated by his miracles and above all by his Resurrection that he was whom he claimed to be.

St John's Gospel, proof of the Incarnation

At the beginning, we mentioned the old-style apologetic. The argument went that Jesus claimed to be God. So, in making such a claim, he could not have been just a good man. He must have been either bad, mad or God. He was neither bad nor mad. Therefore, concluded the old apologetic, Jesus must have been who he claimed to be, God. Faith in Jesus as the divine Son of God become man, therefore, was, according to this traditional argumentation, reasonable. The truth of this claim was demonstrated by the sublime teaching of Jesus, by his miracles, and above all by his Resurrection from the dead.

This argument today would be ridiculed by many. Yet, strange though it may seem, and in spite of the apparent naïvety at least of the presentation of this argument, it is nevertheless the very argument of the Fourth Gospel itself, as we demonstrated right at the beginning of this work.

None of the other three Gospels is as clear in its expressed purpose as is the Fourth, which summons the reader to faith in Jesus Christ as Son of God:

> Now Jesus did many other signs in the presence of his disciples, which are not written in this book: but these are written so that you may come to believe that Jesus is the Messiah, the Son of God, and that through believing you may have life in his name. [John 20:30-31]

The Enigmas of the Fourth Gospel therefore are entirely simple and clear. It is to lead us into faith in Jesus as the unique Son of God. Chapter 21 only serves to underline the veracity of the testimony upon which the previous 20 chapters has been based [21:24], and the solid foundation in the words of the risen Lord upon which the pastoral structures of the new Christian community are founded [21:15-18].[1]

This simplicity and clarity in the intention of the author of the Fourth Gospel is often lost in the maze of discussion concerning possible redaction, and theories of multiple editions and stages, which we have already examined briefly.[2] At this point, we may bypass all such theories, and even the question as to who wrote the Gospel of John. In looking at the finished text, whoever wrote it and however it was written using whatever sources or lack of them, it is quite obvious that St John's Gospel as it now stands is a defence, an *apologia*, of the divinity of Christ, and a consequent challenge to faith in him.

St John's Gospel, idealism or from the real Jesus?

The general belief in historical Jesus research, as we have seen first outlined in our Introduction, and in chapter 1, is that its Christology of the primitive church moved upwards from Jewish prophet to Gentile God. We saw in chapter 2 how Bultmann described a theory of the stages whereby the early church moved upwards in its Christology from the teaching of a Jewish Rabbi to Son of God "in the sense of ascribing a 'divine' nature to him."[3] This still seems to be the general critical position.

Assuming the generally held Two-Source Theory,[4] an ascending Christology has been proposed beginning with Jesus as first and foremost a Rabbi to the Johannine High Christology as the end point of development. This supposed development is traced for us lucidly in Raymond Brown's *Birth of the Messiah*[5]:

1. The hypothetical document Q, material common to Matthew and Luke, not in Mark. Date c.30-50 AD. This document, written originally in Aramaic, presents Jesus as a teacher.

2. From 50 AD onwards, Paul preaches Jesus as Kurios, Lord, cf. Philippians 2:11.

3. Mark's Gospel, c.64 AD, presents Jesus as the Son of God by virtue of his baptism. This could square with an Adoptionist view, namely that Jesus *became* Son of God only when consecrated by God.

4. Matthew and Luke, 70-90 AD, present Jesus as Son of God from his birth from the Virgin Mary.

5. Finally, John, 90-110 AD, presents Jesus as eternal Logos, the Son of the Father from all eternity.

But this general presumption, that the early church moved necessarily upwards in Christology,[6] is challenged appropriately by John McDade:

> It (Life of Jesus Research) also often makes the assumption that early Christology is "low" and later Christology is "high", and therefore the Christological categories closest to Jesus and perhaps deriving directly from him, are the "low" end of the Christological spectrum. Yet the earliest Christian writings, those of Paul, give no evidence that the Christology of the 40s and 50s was "low", quite the reverse in fact. I sometimes wonder if "early low Christology" is not a fantasy of modern exegesis.[7]

Of course, all these critical assumptions are radically challenged if we follow the dynamic researches of Margaret Barker.[8] If she is right, as we have seen, the historical Jesus himself had a "high Christology".

Even more, our own carefully worked conclusions in the previous chapter are a clear demonstration that the historical Jesus saw himself as Son of God; and that in the "high" sense of direct authority divine in origin. Thus Brown's No. 3 moves up to No.1. This answers directly and simply our first two Problems, (1) as to how the first Christians came to worship Jesus as God and (2) now even more important, why his contemporaries wished to put Jesus to death. As we demonstrated in our chapter 8, his Jewish contemporaries thought he was blaspheming. This gives more than Sufficient Reason[9] as to why Jesus was eventually crucified, and authenticates Mark's description of Jesus as Son of God.

This must in its turn radically alter our picture of the development of Christology in the primitive church. If the historical Jesus saw himself as the transcendent Son of God, authenticating Mark's view of him, then the development towards John's Christology is not from early Rabbi or prophet to Logos, but is rather *a further explicitation of Mark's already 'high' view authenticated as from the historical Jesus.*

From thread to golden chain

But what in Mark is a thread running through the narrative, so thin that it seems to be missed by some,[10] becomes in John a kind of heavy gold chain, not only defining the story-line, but permeating every small piece of the story.

There can be little doubt that the plan of the final author of the Fourth Gospel was that the whole of the Gospel narrative was to function as a proof of the thesis expounded in the Prologue, 1:1-18. Throughout the Fourth Gospel all is devoted to the question as to who Jesus is, beginning with the Prologue 1:1-18, and right through to Thomas' confession of faith before the risen Christ "My Lord and my God" (John 20:28). The Prologue states who Jesus is. The remainder of the narrative is intended to demonstrate that indeed Jesus *is* the Logos become flesh.[11]

The seven miracles, recounted in the first twelve chapters of the Fourth Gospel,[12] are carefully selected and carefully staged in terms of the evangelist's purpose, to demonstrate that Jesus is truly the Word become flesh. This we will clarify in the next chapter.

For John, the miracles are "works" (*erga*), linking with the creative activity of God, which demonstrate that "the Father Himself may be said to perform Jesus' works".[13] It is because Jesus works the works of the Father that his hearers see this as a claim to be "equal with God" [John 5:18].[14] This claim of Jesus do the works of the Father is seen itself as blasphemy by Jesus' Jewish hearers:

> Jesus answered, "I have told you, and you do not believe. The works that I do in my Father's name testify to me; but you do not believe, because you do not belong to my sheep. My sheep hear my voice. I know them, and they follow me. I give them eternal life, and they will never perish. No one will snatch them out of my hand. What my Father has given me is greater than all else, and no one can snatch it out of the Father's hand. The Father and I are one." The Jews took up stones again to stone him. Jesus replied, "I have shown you many good works from the Father. For which of these are you going to stone me?" The Jews answered, "It is not for a good work that we are going to stone you, but for blasphemy, because you, though only a human being, are making yourself God." [John 10:25-33]

Since C.H. Dodd's *Interpretation of the Fourth Gospel*, the setting of the recounting of these seven miracles has been called "The Book of Signs",[15] which for Dodd, begins at 1:15 and ends in 12:44-50. This first part is brought to an end with the last Johannine miracle of the raising of Lazarus, itself a presage of the final Resurrection of Jesus.

Dodd sees 12:44-50 as taking up themes from the whole of the first half of the Fourth Gospel; e.g.12:46 with 8:12, Christ as the light of the world.[16] But perhaps even more suggestive is to see 12:44-50 as the author saying "Q.E.D. the Prologue".[17] This would not deny that themes are taken up from the earlier chapters. But the parallels with the Prologue are so striking, words and phrases referring to the Logos now transposed to the mouth of Jesus, this becomes a superb Epilogue balancing off the Prologue, to bring the public ministry of Jesus to a close:

Prologue 1:1-18	Epilogue to the Book of Signs 12:44-50
[1:13] for those who believed in his name…	[12:44] Whoever believes in me believes not in me but in him who sent me."
[1:5] The light shines in the darkness, and the darkness did not overcome it.	[12:46] everyone who believes in me should not remain in the darkness
1:10] He was in the world, and the world came into being through him; yet the world did not know him.	[12:47] I came not to judge the world, but to save the world
[1:12] But to all who received him, who believed in his name, he gave power to become children of God	[12:48] The one who rejects me and does not receive my word has a judge
[1:17] The law indeed was given through Moses; grace and truth came through Jesus Christ.	[12:49] The Father who sent me has himself given me a commandment and I know that his commandment is eternal life
[1:18] No one has ever seen God. It is God the only Son, who is close to the Father's heart, who has made him known.	[12:50] What I speak, therefore, I speak just as the Father has told me.

The reader will note that the evangelist is not actually quoting the Prologue; but it must surely be in his mind. His purpose is twofold:

1. To identify the Jesus who has just performed signs and revealed the mystery of his own being as the Logos of the Prologue. He does not use the word *logos* in 12:44-50. Again, is this because the historical Jesus never used the word *logos* of himself? But he does use equivalent phrases like "my words" (*tón hrématón*) [12:47], (*ta hrémata mou*) [12:48], "that I speak" (*ti lalésó*) [12:49] (*houtós laló*)[12:50]. The Word therefore has truly now become flesh.

2. The Epilogue to the Book of Signs also looks forward to what follows, where Jesus will give his New Commandment to his disciples. Believers like Martha have seen his glory, 11:14, a glory which will be revealed in the Passion, and even more in the appearances of the risen Jesus, leading finally to Thomas' profession of faith, 20:28. Thus for John, the ultimate QED comes with Thomas' acclamation "My Lord and my God." Thus the evangelist is saying to us, "The Word was God, and became flesh. Jesus IS the Word become flesh, and is worshipped as such by Thomas."[18]

Explanation, not new creation

John has a much more explicit Christology than Mark. But Mark has all the elements of the doctrine which we see much more explicitly stated in John. John is not adding to Mark. He is only explaining. After all, in the Parable of the Wicked Husbandmen, the master of the estate says, "They will reverence my son". If Jesus is his natural son, then the formula of Nicea is justified, that the Son is the same nature (*homóousios*). He could be the adopted son, but could also be the natural son; and the latter seems to be the meaning of "my son" which springs first to mind. Our contention here is, as with J.A.T Robinson, that the Fourth Gospel only makes explicit what is already implicit in the Synoptic picture of

Jesus, which, as we have shown earlier, particularly in connection with our discussion on Mark 14:62-64[19] is rooted in the self-understanding of the historical Jesus.

We would go with Oscar Cullmann here, as quoted by Robinson:

> Might we not have a special kind of teaching here? It would not be secret, or systematically withheld from the majority of disciples, but it would have been more intimate teaching which not all the disciples knew (and which they may have barely understood). The author of the Gospel of John may have developed it *freely*, in the way that we know, but still keeping Jesus' teaching as a foundation.[20]

Robinson quotes a perhaps even more enlightening comment on the relationship between John and the Synoptics by T.E. Pollard *St John's Contribution to the Picture of the Historical Jesus* at Knox Theological Hall, Dunedin in 1964, which seems to me to express the matter perfectly:

> On Collingwood's definition of the real task of the historian, it could well be argued that John is a better historian than the Synoptists. John protrays Jesus as the one who at every point is conscious of his Messianic function as Son of God, whose every action, thought and word are governed by this consciousness. There is no need to interpret this portrait as an invention by John or a falsification of what Jesus really was. Rather it is an attempt to portray Jesus as he was, in his earthly life, in and for himself. It is not that this Jesus of St John is any less human than the Jesus of the Synoptics; it is rather that John penetrates with deeper insight into the inner springs of the personality of Jesus. Nor was John's portrait a more highly developed theological interpretation; rather because of his deeper insight he makes explicit what is implicit, and, for the most part, veiled in the Synoptics.[21]

A.M. Hunter makes the same valid point. He notes that on the one hand, the Synoptics like John claim that their Gospel is about Jesus Son of God. He notes further that for John, even more than for the Synoptics, "is the insistence on Jesus' *utter dependence*, at every point, on his heavenly Father".[22] Similarly, Hunter points to the "paradox"[23] which, close to the idea of "parable", *mashal*,[24] is inherent in the very doctrine of the Incarnation itself, God become man, and which is also present in the biblical picture of Jesus, both in John and in the Synoptics. This paradox, Hunter claims, is deepened in John, but not in contradiction to the Synoptics. We will submit in this latter part of our investigation that this deepening of the paradox is not simply the creative work of the Fourth Evangelist, but was part of the historical Jesus' own self-revelation during his life on earth.

What generated this extraordinary vision?

In a most recent and perceptive study, *John's Apologetic Christology: Legitimation and Development in Johannine Christology*,[25] James F.McGrath has fully recognised this apologetic intent of the author of St John's Gospel, which he calls "legitimation". McGrath argues that, in line with the general critical view, the Christology of John's Gospel is the result of a development within the Christian community from the Synoptic and Pauline Christologies. But how is this development to be explained, and above all, what was its cause? McGrath proposes that "these distinctively Johannine developments are best understood as an attempt to respond to objections to Christian Christological beliefs...,"[26] that is objections in particular within Judaism at the close of the first century AD.

But, the fundamental question arises, how did this Fourth Gospel view of Jesus arise at all at the close of the first century? As we saw earlier in chapter 9, the roots of John's Christology become clearly visible as Semitic rather than Greek, as comparative studies of Qumran[27] and even more of Rabbinic Judaism[28] have now demonstrated. And, again in Ashton's terms, once we abandon Bultmann's fantastic Mandaean hypothesis based upon second millenium manuscripts[29] to account for John's Christological development, then, in Ashton's terms, "we must replace it by something sufficiently powerful to have generated the extraordinary, indeed the unique vision of John the Evangelist."[30] But with what can we replace it?

McGrath's own solution to this question is that at the close of the first century, Johannine Christianity was attempting to *legitimise* its own beliefs in the face of a hostile world. St John's Gospel is therefore an exercise in "legitimation/apologetic for its view… Thus the end result will be a more fully developed ideology or doctrine, the existence of which could not necessarily have been foreseen prior to the conflict".[31] In the same way, the Rabbinic Jews after the Council of Jamnia defined their position more clearly *vis á vis* Christianity.

But has McGrath yet given us a *sufficient reason* for the rise of John's exceptionally high Christology? Would not purely Messianic Judaism have been sufficiently provocative as an opposition to the newly clarifying Rabbinic Judaism post-Jamnia? We might argue that believing that Jesus was simply the Messiah would not cause excommunication from Judaism. But presumably a Jew could have been expelled from the synagogue if that particular synagogue or group of synagogues believed that such a Messiah was a false one, or teaching false doctrine.

In terms of McGrath's own investigation above, the best kind of legitimation, the most effective apologetic, would have been that the historical Jesus himself claimed to be what the Fourth Gospel claimed him to be, and that he substantiated those claims, again as the Fourth Gospel claimed, by his miracles, by his saving death, and by his Resurrection. This avoids positing the hypothetical "Johannine Community" as the source of John's ideas. This would certainly provide sufficient reason for the development of John's high Christology, that the historical Jesus' own claims were the beginning of this development. In such a case, also, the Fourth Gospel would be far from anti-Semitic, as we shall demonstrate later in chapter 15, because it simply recounts the conflict which resulted in Jesus' own time on earth which resulted from his claims, which his opponents saw as blasphemous.

Having accepted an historical basis for John's ideas, we could accept a modified version of an ascending Christology. We see Ashton's problem:

> The original message proclaiming Jesus as Messiah was certainly much weaker than the one later rejected as blasphemous by the Jews. Otherwise it would never have gained a footing among them in the first place. To make sense of what evidence there is we have therefore to postulate a period of development in which the followers of Jesus moved from a low to a high Christology. But that came later.[32]

We could accept that it took time for the primitive Christian community to come to terms with what the historical Jesus had actually said and done during his life on earth. This would be a legitimate argument for the late date of John, which we accept with the vast majority of Johannine scholars. What we cannot accept is that somehow this Johannine Community was able to invent these amazing ideas about Jesus, when a simple explanation is easily to hand, namely that these ideas came from a superbly creative mind, Jesus himself.

If the author of the Fourth Gospel tells us that he is attempting to demonstrate that truly the Word has become flesh, *in history*, this in itself would justify us in taking the question of the historicity of the Fourth Gospel as more than possibly seriously, since the evangelist's whole thesis is that the Word has entered our history precisely in Jesus of Nazareth. If the Fourth Gospel was rooted in Gnostic ideas, then we would expect a mythical story, such as the Cybilene cults provide us, and there would indeed be much more justification for a Bultmannian style Gnostic or semi-Gnostic redaction. But if the thesis of the Fourth Gospel is totally unique, as we have just demonstrated, that the Word has truly become flesh, then we must look to the possibility that the author is writing sober historical fact, even if, no doubt, he is writing in dramatic form.

Our plan

This book is far from fundamentalist. We are not claiming that in the long discourses of Jesus in the Fourth Gospel, we have his *ipsissima verba*, a tape-recording of his very words. As we have earlier explained,[33] we accept Schnackenburg's view that the Johannine speeches are in the reported speech of the evangelist. All we would claim that, similarly to the Synoptic evangelists (even if there may be less original material in John than in Matthew, Mark, and Luke), we may find genuine sayings, even *ipssisima verba Jesu*, within those discourses recoverable by the use of criteria which we have already seen as developed by historical Jesus research.[34]

Likewise, we would not claim that we have strict chronological sequences necessarily in John; even though modern scholarship is, as we have seen,[35] quite ready on occasions to prefer John to the Synoptics in some matters of historical detail. In this connection, particularly important are the short and pithy accounts of miracles and of Synoptic-like sayings, as studied in Dodd's *Historical Tradition in the Fourth Gospel*.[36] Dodd sees this "pericope" like format in the Fourth Gospel as evidence of a tradition of Jesus' words and deeds early and independent of the Synoptic tradition. We shall find for instance with Dodd that John's account of the Walking on the Water [John 6:16-21][37] and of the Multiplication of the Loaves [John 6:1-14][38] is evidence of this early historical tradition, and we shall further attempt to argue that the story is intended to be conveyed as factual by both the tradition and by the evangelist.

Finally, the Fourth Gospel, as the other three, is written in the form of a history, that of the public ministry, the death, and the Resurrection of Jesus. We have earlier noted that Christian tradition has always maintained the substantial historicity of the four Gospels, reiterated in paragraph 19 of the *Dogmatic Constitution: Dei Verbum*,[39] This is granted the fact, as asserted by DV 19, that the evangelists "selected, synthesised, explicated, and wrote everything in the form of preaching". In our study of the Fourth Gospel, by this we take to mean that the fourth evangelist, while writing that

Gospel in dramatic form, was writing about what actually occurred in historical fact, including the miraculous dimension, which was part of the whole amazing true story of Jesus.

Our aim is to demonstrate historically the Gospel, the Good News, as presented by the Fourth Evangelist, the Gospel within the Gospel.

• The miracles of Jesus, particularly the Walking on the Water and the Multiplication of the Loaves, demonstrated to the disciples, at least as they understood it after the Resurrection, that he was the manifestation of the divine logos.

• Jesus was fully aware of his own divine nature, and proclaimed it explicitly in the Temple courtyard just prior to his arrest, identifying himself with the YHWH God of the old Testament, the I AM, a claim which was seen as blasphemous by many of his hearers.

• It was first and foremost because of these claims that Jesus was arrested and then handed over to Pontius Pilate the Roman Governor.

• Jesus made these claims in the Jerusalem Temple courtyard because he believed that "the Jews", that is those of God's chosen people who had the privilege of living in Jerusalem and Judea, had the right of hearing the message of salvation and of forming the renewed people of God following Jesus "the light of the world."

• Jesus after his death appeared bodily to the women and his disciples, who discovered his tomb empty. This demonstrated to the apostles that Jesus was precisely who he claimed to be during his life, the Word become flesh, fully worthy of doubting Thomas' worshipful proclamation "My Lord and my God" [John 20:28].

• Thus all the readers of the Fourth Gospel are invited to share in the faith of once doubting Thomas.

1 Bultmann, 712, "The story (i.e. the rehabilitation of Peter by Jesus after Peter's denial, 21:15-23) rather is a variant of Peter's commission to be the leader of the community, Mt.16:17-19; cf. also Lk.22.32".

2 Cf. p. 176.

3 Cf. p. 57. JW, 1934, 152.

4 Cf. p. 51.

5 Brown, R.E. *The Birth of the Messiah. A Commentary on the Infancy Narratives in Matthew and Luke.* London, Chapman, 1977, 141.

6 The model of an ascending Christology depends first and foremost on a *unilinear* concept of Christological development in the early church. If we accept that the hypothetical early source Q, NJBC, **40:13**, 590, pre-dating Matthew and Luke, has a low Christology, this would mean that the whole of the primitive church had a low Christology, and any evidence of a higher Christology must be later than Q.

7 McDade, 1998, 502.

8 Cf. pp. 222-3.

9 Cf. pp. 116, 124.

10 So JPGG, 24. But we have already seen how Mark's description of Jesus is close to being an expression of his divinity, cf. pp. 139-40.

11 We quoted Lightfoot. "These verses give the key to the understanding of this gospel, and make clear how the evangelist wishes his readers to approach his presentation of the Lord's work and Person; and equally the rest of the book will throw light on the contents of these verses". Lightfoot, 78.

12 2:1-11, 3:46-54, 5:1-15, 6:1-15, 6:16-21, 9:1-7, 12:41-44.

13 Brown, I, 527.

14 As Barrett, 256, says, "the assumption of a uniform activity common to Jesus and to God could only mean that Jesus was equal to God".

15 IFG, x.

16 IFG, 381.

17 This idea of linking 12:44-50 with 1:1-18 I took from a lecture I attended while studying at the Pontifical Biblical Institute given by Ignace de la Potterie, one of the finest Johannine scholars of his generation. Unfortunately, I have not found that idea published anywhere, so cannot give the reader any reference.

18 Brown, II, 1026.

19 Cf. pp. 35-6.

20 Cullmann, O., *The Johannine Circle: Its Place in Judaism, among the Disciples of Jesus and in Early Christianity.* London and Philadelphia, 1976, 82.

21 PJ, 363. Pollard's lecture St.John's Contribution to the Picture of the Historical Jesus.appeared in Forum 6, August 1964, 2-9.

22 Hunter, 1968, 115.

23 Hunter, *ibid.*

24 Cf. p. 134.
25 McGrath, J.F. *John's Apologetic Christology: Legitimation and Development in Johannine Christology.* Society for New Testament Studies, Monograph Series 111. Cambridge University Press, 2001.
26 McGrath, op.cit., 40.
27 Cf. pp. 162-3.
28 Cf. pp. 163-4.
29 Cf. p. 175.
30 UFG, 66.
31 McGrath, op.cit., 38.
32 UFG, 169.
33 Cf. p. 175.
34 Cf. pp. 114-8.
35 Cf. p. 26.
36 Cf. pp. 170-2.
37 HTFG, 196-199.
38 HTFG, 199-217.
39 Cf. p. 158.

CHAPTER 11

MIRACLES IN JOHN

The seven miracles reported in St John's Gospel all serve his Christology, in that they are signs *(sémeia)* that Jesus was truly the only-begotten Son of God. However, the narration of these miracles in John is sober, and not unduly influenced by his theology, thus making them credible historically.

Jesus the miracle worker: the critical minimum

In one sense, miracle was *the* question of questions regarding the historical Jesus. As we saw in Chapter 1, the first Questers such as Reimarus and the Rationalists were unable to accept either miracles or Incarnation. Thus a truly "historical Jesus" would be for them a Jesus bereft of his divine "robes of splendour with which he had been apparelled", and clothed "once more with the coarse garments in which He had walked in Galilee,"[1] a wandering Jewish preacher put to death for one reason or other by a cruel Roman and Jewish establishment.

Yet the critical movement has mostly acknowledged that at least Jesus was renowned as a miracle worker. That is because the evidence that Jesus did at least have the reputation of being a miracle worker is overwhelming. Also, a rationalist could accept that a man could have healing powers as yet unexplained by science. Faith healing is accepted by many as a scientific fact, whether healing is by auto-suggestion or from the subject's own inner resources. And regarding Jesus' powers of casting out devils, those could be explained in Freudian terms as release of the sub-conscious.

Meier is totally convinced that the historical Jesus was renowned as a miracle worker: "The single most important criterion in the investigation of Jesus' miracles is the criterion of *multiple attestation of sources and forms.* As for multiple sources, the evidence is overwhelming. Every Gospel source (Mark, Q,M,L, and John), every evangelist in his redactional summaries, and Josephus to boot, affirm the miracle-working activity of Jesus. Indeed, each Gospel source does so more than once, and some do it repeatedly." [2]

Meier emphasises the importance of miracles in the Gospel presentation of the life of Jesus. In the reckoning of Alan Richardson, 209 verses of a total of 666 in Mark's Gospel deal with miracles directly or indirectly.[3] "When one looks at this vast array of disparate streams of miracle traditions in the first Christian generation, some already grouped in collections, some still stray bits of material, Mark alone – writing as he does at the end of the first Christian generation – constitutes a fair refutation of the idea that the miracle traditions were totally the creation of the early church after Jesus' death."[4]

To the criterion of multiple attestation[5], Meier adds the criterion of coherence.[6] The miracles of Jesus explain his extraordinary success, as compared with John the Baptist, who, as we saw in the previous Chapter, faded soon from the picture.

John the Baptist, according to Christian tradition – and Christian tradition is nearly everything we have about John the Baptist, apart from Josephus[7] – performed no miracles. But Christian tradition is equally clear in affirming Jesus as a miracle worker, and the Talmud stated that Jesus was put to death for sorcery,[8] implicitly acknowledging for Jewish tradition that Jesus reputedly performed miracles.

The parallel claims of miracle-working in the ancient world do not cast doubt on the general historicity of Jesus miracle-worker, but rather they set up a contrast between the usually trivial circumstances of miracle-working and the whole context of Jesus and his miracles as signs of the coming kingdom of God. It is really irrelevant whether anyone else performed miracles at a time contemporary with Jesus.[9] Just because miracle stories have some parallels in terms of form with the Gospels cannot decide whether the miracles of Jesus are history or legend.[10] That is to make the mistake identified by Schweitzer a century ago as between the *form* of a narrative and its *origin*.[11] Having established the fact that Jesus was renowned as a miracle worker, what matters is the validity of the understanding which Jesus gives to his miraculous actions, and, from the historical Jesus viewpoint, how faithful the Gospels have been in transmitting that self-understanding.

Miracles in John as proofs of Christ's divinity

But criticism right up to the present will generally agree with post-Reimarus conclusions, namely that Jesus' miracles cannot be used in any sense to demonstrate his Incarnation. But this is precisely the meaning of Jesus' miracles in the Fourth Gospel itself.[12]

Barrett brings out strongly the divine aspect of Jesus' *erga*. "The miracles of Jesus are described as his works (*erga*). As such, they are also the works of God himself; there is a complete continuity between the activity of Jesus and the activity of the Father (see, e.g. 5:36, 9:3, 10:32, 37f.: 14:10).[13] Thus when Jesus says in justification for performing a miracle on the Sabbath, "My Father is working still, and I am working." [John 5:17]. John tells us, "This was why the Jews sought all the more to kill him, because he not only broke the sabbath but also called God his Father, making himself equal with God." [John 5:18]. Jesus is linking his own miracles with God's creative work which always goes on, even on the Sabbath. His Jewish opponents saw that as blasphemy.

Likewise Haenchen in his commentary on John insists that whatever tradition the evangelist utilized in writing his Gospel contained the intention throughout to legitimize Jesus through miracle. Thus for Haenchen, surely correctly, the intention of the evangelist is to use the miracle stories in his Gospel to demonstrate who Jesus is, to stimulate faith in his readers.[14]

After the first miracle, the Turning of Water into Wine [2:1-11], we read that his disciples believed in him [John 2:11]; then after the Cure of the Official's Son at Capernaum [3:46-54], John tells us that "he himself believed, and all his household" [John 4:53]; after the Cure of the Sick Man at the Pool of Bethesda [5:1-15], his enemies think that he was "making himself equal with God" [John 5:17-18] because he identified himself with his Father who as Creator never stops working; the fourth and fifth miracles, the Multiplication of the Loaves [6:1-15], and the miracle of the Walking on the Water [6:16-21] are followed by the Bread of Life discourse, where Jesus says "This is the work of God, that you believe in him whom he has sent." [John 6:29]; then the miracle most of all related to faith in Jesus as divine, the Cure of the Man Born Blind [9:1-7], followed in the narrative eventually by the blind man worshipping Jesus [John 9:38]; and in the seventh and last miracle The Raising of Lazarus, immediately after the story of the rolling away of the stone and the dead man coming out alive dressed in his grave-clothes, we read: "Many of the Jews therefore, who had come with Mary and had seen what he did, believed in him" [John 11:45].

Presuming that John knew the Synoptic tradition of Jesus' miracle stories, which is certainly most plausible, he has removed every reference to the kingdom of God.[15]

Post-Easter Christianity did not see the concept of the "kingdom of God" as central as did the historical Jesus in his teaching, which Dunn argues had both a present sense of being fulfilled in that "Satan's rule was already broken"; and "At other times Jesus spoke in still future terms,"[16] that "the kingdom of God as a post-mortem state; to be 'entered into' after suffering and self-sacrifice." No doubt by the end of the first century AD, Christians were thinking of the kingdom of God mainly as their heavenly inheritance; e.g. 1 Corinthians 6:10, 1 Corinthians 15:50, Galatians 5:21. Christ's miracles were first and foremost a challenge to present faith in him, rather than the inauguration of the kingdom by the public ministry of the historical Jesus, which by that time was a memory.

The circumstances of the church situation did of course have an effect on the writing of the Gospel, on what material was selected or de-selected, and on the way it was presented. We would never wish to deny that. A more serious question is as to whether the situation of the church at the close of the first century AD and the beginning of the second, led to the evangelist losing his touch with what actually happened in the life and ministry of Jesus two generations before. We shall now find that there is no proof of that, rather of the opposite.

There is no evidence for a "signs source"

The use of sources does not of itself exclude the possibility that the writer or writers of a document were eye-witnesses. All of us know how we often need to use sources to write up an account of a meeting or of a lecture we might have heard.

However, there are sources and sources. Without doubt, Bultmann's positing of a 'Signs Source' for the Fourth Gospel served his general purpose of denying any historical worth to John. He requires us to imagine some unknown Christian at the turn of the second century AD. picking up a book of legends about the wonderful miracles of Jesus of Nazareth, a Hellenistic Divine Man (*theios anér*) and gradually putting together the patchwork quilt of the Fourth Gospel. This Christian had no eye-witness contact with Jesus of Nazareth, any more than had the writer or writers who put together the Signs Source. But he (or she perhaps) did have one virtue: the ability to put together an incredibly complicated scissors and paste job, working the various traditions and redactions together into what we read now as the Fourth Gospel. Even more amazingly, those redactions have been integrated so well that the Fourth Gospel reads as a unity, written by one person, a "seamless garment" as Strauss said so long ago. Bultmann's X who finally put the Fourth Gospel together was at least a most intelligent, if a somewhat mentally contorted, individual.

But what evidence is there for the existence of such a Signs Source? In a judicious and well-researched article, Daniel Marguerat[17] concludes that there is no compelling evidence in the Fourth Gospel for a pre-existent Signs Source which the author of the Fourth Gospel drew upon for his narrative:

> We have affirmed that the model of an autonomous and coherent source is plausible from the viewpoint of the literary form, but not in the sense in which Fortna understands by his Gospel of Signs. The inclusive attribution of the accounts of miracle in John as a single source constitutes a reductional enterprise, which the formal, theological and and ideological diversity of the texts concerned does not verify. One must not speak of a source, but rather of many traditional currents from which

John has drawn. The capacity for integration of the evangelist appears, as a result, much stronger than one had thought.[18]

What Marguerat is saying, therefore, is that, whatever sources the Fourth Evangelist might have used to write his miracle stories, he did not just pick them straight out of a first century 'Jesus Wonder Book'. Something such as this has been proposed by Robert Fortna and others,[19] following the Bultmann tradition. Marguerat carefully examines the reasons for such a hypothetical source, and discards those reasons for it one by one.[20] Rather, Marguerat concludes closer to Barrett's opinion, if not identical with it,[21] who saw no reason to doubt that the evangelist used sources, but which sources were not now identifiable with any certainty; and who maintained the essential unity of the finished product of the Fourth Gospel.

The Johannine miracles: Incarnation in the concrete

What Marguerat concludes is vital for our purposes. Firstly, he concludes, as we have already noted, from his in-depth study of the material that "One must not speak of a source, but rather of many traditional currents from which John has drawn. The capacity for integration of the evangelist appears, as a result, much stronger than one had thought."[22] There is not one homogeneous theology of miracle in the Fourth Gospel. Rather, there is a diverse theology which cannot be fitted into any particular theological category. It cannot, according to Marguerat, even be fitted into the category of the evangelist's theology:

> Apart from the (secondary) redaction of John 21, the seven accounts of miracle which have been transmitted from the evangelist by the communities of the Johannine circle, are co-existent as much as with a current near to the synoptic data (John 4; John 6) as with a tradition more specific to Johannine Christianity (John 2, John 5, John 9 and John 11).[23]

This is consistent with Dodd's conclusions in *The Historical Tradition of the Fourth Gospel*, which we have examined earlier in this book,[24] and is an important corroboration and development of it. The importance of Dodd's conclusions was not only that in the texts he examined, he posited that the Johannine accounts were independent of the Synoptic record. Perhaps even more important, he was convinced that these accounts in the Fourth Gospel went back to an early historical tradition in the life of the primitive church. He included some of John's accounts of miracles in his investigations, for instance the Feeding of the Multitude[25] and the Miracle of the Wine.[26] In particular, his conclusions regarding the narrative of John 5:1-9a is strikingly evocative of Marguerat's conclusions, though putting them in an entirely different way:

> The whole story, then, from the introduction of the patient at verse 5 to the establishment of the reality of the cure at verse 9 (with or without the note which follows, "and it was the sabbath day") moves entirely within the ambience of traditional narratives of healing as they are amply known to us from the Synoptic Gospels. Yet it does not simply imitate Synoptic forms, but develops them in an individual way. In particular, the dialogue is intimately related to themes intrinsic to the tradition of narratives of healing, and supplements the discussion of such themes in the Synoptics by making explicit a point which they left just beneath the surface.[27]

We could put the conclusion another way, but equally consistent with Marguerat's conclusions if we were a little sceptical about the Johannine Community and were closer to thinking that John the Son of Zebedee might be behind the Fourth Gospel. We would conclude that in writing the Fourth Gospel, the evangelist wrote the narrative of the seven miracles, perhaps using a source or sources to write them, without any particular theology in mind, even his own. We may put it this way; he wrote them neat and straight. He was rather dominated by the action which had occurred, than by attempting to get across pre-conceived ideas in the narrative.

That is not to say that the Fourth Evangelist wrote the miracle stories, with or without sources, or without any pre-conceived ideas. It is not possible to write anything without pre-conceived ideas. Even in the miracle story about the man at the pool of Bethesda, the evangelist cannot avoid mentioning the supernatural knowledge of Jesus. But he presents his theology, if he presents it at all, almost in passing, to focus on the action. To say "When Jesus saw him and *knew* that he had been lying there a long time, he said to him, "Do you want to be healed?" [John 5:6] is hardly a massive theological gloss. It is what the young person today would describe as a "cool" reference, laid back, off-beat, lest we should think of the theological concept of Jesus' knowledge rather than go on to think of the wonder of that man's healing by Jesus.

There is no legend-building in John

This takes us immediately to the other vital point made by Marguerat. He concludes that the miracle accounts in John are welded into the discourses. The discourses have not created the miracle stories, but only used them.[28] Marguerat quotes Schnackenburg[29] in referring to the massive *Dinglichkeit* ("thingness", "touchableness") of the *sémeia*, the miracle-signs of the Fourth Gospel.[30] It is because for the Fourth Evangelist the Word has become flesh, and a reality, that the Word has also become *Dinglichkeit*. But the reality it has become is not ordinary. It is full of the power of the Father, who works his creative, healing work in his Son Jesus.

It is for this reason that, as Marguerat says, John has to include miracles in his discourse, to concretise Jesus the Word become flesh in his divine action. This approach to the miraculous in John overturns many commonplace attitudes in New Testament scholarship if we reflect on it further. If criticism were right, we would expect the opposite to what we actually find. St John's Gospel being later than the other Gospels, we would expect a heightening of the miraculous, as a function of the propaganda for the Word become flesh. "One must allow for legend-building in the Gospel tradition."[31] So says one eminent scholar. But where is the evidence for this "legend-building"?

Certainly, there is no evidence in the Johannine tradition. If the critical dating is right, the Johannine Community had eighty years after the Resurrection of Christ to "legend-build" (110 AD[32]) and some forty years after Mark's Gospel (64[33]). The Johannine Community made a pretty poor effort at it, if the Fourth Gospel is any evidence.

Of the seven miracles recounted in John, three are healing miracles; the Cure of the Offical's Son at Capernaum 3:46-54, the Cure of the Sick Man at the Pool of Bethesda 5:1-9a, and the Cure of the Man Born Blind 9:1-7. Each of these three miracles has parallels in the Synoptic Gospels and John narrates them no more dramatically. Matthew 8:5-13 and Luke 7:1-10 has a parallel cure of Jesus to John's Cure of the Official's Son.[34] The Cure of the Sick Man at the Pool of Bethesda is difficult to parallel, because we are not told in detail the nature of his sickness; but he obviously cannot move by himself, and his cure is hardly more dramatic than that of the man let down through the roof of a house, with Jesus simply saying "I say to you, stand up, take your mat and go to your home" [Mark 2:11]. Matthew 9:27-8 has two men rather than the one in John 9:1-7 cured of their blindness, both at the same time. So John is hardly increasing the "legendary" character of the narrative there.

The two miracles recounted in chapter 6 of the Fourth Gospel – the Walking on the Water, 6:16-21, and the Multiplication of the Loaves 6:1-15 – have exact Synoptic parallels, which we will be examining in detail shortly. But certainly those miracles are given no extra gloss in the Fourth Gospel account. The number of people fed remains the same, 5,000, and Jesus walks on the water, and no more, in John's account as well as in the Synoptic parallels. Where is the "legend-building" here?

Not even the raising of Lazarus, 12:41-44, is demonstrably an example of legend-building. Compared with any Synoptic miracle story, the drama is heightened, but the drama is heightened mainly by the long dialogue and discourses of Jesus, which serve the evangelist's theological purpose, not by the action itself. Is the raising of Lazarus more dramatic than the raising from the dead of the widow's son at Nain where we read, "Then he (Jesus) came forward and touched the bier, and the bearers stood still. And he said, "Young man, I say to you, rise!" The dead man sat up and began to speak, and Jesus gave him to his mother" [Luke 7:14-15]. We might well find a dead man sitting up in his coffin in the midst of his own funeral procession quite as startling as seeing a man walk out of a tomb bound in his grave-clothes.

Only the Turning of the Water into Wine, 2:1-11, which is an isolated miracle in John, could possibly be seen as legend-building; because John alone has this particular miracle, and also because the nature of the miracle in itself might seem to be a slight denigration of the type of miracle usually performed by Jesus. Compared with raising the dead, and healing a blind man, making sure that the drink did not run out at a party might seem to be the lowering of a miracle-worker's image. On the other hand, it might be seen as a nice touch that the Son of God was concerned that the people at the wedding did not have their party spoilt. It makes Jesus very human and concerned. The messianic and eschatological symbolism of the miracle justifies it from a theological point of view.[35] And, as a prodigy, turning water into wine hardly rates higher on the Richter scale than the Synoptic miracles of healing, exorcism, and above all the Walking on the Water and the Multiplication of the Loaves.

John's straightforward accounts of miracles

If there is paltry evidence, if any, for legend-building, therefore, regarding the miracle stories in the Fourth Gospel, is there any contrary evidence? Could we try out a completely contrary hypothesis; that in fact, far from legend building, the evangelists were concerned *not* to build legend? Rather, they were concerned to emphasise the facticity of what they reported. There was enough drama in the events themselves, without creating any. It is surely worth trying out such an hypothesis, which we can do in the following way.

It is difficult for us, so far removed from the events, to tell. But the fact that Jesus chose fishermen, whose life is dangerous, and who have to stay very close to reality if they are to stay alive, may indicate that he did not have on his hands a set of Holy Joes, ready to believe any pious story. Having read the Gospels all my life: heard them read in the liturgy, and studied them in depth, the miracle accounts seem to me as close to the report of a miracle at Lourdes, for a panel of doctors including agnostics, as they do to a spurious legend. There is certainly no indication that the miracle story is myth from the form of the narrative.

Indeed, the distinction so sagely propounded by Schweitzer a hundred years ago between the *origin* and the *content*[36] of the narrative is essential once more to reiterate, as we note again the form of the miracle story in John 5:1-9a, which was analysed by Theissen as Introduction – Narration of Situation of Distress – Healing Intervention by Jesus – Reaction to the Miracle.[37]

Theissen entitles his book *Urchristliche Wunder-geschichten*;[38] "Early Christian Wonder Stories". The very title *could* suggest a book of fairy tales when translated into English. But, as Latourelle insists, we cannot recount a history of a miracle at all, one which we insist really happened, without those four elements present. Latourelle quotes R. De Solages: "I challenge Bultmann himself to give a factual account of an extraordinary healing without first telling us that the sick person was seriously ill, then that he or she was cured, and finally, without showing that the cure really took place. This necessity arises not from the form of the story but from the nature of things."[39]

Latourelle[40] quotes the extraordinary cure of Marie Ferrand, who went to Lourdes in 1902 as a very sick woman with all the signs of tubercular peritonitis. Throughout her life, she had suffered from consumption, complicated by recurring pleurisy. By the time Marie reached Lourdes, the sceptical doctor Alexis Carrel had to give her cocaine to deaden the pain. But later when Carrel approached her and was amazed to see an obvious improvement in her general condition; skin colour, speedy reduction in the swelling of the abdomen. "He said nothing; he was startled, immobilised, and thought he must be dreaming."[41] Had the incurable Marie Ferrand actually been cured? He examined her abdomen, and found that it had returned to normal. Eventually, Carrel submitted to what he saw as the evidence of a miracle, and returned to a living faith.

If we parallel Latourelle's narration with John's account of the Miracle at the Pool of Bethesda, we see how both accounts are equally sober and matter-of-fact:

The Miracle at the Pool of Bethesda	The Cure of Marie Ferrand
The Situation at the Pool Described, 5:1-3a	The Pilgrimage to Lourdes
Narration of the Situation of Distress, 5:2-5	The Serious Medical Condition of Marie
The Healing Intervention by Jesus, 5:6-9	The Cure of Marie at the Grotto
The Reaction to the Miracle, 5:10 ff.	The amazement of Alexis and his eventual conversion to faith.

The cure of Marie Ferrand took place in 1902. We could verify the reliability of the account by going to Lourdes and examining the medical records in the Medical Bureau, which are meticulously kept. Whether or not we believed that something extraordinary happened, we would know that a whole group of expert opinion, including agnostic doctors, would verify at least the seriousness of the documentation: that something very difficult to explain did actually occur.

However, if we did not know this, and could not verify the actual witnesses in any way, would there not be a temptation to believe that the story of the apparently miraculous cure of Marie Ferrand which we have just told was generated by the credulity of the Lourdes pilgrims, flocking to the shrine in their hundreds of thousands, and that faith fictionally produced the myth?

Now that is precisely the situation we are in when we examine the miracle stories in the Gospels. Chronologically, the writer of the Fourth Gospel was closer to the events than we are to the narrative of the cure of Marie Ferrand, which took place one hundred years ago from the writing of this book. If, as New Testament scholarship unanimously accepts,[42] the Fourth Gospel was written at the latest in the first decade of the second century AD, the writer of that Gospel was at the most seventy years removed from the events which took place c.30 AD. There can be no doubt that the author himself could have been an eye-witness, or at least could have known eye-witnesses personally. But all we have are the documents recounting the miracles themselves. We have no living witnesses, or process of documentation checking that we have regarding the miracles attested at Lourdes.

From Bultmann onwards, it has been the standard position in critical scholarship to say that these miracle stories are legends, unless it can be proved otherwise. But has the academic world been brainwashed by Bultmann's *History of the Synoptic Tradition*? We just cannot tell from the form of the story whether we have a mythical creation by the early church, or a serious account of what factually happened such as a Lourdes-type record which aims to be scientific, describing in detail the sequence of events. All we have are the indications so far that the author of the Fourth Gospel did not indulge in legend-building, but wrote a brief and basically unembellished account of what apparently took place during the life of the historical Jesus.

We will now proceed further in this direction, and test the miracle of the Walking on the Water, to see whether the evangelist is telling us that these wonderful things actually happened, and of course why they happened. We will then attempt to establish criteria whether or not we should believe him.

1 QHJ, pp. 4-5. 2. 3.
2 MJ2, 619.
3 Cf. MJ2, 636, n.11 and 12 regarding counting the miracles.
4 MJ2, 620-622.
5 Cf. p. 115.
6 Cf. p. 116.
7 Meier, MJ2, 20, translates Josephus *Antiquities* Book 18. "§116. But to some of the Jews it seemed that the army of Herod was destroyed by God – indeed, God quite justly punishing [Herod] to avenge what he had done to John, who was surnamed the Baptist."
8 Cf. p. 110. Babylonian Talmud's tractate *Sanhedrin* 43a. Translation HJCG 75.
9 For a searching analysis of Crossan, cf. JVG, 2.4, 44-66.
10 JVG, 190-1.
11 QHJ, 84.
12 Aquinas neatly summarises the reasons why for him "the miracles which Christ worked were sufficient to demonstrate his divinity" (miracula, quae Christus fecit, sufficientia erant ad manifestandam divinitatem ipsius). S.T. III, q.43, a.4. Firstly, he argues, "according to the very nature of the works, which surpass totally the capability of any created power", (primo quidem secundum ipsam speciem operum, quae transcendebant omnem potestatem creatae virtutis; et ideo non poterant fieri nisi virtute divina). Aquinas quotes John 9:32, when, in reaction to the scepticism of the official religious reaction, the blind man says "Never since the world began has it been heard that anyone opened the eyes of a man born blind."
13 Barrett, 75.
14 Haenchen, 85.
15 FG, 329. For a thorough discussion of the "Kingdom of God" in historical Jesus research, cf. JR, 383-92.
16 JR, 466.
17 CJH, 70-93. *La Source des Signes. Existe-T-Elle?*
18 CJH, 87
19 Cf. CJH, 71, n.12.
20 CJH, 86.
21 Barrett, 26.
22 CJH, 87.
23 CJH 88.
24 Cf. p. 170.
25 HTFG, 196-222.
26 HTFG, 223-232.
27 HTFG, 178-9.
28 CJH, 92.
29 CJH, 92, n.88. Schnackenburg, 1964, 66.

30 CJH, 92.
31 MJ2, 629.
32 Cf. p. 161.
33 Cf. p. 170.
34 Barrett, 245, discusses those parallels.
35 Cf. Brown I, 105. "One of the consistent Old Testament figures for the joy of the final days is an abundance of wine (Amos 9:13-14, Hosea 14:7, Jeremiah 31:12)."
36 Cf. p. 45, chapter 2.
37 Theissen, G., *Urchristliche Wundergeschichten*, STNT8, Gotersloh, 1974, 57-83.
38 Ibid.
39 MJTM, 35. Solages, 1972, 82.
40 MJTM, 304.
41 MJTM, 305.
42 Cf. p. 45.

CHAPTER 12

JESUS WALKED ON THE WATER

> The miracle of the Walking on the Water was a key event in the disciples' memory of the historical Jesus. In a rough sea, they saw him walk on the water, and say to them "Fear not, I AM" They recognised that he was the YHWH God of the Old Testament bestriding the sea. This became an important foundation of their Christology.

Walking on the water? You cannot be serious.

Jokes regarding Jesus' walking on the water are themselves legendary; such as the story, told in the Holy Land, that a tourist down by the shore of Tiberias was given a sales pitch by a man in a boat, offering him a trip on the lake for twenty dollars. "Twenty dollars?" asked the tourist. "Is that not a little expensive?" "Well, sir," replied the boat-man, "This is no ordinary lake. Jesus walked on the water on the Sea of Galilee." "Well, now," said the tourist, "it is not surprising that he walked on the water if it would cost him twenty dollars to go in a boat."

Indeed, to many people it may be at least initially ridiculous to believe that a man walked on the water and fed five thousand people with five loaves and two fishes. But the matter may be put another way. If a person claimed to be the Incarnate God, he would surely have to do something like walk on the water and feed a multitude miraculously in order to validate his claim. A Jesus divested of his miracles holds only tenuously on to his divinity in the minds of his followers. To demonstrate that a person is morally exceptional does not demonstrate his full divinity. Jesus performing great miracles and so manifesting his divinity impressed not only weather-beaten fishermen in the first century, but people of all levels of intelligence over two millenia.

We choose therefore to select the miracle hardest to believe in order to illustrate a point. This miracle is well authenticated in the Jesus tradition. It is truly a prodigy, a marvel; and yet less than the miracle of the Incarnation itself, God becoming a tiny baby for us. After all, some insects, such as water boatmen, walk on the water. Finally and most important, Jesus used this miracle to manifest to his disciples precisely who he was, and is.

The miracle story: an early tradition

We agree with Meier that the narrative of the Walking on the Water was not a late legend. Rather, "Sometime in the first Christian generation it already stood attached to the feeding of the five thousand."[1] And, regarding the Fourth Gospel account, Meier concludes that, "The connection between the feeding of the five thousand and the walking on the water in Mark and probably Mark's source makes it practically certain that the two miracles were also already connected in John's source as well."[2]

To demonstrate this, Meier sets out the parallels in all four Gospels of what he considers to be a primitive pattern of events.[3] We will include Luke, even though he is the one evangelist of the four who does not recount this miracle of the walking on the water, for the purpose of comparison. Meier has a more complex comparison of Matthew, Mark, Luke and John than the one set out below; but, for our purposes, we can draw important conclusions from seeing clearly the main lines of the development of the narrative in the four Gospels:

The Multiplication of the Loaves	The Walking on the Water	A Dialogue about Bread	Peter's Confession
Matthew 14:13-21	Matthew 14:22-27	Matthew 16:5-12	Matthew 16:13-20
Mark 6:30-44	Mark 6:45-52	Mark 8:14-21	Mark 7:27-30
Luke 9:10-17	–	–	Luke 9:18-22
John 6:1-15	John 6:16-21	John 6:22-65	John 6:66-71

Meier concludes his analysis by saying "What is especially intriguing about the independent agreement between Mark and John is that it extends not just to this one story but to a whole primitive pattern or grid of stories about Jesus' ministry in Galilee."[4]

How are we to evaluate historically this sequence of events as recounted in the four evangelists? For Meier, "It would appear that Mark, who loves 'duality' large and small, knew two versions of an early catechetical pattern recounting Jesus' ministry in Galilee and incorporated both versions – with a good deal of his redactional theology added – into his account of the Galilean ministry as it approaches its climax."[5] If we accept at least for the moment this "doubling" of Mark, is it not significant that John has followed the same pattern without such doubling? Is it also perhaps significant that Luke, who never claims himself to be an eye-witness,[6] does not follow this sequence; perhaps because he had not experienced these events personally?

Is it not possible, granted the primitive nature of this tradition as avowed by Meier, that this reflects an historical sequence of events remembered by the apostles? This is particularly because there are geographical notes and links in all the stories. Why should these always be seen as editorial additions, and not historical reminiscences? Particularly interesting is the link we see between the Miracles of the Walking on the Water, the Multiplication of the Loaves, and the confession of Peter after the Discourse of Jesus. Is there not at least possibly an historical reminiscence there; at a crucial time in the ministry of Jesus after the death of the Baptist and before Christ's final journey to Jerusalem? Note that John, even though he has more than one visit of Jesus to Jerusalem recounted in his Gospel, makes the visit recorded in Chapter 7 immediately after the Miracles of the Multiplication of the Loaves and the Walking on the Water. Thus the Christological significance of these miracles is further enhanced by their situation in the narrative.

The walking on the water: a primitive epiphany

In any case, the tradition is early, and John's version is at least possibly the earliest: "In agreement with Schnackenburg and many other critics, I think that John's version of the story is on the whole more primitive than Mark's."[7]

What is the point of the story, then, granted that it is from an early tradition? We have noted the essential and simple points of an extraordinary story, of a man appearing walking on the water to a terrified group of his disciples in a boat. Very clearly, says Meier, it is an Ephiphany of Jesus. That is the sole point of the narration, and in each of the three Gospels it can be understood only that way:

> 2. The Miracle Proper: The word and deed of Jesus effect an epiphany that overcomes the separation. Separated from Jesus and rowing at night in the face of a strong wind, the disciples make painfully slow progress across the sea. Suddenly, out of the darkness they see Jesus walking toward them on the sea. As elsewhere in the Bible, the typical reaction of those receiving the epiphany is fear, just as Jesus' response to their fear is the *typical* word of identification, revelation, and comfort: "It is I [or: I am], fear not." It is noteworthy that here, at the heart of the story, John and Mark agree closely.[8]

We have here, says Meier, "a concise miracle story belonging to the form-critical category of epiphany, the only epiphany miracle Jesus performs in the public ministry."[9] That gives the walking on the water its *raison d'etre*. It is truly a manifestation of the divinity of Christ, not a Houdini act on the part of Jesus.

Meier notes a rich assortment of Old Testament texts which explain this phenomenon as an appearance of YHWH. He mentions first Job 9:8b, where God is described as "trampling upon" the sea, "which in ancient Near Eastern mythology was often depicted as the monster of chaos, the principle of evil, disorder, and death that opposed the creator god(s)."[10] Even more, there is a linguistic parallel between the

214

Greek Septuagint version of Job 9:8b and Mark 6:48, which says that Jesus "walked on the sea". This conveys God's "unlimited power over the sea and indeed over all the forces of creation – a power humans do not have. The same imagery is applied to Jesus in the Gospel miracle."[11] Similarly, Habakkuk 3:15 has God displaying his power, "You trampled [or tread] on the sea [with] your horses."[12]

Deutero-Isaiah,[13] Isaiah 43:16, links the power of Yahweh over the sea with the redemption of his people. "Thus says Yahweh, who provides in the sea a way, and in mighty waters a path", cf. Wisdom 14:3. The later Wisdom literature also linked God's creative power with God leading his people through the Red Sea [Wisdom 10:17-18].

Above all, when Jesus says "It is I; do not be afraid."[John 6:20], he is using the words which YHWH himself uses when announcing his saving presence in a theophany. In the context of his walking on the water, we could interpret: "It is I; do not be afraid" as "Don't worry, chaps, it's only me." But in the context of Exodus 3:14-15, where YHWH declares to Moses I AM WHO AM, the Septuagint translating as *egó eimi ho ón* (I am the One who is")[14] and the person speaking is walking on the water in a choppy sea, then we have the combined elements of one at least like YHWH speaking in a revelation of his power and glory as the master of the elements.

"Fear not" was the traditional opening to a theophany or a vision in the Old Testament; because one could not see God's face and live [Exodus 3:6]. Meier outlines an impressive sequence of God stating who he is, plus the reassurance not to fear, from a key text Isaiah 43:1-13:

v1: Fear not (LXX: *mé phobou.*), for I have redeemed you.

v2: When you pass through the water, I will be with you; the rivers shall not overwhelm you.

v3: For I am Yahweh, your God.

v5: Fear not, for I am with you.

v10: You are my witnesses... to know and believe in me
and understand that it is I [or: I am he] (MT: *ᵃni hu'*; LXX: *egó eimi*).
Prior to me no god was formed, and after me there
shall not be [any].

v11: [It is I, I Yahweh (MT: *nóki, nóki YHWH;* LXX *egó ho theos* ["I am God"]
There is besides me no Saviour.[15]

Literally, Jesus was speaking to the terrified disciples in
their own language, the theological language of what we
Christians call the Old Testament. It was this which was the
foundation of the early Christology, not some Hellenistic
concept of the *theos anér*.[16] But that judgement will now
depend upon our estimation of the historicity of the account
of the miracle. In terms of Dodd's investigations, we have
only demonstrated that the tradition of the Miracle of the
Walking on the Water is an early one. We have not demonstrated that this early tradition recounted history rather than
myth or *theologoumenon*.

There seem to be three possible types of explanation:

- There is a naturalistic explanation. This would be similar
to the rationalistic explanation of the miracles by the early
Questers such as Reimarus and Paulus.[17]
- The narration is a *theologoumenon*, a fictional theological
narrative, a legend, in Strauss' terms[18] a myth.
- A miracle actually occurred. Jesus walked miraculously
on the water.

The naturalistic explanation

Since we are dealing with a very ancient story which we
cannot verify, the naturalistic explanations could be infinite.
The disciples could have had an hallucination, could have been
drunk. Especially in a stormy sea, their imagination might
have run riot. All we can do in this case is to put reasonable

trust in their seriousness; and say that, on the contrary, they would not have recounted this episode had, in their opinion, something extraordinary not occurred.

One explanation, which we might call naturalistic, is from the language used by the Fourth Gospel in its account of Jesus "walking *on the water*". The crucial phrase is [John 6:19] "When they had rowed about three or four miles, they saw Jesus walking on the sea and coming near the boat, and they were terrified." The crucial phrase "on the sea" is in Greek *epi tés thalassés*,[19] which could also be translated "by the side of the lake", i.e. on the shore or beach of the lake. Dodd comments "The story therefore *could* be read in the sense that the disciples had rowed the greater part of the distance across the lake when they saw Jesus walking on the beach (which they were now approaching, though in the darkness and confusion they were unaware of it), and prepared to take him on board, but found that by this time the boat had touched land."[20]

Dodd admits "Not that this is how John intended it to be read..."[21] Dodd here refers forward to 6:25, where we are told that the evangelists found Jesus on the other side of the lake. John obviously intends to tell us that Jesus arrived there miraculously by walking on the water. Dodd however tries to wriggle out by saying that: "the element of miracle is not here the main motive. For that we must look elsewhere. It is surely the *Egó eimi* (I AM) that stands out."[22] But if, as Dodd admits, the intention of the evangelist is clear, to recount the miracle of Jesus walking on the water, then the I AM must be seen in that context. Jesus is demonstrating that he truly has the power of God over the water by walking on it in a stormy sea. That is why he can say *egó eimi*. As Meier rightly says, "That it is not the sense in any of the Gospel versions of the story is evident to anyone who has explored the OT background to the story", i.e. of God bestriding the sea.[23]

Other explanations are more bizarre. Derrett, in answering the question "Why and How Jesus Walked on the Sea"[24] suggests that Jesus actually walked on a shelf underneath the sea, at a more shallow part. Since the disciples in the boat were fishermen with a great deal of experience of that particular

217

sea, it is difficult to believe that they would not have known about it.

These naturalistic explanations, either have to cast doubt on the common-sense of the disciples – and they, as fishermen, would need to have had a great deal of it – or the explanation of what actually happened becomes more incredible than any miracle. We turn then to the second possible explanation, namely that the evangelist has written a *theologoumenon* (or in this case perhaps recorded a traditional and very early *theologoumenon*), that is a fictional story with a theological meaning.

The mythical explanation (*theologoumenon*)

This view at least has the virtue of obviating the necessity of performing the mental contortions necessary to give the story a naturalistic explanation, and is espoused by Meier, who thinks "that the story came into existence precisely as a miracle story that was created by the church to comment on another miracle story"[25] i.e. the Multiplication of the Loaves. Meier assures us that he does not come to this opinion with any philosophical presupposition against the miraculous:

> In this whole process it should be emphasised that my decisions have been and will be reached not on the basis of an *a priori* philosophical judgement (e.g. that such miracles did not happen because they simply could not happen) but rather on the basis of the same criteria of historicity that have been applied to the Jesus tradition in general and to other categories of miracle stories in particular.[26]

Meier gives two objections which to him are decisive against the historicity of the narrative of the Walking on the Water:

1. "The criteria of discontinuity and coherence, used in tandem, tell against historicity,"[27] says Meier. He argues that in all the other genuine miracle stories in the Gospels, Jesus responds to a person in dire need, e.g. healing miracles,

"They do not focus on Jesus' person and status or seek his self-glorification."[28] Rather, this miracle story of the Walking on the Water is "continuous with the Christology of the early church, especially with an early thrust towards high Christology that tended to associate Jesus with Yahweh or make Jesus the functional equivalent of Yahweh."[29]

But, why should miracles all have to be of a particular pattern? What greater healing is there than a divine epiphany of Jesus which at first creates fear in the disciples and then does away with that fear by their recognition that their Rabbi is, after all, the Son of God who has the creative power of God his Father over the sea? Surely, Jesus is not seeking his own self-glorification, but rather that the disciples should recognise him for whom he is. Christ himself would surely reply to this objection, in Johannine terms "If I glorify myself, my glory is nothing. It is my Father who glorifies me, he of whom you say, 'He is our God,'" [John 8:54]. Through this miracle and on further reflection upon it, the disciples would have come to a faith in Jesus as the only begotten of the Father, not to Jesus as God in isolation from the Father.

Regarding Meier's assertion that this miracle is continuous with early Christology, and so more likely to have been invented by the primitive church, one would ask the reader to wait until the analysis of Latourelle is considered below, who comes to a different conclusion to Meier regarding this particular criterion.

2. Meier's second objection against the historicity of the narrative of Jesus walking on the water is that "the elements of epiphany and of OT allusions have moved to centre stage and have become the very stuff of the narrative. In stories like the walking on the water Jesus is becoming the very epiphany of God; what the OT texts said of God displaying his power in theophany is being applied directly to Jesus in his public ministry. When the OT material, especially the OT portrayal of Yahweh, enters so massively into a NT miracle story, we have a fairly good indication that we may be dealing with a theological creation of the early church."[30]

But Meier has already had to dig fairly deep into the Old Testament to find those allusions. The early Christian writing this *theologoumenon* would have had to follow a process of thinking something like this:

- "Jesus is God, with the power of YHWH. That is our faith."
- "In the Old Testament, God is described as having the power to bestride the sea."
- "Therefore, we will invent a story telling how Jesus walked on the water, showing that he was YHWH."

What would be the point of inventing this story if they believed already that Jesus was God? This is where Meier runs into difficulties more severe even than those who opt for a naturalistic explanation. "To say that the story of the walking on the water was created by the early church leaves many questions unanswered, perhaps unavoidably so. What was the function and setting in the early church? These questions of *Sitz im Leben* are both legitimate and easy to raise, but I doubt whether we have sufficient indication in the text or in the history of early Christianity to answer them."[31]

Meier floats a possible idea that the walking on the water was connected with the celebration of the Eucharist; "it is actually a symbolic representation of one way in which the church experienced the risen Christ in its celebration of the Eucharist."[32] He admits the totally "tentative and speculative"[33] nature of this suggestion. He is right so to do. The only factor even possibly in its favour is that, as we have seen, in Matthew, Mark, and John, the Multiplication of the Loaves is followed by the Walking on the Water, and the Discourse on Bread follows.[34] But Meier has already expertly shown how the account of the Walking on the Water sits somewhat uneasily in John Chapter 6, breaking an even flow from the narration of the Multiplication of the Loaves 6:1-15 to the Discourse on the Bread of Life, 22-65. There is also a fair amount of physical movement described both for Jesus and for his disciples, which is all necessitated by the insertion of the miracle of the Walking on the Water. Are we to say that all this geography is only a function of the myth, and that there was not something which actually occurred which historically linked the two miracles, that of the multiplication of the loaves and the walking on the water?

Finally, we must ask what kind of primitive church would invent such a myth? That is truly a moral question, which it is right to address to Christians who try to persuade others as to the truth of their religion. The standard reply would be: "You must understand that the attitude of the early church to history was different from ours. They would quite happily invent legend in order to increase their faith." But again, where is the evidence for this? We must truly think the ancients were stupid (*Urdummheit*) if we posited that they did not realise the difference between a man walking on the water and a mythical story that he did so; and that the difference is important.

They themselves wished to persuade people of the truth of who Jesus was, and were very successful in doing so, more spectacularly than we are in the modern world. Why should we take them seriously if they told us that Jesus walked on the water, that he had the creative power of God and so demonstrated it; but then afterwards told us that this was mythical? What kind of reaction would they have had among intelligent Romans and Greeks, with whom they were most successful in drawing into the new faith? We could almost invoke the criterion of embarrassment[35] to authenticate the historicity of this story. Would the early Christians invent a story about Jesus which, unlike the healing miracles and the miracles of exorcism, would make them a laughing stock in the Roman Empire?

Meier insists again that he has not rejected the historicity of the miracle story of Walking on the Water because he has a philosophical presupposition against it. He tells us that he has made his decision rather on the basis of "criteria of historicity that have been applied to the Jesus tradition in general and to other categories of miracle stories in particular."[36] However, as we shall see now, another scholar sees those criteria in a different way.

221

A genuine miracle story

Latourelle, on the other hand, lists an impressive array of criteria which, quite apart from the question of the credibility of the account, for him should lead us to a decision as to its historicity on literary-critical grounds. After all, Meier has himself admitted the frail nature of his hypothesis to explain how the Walking on the Water could be explained as a *theologoumenon*, while at the same time insisting, also rightly, that naturalistic explanations are often strained.

Latourelle first claims that the narrative of the Walking on the Water passes the test of multiple attestation.[37] In this, Latourelle uses only conclusions already made, and incidentally agreed by Meier, concerning the primitive nature of the account of the Walking on the Water in Matthew, Mark, and John. "Within this larger section the three recensions link the multiplication of the loaves, the walking on the sea, and the confession of Peter."[38]

Secondly, Latourelle also claims that the miracle story passes the test of discontinuity.[39] We have seen already how Meier disputed the historicity of the account because of what he claimed was its continuity with the Christology of the early church. But Latourelle argues the opposite way. He claims "He who 'walks on the sea' is not the YHWH of the Old Testament (Job 9:8, 38:16, Habbakuk 3:15, Psalm 77:19-20, Isaiah 43:16), but a man, Jesus of Palestine, who can be described as one who daily shares the life of his disciples but who appears here as *wholly other*. The man Jesus, walking on the sea like Yahweh, yields an image that is in conflict with the rigid monotheism of Israel."[40]

We have seen earlier that, following Margaret Barker's fascinating researches, we should perhaps modify this usually accepted opinion of the "rigid monotheism of Israel", with her view that Jesus had the experience of rising up to heaven at his baptism and realising himself as the adopted Son of God.[41] She saw the roots of this belief in pre-Christian Judaism, where the Metatron was called "The Lesser Yahweh". "Enoch was an enthroned high priestly figure, bearing the divine name."[42] Even though there is a dispute as to whether such ideas pre-dated the rise of Christianity, and even if we admit Dunn's view that the "two powers heresy", of a greater and a lesser God, was manifest at the earliest in late first to early second century AD,[43] Barker still provides a *cauté* against assuming that, at the time of Christ and immediately before it, Judaism was so rigidly monotheistic that Jesus claiming divinity was totally contrary to Jewish ideas.

Could Jesus walking on the water therefore be seen as a "Lesser Yahweh"? We cannot say, if Margaret Barker is even close to being right, that such is an historical impossibility. To make more precise the nature of Jesus' identity, we must wait until the next chapter. But this is really the difficulty of using the criteria as outlined above.[44] What one scholar uses as a criterion for authenticity can be opposed by another using another criterion. Margaret Barker, if she is right, would no doubt argue to the *historical coherence* of the disciples recognising Jesus as Yahweh, or at least perhaps as a lesser Yahweh. Surely we cannot believe that everything authentically historical about Jesus was either an embarrassment to the early church or was discontinuous with Judaism and with the post-Easter confession of faith of the primitive church?

What we can say is that there is no figure in Judaism, however exalted in its most imaginative apocalyptic literature investigated by such as Margaret Barker, who exists as a living human on this earth and who walks on the water. We can also say that in the literature of the early church, there is also no confession of faith in Jesus as I AM. Their confession of faith always took other verbal forms.

Are miracles possible and verifiable?

It is right, therefore, for us to first examine critically,[45] the theology of miracles, precisely in order to test further our exegetical decision that the Walking on the Water was a genuine miracle, that it was in this case historically credible. This does of course presuppose our belief in an omnipotent and personal God; not a deistic God, who is restricted to the laws of nature he himself has created; nor a pantheistic God who is identified with the world or its process as with the radical Hegelianism of Strauss.[46] Malevez, in his *Christian Message and Myth*, outlines three common objections to the miracle, and gives his reply. We will take these objections, and Malevez's answers to them, with our own comments.

A. *First Objection: the Physical Determinism of Nature.*

Malevez explains: "A primary reason which Bultmann could invoke, and which he does actually invoke,[47] is the scientific postulate of determinism: for modern science the world is rigorously determined, governed by immutable laws; thus any breach in the course of phenomena, even one provoked by a transcendent agent, is, properly speaking, inconceivable."[48]

Malevez first says that Heiselberg's Uncertainty Principle: "the impossibility of determining exactly the position of particles at the same time as their momentum"[49] is no real objection to scientific determinism. This simply is a defect of knowledge, not of scientific law. Heiselberg's Uncertainty Principle has shaken post-Newtonian physics to the core. "But this does not mean that contemporary science henceforth considers that physical reality is open to the action of agents which are not within it."[50]

The objection of physical determinism, in Malevez's opinion, can be answered only by a true notion of God's omnipotence. Science needs to accept the hypothesis of an ordered world, otherwise continuity is impossible to establish. We might say that God has created nature to follow its own laws in order for there to be an unchaotic world. "But he (the scientist) can only accept this idea as a norm for discovery, as the necessary means for his inductions and his generalisations; if he goes further, sets it up as a necessary principle of physical reality, and asserts that the physical world is not intelligible save on the condition of being conceived as a strictly closed system, and he has gone further than he has any right to do; he has left his own sphere, and now claims to be a metaphysician…"

He quotes Aquinas: "For God can act beyond the order of created nature, and when he so acts, he does not act against nature, but according to the obediential potency, by which any creature whatsoever is made to obey God, to accept whatever God wills."[51] This is why we have said that to accept the possibility, and actuality, and discernability of a miracle is a radical challenge to modern thinking; precisely because it sees the transcendent God as summoning creatures to be what they truly are, creatures open to do and to be whatever God calls them to be and to do. It makes God, and them, truly free.

B. *Second Objection: A miracle breaks the order of visible phenomena.*

This is close to the first objection, but not entirely the same. The first objection related more to the individual nature; the second relates more to the cosmos considered as a created unity. The objection to the miracle by the eighteenth-century Enlightenment was that it broke the necessary order and interconnection of the world, and so was in some way demeaning as far as God was concerned. The architect of the universe had not built a very good house if he had to keep intervening himself to mend the fuses.

Malevez replies "that in point of fact a phenomenon is inconceivable save as part of a whole, like a chord in a vast concert... this order of nature has been integrated by God into an order which transcends it by encompassing it... in this instance, the phenomenon which makes the breach would be a miracle produced by God in order to signify to the spirits this superior order to which he has assumed them... it will be both the manifestation and the expression of the supernatural order..."[52]

Another analogy we could use is that of the body. There are many mechanisms in the body which work whether we are conscious of them or not: digestion, waste disposal, life-blood coursing through our veins. A person observing these functions, if that was all that person did observe, might come to the conclusion that the human body works mechanistically and automatically. Then, when the body stands up and begins to act as if apparently freely, "telling" its feet and hands to move, then we realise that there is a "higher intelligence" not breaking the order but directing the body to a higher end than just eating and digesting. However philosophically we might explain it, this creature has apparently "free will".

Likewise the miracle does not rupture the order of phenomena, but indicates that directing the universe there is a God, its transcendent supreme intelligence, who has a higher plan, and who sometimes works directly according to that higher plan. In this way, Jesus walking on the water did not disrupt the order of phenomena, i.e. the natural order, whereby human beings walk on land rather than on water, but manifested that he himself was that very God from God, come to save us and take away our fear.

C. *Third Objection: it is impossible to know whether a miracle has occurred.*

The third objection is the strongest. As Malevez says, "in order to recognise the breach, the exception, it would be necessary first of all to know, with absolute certitude, the laws of nature; but this certitude is not our concern."[53] It is not only not our concern, it would seem at first sight to be impossible. From whatever illness a person is cured, is it not possible to say that it was a natural cure, not a miraculous one? We simply do not know enough about the human body to say whether or not it was a miracle or a new type of cure, which was a chance occurrence, unknown at present to science. Even we could posit that Jesus, in walking on the water, had a physical ability denied to other human beings. After all, as we have said, some insects apparently walk on water.

Malevez answers this by emphasising the fact that to estimate that there has been a miracle must be an *empirical judgement.* "As has been said, the laws established by science doubtless only express one part of the laws of nature, but a part which is certain: it follows from this that a strange fact cannot be without doubt antecendently declared to be mathematically improbable; but its probability can be treated as a negligible quantity: to such an extent that it can be affirmed that we shall never observe scientifically the spontaneous elevation of a brick to the first storey by the Brownian movement."[54]

Thus, in the first century AD province of Syria, if we see a man born blind cured after a meeting with Jesus when Jesus spat on the ground and told him to wash in the pool of Siloam, then, if that same man, Jesus, has cured blind people before by his word, cast out devils, and even raised the dead: quite legitimately, therefore, as an empirical and an *historical judgement*, we are justified in concluding that the source of this power is Jesus himself. This judgement is relative, nor absolute, as is any historical judgement. But it is yet reasonably certain, as some historical judgements are reasonably certain.

The disciples following Jesus had by the time they were in the boat crossing the lake on the stormy sea become convinced that Jesus was at least a very special prophet, by the number of miracles they had witnessed him perform. One might say that a scientific law was beginning to operate, which connected the word of Jesus with things happening beyond the natural. Then, when they saw him walking on the water, that was a sign to them that the man performing these miracles was not simply a prophet, but YHWH bestriding the sea. In a sense, we are reaching a judgement in the same way that any empirical judgement is reached, by the "constant conjunction" as David Hume would put it, of events. But in this case we are coming to the conclusion that there is a direct action of God. And this conclusion is reasonable.

A "one-off" event

This event, of Jesus walking on the water, is as far as we can humanly tell, an entirely unique event. It is unique for two reasons; that a man has walked on the water, which as far as we can tell has never happened before, and will never happen again.[55] Yet it is unique not for that reason alone. Perhaps a very clever swimmer might be able to perform such a feat after years of practice. It is unique also because thereby Jesus of Nazareth declared himself to be God Incarnate. But, according to our criteria, such a "one-off" event might be unlikely, but it can never be excluded *a priori*.

We remind our readers once more of our definition in

general of the historical, and of the criteria of historicity. To make an historical judgement of any kind is to make an act of credibility in the human witness who has written the particular document in question, in this case the Fourth Gospel. The following is the judgement we are making in this case, following the criteria we established in chapter 4 above.[56]

• **The Document is not false.** We have systematically tested the tradition underlying John's account, together with Matthew and Mark, and concluded that the account of Jesus walking on the water is very early, going back at least to the earliest Christian tradition, and indeed quite possibly to the historical Jesus himself.

• **The Witness has not been misunderstood.** The Writer of the Fourth Gospel said that Jesus Walked on the Water. We did not misunderstand him by thinking that he was saying that it really happened when in fact he was only reporting a theological fiction, a *theologoumenon*. He actually meant to say that the disciples including himself saw Jesus actually walking on the water.

• **The Witness was not deceived.** We do not think that he was drunk or hallucinated, but in a sober state of mind, although distressed by a rough sea. We believe him, when he says that he saw Jesus walking on the water.

Now why should we believe him? If an Olympic swimmer was reported as having walked on the water, and we were told by an apparently sober witness that such had happened, we would still have difficulty in believing that witness. We would think that perhaps that swimmer had invented a new type of swimming stroke, which made it look as if the swimmer was walking on the water. The act would be even less credible if it was reported that a non-swimmer had walked on the water. This raises the criterion established by asking the question: are the circumstances credible? In this case Who actually it was claimed had walked on the water? As we said above, the Who of an event to a very large extent determines its credibility.[57]

The Who in this case is the one claiming by this very act to be YHWH incarnate. We can make a positive judgement concerning the historicity of the account. We can make an act of historical credibility in Jesus walking on the water, because the person who it was claimed did walk on the water could do so as the incarnate Son of God, and wanted to do so at that point in time in order to reveal himself as the incarnate Son of God to his disciples. We have made an *exegetical decision* here, a decision as to the historicity of the account. But that positive decision as to historicity is made on the basis of a theological presupposition, that Jesus truly was, or at least possibly was, the God the Son. Thus we would have to admit that, in this case, at least a *conditional faith* [58] that Jesus might be the Son of God would be necessary to concur with this judgement. Yet the decision is nevertheless exegetical, and nevertheless about the historical Jesus. Our presupposition is that, in Jesus, God has actually entered our history as Man, and wanted to reveal that fact to his disciples likewise in history. This is as objective a criterion as the opposite presupposition, that miracles do not occur, or that this particular miracle could not have occurred.

Conclusion: it really happened

We do not know how much the disciples understood at that particular point. Perhaps, as loyal Jews, they were not yet really sure, but believed that God was present to them in some special way in Jesus; that he was the Son of God, but they were not absolutely sure what that meant. It was after the Resurrection that this became clear. But their faith in Christ was grounded not in evolutionary idealism, but in the *divine fact* of having seen YHWH walking on the water.

One is not surprised to learn that Latourelle also classifies the multiplication of the loaves as a genuine miracle of Jesus;[59] thus the two miracles recounted in John 6 assume their historical character, and therefore are both pre-paschal. Nor, for Latourelle, is there a theophany, a manifestation of God to an individual as at Sinai. "What we have is rather an *epiphany*, as in Habbakuk 3:3-15. Jesus comes to his disciples, who *see* him, and he manifests his divine power to them."[60]

Already the so-called "high Christology" of the Christian Church was formed, long before the Resurrection, on a stormy night on the Sea of Tiberias, when the disciples saw their Lord walking on the water, and when the loaves and fishes which fed five thousand people on the plains recalled the manna sent down from heaven by the Word of God, now become flesh in Jesus.

One might even add that an agnostic could concur with this judgement as to the historicity of the account, while not coming to the same conclusion as the disciples, faith in Jesus. An agnostic could conclude that the disciples genuinely thought that they saw Jesus walking on the water, and saw him feed five thousand people from a small quantity of loaves and fishes. An agnostic could therefore conclude that the disciples were not writing a mythical account, and that they genuinely believed that this demonstrated that Jesus was the divine Son of God. The agnostic, however, could conclude finally that either there was some non-supernatural explanation for these amazing events (equivalent to the early rationalists such as Paulus), or that we just do not have any explanation within the compass of our limited human cognition. We would reply that already as potential believers, we are building up a coherent set of facts reasonably well authenticated towards a rational conclusion that this man Jesus of Nazareth was whom John's Gospel said he was.

Thomas Aquinas neatly summarises the reasons why for him "the miracles which Christ worked were sufficient to demonstrate his divinity."[61] Firstly, he argues, "according to the very nature of the works, which surpass totally the capability of any created power." Secondly, because Christ worked miracles by the power which came out of him, and not by praying [Luke 6:19]. And thirdly because "from his teaching by which he said he was God". It is to this teaching concerning himself to which we now turn, by which Jesus explained the full meaning of his miracles as manifestations of his divinity.

1   MJ2, 906.
2   MJ2, 908.
3   MJ2, 907-8.
4   MJ2, 905.
5   MJ2, 906.
6   Brown, I, 239, Barrett, 43.
7   MJ2, 908.
8   MJ2, 913.
9   Is not the Transfiguration, Matthew 17:2, Mark 9:2 also an epiphany? Meier prefers to call that a "vision" following the Synoptic vocabulary, rather than a "miracle" that Jesus "performs". MJ2, 999, n.135.
10 MJ2, 914.
11 MJ2, 914.
12 MJ2, 915. I am following Meier's translation of Habbakuk 4:15 here.
13 NJBC, **21**, pp. 329ff.
14 MJ2, 918.
15 MJ2, 918.
16 NTHIP, 270, cf. p. 56.
17 Cf. p. 45.
18 Cf. pp. 42-9.
19 Dodd says that the same phrase *epi tés thalassés* in 21:1 certainly does mean "off shore". HTFG, 198.
20 HTFG, 198.
21 HTFG, 198.
22 HTFG, 198.
23 MJ2, 1002, N.150.
24 J. Duncan N. Derret, *Why and How Jesus Walked on the Sea*, Novum Testamentum 23 (1981), 330-48.
25 MJ2, 1002, N.150.
26 MJ2, 880.
27 MJ2, 920.
28 MJ2, 920.
29 MJ2, 921.
30 MJ2, 921.
31 MJ2, 921.
32 MJ2, 923.
33 MJ2, 922.
34 Cf. p. 212.
35 Cf. pp. 113-5.
36 MJ2, 880.
37 Cf. p. 115.
38 MJTM, 144.
39 Cf. p. 115.
40 MJTM, 145.

41 Cf. pp. 149-50.
42 RL, 21.
43 CM, 80.
44 Cf. pp. 114-8.
45 QHJ, 396.
46 Cf. p. 44.
47 Cf. in particular the fascinating discussion in Roberts, C. Robert: *Rudolf Bultmann's Theology: A Critical Interpretation.* London, SPCK, 1977.
48 CMM, 1958, 133.
49 CMM, 1958, 134.
50 CMM, 1958, 1345.
51 CMM 1958, 135. S.Th. I, q.105, a.6, ad 1.
52 CMM, 1958, 135-6.
53 CMM, 1958, 136.
54 CMM, 1958, 137-8.
55 Cf. p. 90.
56 Cf. especially pp. 86-90.
57 Cf. pp. 86-7.
58 Cf. pp. 88-9, Kereszty, *Communio* 598.
59 MJTM, 72-78.
60 MJTM, 144.
61 *miracula, quae Christus fecit, sufficientia erant ad manifestandam divinitatem ipsius.* S.T. III, q.43, a.4.

CHAPTER 13

ACCORDING TO JOHN, JESUS CLAIMED TO BE GOD

The Fourth Gospel teaches that Jesus was and is God Incarnate.

Did he really say "I am"?

We said earlier[1] that "in one sense, miracle was *the* question of questions regarding the historical Jesus." But it was only in one sense. In another sense, miracle was not the most important question of the historical Jesus. It was the question of the Incarnation. We repeat Schweitzer's assertion with which we began our investigation:[2] "This dogma had to be shattered before men could once more go out in quest of the historical Jesus, before they could even grasp the thought of his existence. That the historic Jesus is something different from the Jesus Christ of the doctrine of the Two Natures seems to us now self-evident."[3]

That the doctrine of the two Natures in Christ, human and divine, was more important to the Quest even than the question of God's supernatural intervention through the miracle is also proven by the history of Fourth-Gospel criticism. As we saw also at the beginning of this book,[4] the first Questers, including the great Schleiermacher himself – the "father of modern theology"[5] – considered that the Fourth Gospel was superior historically to Matthew, Mark, and Luke, because it had fewer miracles and as we saw confirmed in our study in the previous chapter, those miracles are recounted quite soberly.

What changed scholarly opinion against the Fourth Gospel was precisely the doctrine of the Incarnation in it. As we saw, for Strauss, the fundamental myth was the Incarnation itself. Strauss was one of the first to attempt to demythologise the

Incarnation, seeing human history in Hegelian terms, as "the individual man participates in the divinely human life of the species."[6]

It is the long discourses and dialogues where Jesus makes the extraordinary claims for his divinity which is the real scandal of post-Enlightenment criticism. Thus, if we are to consider the historical Jesus in the Fourth Gospel, there is no more important subject than this. How far are those dialogues in any sense attributable to the historical Jesus? Or must we still concur with the view first posited by Strauss in 1834, and still the general opinion among scholars now, that the discourses are in Strauss' terms myth, that they tell us a great deal about the Johannine Community, but little about the historical Jesus?

As we also saw at the beginning, the question is not merely an academic one. The *Jesus Seminar,* and earlier the *Myth of God Incarnate,* even if milder in tone, had a clear agenda, to rid the Church of incarnational dogma just as much as Reimarus and the early Questers. And we saw an equally radical point made by Maurice Casey, invited to give the Cadbury Lectures in Birmingham in the autumn of 1985, that belief in Jesus as incarnate and divine will lead to "official Christianity" being less and less credible.[7] If we can demonstrate the possibility, even more the likelihood, that the historical Jesus made incarnational claims for himself, then the debate takes a new post-critical turn.

But first, we must look at the text of the Fourth Gospel itself, to see what it claims for Jesus.

John says Jesus is the *logos,* equal *theo*

In the beginning was the Word, and the Word was with God, and the Word was God [John 1:1]. *En arxé én ho logos, kai ho logos én pros ton theon, kai theos én ho logos.*

Not all followers of Jesus understand that John's Word (*logos*) is equal with God. Sects such as the Jehovah's Witnesses claim that, because in the final phrase "and the Word was God", "God" (*theos*) is without the definite article (*ho theos,* "the God") otherwise with *theos*, Jesus Christ is not fully God, but only "a god".

This idea is not entirely original. The first to hold such a view was an Alexandrian priest named Arius, (c.250-c.336) who held that God is totally other, alone ingenerate, judge of all, etc. "For God to impart His substance to some other being, however exalted, would imply that he is divisible, and subject to change, which is inconceivable".[8] Thus any other being than God the Father "must have been called into existence out of nothing." In consequence, for Arius:

- The Son must have been created.
- The Son must have had a beginning, when he came into existence.
- The Son is different from, and cannot fully know, the divine Essence.
- The Son could in principle at least have sinned.

So, for Arius, when John's Gospel said "The *logos* was God", he would have replied that the *logos* was a created idea, albeit the most sublime and powerful, in the mind of God. The Council of Nicea responded by excommunicating Arius, insisting that Jesus was 'of the same substance as the Father (the famous phrase *homóousios*, translated in the present day Creed 'of the same being' with the Father). For the Council of Nicea, therefore, Jesus was not only divine in some sense or other. He was actually God, the eternal Word of the Father, the Second Person of the Trinity.

Bultmann, perhaps to our surprise, nonetheless pleasant, defends vigorously and convincingly the Nicene interpretation of *kai theos én ho logos*. He insists:

> "The status of the *logos* is one of equality with God: he was God. For it cannot be taken as meaning: he was a god, a divine being, as if *theos* were a generic concept such as *anthrópos* or *animal*, so that there could be two divine beings, either in the naïve polytheistic sense, or in the sense of the Gnostic idea of emanation. This is clearly out of the question, because in the phrase *én pros ton*

theon, which both precedes and follows *kai theos én ho logos,* the word *theos* is intended in its strict monotheistic sense; furthermore, what comes afterwards shows that all polytheistic conceptions and emanationist theories are foreign to the text. And one can hardly translate "of divine being" "of the divine species"; for in that case, why was not *theios*[9] "divine") *used?...* The Logos is therefore given the same status as God, just as faith confesses the Son, who has been raised again to the glory that he had before (17:5) to be *ho kurios mou kai ho theos mou* ("my Lord and my God" [20:28].[10]

The logos pre-existing and becoming flesh

What is important to recognise at this stage of our argument is that we claim that for John, in his Prologue, whether he wrote it himself[11] or took an already-existing Logos Poem,[12] was proclaiming that Jesus, the subject of his Gospel, enjoyed the full existence of God with his Father. *This is not so much a question of temporality as of quality.* We must be clear at the outset, because some theologians, in discussing the Incarnation, over-emphasise the question of *pre*-existence. John Knox thinks that it is not logically possible for a person to be both fully God and fully Man: "We can have the humanity without the pre-existence and we can have the pre-existence without the humanity. There is absolutely no way of having both."[13]

Presumably, Knox means that it is absolutely impossible for one to be both fully God and fully Man in one and the same being. The notion of "pre-existence" can be confusing, since in the Jewish worldview of the time of Jesus, it was thought that Elijah would return for the great and terrible day of the Lord [Malachi 4:5]. Elijah was now waiting in heaven somewhere, ready to descend in his chariot, where he had ascended assumed into heaven in the sight of his prophetic son and successor Elisha [2 Kings 2:12]. Presumably Knox, or anyone else for that matter, would not think it logically impossible for a human being to pre-exist, whether or not one actually believed that a human being pre-existed. After all, anyone who believes in re-incarnation – and such a belief continues to have its followers – must by implication believe in the pre-existence of that individual in some form or other. Louis Bouyer, the celebrated French theologian, floated the idea that Christ *as human* might have pre-existed.[14] The real problem therefore is not pre-existence, but rather the ontological problem of a person being both God in the full sense and Man in the full sense.

And, already in the Prologue, John is providing the contrast between the infinite limitless existence of the Logos with *ho theos,* and the temporary becoming of that Logos into our world. John does not see this contrast as contradictory, as apparently does John Knox. On the contrary, all comes to a conclusion and climax with the *union* of the Logos becoming flesh.

There is a constant contrast in the Prologue between the Logos who <u>is</u> (*én*) existent permanently and eternally, with created beings, who only <u>came to be</u> (*egeneto*) through the Logos. So John the Baptist was a man who <u>came to be</u> (*egeneto anthrópos*). He came only "to bear witness concerning the light", [1:6] because he was (*én*) not that light himself. That was the Logos, who was (*én*) the true, the genuine (*aléthinos*) light which was coming into the world. This Logos was now coming into the world; but coming to his own, his own did not receive him. But to those who did receive him, he gave power to become (*genesthai*) children of God...

1:14: "And the Logos became (*egeneto*) flesh." It is a superb climax. That Word which ever was (*én*) with God has now come to be (*egeneto*)with creation as flesh (*sarx*). Flesh for John simply means weak human nature; "the sphere of the human and the worldly as opposed to the divine."[15] The Logos, eternal with God through whom all things came to be, actually entered the sphere of the human and the worldly, became flesh.

So for John, the Logos was not only pre-existent. The Logos shares in the infinite and eternal being of God, but not in such a way that union is impossible. On the contrary, the Logos becoming (*egeneto*) flesh shares that being (*én*).

This union is called in Christian tradition the *hypostatic or substantial union of divine and human natures in Christ.* Dermot Lane is particularly perceptive in drawing us away from thinking of the nature of Christ as God and man rather like a two-headed monster, and sees the key precisely in the doctrine of the hypostatic union:

> Consequently the involvement of God and man in Jesus should not be thought of as a synthesis or mixture or some hybrid-reality resulting from a combination of the human and the divine. Each of these combinations is ruled out by the Chalcedonian clause "without confusion and without change, without division and without separation."[16] The unity between God and man in Jesus is much more real and intensive than such a synthesis mixture or hybrid-reality. It is a unity which is so real, comprehensive and inclusive that we can justifiably say in all truth that Jesus is true God and true man as a single assertion about the one reality of Jesus. It was precisely this point concerning the reality of the unity between Jesus and God that the doctrine of the hypostatic union was trying to preserve and communicate.[17]

It is precisely this union which is described by John when he says "And the Word became flesh and lived among us, and we have seen his glory, the glory as of a father's only son, full of grace and truth" [John 1:14].

John's story-line: the golden chain

Thus, as Carson says "The Prologue is a foyer to the rest of the Fourth Gospel."[18] Perhaps best of all Lightfoot:

> These verses give the key to the understanding of this gospel, and make clear how the evangelist wishes his readers to approach his presentation of the Lord's work and Person; and equally the rest of the book will throw light on the contents of these verses.[19]

The key to such understanding is the story told by the Fourth Evangelist which develops the central theme of the Prologue, namely that in the public ministry of Jesus of Nazareth, the Logos, who was ((*én*) with God and who was (*én*) God, reveals himself in the present tense of the verb to be, I AM, *ego eimi*. Because, after all, the infinite God was, and is now, and shall be. "I am the Alpha and the Omega," says the Lord God, who is and who was and who is to come (*ho ón kai ho én kai ho erchomenos*), the Almighty [Revelation 1:8].[20] That, John now tells us in his Gospel, has become flesh in Jesus of Nazareth.

Earlier,[21] we traced the "story-line" of Mark's Gospel. The "story-line" of John's Gospel is the progressive revelation of who Jesus is in the course of his public ministry from his Baptism by John the Baptist [John 1:29] until the confession of faith of doubting Thomas' "My Lord and my God" [John 20:28].[22] This progressive revelation takes place in stages:

• **The Messianic Secret**. During the early part of Jesus' ministry, he did not reveal explicitly who he was. This was to avoid misunderstanding, to avoid being presented as a political Messiah. We note that not only in the Synoptics, but also in the Fourth Gospel Chapters 1-4, Jesus himself gives no explicit statement as to who he really is, apart from to the Samaritan woman [John 4:25[23]], privately and away from the multitude of his own people.

• **The Death of John the Baptist**. Again, in all four Gospels, the death of the Baptist leads to a crescendo in Jesus' self-revelation. In all four Gospels, the sequence we have discussed in this book connected with the Miracle of the Loaves and of the Walking on the Water leads to the Confession of Faith of the disciples led by Peter.[24]

• **The Self-Revelation of Jesus in Jerusalem**. The account of this self-revelation is not in the Synoptic account of the last days of Jesus on earth. But, as we have seen earlier, the Synoptics do record the self-revelation of Jesus at his trial, which causes the high priest and the Sanhedrin to condemn him for blasphemy, and which we have argued in chapter 8 is historically authentic. Mark and Luke have Jesus saying that

"Day after day I was with you in the temple teaching, and you did not arrest me. But let the scriptures be fulfilled" [Mark 14:49, Luke 22:53].

It is clear that this Temple teaching is not fully set out in the Synoptic Gospels. At first sight at least, therefore, it seems that in Chapters 7-12, John is filling this gap by outlining the dialogue with his adversaries in the Temple. And this dialogue appears as an extended exposition of the theme so briefly stated in Mark 14:60-64, where the high priest asks Jesus whether he is the Son of God, Jesus replies "I am..." and the high priest tears his garments declaring that Jesus has uttered blasphemy. A.E. Harvey thinks that: "it is possible to understand the Fourth Gospel as a presentation of the claims of Jesus in the form of an extended 'trial'."[25] Certainly, John 7-10 conveys every appearance of being such a polemical conversation.

According to John, did Jesus claim to be God?

In the final pages of his stimulating book *The Priority of John*, J.A.T. Robinson asks whether the Fourth Gospel really teaches the doctrine of the Incarnation, the main written source, in fact, for the doctrine eventually set out at Chalcedon. "This is of a pre-existent divine being, subsequently confessed as the second Person of the Trinity, who descended from heaven and became man by assuming a human as well as his own divine nature."[26] Robinson mentions first that this view of the doctrine of the Incarnation being rooted in the Fourth Gospel has had recent confirmation by the distinguished scholar James Dunn in his book *Christology in the Making.*

However, Robinson is somewhat confusing at this point.[27] He quotes John 6:42, where Jesus begins by answering those who say that he is only "Jesus, son of Joseph", by replying that he has come from God the Father [6:46]. Robinson seems to agree: "He is from or out of Nazareth *and* he is from or out of the Father, and not one at the expense of the other."[28] That looks as if Robinson is going to make a classic defence of the doctrine of the Incarnation as found in the pages of the Fourth Gospel. But he then goes on to argue as if the full humanity of Christ was incompatible with the doctrine that Jesus was God; whereas, as anyone with the most elementary knowledge of the history of Christian doctrine will know, the full humanity of Jesus was affirmed in Christian tradition as strongly as his divinity. The defence of the humanity of Christ was expressed rigorously against the Docetist,[29] the Apollinarian,[30] and the Monophysite[31] heresies.

Curiously, regarding the Fourth Gospel, Robinson says: "But it is important to recognise what is happening here. Otherwise the impression will quickly be given that Jesus is *not* truly an earthly, historical human being at all. And John more than anyone else can be quoted for statements of pre-existence which appear to throw doubt on the genuineness of his humanity – such as his being before Abraham [8:58] or sharing the Father's glory before the world began [17:5, cf. 17:24]. How could such a man be normally human, let alone normative of humanity?"[32]

One would have thought that the Fourth Gospel asserting both Jesus' divine and pre-existent origin together with his humanity is a strong argument for saying that the doctrine of the Incarnation is well founded in John. Certainly the Fathers of the Church thought so. But Robinson seems to think that the divinity and the humanity are incompatible, and goes on to attempt to reduce the significance of statements in the Fourth Gospel which proclaim Christ's full divinity, on the ground that John asserts the full humanity of Jesus.

Robinson concludes differently from Dunn at this point. For Dunn, surely correctly, the Fourth Gospel is already teaching what became orthodox Incarnational theology. But for Robinson, regarding Jesus' saying "Before Abraham was, I am" [John 8:58], there is so far nothing to suggest any claim to divinity. Likewise, Jesus saying "I am He" when walking on the water [John 6:20], and any other "I am" references. "That Jesus is arrogating to himself the divine name is nowhere stated or implied in this Gospel."[33]

Regarding John 5:18, where it is said that the Jews considered that Jesus calling God his Father was making him "equal with God" (*ison…to theo),* Robinson goes with H. Odberg as interpreting this from Rabbinic parallels, "rebellious independence, being 'as good as God'."[34] And regarding John 10:33, where the Jews accuse Jesus of blaspheming because, being a man, literally "you make yourself God" (*poieis seauton theon*), Robinson says that the Jews simply have misunderstood Jesus. "What they take to be the blasphemy of making himself 'a god' in 10:33 is again made clear to be a misunderstanding of Jesus calling himself 'God's Son'. For Robinson, it is inconceivable that, if Jesus really made what to the Jews was a blasphemous claim to divinity, this would not have come out in his trial, "where again the worst that can be said about him is that he claimed to be 'God's Son'."[35]

What do these various "I AM" sayings mean, therefore, according to Robinson, if they are not a claim to divinity? Robinson quotes Dom Bede Griffiths, a monk who practised his monastic life in India, with the explicit aim of contacting close at hand the Eastern mystical tradition:

> In the depths of his being, like every human being, he was present to himself, aware of himself, in relation to the eternal ground of his being. In most people this intuitive awareness is inchoate or imperfect, but in the great prophet and mystic, in the seer like Gautama Buddha or the seers of the Upanishads, this intuitive knowledge of the ground of being becomes a pure intuition, a total awareness. Such according to the tradition of St John's Gospel (which in its origin is now considered to be as old as that of the other gospels) was the nature of the knowledge of Jesus. He knew himself in the depth of his spirit as one with the eternal ground of his being.[36]

Robinson deals with an immense array of texts in the final pages of his book, demonstrating how each text could have been less than a claim to the full divinity of Christ. It is not necessary for us to go laboriously through each text to prove that the meaning goes higher than Robinson claims. Our task is easier than Robinson's to this extent, that, if we discovered even a few texts where the full divinity of Christ is expressed, this would be sufficient to demonstrate our thesis.

Regarding Jesus' own claims at his trial, it is true that, as Robinson says, it is said no more than that Jesus claimed to be "Son of God". According to John's account of the trial of Jesus, his Jewish opponents say to Pilate, "We have a law, and according to that law he ought to die because he has claimed to be the Son of God" [John 19:7]. But surely this phrase "Son of God" has to be interpreted in context, as we have so interpreted "Son of God" in Mark.[37] It is Jesus' own understanding of what "Son of God" means as expressed in his public teaching which causes his enemies to accuse him of blasphemy, and according to this particular law, to be worthy of the death sentence. And Jesus' own understanding of "Son of God" with reference to himself in John's account, is precisely a claim to identify himself as I AM, and so equivalent to the divine Name. This surely means much more than Bede Griffith's affirmation that Jesus "knew himself in the depth of his spirit as one with the eternal ground of his being". This would be no more than the union of the mystic with the divine. But the mystic, however holy, will never say I AM, only that he or she is united with I AM, considered as Eternal Other.[38] But, I AM, as we shall now see, is precisely what Jesus claimed.

He said "I am"

We will focus on the I AM sayings of Jesus, following the most important study by David Mark Ball published in 1996.[39]

Ball begins his study with a history of Johannine scholarly opinion regarding the I AM sayings, by assessing the monumental work of E. Schweizer,[40] who was the first to distinguish between the I AM sayings accompanied by an image ("I am the bread of life" John 6:35), and the I AM without an image. It will perhaps be useful to list the occurrences of I AM in the absolute sense, quoting from Raymond Brown's article on that subject in Appendix IV of his commentary Vol I, and using his translation:

8:24: "Unless you come to believe that I AM, you will surely die in your sins"

8:28: "When you lift up the Son of Man, then you will realise that I AM"

8:58: "Before Abraham even came into existence, I AM."

13:19: "When it does happen, you may believe that I AM."

Brown puts under a separate category the Walking on the Water, John 6:20, where he comments:

> Jesus assures them "*Egó eimi:* do not be afraid". Here the expression may simply mean: "It is I, i.e. someone you know, and not a supernatural being or a ghost." We shall point out, however, that divine theophanies in the OT often have this formula: Do not be afraid; I am the God of your ancestors. As we have said in the COMMENT on # 21, in 6:20 John may well be giving us an epiphany scene, and playing on both the ordinary and sacral use of *egó eimi*. [41]

Ball examines the proposed parallels which scholars have found with extra-biblical sources. Ball is unconvinced by these extra-biblical parallels.[42] He counters by referring to scholars who see the background to the I AM sayings in John rather in Judaism contemporary with Jesus and the writing of the Fourth Gospel. He cites Dodd's *Interpretation of the Fourth Gospel,* where Dodd links *ani hu* with Rabbinic expression of the divine Name.[43] Stauffer agrees with Dodd, and links Isaiah 40-55 with the Dead Sea Sect, e.g. the *Manual of Discipline* which states in 8:13f. "They are to be kept apart and to go into the wilderness to prepare the way of the HUAHA there…" cf. Isaiah 40:3. HUAHA is therefore the Dead Sea Sect's reference to the divine name. "Presumably this is made up of the HUAH (HE) and A (signifying *Elohim*, God)."[44]

Daube takes the same line, and links the I AM of the Passover Midrash with Jesus' claims to divinity in John. Daube claims that I the Lord implies God's own personal intervention and no one lower in being:

"For I will pass through Egypt – this means, I and not an angel; and I will smite all the firstborn – this means I and not a seraph; and I will execute judgement – this means I and not the messenger; I the Lord – this means I am and no other."[45]

Consequently, says Daube, when God says "I am and no other" [*ani hu we ló ehad*] we must translate with God's own person being present and no other."[46] All this, of course, depends on how cognisant the author of the Fourth Gospel was of Rabbinism, and of the Dead Sea beliefs.[47] We cannot know that for certain that he was; but it is not impossible, and perhaps it is even likely. Schnackenburg sees a double influence, both Hellenism and Judaism: "The formal structure of the revealer's utterance was probably influenced by the soteriological type of discourse current in Eastern Hellenism."[48] An educated Jewish Christian writing the Fourth Gospel[49] would have had these influences in his thinking, to a large extent assimilated and unconscious. We are not here speaking of a "source", either Jewish or Hellenistic or a mixture of both, but rather of influences on the mind of the writer of the Fourth Gospel which were part of the grammar of his thinking.

These studies, for Ball, cannot be conclusive without looking at the narrative context of the I AM sayings in the Fourth Gospel, and in particular the narrative context of the I AM sayings in the absolute sense, as listed by Brown above. Conventional methods of finding linguistic parallels can usually only produce a number of possible backgrounds.[50] It is only the narrative itself which will tell us more precisely what the author intends us to understand by, e.g. "Before Abraham was, I am."

"I am" in context

Particularly significant for Ball is 6:20, the Walking on the Water, when Jesus says that they are not to fear: *egó eimi mé phobeisthe* 6:20b. Ball quotes the important thesis by J.P. Heil,[51] who sees the dramatic connection between Jesus' statement as divine revelation[52] *egó eimi mé phobeisthe,* and Peter's confession in 6:69b:

> Peter's confession functions as the climactic response which concludes the paradigmatic series of revelatory words introduced by the self-identification formula *egó eimi.* Peter confirms these self-identifications of Jesus in 6:69b with 'You are (*su ei*) the Holy One of Israel.'[53]

Peter's confession 6:69b thus forms a kind of dramatic inclusion with "I am, fear not" *egó eimi mé phobeisthe* 6:20b and "I am the bread of life", *egó eimi ho artos tés zóés,* 6:35. Peter responds to give Jesus the acknowledgement in faith that his wonderful deeds of Walking on the Water and Feeding the Five Thousand have revealed Jesus as truly I AM.

Ball comments in the same way: "The narrator's point of view concerning Jesus' divine origin is confirmed by Jesus' action of walking on the water as well as by his claim to be the bread come down from heaven. It is surely significant that by means of *egó eimi* Jesus again applies a thoroughly Jewish concept to himself."[54]

A similar meaning becomes clear if we look, with Ball, at Chapter 8, the dramatic dialogue in Jerusalem between Jesus and "the Jews". We see first a similar inclusion: *egó eimi* in 8:12, where Jesus says that he is the Light of the World, and 8:58, where he says, "Before Abraham was, I am." Ball claims that "the striking similarities between John 8 and Isaiah 42-43 suggest that the narrator expected the understanding reader to have a knowledge of the same"[55] that is to Isaiah's use of *ani hu,* the statement of the divine name which Jesus applies to himself, and thus incurs not surprisingly the reaction from his unbelieving audience that he is blaspheming. Even more significant for Brown is John 8:28, which looks back to Isaiah 43:10. YHWH says that He has chosen his servant Israel "that you may know and believe me and understand that *egó eimi.*"[56]

We have already noted when looking at St Mark's Gospel this same phenomenon, as to how the claims of Jesus cause the reaction of his hearers that Jesus is blaspheming; and we concluded that the narrative context of the use of "Son of

God" in Mark must therefore lead us towards considering its higher meaning, that Mark means us to understand "Son of God" in terms of Jesus' direct divine authority from his Father. This narrative context in John of course is many times more obvious than in Mark. The "understanding reader" of John's Gospel is surely expected to realise that the absolute I AM, the cause of Jesus' hearers thinking he is blaspheming, is a statement by the Fourth Evangelist that Jesus of Nazareth was truly God, the Word become flesh. That becomes even more obvious when we look at John 10:30, "The Father and I are One."

"The father and I are one"

Some, such as Robinson, have attempted to demonstrate that "The Father and I are one" [John 10:30] means no more than a *moral unity*.[57] If so, it is difficult to see why there should be any blasphemy at all in such a statement. Yet it is immediately upon this statement of Jesus that the Jews take up stones to stone him [John 10:31]. If Jesus claimed only moral unity with God, union of wills, then he would be claiming to be no more than a just man, as for instance Tobit in the Old Testament. It would be no more than the sinlessness claimed by Roman Catholics for Mary the Mother of Jesus, and in the Middle Ages for Jeremiah and John the Baptist. If Jesus claimed merely human sinlessness, his hearers might think him arrogant, even manifesting the sin of pride. But they would not think of him as a blasphemer.

Schnackenburg is, at first sight, less hesitant. He comments on 10:30, "I and the Father are One": "In the short sentence a vista appears of the metaphysical depths contained in the relationship between Jesus and his Father."[58] It might seem that Schnackenburg is saying that the relationship is metaphysical, therefore perhaps of identity of being. However, Schnackenburg himself draws back slightly in his footnote on this verse, when he notes "The verse has played a not insignificant part in relation to the doctrine of the Trinity... It is upon the *ek tés chairos*, which is predicated jointly of the

Father and the Son, that Ammonius of Alexandria bases his interpretation to the effect that the unity relates not to personhood *(hupostasis)*, but to nature *(ousia)*" Yet, concludes Schnackenburg, "These speculations exceed the scope of what the evangelist had in mind."[59]

But what *did* the evangelist have in mind? There is a double usage of *ek tés chairos* in the following verses:

> I give them eternal life, and they will never perish. No one will snatch them out of my hand *(ek tés chairos mou)*. What my Father has given me is greater than all else, and no one can snatch it out of the Father's hand *(ex tés chairos tou patros mou)*. The Father and I are one *(egó kai ho patér en esmen)*. The Jews took up stones again to stone him. [John 10:28-31]

In 10:28b, "out of my hand", *ek tés chairos mou* is a promise from Jesus that his sheep will never be snatched out of his hand. Parallel to this, in 10:29b, *ek tés chairos tou patros mou*, there is a promise that no one will be snatched out of the Father's hand. That is followed by Jesus saying that he is one with his Father. Was Ammonius of Alexandria being over-literalist when he saw a unity of nature between Father and Son precisely in that parallelism: that Jesus' hand and the Father's hand are by nature one and the same? It is a strange way of speaking if such was not meant. Jesus would have said something like "My will is one with God's will. If people come to me, they will be safe in my hands. That means they will be safe in God's hands too." But to say "The Father and I are One", just like that, after a straight parallelism between his hands and the hands of his Father, seems to say much more; and it is understandable why Jesus' opponents take up stones to stone him.

Exegetes seem to be nervous about metaphysical statements in scripture. But what of the statement that YHWH is one, the Jewish *sh'ma*? This seems to have an explosive combination with Jesus saying that he and his Father are one: *egó kai ho patér en esmen*. It most certainly *could* be patient of a blasphemous interpretation by Jesus' Jewish hearers. The

NRSV translates [Deuteronomy 6:4] "Hear, O Israel: The LORD is our God, the LORD alone." But the older RSV translates, as usual, more literally "Hear, O Israel: The LORD our God is one LORD." The Hebrew is *sh^ema' yisra'él, yhwh 'elóhéynu yhwh 'ehad.* That could also be translated, "Hear O Israel. YHWH is our God. YHWH is One." The latter seems to be the best translation.[60] It seems to be a highly ontological statement, that YHWH is one. Whether it implied total monotheism prior to the Exile is a point of discussion among Old Testament exegetes.[61] But that YHWH is one, and so the only God for Israelites to love with all their heart, soul, mind, and strength, that was certainly the Deuteronomic meaning.[62] And certainly the verse was interpreted in a total and metaphysically monotheistic meaning by Judaism at the time of Christ.

But what does it mean when Jesus says that he and the Father are one? Is there not a clear implication that Jesus is joining the Father as *yhwh ehad,* sharing in the oneness of YHWH? This would be a form of idolatry, and so certainly blasphemous. If Jesus' hearers take it that way, and want to stone him, we could hardly blame them. If Jesus wanted to avoid such an implication, surely he should have been much more careful in his language. Again, he is using a highly Semitic form of stating his identity. If "I and the Father are one" does go back to the earthly Jesus, then what does this say about his knowledge of God and of himself while on earth? And could we argue that Chapters 7-10 are substantially historical, albeit written in dramatic form, in that the historical Jesus, towards the end of his earthly life, manifested to his Jewish hearers publicly his knowledge of himself being I AM? In other words, did he really claim to be God?

1   Cf. p. 196.
2   Cf. p. 39.
3   QHJ, 4.
4   Cf. pp. 43-4.
5   Hodgson, P. and King, R. ed., *Christian Theology: An Introduction to its Traditions and Tasks*, London, SPCK, 1983, 12-13.
6   LJCE, 780.
7   Cf. p. 25. JPGG, 178.
8   ECD, 227.
9   Brown, I, 5, Barrett, 156, Schnackenburg, 232, "The Logos is God as truly as he with whom he exists in the closest union of being and life. Hence *theos* is not a genus, but signifies the nature proper to God and the Logos in common."
10   Bultmann, 35-36.
11   This is the view of Barrett, 151.
12   This, famously, is Bultmann's view: Bultmann, 17. Cf. Schnackenburg, I, 220 Brown, I, 22.
13   HDC, 106.
14   TGC, 149. Mascall is not too happy about this speculation on the part of Bouyer.
15   Bultmann, 62
16   Tanner, I. *86.
17   Lane, D., *The Reality of Jesus: An Essay in Christology*, Dublin, Veritas, 1975, 119-120.
18   Carson, 111.
19   Lightfoot, 78.
20   Brown, INT 773-813. INT 803-4.
21   Cf. pp. 140-1.
22   We have accepted earlier that Chapter 21 is an Appendix, added later, whether by the original author or by another author.
23   Brown, I, 172-3.
24   Cf. p. 212.
25   Cf. p. 151, n.11. Harvey, op.cit, 17.
26   PJ, 365.
27   PJ, 367.
28   PJ, 367.
29   ODCC, 413.
30   ODCC, 72. Apollinarius was Bishop of Laodicea c.360, seceded from the Catholic Church 375.
31   For *The Tome of Leo* 13 June 449, cf. ND **609-612**.pp.151-153. Cf. Tanner I, 77-82, which gives the full Letter of Pope Leo to Flavian, Bishop of Constantinople, about Eutyches.
32   PJ, 383.
33   PJ, 385, 386.

34 PJ, 387.

35 PJ, 387.

36 Griffiths, B., *The Marriage of East and West*, London, 1982, 189.

37 Cf. pp. 140-1.

38 Nevertheless, there is a close connection between the Incarnation, which is a *union of hypostasis*, where that union results in Jesus truly *being* God become man, and the union with God of the mystic, where God is seen as dwelling in the soul, while the individual soul in this case retains its own distinct nature and also its own human being. This union is described poetically by the great Spanish mystic St John of the Cross, who calls the divine presence in his soul the "living flame of love that tenderly woundest my soul in its deepest centre." Peers, E.A., *The Complete Works of John of the Cross*, Wheathamstead, Vol III, 16.

39 Ball, D.M. 'I am' in John's Gospel: Literary Function, Background and Theological Implications. JSNTS, 124, Sheffield Academic Press, 1996.

40 IAM, 29.

41 Brown, I, 533-4.

42 IAM, 30.

43 IFG, 94-5.

44 IAM, 36.

45 IAM, 38.

46 IAM, 39.

47 Cf. p. 150. Brown, I, LXIV.

48 IAM 43, Cf. Schnackenburg, II, 86.

49 Cf. PJ, 300-303

50 Although sometimes the formula itself is an indication as to meaning. Cf. UFG, 187.

51 Heil, J.P., Jesus Walking on the Sea: Meaning and Functions of Matt. 14.22-33, Mark 6.45-52 and John 6.15b-2. Analectica Biblica, 87 Rome, Biblical Institute Press, 1981.

52 Cf. p. 214, The Walking on the Water: A Primitive Epiphany.

53 Heil, op.cit. 169.

54 IAM, 79.

55 IAM 93,

56 "Jesus is presented as speaking in the same manner in which Yahweh speaks in Deutero-Isaiah." Brown, I, 537.

57 PJ, 375. "Any attempt to establish an ontological *as distinct from* a moral basis for the unique sonship of Jesus in this Gospel is I believe wrong-headed and purely on linguistic grounds doomed to failure." On the contrary, to try to argue linguistically any other way than towards the ontological implications of "I and the Father are one" is surely to go up a linguistic *cul-de-sac*.

58 Schnackenburg, II, 308.

59 Schnackenburg, II, 511, n.121.

60 Driver, S.R., *A Critical and Exegetical Commentary on Deuteronomy*, Edinburgh, T and T Clark, 1902, puts this as one of four possible translations, 89, n.30, (a) "J. our God, (even) J., is one." (b) "J. is our God, J. is one." (c) "J. is our God, J. alone." (d) "J. our God is one J." But Driver favours (d) "J. our God is one J.", which is materially the same as "J. is our God, J. is one.", which seems to me to read more easily.

61 NJBC, **6:22**, 99

62 Driver, S.R., op.cit. 90. "This verse is thus a great declaration of Monotheism (in the sense both that there is only one God, and also that the God who exists is truly one)."

CHAPTER 14

THE HISTORICAL JESUS REALLY SAID "I AM"

The historical Jesus claimed to be God the Son

The Gospel truth of God incarnate

Having seen the clear reference to the divine name throughout the texts we introduced above where *egó eimi* is used in the absolute sense without a predicate, it is difficult to see a stronger exegetical argument for the claim that the author of the Fourth Gospel provides the full foundations for the doctrine of the Incarnation, eventually to be defined at Chalcedon AD 451.

It also clarifies other texts where scholars have attempted to say that there was a misunderstanding of Jesus' words; in particular, John 5:18, where it is said by the evangelist that the opponents of Jesus pursued him because he made himself equal with God, and John 10: 33, where they wish to stone him because, they say, being a man, he makes himself out to be God.[1]

Ball's conclusion, for which he has produced a huge mass of evidence only a small portion of which could be summarised in the previous chapter, is that, in the Fourth Gospel, Jesus actually claims to be God, the *ani hu* of the divine name in the Old Testament. His hearers therefore do *not* misunderstand him. Note that Jesus never makes it clear that he is *not* equal with God, or *not* God. His statement that he is the "Son of God" does not let him out of that highest of all claims either, because it is in the context of his being the *monogenés theos,* the only-begotten Son of God, the Logos, in John 1:18, which, as we have just demonstrated with Ball, links with the I AM sayings of the main body of the Gospel, and means that Jesus is the divine Son of God eternally existing with the

Father. He is therefore accurately described *both* as God *and* as the Son of God.

Surely, if the author of the Fourth Gospel wished to reduce the force of such high Christological statements, he would have qualified them in some way; but he does not. Either, then, he is guilty of a massive deception, or he really intends us to believe that Jesus claimed what was blasphemy to his hearers, namely, that he was the I AM of the Old Testament, the sacred name of YHWH become flesh.

The Gospel itself, therefore, is unambiguous. Jesus of Nazareth actually claimed to be God the Son. This now, therefore, pushes us back to the final question, concerning the historical authenticity of the Fourth Gospel's Christology: was the historical Jesus aware of his own full divinity? Or is the *Jesus Seminar* right, and the Fourth Gospel is only expressing a myth, however pious, that a Jewish prophet called Jesus of Nazareth who saw himself as no more than a prophet was elevated by his followers (in particular "the Johannine community") to be the Incarnate Son of God?

Did the historical Jesus know that he was God?

Some approaches to Christology in the twentieth century would be very happy that Jesus did not know that he was God during his life on earth, even presuming that he was God. A text from St Paul says that Jesus "emptied (*ekenósen*) himself, taking the form of a slave, being born in human likeness." Philippians 2:7 has been used to produce a "kenotic" Christology. In becoming man, Christ emptied himself of divine attributes, becoming like us in everything "except sin". Part of this self-emptying, it could be argued, was divesting himself of his divine knowledge, Jesus only knowing that he was specially sent by God his Father for a very special mission, but not being aware that he was fully divine.

Furthermore, F. Dreyfus, a loyal Roman Catholic, is convinced that there is no magisterial decision of the Church which says that a Catholic must believe that Jesus knew that he was divine.[2] That Jesus was divine is, of course, Catholic faith defined at the Council of Nicea 321 and again at Chalcedon 451. But that the *historical Jesus* knew that he was divine is not defined Catholic faith; therefore, Dreyfus argues, it is still open to debate.[3]

Christian tradition has always asserted that Jesus had "acquired knowledge". Luke's Gospel tells us that Jesus increased in wisdom and stature, and in favour with God and man [Luke 2:52]. He also had divine knowledge; but how was this divine knowledge to be communicated in his human life? Without indulging in the Quest of the Historical Jesus, the mediaeval scholastics did face the problem as to Jesus' divine and human knowledge. Aquinas quite radically stated that, if Jesus did not have human knowledge, he would not have divine knowledge either.[4] As Dreyfus says, "In fact, knowledge is an act of the Person of Christ, but acting through the faculties of his nature."[5]

Theoretically, therefore, it would have been possible for Jesus to have been God, and not to have known it, if that knowledge was not in some way communicated to his human nature. Dreyfus concludes, "The mystery of the Incarnation does not imply intrinsically, in its intimate structure, the knowledge of his divine nature by Jesus."[6]

However, the present Pope is much more in line with the general teaching of the Catholic Church (its "ordinary magisterium") in affirming without doubt that the historical Jesus did know that he was God. In his Apostolic Letter inaugurating the New Millennium,[7] Pope John Paul II states with full confidence that Jesus of Nazareth, whom Christian faith affirms to be fully divine and fully human, was aware of his own identity as the "only begotten Son of God" [John 1:18]. In this, the Pope was expressing not only the belief of Roman Catholics, but traditionally of all Christians, Protestant, Orthodox, and Catholic:

> However valid it may be to maintain that, because of the human condition which made him grow "in wisdom and in stature, and in favour with God and man" (Lk 2:52), his human awareness of his own mystery would also have progressed to its fullest expression in his glorified

255

humanity, there is no doubt that already in his historical existence Jesus was aware of his identity as the Son of God. John emphasises this to the point of affirming that it was ultimately because of this awareness that Jesus was rejected and condemned: they sought to kill him "because he not only broke the Sabbath but also called God his Father, making himself equal with God" (Jn 5:18). In Gethsemane and on Golgotha Jesus' human awareness will be put to the supreme test. But not even the drama of his Passion and Death will be able to shake his serene certainty of being the Son of the heavenly Father.[8]

Dreyfus himself is convinced that Jesus did know that he was God. Indeed, it seems to me nonsense to think that Jesus could have been God the Son and not to have known it while on earth. If a man does not know who he is, we usually arrange for a course of psychotherapy for his benefit. Jesus' *kenósis,* his self-emptying, would surely have even been greater if he had known that he was God, but submitted himself to death as a common criminal for our salvation.

It is not necessary to interpret Philippians 2:7, *he emptied himself,* as being a reference to Jesus' loss of the attributes of divinity apart from the loss of his divine glory and status.[9] As Brendan Byrne says regarding Philippians 2:7:

> This expression has contributed to the development of 'kenotic' Christologies, but here it probably has a metaphorical sense along the lines of Paul's use of the same verb (*kenoun*) in the passive to mean 'be rendered powerless, ineffective'. (cf. Romans 4:14). The meaning would be then that Christ freely rendered himself powerless – exactly as a slave is powerless, *adopting the condition of a slave:* In the thought of the hymn (Galatians 4:1-11; 4:21-5:1; Romans 8:15) unredeemed human existence is essentially a slavery, a bondage, to spiritual powers, ending in death.[10]

The scholastic explanation seems to presuppose some kind of infused knowledge in the historical Jesus' mind, to communicate this Beatific Vision of God to Christ's human knowledge.[11] It is here perhaps that the post-Enlightenment Quest can render such extrinsic knowledge as no longer necessary. A constant question in the Quest has been how the historical Jesus developed his knowledge about himself and of his own being and nature. As a result of our researches, we would easily see how Christ's knowledge of his divine identity developed as human and as divine. It was acquired in the way in which human knowledge is customarily acquired, by sense-experience, which was assimilated by his human mind. As we have seen in this chapter, Jesus expresses his self-understanding in Semitic terms. His awareness of his own divine identity grew by his own reflection on the scriptures. In reading about the YHWH God of salvation history, he became increasingly aware that these were references to himself.

Modern Christology has added a further insight to this debate about Jesus' self-understanding. Our senses communicate knowledge to us, and we need our senses for any act of knowledge. In the words of the old scholastic adage "nothing is in the mind which was previously not in the senses" (*nihil sit in intellectu quod prius non erat in sensu*). But we receive this knowledge as part of our human consciousness, our ego. Now, as Galot argues, regarding Jesus, because of the Incarnation, "In his human consciousness Christ perceives his ego, which is that of the Son of God. Thus there is in him no human ego; there is human consciousness of a divine ego."[12] Thus, for Galot, Christ possessed "the intuitive knowledge of a divine ego in its intimate relation to the Father."[13] This would be a divine gift, a grace, as Dreyfus realises; but it would for Galot be less apparently extrinsic than it appears in the scholastic theory that Christ was given "from outside of his being" as it were the Beatific Vision. Rather, it would be an essential consequence of Christ being who he actually was, the Word become flesh. Our mode of knowing fits our mode of being.

This fits in perfectly with the I AM of the Gospels, and particularly of the Gospel of John. The "I am" heard by the frightened disciples in the boat was that divine self-consciousness communicating itself to them. There is even a double discontinuity[14] here. *Egó eimi*, the Hebrew *ani hu*, never formed part of the Christian confession post-Easter. Nor was there a complete identity between Jesus and the divine figures quoted by Margaret Barker. Metatron was called "The Lesser Yahweh". Metatron is appointed "in the height as a prince and a ruler among the ministering angels."[15] But Metatron is not simply and unequivocally stated to be *egó eimi* without qualification and without predicate, as Jesus names himself.

In the beginning was the grab bag

When I began to write this book, I had no idea at all how crucial the Miracle of the Walking on the Water would prove to be. That was almost as surprising as the event itself, the bewildered disciples, two thousand years ago on the Sea of Galilee. Even the selection of the miracle for special analysis was originally to some extent accidental. One could not discuss each of the seven miracles in John. There just was not space. My main focus in that chapter was originally intended to be the Multiplication of the Loaves; but I never really got past the Walking on the Water.

If the Walking on the Water was truly an historical event, as we have attempted to demonstrate earlier, then all the elaborate theories of the evolution of New Testament Christology would be blown away. Even if the miracle were only a *theologoumenon,* as Meier thinks it is,[16] a fictional epiphany tale, a challenge is thrown out at "evolutionary" Christologies, precisely because, as Meier himself says, the story itself is so primitive, going right back to the beginnings of the Christian faith just after the death and Resurrection of Jesus; and its Christology is so high.

Meier himself realises the implications of this for early Christology, in terms of his "grab bag":

> Instead of engaging in artificial rectilinear patterns of development, we should recognise that, once the early Christians believed that Jesus had been raised from the dead, a theological explosion was set off that assured

both creativity and disorder for the rest of the first century AD. When it comes to understanding NT Christology, it is best to recite this mantra: in the beginning was the grab bag. Many early Christians were quite content to make both "low" and "high" affirmations about Jesus, with no great concern about consistency, systematisation, or synthesis. Hence we need not be surprised to find in a pre-Marcan and pre-Johannine miracle story a presentation of Jesus that basically depicts him as Yahweh bestriding the waters of chaos in a theophany and proclaiming his identity with the words of Yahweh in Deutero-Isaiah: "It is I [or I am]; fear not". The same Mark who takes over this portrayal of Jesus has no difficulty in speaking of Jesus' inability to heal people because of their unbelief or of Jesus' ignorance of the date of the parousia. In the beginning was the grab bag."[17]

What that means, as Meier so rightly says, is that it makes the neat schema of the development of Christology in the early church, from low to high, quite simply a house of cards, collapsing before any serious investigation based upon the evidence. This is because the evidence is that Jesus is presented as I AM in all the strands of tradition, in Matthew, Mark, and John, through the Miracle of the Walking on the Water, and is so presented in the earliest tradition. It is true that, in itself, the phrase I AM could mean no more than a reassurance by Jesus that he was there. But, in the context of what we have seen to be the earliest understanding of the miracle itself, the I AM of Jesus becomes an epiphany with high Christological import.[18] High and low Christology as theological tendencies were there from the beginning.

Furthermore, is not this existence of the various Christologies at least to some extent inherent in the very doctrine of the Incarnation itself? Jesus is fully God and fully Man, in a single divine identity of person. The dialectic of opposites was working almost in Hegelian fashion in the history of the early church, torn apart by the Christological disputes of the fourth and fifth centuries. The Alexandrians[19] such as

Athanasius and Cyril[20] pulled the church so far towards the divinity that the heresies of Apollinarianism[21] and Mono-physitism,[22] compromised the full humanity; while Antio-chenes[23] such as Theodore of Mopsuestia[24] pushed the humanity of Jesus so far that Adoptionism[25] – the belief that Jesus was the adopted Son of God and not his Son from all eternity, and Nestorianism[26] – the denial of the full personal divine identity of Jesus – almost inevitably arose.

It is not only "in the beginning was the grab bag", but the grab bag was there throughout the history of Christology. Any presentation of the Incarnation has to some extent to be a "grab bag". The pre-scientific mind loved unexplained paradoxes, riddles.[27]

This is not to say that the early Christology was not primitive and needed development. But perhaps it presented the doctrine of the Incarnation better precisely because it left the opposites in tension, and mostly without explanation in the New Testament. It had met Jesus, and that itself was the greatest mystery, if you like the greatest riddle.[28] To do justice to that meeting, they simply described, they did not try too hard to explain.

This makes even more apposite the affirmations of the *Instruction of the Pontifical Biblical Commission Concerning the Historical Truth of the Gospels,* April 21, 1964. *The Instruction* admits freely that there was a three-stage process in the writing of the four Gospels:

Christ commanded the Apostles to preach

|

The Apostles preached as Christ commanded

|

The *apostolici viri* gave us the four Gospels inspired
by the Holy Spirit

What *The Instruction* denies strongly, however, is that there was any process of "mythicalisation" of Christ in that process:

The apostles proclaimed above all the death and resurrection of the Lord, as they bore witness to Jesus. They faithfully explained His life and words, while taking into account in their method of preaching the circumstances in which their hearers found themselves. After Jesus rose from the dead and his divinity was clearly perceived, faith, far from destroying the memory of what had transpired, rather confirmed it, because their faith rested on the things which Jesus did and taught. Nor was he changed into a 'mythical' person and His teaching deformed in consequence of the worship which the disciples from that time on paid Jesus as the Lord and the Son of God.[29]

Did Jesus reveal that he was God?

We have demonstrated that it is most reasonable that the historical Jesus knew that he was God, with a knowledge that grew as a Jewish man who knew the scriptures and recognised himself as the I AM of the Old Testament. The question now arises as to whether he revealed his divine identity personally during his life on earth; or whether his disciples were left to draw this out by implication after the Resurrection.

We return to consider that crucial text "I and the Father are One" [John 10:30].[30] As we have discussed previously, what does it mean when Jesus says that he and the Father are one? Is there not a clear implication that Jesus is joining the Father as *yhwh ehad*, sharing in the oneness of YHWH? This would be a form of idolatry, and so certainly blasphemous. If Jesus' hearers take it that way, and want to stone him, we could hardly blame them. If Jesus wanted to avoid such an implication, surely he should have been much more careful in his language.

There seems no reason, therefore, apart from dogmatic prejudice against the historical Jesus having a high Christology himself, why "I and the Father are One" should not go back to the historical Jesus, *together with the reaction of the hearers of Jesus that he was committing blasphemy by saying those words.*

It fulfils the criteria:

1. **Double Discontinuity.**[31] As we have just demonstrated, it is doubly discontinuous both with Judaism and with the early church formulations.

2. **Coherence.**[32] Thirdly, it also satisfies the criterion of coherence. Jesus was accused of blasphemy. Jesus saying "I and the Father are one" This is coherent with Jesus being accused of blasphemy since it gives a more than sufficient reason why he was accused, as we have demonstrated above.

3. **Multiple Attestation.**[33] It also satisfies the criterion of multiple attestation, because it links in with a small but significant group of texts already mentioned which speak of this ontological relationship between Jesus and his Father, which we will look at again now. Each text clarifies the other.

Before we even look at John, we have already demonstrated how Jesus' statements in the Synoptic Gospels are potentially blasphemous as far as Jesus' hearers are concerned because they identify too closely Jesus' actions and his authority with those of God his Father. To the crowd watching Jesus cure the paralytic, Jesus is blaspheming by saying he has the power to forgive sins. [Mark 2:5-7, Matthew 9:2-3\\]. To the high priest at his trial, Jesus is blaspheming because he is equating his own power in heaven too closely with God. We must add the text we have already referred to earlier,[34] the Parable of the Wicked Husbandmen [Matthew 21:33-46, Mark 12:1-12, Luke 20:9-19], and whose authenticity we have demonstrated. This is about the master of the vineyard sending first his servants (i.e. the prophets) and then finally sending his own Son, who is killed by the wicked tenants. The hearers of Jesus do not accuse him of blasphemy; but they wanted to arrest him after he told this parable. Was this because of the implied identification of Jesus with the son? [Matthew 21:46].[35]

Finally, we must add the stray "Johannine" text in the Synoptic tradition, which produces no reaction from Jesus' hearers, but speaks of the same exclusive relationship between Jesus and his Father which in other circumstances certainly produced the reaction of the charge of blasphemy.[36]

All things have been handed over to me by my Father; and no one knows the Son except the Father, and no one knows the Father except the Son and anyone to whom the Son chooses to reveal him. [Matthew 11:27]

The only reason of substance to leave it out of the authentic sayings of Jesus is that its Christology is too high: again, a circular argument. Casey would deny its authenticity because it does not occur frequently enough. "If the historical Jesus had used this key term extensively as John says he did, the faithful Christians who transmitted the synoptic tradition would have transmitted it extensively."[37] Scholars all admit that the argument from silence is flimsy. Surely, Casey's argument from infrequency of mention is even more hazardous.

From our researches into Mark's Gospel, we found a high Christology already operating, which authenticates Matthew 11:27 by the principle of coherence. We concluded[38] that Mark considered that the historical Jesus was put to death for blasphemy; and that blasphemy was precisely to claim to be the exalted Son of Man at the right hand of God.[39] We concluded that Jesus kept the so-called "Messianic Secret" up to that point because, if he had declared himself earlier, he would have been put to death before he had completed his mission.[40]

What is common to these texts is that Jesus is claiming a unique relationship with his Father, which is much more than his being simply a prophet. This comparison with prophecy is most important, because in the Jewish context the usual type of relationship with God, which was special and charismatic, was that of prophecy. The typical expression of the Old Testament "The Word of YHWH came to…" [Jeremiah 1:2, Ezekiel 12:8, etc].[41] The Word of God was something external, which acted upon and which directed, even took possession of them. With Jesus, however, this Word is not external to him, but is always in him and with him. It is the Father himself.

In the Parable of the Wicked Husbandmen, Jesus compares himself, as a Son, with the servants, the prophets. We find this same comparison significantly now in John, in the passage in question. Jesus wishes to know why his hearers think that he is blaspheming when in the Old Testament judges are called "gods". [John 10:34]. What Jesus does in Rabbinic fashion is to argue from the lesser to the greater. Even the judges, Jesus says, are said to be "gods" because the Word of God came to them. He is using a Rabbinic type of exegesis of Psalm 82:1-8. But this comparison in no way satisfies Jesus' hearers. They obviously think that Jesus calling himself a *Son* in status higher than the prophets, together with the absolute I AM statements, was blasphemous.

The answer is simple and clear. Not only is Jesus Son in his own eyes, but fully God as Son. We saw at the close of the last chapter that Jesus' claim to be one with his Father is a claim to divinity, and that historically it is authenticated by being discontinuous both with Judaism before Christ, which never identified a living human being as one with YHWH, and with the primitive church's Christology, which did not use this formulation in developing its doctrine about Christ. This is even more evident regarding the absolute I AM sayings in the Fourth Gospel.[42] No Old Testament figure was identified as the *ani hu* of Deutero-Isaiah in the history of Judaism; nor did the primitive church describe Jesus that way. The I AM sayings are therefore authenticated historically by the principle of double discontinuity.

We do not claim that the disciples of Jesus understood the full implications of Jesus' claims during his life. There was a genuine development in the mind of the evangelist himself, which enabled him to take the hints given earlier by events such as the Walking on the Water, and to express that divinity more explicitly in the dialogues and monologues of the Fourth Gospel. This would allow for a role to be played by the "Johannine Community", since surely the evangelist's mind would have developed with the help of his own Christian community. If Jesus was truly the incarnate Son of God, as a man on this earth, then he would have to let them know this somehow during his life on earth; even if his disciples could only fully understand the message after the Resurrection.[43] Once more, as we shall see again in our next chapter, the Fourth Gospel is entirely historically coherent.

1 Brown, I, 408. It is not easy to understand what Brown means here. How can a statement such as a claim to be "equal with God" be "primarily functional"? Are not its "ontological implications" primary, as it seems those who heard Jesus originally, as John tells us, thought it to be?

2 JSD, 13.

3 JSD, 38. The position would be similar to that of the Assumption of Mary, the doctrine that Mary was assumed into heaven body and soul. It was considered *definable* before it was *defined*.

4 S.T. IIIa, q.9, a.1 ad 1.

5 *En effet, la connaissance est un acte de la Personne du Christ, mais agissant avec les facultés de sa nature.* JSD, 31.

6 *Le mystère de l'Incarnation n'implique pas intrinsequement, dans sa structure intime, la connaissance par Jésus de Nazareth de sa nature divine.* JSD, 34. There would, however, surely be some incongruity, indeed some defect in Christ's being on earth, if he did not know his identity as God become man, even granted that this had to be communicated to him by God the Father.

7 *Apostolic Letter* Novo Millenio Ineunte *of His Holiness Pope John Paul II to the Bishops Clergy and Lay Faithful at the Close of the great Jubilee of the Year 2000,* Vatican, 6 January, 2001.

8 Ibid. para 246.

9 INC, 62-63.

10 NJBC, **48:20,** 794-5.

11 INC, 84.

12 *La Conscience de Jésus,* 1971, 115f. Translated by Mascall, TGC, 164.

13 *La Conscience de Jésus,* 1971, 152. Translated by Mascall, TGC, 166.

14 Cf. p. 115.

15 Cf. pp. 149-50. RL, 18.

16 Cf. p. 216. MJ2, 920-21.

17 MJ2, 919.

18 Cf. p. 214.

19 Cf. "Alexandrian Theology", ODCC, 35.

20 Athanasius, Bishop of Alexandria, defender of the divinity of Christ as of "one substance *(homóousios)* with the Father, cf. ODCC, 101. And for Cyril of Alexandria, defender of the doctrine of the hypostatic union, cf. ODCC, 369.

21 Cf. "Apollinarius and Apollinarianism", ODCC, 72. For Apollinarius, a close friend of Athanasius, he so emphasised the doctrine of Christ as of one substance with the Father that he denied a human spirit in Jesus.

22 "The doctrine that in the Person of the Incarnate Christ there was but a single, and that a Divine, Nature, as against the orthodox teaching

of a double Nature, Divine and Human, after the Incarnation."
ODCC, 931.

23 Cf. "Antiochene Theology", ODCC, 65-66." The tendency of the
school was to incline towards belief in a loose union of the divine and
human natures in Christ..."

24 ODCC, 1358-9.

25 A typical Adoptionist was Paul of Samosata, third century Bishop of
Antioch, cf. ODCC, 1052.

26 ODCC, 961.

27 Cf. p. 134, cf. JR, 494.

28 EBT II, 625.

29 BI 394.

30 Cf. p. 247f.

31 Cf. p. 115.

32 Cf. p. 116.

33 Cf. p. 115.

34 Cf. pp. 130-1.

35 Brown, I, 409-410.

36 Perhaps we might well put this text, following Dreyfus, into the
category of a private communication of Jesus to his own disciples.
Cf. JSD, 71. Even if we maintain, against Dreyfus, that Jesus revealed
his divine identity not only privately to his disciples, but publicly.

37 JPGG, 25. Bultmann HST, 166* only says that Matthew 11:17
seems "at first sight" to be a Hellenistic formulation, for him an
extraordinarily cautious remark. Viviano says, *I praise you Father,*
"This is a typical Jewish blessing formula, but with Jesus' intimate
Abba-Father address added (five times in three verses", NJBC, **42:75**,
653).

38 Cf. p. 145.

39 Cf. p. 146.

40 Cf. p. 141.

41 E.g. Psalm 105:19, Isaiah 38:4, Jeremiah 1:2. 1:4, Ezekiel 1:3, 3:16,
6:1, 7:1, 11:14, 12:1, Haggai 1:1, 1:3, 2:1, 2:10, 2:20.

42 Cf. p. 243f.

43 JSD, 71.

CHAPTER 15

"THE JEWS" (*HOI IOUDAIOI*) AND THE DEATH OF JESUS

> Jesus, as presented in John 7-12, makes his final appeal to *hoi Ioudaioi* to fulfil their destiny of leading the whole world to faith in Zion. But, in order to fulfil that destiny, they had to accept Jesus himself as the Light of the World. Tragically, they reject Jesus as a blasphemer, and he is handed over to Pilate for crucifixion.

Was St John's Gospel anti-Semitic?

In the past twenty years, there has been a gathering momentum of scholars asserting that the Fourth Gospel is anti-Semitic.[1] This is a very serious charge against a foundation document of the Christian religion, and must be seriously heard and acted upon if it is true.

The Fourth Gospel's "anti-Semitism" leads Kysar to challenge whether the Gospel of John should remain in the Christian canon of scripture. Kysar argues that "In its canonical status the Gospel of John has nurtured (if not conceived) repugnant attitudes and evoked abhorrent actions on the part of Christians toward their Jewish colleagues."[2] The matter is deemed particularly urgent since the Holocaust of the Second World War 1939-45, when millions of Jews died in Nazi concentration camps. Maurice Casey joins his voice to this call to remove St John's Gospel from the canon of scripture for basically the same reason, its anti-Semitism, together with its misrepresentation of the facts.[3]

The Johannine Community, in the view of both Brown and Martyn, as Kysar says, "took the references in the Gospel to expulsion from the synagogue (*aposynagógos,* John 9:22, 12:42, 16:2) as indications that the Christian community of which the fourth evangelist was a part and for which the Gospel was written had been part of a Jewish synagogue but was then expelled from its religious community there."[4] For

Martyn, the Gospel "seems to reflect experiences in the dramatic interaction between the synagogue and the Johannine church."[5]

The result of this conflict for Kysar is "a defensive and threatened Christian community, attempting to reshape its identity isolated from the synagogue and its Jewish roots."[6] Kysar claims this feeling of threat in the face of Judaism makes the Gospel itself defensive and polemical.[7]

From the historical viewpoint, of course, as we have already discussed,[8] the 'Johannine Community' is sheer speculation. The Fourth Gospel presents itself, we have seen, as an historical drama about Jesus of Nazareth, not in any way as a story of the loves and hates of the Johannine Community. Any reflections on the Johannine Community must be in the nature of hypothesis.

Furthermore, J.A.T. Robinson challenges the view that the Gospel of John can be dated with reference to the excommunication of Christians by Jews at the close of the first century.[9] Rather, such excommunication practice could well, according to Robinson, go back to the time of the historical Jesus.

If, as Kysar argues, "the Jews" are a fictional group in the Gospel story who exist there to support the flagging faith of the Johannine community, the Johannine community itself becomes a prototype, even *the* prototype, of two thousand years of anti-Semitism.

But, if, as we shall now demonstrate, "the Jews" in the Fourth Gospel are defined in terms of the role they played as a group limited in the place and time of the historical Jesus, then the author of the Fourth Gospel can in no way be accused of anti-Semitism. Rather, the Fourth Gospel described a situation of conflict *within Judaism itself,* and a situation of conflict which existed before, even if only just before, Christianity was born. Once again, the Fourth evangelist is telling us about the historical Jesus, and in this case a vitally important set of facts about the opposition to him during his own day, from his own people.

Our investigation so far: summing up

Our conviction throughout this investigation is that, if we follow modern historical Jesus research methods, but divest ourselves from anti-miraculous and anti-supernaturalist presuppositions, we will achieve positive results in attempting to prove the divinity of Christ. So far, results have confirmed the validity of such an approach.

We began in chapter 6 by following the generality of historical Jesus research, to arrive at the critical minimum. Jesus of Nazareth existed; he was baptised by John the Baptist; he was renowned as a miracle worker; he preached the imminent kingdom of God; he was a popular preacher who offended the religious leaders of his day; he was condemned to death by Pontius Pilate; and his followers proclaimed that he had risen from the dead.

We saw that this left three Enigmas:[10] (a) how did his followers come to acknowledge him as Son of God, if we rightly reject the "Bousset" solution, that the primitive Christian community applied Greek categories to one who was only a Jewish prophet?; (b) what was the reason for his death?; and (c) why did the early Christians believe that he had risen from the dead?

We must leave the third Enigma until the next chapter. But already, we are well on the way to solving the first two Enigmas. Going on from the critical minimum, in chapter 7, we followed the Wright Way, building up a profile of the historical Jesus using N.T. Wright's *Jesus and the Victory of God*. We saw that Jesus was a most extraordinary Jewish prophet, indeed much more than just a prophet. He foresaw the downfall of the Temple and all that Judaism held most dear with it. But he saw this catastrophe as only the prelude to a new return and restoration for Israel, *led by himself.*

At this point, we adopted an entirely new methodology as far as historical Jesus research is concerned. In chapter 8, looking at Mark's account, we argued that his intention was to tell us that Jesus claimed to be Son of God in a sense which seemed blasphemous to those who heard it. Thus, right at the beginning of his Gospel,[11] Jesus is accused of blasphemy because he tells the paralytic that his sins are forgiven [Mark 2:5]; and close to the end, the high priest tears his garments and declares that Jesus is a blasphemer because he admits to being the Son of God, and explains that affirmation in claiming that he as Son of Man will sit at the right hand of God and come in the clouds of heaven [Mark 14:64]. We argued that in this case, to take the Gospel of Mark at its face value, a simple and coherent answer is given to the question as to why Jesus died – because he was a blasphemer in the view of his hearers. It also answers the first question as to how the first Christians came to believe that Jesus was God become man; because he himself had claimed such during his earthly life.

We admitted that it remained uncertain in Mark's account precisely what Jesus meant by "Son of God", even if Mark saw "Son of God" very much as Jesus being supernatural in the sense that he acted with the authority of God's own Son. But we saw in chapter 13 how this meaning of "Son of God" is filled out in John's Gospel. Jesus is the I AM, the *ani hu* of the Old Testament, the secret divine name revealed. This he declares to the frightened disciples in the boat; and most of all, he tells his Jewish hearers that he and the Father are One, and that "before Abraham was, I AM", which we argue with Ball is nothing less than a claim to full divinity. We argued to the historical credibility of Jesus' knowledge and understanding of his own self and his own mission; that Jesus as I AM is not the creation of the Johannine Community, but the supreme example of the originality of the ideas of Jesus about himself.

We have therefore built up our case using the various criteria outlined,[12] and particularly the criterion of coherence,[13] and the criterion of sufficient reason.[14] We have found that a coherent picture of Jesus emerges, which explains the problems which are such in critical scholarship only because the world of scholarship will not accept the text as it stands. This we have argued, not from a Fundamentalist viewpoint, but strictly from historical/critical reasoning.

Why they wanted to arrest Jesus

So far, in chapter 8, we answered the question:

Who delivered Jesus up to Pilate for Trial?
Answer: The Sanhedrin

Why? Because they were convinced that he was a blasphemer (Mark 14:64\\).

But this leaves the question unanswered. Why did they want to arrest Jesus in the first place?

We have argued to the historical authenticity of Mark 14:57-65. In the Marcan version of the trial of Jesus, the high priest asks Jesus whether he is the Christ, the Son of the living God. Jesus replies "I am; and 'you will see the Son of Man seated at the right hand of the Power,' and 'coming with the clouds of heaven.'" It is this which the high priest sees as blasphemous. All condemn him as worthy of death.[15]

But why did the high priest ask him that particular question? Mark himself indicates that, right at the beginning of Jesus' public ministry, he offended his Jewish hearers by saying to the paralytic let down through the roof "Your sins are forgiven you" [Mark 2:5]. As we have seen,[16] throughout the Gospel of Mark, there is cast the shadow of Jesus' impending death. But we would have to say that Mark does not give us a clear lead-up to Jesus' arrest. Surely, if Jesus were to be indicted for blasphemy, there would have to have been some kind of climax whereby Jesus' enemies in high places came to realise that the only solution would be to arrest him.

This is precisely the information given us by John, particularly in Chapters 7-10. We must again repeat that we are not claiming that the Fourth Gospel record gives us strict chronology, any more than the Synoptic Gospels. We would admit, with F.F. Bruce, that the Gospel of John is written as a drama, not like a tape-recording of the words of Jesus.[17] Yet we would insist that, in recounting the story of Jesus in dramatic form, any historical drama can contain significant

271

historical facts. We maintain here, therefore, that John's account gives us a sufficient explanation for the unanswered question as to why Jesus was arrested.

John tells us that, in the weeks prior to his arrest, Jesus went up to Jerusalem, even though he knew that a group called "the Jews" (*hoi Ioudaioi*) were looking out for him [John 7:11]. John has already told us that "the Jews" were offended when, after curing the sick man at the pool of Bethesda, Jesus had said "My Father works, and I work", thus apparently making himself equal with God [John 5:18]. These same "Jews" had seen Jesus in Galilee multiply the loaves and fishes to feed the multitude, and were similarly offended when Jesus had promised to give his own flesh for the life of the world [John 6:52]. Thus Jesus had been warned already to keep out of their way, presumably to avoid being harmed or arrested by "the Jews". Nevertheless, Jesus goes up to Jerusalem, and declares himself openly in the Temple as "the light of the world" [John 7:12].

Things go only from bad to worse after Jesus proclaims his own being and mission at the feast of Tabernacles. He tells "the Jews" that, where he is going, they will not be able to find him [John 7:31-36]. Then the "temple police"[18] take a report to the chief priests and Pharisees of the Sanhedrin, who have power to arrest Jesus.[19] "The officers do not see Jesus as a deceiver of the people, but as a man proclaiming the truth of God (cf. 8.40), and have decided for themselves not to carry out their instructions."[20] John tells us therefore that there are tensions arising from different estimates of Jesus; but the authorities are determined to press ahead to arrest Jesus, retorting to Nicodemus, who protests that "Our law does not judge people without first giving them a hearing to find out what they are doing", that "prophets do not come out of Galilee" [John 7:52].

But Jesus' accusers had not long to wait before Jesus condemned himself out of his own mouth, as far as they were concerned. Jesus declares publicly that he will be leaving them soon [John 8:21-26]. He is obviously aware of his impending death, but much more that he is returning to his Father. Then, when they have lifted him up (i.e. crucified him), they will

272

know that I AM (*egó eimi*) [John 8:28]. "As he was saying these things, many believed in him." [John 8:30]. But, as he have already seen,[21] Jesus only inflames those Jews who believed in him by claiming "Before Abraham was, I AM" [John 8:58]. They try to stone him, thinking that he was a blasphemer, "So they picked up stones to throw at him, but Jesus hid himself and went out of the temple" [John 8:59].

The climax is reached when, after curing the man born blind in Chapter 9, and making claims about his relationship with God his Father which cause some of "the Jews" to think that he is possessed, while others were not so sure [John 10:20], Jesus claims that he and the Father are one [John 10:30],[22] "Then they tried to arrest him again, but he escaped from their hands" [John 10:39]. Jesus retires to nearby Bethany, knowing that if he appears any more in public, he will most likely be arrested. It is hardly surprising that, as John says, as the Feast of the Passover drew near, "the chief priests and the Pharisees had given orders that anyone who knew where Jesus was should let them know, so that they might arrest him" [John 11:57].[23]

Throughout my life's reading of St Johns Gospel, I have always been convinced that these chapters read like fact, even if dramatically presented. There seems little reason why the evangelist should have recorded them except to explain a fact, namely why Jesus was arrested. We have here a supreme example of historical authentication:

- Firstly, by the criterion of sufficient reason,[24] since the evangelist tells us why Jesus was arrested; the only reason given by any of the evangelists.
- Second, by the criterion of multiple attestation,[25] since John's testimony that Jesus was arrested for blasphemy is, as we have already seen, the only reason given for his being handed over to Pilate for punishment in the Synoptic record.[26]
- Third, by the criterion of historical coherence,[27] because Chapters 7-12 of John build up a coherent picture of a Jesus who makes claims for himself unacceptable to his hearers.

The only other possibility immediately evident is that the author of the Fourth Gospel is targeting "the Jews" as a hate object, by fictionally presenting them as unable to believe in Jesus. This was in order to bolster Christian faith over against the increasingly reactionary Synagogue after Jamnia. Thus it is hardly surprising that, with a critical scholarship increasingly viewing the Fourth Gospel as "the loves and hates of the Johannine community", rather than as in any sense a faithful record of the life and death of the historical Jesus, cries of "anti-Semitism" against the Gospel of John multiplied towards the close of the twentieth century. Thus it becomes vitally important for us to attempt now to determine who these *Ioudaoi* were in the mind of the Fourth Gospel writer.

Who were *hoi Ioudaioi*?

There is an immense scholarly debate as to who "the Jews" (*hoi Ioudaioi*) are in the Fourth Gospel. It is difficult to determine a single meaning for all the 71 times that *hoi Ioudaioi* occurs in John. The reader is referred to the full discussion in Gérald Caron's most important recent study *Qui sont les* Juifs *de l'évangile de Jean?*[28]

It is clear from the outset that *hoi Ioudaioi* in the Fourth Gospel does not refer to all members of the Jewish religion, at least one present-day meaning of the term "Jew". Jesus and his disciples, although clearly what we would call "Jews", since members of the Jewish race and religion, are not referred to as *hoi Ioudaioi*, except in John 4:22, where Jesus says to the Samaritan woman, "You worship what you do not know; we worship what we know, for salvation is from the Jews." As Brown says:

> "People who are ethnically, religiously, and even geo-graphically Jews (even in the narrow sense of belonging to Judea) are distinguished from 'the Jews'. For instance, in ix 22 the parents of the blind man, obviously Jews themselves, are said to fear 'the Jews', that is, the Pharisees who are investigators. The former cripple, a Jew himself,

is pictured in v 15 as informing 'the Jews' that Jesus was his benefactor."[29]

What, then, did John mean by *hoi Ioudaioi?* With Caron, but slightly broadening his classification, we may divide views about what John meant by *hoi Ioudaioi* into three:

1. *hoi Ioudaioi* refers to the Jewish Authorities.

As Caron says, "For the great majority of commentators today as yesterday, this expression designates the *Jewish authorities* (hostile to Jesus)."[30] There are, of course, many instances where it could well mean the Jewish authorities, e.g. John 8:52, 57, where *hoi Ioudaioi* dialogue with Jesus, and end up by attempting to stone him. Presumably *hoi Ioudaioi* were Jews with some authority.

But there are difficulties with this view, if we wish to apply all the 71 references of *hoi Ioudaioi* in the Fourth Gospel to mean the Jewish authorities. Urban von Wahlde has put together well the reasons why: "A current trend in scholarship is to see the Johannine Jews as comprising both the common people and the authorities."[31] The main problem with a simple identification of *hoi Ioudaioi* with the authorities is that the Fourth Gospel sometimes distinguishes between them and the Pharisees, the chief priests, and the scribes:

> The Pharisees heard the crowd muttering such things about him, and the chief priests and Pharisees sent temple police to arrest him. Jesus then said, "I will be with you a little while longer, and then I am going to him who sent me. You will search for me, but you will not find me; and where I am, you cannot come. "The Jews (*hoi Ioudaioi*) said to one another, "Where does this man intend to go that we will not find him? Does he intend to go to the Dispersion among the Greeks and teach the Greeks?" [John 7:32-5]

The Pharisees and the chief priests seem in the above text to be distinct from *hoi Ioudaioi.*

2. *hoi Ioudaioi* refers to the people who lived in the Jerusalem/Judea area.

As we saw above, Jesus and the disciples are not part of *hoi Ioudaioi* in the Fourth Gospel. Is this because geographically they were Galileans, not Judeans? The simplest suggestion, therefore, is that *hoi Ioudaioi* refers to those Jews who lived in the Jerusalem-Judea region. If this is the case, *hoi Ioudaioi* should really be translated "the Judeans", and there could be no hint of anti-Semism in the Fourth Gospel. *Hoi Ioudaioi* would simply refer to those who lived in a particular area, and who were hostile to Jesus during his life on earth.

As early as 1828 Bornhaüser held this view.[32] He argued that *hoi Ioudaioi* has a geographical meaning.

This is undoubtedly the case in e.g John 7:1 "After this Jesus went about in Galilee; he would not go about in Judea, because the Jews (i.e. the Judaeans) sought to kill him." *Hoi Ioudaioi* here mean "geographically Judaeans", and this geographical reference works for an extraordinarily high number of 69 out of 71 uses of the word *hoi Ioudaioi* in John. The two exceptions are John 6:41 and 52, groups of Jews being in Galilee when Jesus feeds the multitude. But even here, *hoi Ioudaioi* could at least possibly mean "those living geographically in Judaea, but who were paying a visit to Galilee." Many authors agree substantially with this geographical view. Dekker explains 6:41 and 52 as the work of the redactor.[33] He claims that the author of the *Grundschrift* used the Palestinian terminology throughout, whereas the redactor has used the expression common to the first Christians. In 1971, Lowe revised this view, which he presented thoroughly and convincingly. Some even think that the Gospel represents a tension between the Judeans and the Galileans (also the Samaritans).[34]

But this "geographical interpretation" of *hoi Ioudaioi* has not been universally well received by the scholars. Ashton gives his reasons for disagreeing with Lowe as follows:

> Unfortunately, however, although there is plenty of evidence in contemporary writing (above all Josephus)

for the use of the term *Ioudaioi* to refer to the people of Judaea. it is nowhere used to distinguish them from Jews of the diaspora or of other parts of Palestine. Indeed, the *Ioudaioi* who debate with Jesus on the shore of Lake Tiberias in John 6 can scarcely be anything other than Galileans. And the term is just as proper a designation for the people of Galilee as it is for the Jewish communities of, say, Antioch or Alexandria.

A further drawback to Lowe's solution is that it offers no satisfactory answer to the puzzling question of the source of John's hostility towards the *Ioudaioi*. Even if some degree of local antipathy between Galileans and Judaeans may be said to have crept into the Gospel, it has done so only fleetingly; it is certainly not sufficiently pervasive to account for the continual enmity and distrust of the evangelist towards those he calls *hoi Ioudaioi*.[35]

It is not quite clear why, in Ashton's terms, *hoi Ioudaioi* in debate with Jesus have to be Galileans. Could they not have just come up from Jerusalem to meet Jesus in Galilee? But Ashton is certainly right, that Lowe has not adequately accounted for the important role of *hoi Ioudaioi* in the Fourth Gospel simply in geographical terms. There must be some other reason for their central, and apparently hostile, part in the Fourth Gospel drama.

3. *hoi Ioudaioi* is primarily a symbolic description of those lacking in faith.

This is the view of Bultmann. "According to Bultmann, the cosmological dualism of Gnosis is changed into a dualism of decision."[36] In one sense, this could remove any anti-Semitic suggestion in the Fourth Gospel. The writer(s) of the Gospel for Bultmann do not have the Jews as such as an object of hostility. *Hoi Ioudaioi* for Bultmann simply become a dramatic symbol for those who refuse the decision of commitment to existential faith.

Wolfgang Trilling takes this even further. For him, the Fourth Gospel presents a dualism between good and evil, *hoi Ioudaioi* representing the evil world.[37] For Schram[38] and

277

Culpepper,[39] performing a literary analysis of the Fourth Gospel, *hoi Ioudaioi* represent both those who believe and those who do not.[40]

However, Caron, to my mind correctly, takes Bultmann to task for ignoring ultimately the problem of the particular role of those called the "Johannine Jews". As Caron says, "It is primarily and above all this narrative role which comes to define or identify the Johannine Jews.[41] But there seems to be no relationship with the other actors in the drama, the Pharisees, etc. In order to sustain his view, Bultmann has to ignore the concrete dramatic function of *hoi Ioudaioi*.

Where Culpepper and Schram are concerned, the problem is precisely the opposite. Culpepper for Caron pays insufficient attention to the actual meaning in context of the word *hoi Ioudaioi*. Philology must be satisfied as well as dramatic and literary analysis, he says. In this, the differences in the use of *hoi Ioudaioi* in the different individual texts of the Fourth Gospel must never be forgotten. Caron is surely right here.[42]

Although anti-Semitism is obviously far from Bultmann's mind especially, for him *hoi Ioudaioi* only representing those lacking faith, yet, with any fictional presentation of *hoi Ioudaioi* as with Bultmann, Culpepper, or Schram, the charge of anti-Semitism will never lurk far behind; as it has not, as we have already seen, in Johannine studies at the close of the last century. If *hoi Ioudaioi* has primarily a symbolic meaning and not any reference to the time of the historical Jesus, then why does the drama of the Fourth Gospel pick on the Jews precisely for this dark and evil role? A fictional presentation makes the Jews the "bad guys", and forms the basis of future anti-Semitism, without any factual justification.

Obviously, if *hoi Ioudaioi* proves to be primarily a fictional symbol, then we as Christians have to live with that, and deal with its potential anti-Semitism also. But, one would suggest, we should look to the Fourth Gospel, not primarily for answers to the problems of the Johannine Community, except insofar as those problems are solved with reference to the life and times of the historical Jesus, but to clues as to the real historical situation at the time of Jesus. Here, one would suggest, we have the key to the meaning of *hoi Ioudaioi*.

And then, in consequence, the question of anti-Semitism, and its resolution in our own time, can be dealt with more rationally.

"The Jews" in the Old Testament

The term "Jew" is by no means simple to define. Merriam Webster's Collegiate Dictionary[43] gives four possible meanings, all in current usage:

1. *a:* a member of the tribe of Judah, *b:* Israelite.
2. a member of a nation existing in Palestine from the sixth century BC to the first century AD.
3. a person belonging to a continuation through descent or conversion of the ancient Jewish people
4. one whose religion is Judaism

The complexity of the definition arises from the fact that being a Jew is itself not a univocal idea. It refers not only to a religion, but to a nation, and therefore to lineage within that nation. Thus if a person is a "Catholic" or a "Baptist", it is first and foremost his or her religion which is being nominated. Thus if a Catholic or a Baptist becomes an atheist, they will usually say something like "I was baptised a Catholic, but now I am an atheist", or "I was brought up a Baptist, but I became an atheist as a youth and was never baptised". But a Jew who becomes an atheist would still be called a Jew because of Jewish descent.

In the Scriptures of the Old and New Testament also, the term "Jew" and "Judean" is likewise multi-faceted; because the tribe of Judah from originally being one of the twelve tribes eventually comprised in effect all the people of God by the time of Christ. The word Judah is further complicated by the fact that in the Old Testament it is a frequently used personal name. Thus, in Zorell's Hebrew Lectionary,[44] there are eleven meanings given for the word *yᵉhudah,* and five meanings for *yᵉhudiy:* which latter is more obviously translated "Jew": even if on occasions *yᵉhudah* can also be a personal name [Nehemiah 12:36]. We will set out the parallel meanings in a grid:

y^ehudah ("Judah")	y^ehudiy ("Judean")
One of the twelve tribes. Genesis 49:8-10, Deuteronomy 33:7[45]	One born from the tribe of Judah. 1 Chronicles 4:18
The kingdom of Judah after the Schism of the Twelve Tribes. Isaiah 44:26.	A citizen of the kingdom of Judah after the Schism. 2 Kings 16:6, Jeremiah 32:12.
Member of the post-exilic community. Nehemiah 4:10[46]	Member of the post-exilic community. Nehemiah 2:16.
Province of the region of Persia. Haggai 1:1	Citizen of Judah a province of Persia. Nehemiah 1:2.

Nehemiah 1:2 contains both y^ehudah ("Judah") and y^ehudim ("Judeans"), plural of y^ehudiy, and illustrates the usual difference between the two terms:

> One of my brothers, Hanani, came with certain men from Judah (miyhudah); and I asked them about the Jews (hayy^ehudim) that survived, those who had escaped the captivity, and about Jerusalem. [Nehemiah 1:2]

y^ehudah therefore is first and foremost a place, Judah, and y^ehudiy is first and foremost a person, a Judean, or as the NRSV translates on occasion, "Jew":

Thus says the LORD of hosts: In those days ten men from nations of every language shall take hold of a Jew, (*ish y*ᶜ*hudiy*)[47] grasping his garment and saying, "Let us go with you, for we have heard that God is with you." (Zechariah 8:23)

It will be worth going through the four stages of the development of the terms *y*ᶜ*hudah* and *y*ᶜ*hudiy* in order to understand the evolution of the meaning of the word by the time of Jesus:

1. Judah. One of the twelve tribes.

This was the original meaning of *y*ᶜ*hudah* and *y*ᶜ*hudiy* [Genesis 49:8-10]. It seems at the beginning that the tribe of Judah was no more special than any of the other tribes, Moses giving Judah a blessing with the other eleven tribes, cf. Deuteronomy 33:7; although Genesis 49:10 has a prophecy to the effect that "the sceptre shall not depart from Judah, nor the ruler's staff from between his feet, until tribute comes to him; and the obedience of the peoples is his."[48] It was the choice of Saul as the first king of the twelve tribes, as a Benjaminite, [1 Samuel 9:1-2] which brought the kingdom of Judah into close geographical proximity with the royal house of Saul, the Benjamin tribal area adjacent to Judah.

After the failure of Saul came the promotion of David the Judean by the prophet Samuel as king over the twelve tribes [1 Samuel 16:1 ff], first at Hebron, [2 Samuel 2:11] and then at Jerusalem after conquering that city [2 Samuel 5;6]. Jerusalem became the "city of David" [2 Samuel 6:16], and David made it the religious and regal centre of his growing kingdom. The aggrandisement of the Davidic kingdom of Judah reached its height with David [2 Samuel 8:14]; but with David's death (c.970 BC)[49] and the accession of his son Solomon, the kingdom of the twelve tribes assumed all the pomp of a Near Eastern state, Solomon building both his own palace and a Temple in Jerusalem [1 Kings 7-8], with Solomon forcing the northern tribes into heavy labour. On Solomon's death, his son Rehoboam provoked a revolt of the northern tribes (c.951 BC), all except Judah and Benjamin breaking away [1 Kings 12:16] and forming what was known as Israel; the kingdom of the two tribes of Judah and Benjamin in the south being called Judah.

2. Judah. The Kingdom of Judah after the Schism [Isaiah 44:26, Jeremiah 23:6. Isaiah 3:8].

After the breakaway in the tenth century BC. of the ten Northern Tribes to form the kingdom of Israel, with its capital in Samaria, Judah turned into a kingdom comprising Jerusalem and its environs, with the land of the tribe of Benjamin more and more merged with it. The kingdom of Judah was focussed on Jerusalem, and on the promise to David of an everlasting dynasty by the prophet Nathan [2 Samuel 7]. The king in Jerusalem was the successor of David, the Messiah, the anointed of YHWH, his religious power symbolised by the Temple. "Your house and your kingdom shall be made sure forever before me; your throne shall be established forever" [2 Samuel 7:16].

In 721, the kingdom of the north was devastated by the Assyrian power, and its inhabitants carried off to Assyria [2 Kings 17:1-6]. Effectively, therefore, Judah was beginning to be identified with all the hopes of the people of God, Israel. The miraculous deliverance of Jerusalem from the Assyrian siege in 705 [2 Kings 19:35-37] further fuelled the Judeans' faith in the inviolability of the promise of Nathan to David. But this faith would be of no avail, Jeremiah the prophet told them, if they were unfaithful to God. God would make Jerusalem like Shiloh, the sanctuary which was destroyed by the Philistines in the days of Samuel [Jeremiah 7:12]. This is precisely what happened, first in 598 [2 Kings 24:10] and then in 587 [2 Kings 25:1], as successively the new Babylonian superpower conquered Judah, desecrated the Temple and carried off effectively the last King of Judah Zedekiah together with the flower of the people, the king of Babylon leaving "some of the poorest of the land to be vinedressers and ploughmen" [2 Kings 25:12].

3. The post-exilic Community [Nehemiah 4:4].

The kingdom of Judah was never again to rise as a political power as it was under David and Solomon. An over-simplification, but at least half of the truth, is the adage that "Judah went to Babylon a nation and came back a church". The Exile was a fruitful time religiously, where it is conjectured the first five books of the Bible, the Pentateuch, were put into shape, and Judah became more aware of its spiritual destiny. The unknown prophet, whose inspired encourage-ment found its way somehow or other into the book of Isaiah, as Isaiah 40-55, or "Deutero-Isaiah" told them that they would be returning home to rebuild their land. In 538 BC, the first group did return from Babylon, after Cyrus the Persian Emperor (seen by Deutero-Isaiah as the Messiah, the Anointed, Isaiah 45:1) walked into Babylon virtually unopposed. *y^ehudah* and *y^ehudiy* now therefore were the returning exiles, the renewed and reformed chosen of YHWH.

4. The province of an occupying power [Haggai 1:1,14. 2:21].

When the exiles returned home, they occupied a province of the Persian Empire. So far were they from the old empire of David and Solomon and its power. After the return from Exile, to the time of Christ, Judah never lost its occupied status. First the Persians, then the Hellenic forces of Alexander the Great (333 BC), then finally the Romans led by Pompei marched into Jerusalem and once more desecrated the Temple (64 BC). Judah politically was from then on merely the province of an occupying power with Jerusalem as its capital. Even though "Jew" became the title of an exiled Judean (and large numbers did immigrate, particularly to Alexandria in Egypt) "Judah" or "Judea" remained a geographical description of the province of Judah.

But it was more than a geographical description. Together with the geographical description grew also the vision of a redeemer and of a Messiah in the line of David. This theo-logical vision was in no way divorced from the geography. The geography was part of the theology, and the geography concretised the theology. The hope of all Jews was "For God will save Zion and rebuild the cities of Judah; and his servants shall live there and possess it" [Psalm 69:35]. The land of Judah, together with Jerusalem the city of the Messiah David, and together with the Temple on the hill of Zion, were the sum of the hopes of the first century AD Jew. "Jew" in this instance meaning a Jew living anywhere in the Roman Empire, but sharing in the hope of Judah the place.

Those waiting for a restored Zion

All this is a necessary background to understanding the meaning of *hoi Ioudaioi* in John. My contention is that the author of the Fourth Gospel is using *hoi Ioudaioi* as a precise description of a group of people at the time of Christ, who by the time he wrote his Gospel had lost their sacral focus, the Temple and its divinely ordained ritual.

The theological destiny of the Judeans is best of all expressed by Isaiah:

> The word that Isaiah son of Amoz saw concerning Judah and Jerusalem.
>
> In days to come the mountain of the Lord's house shall be established as the highest of the mountains, and shall be raised above the hills; all the nations shall stream to it.
>
> Many peoples shall come and say, "Come, let us go up to the mountain of the LORD, to the house of the God of Jacob; that he may teach us his ways and that we may walk in his paths." For out of Zion shall go forth instruction, and the word of the LORD from Jerusalem. [Isaiah 2:1-3]

I suggest that the key verse of the Fourth Gospel which explains *hoi Ioudaioi* is at first sight the odd one out, namely the words of Jesus to the Samaritan woman "salvation is from the Jews" [John 4:22]. Jesus is saying to her that it is from Judah and Jerusalem that salvation will come. Brown comments on this verse:

284

salvation is from the Jews. Cf. Ps lxxvi 1: "In Judah God is known." Bultmann would reduce this to a gloss since it does not fit in with Johannine hostility to "the Jews". However, the Jews against whom Jesus elsewhere speaks harshly really refers to that section of the Jewish people that is hostile to Jesus, and especially to their rulers. Here, speaking to a foreigner, Jesus gives to the Jews a different significance, and the term refers to the whole Jewish people. This line is a clear indication that the Johannine attitude to the Jews cloaks neither an anti-Semitism of the modern variety nor a view that rejects the spiritual heritage of Judaism.[50]

Brown's positive note is indeed welcome. But has the author of the Fourth Gospel changed from his usual use of the term *hoi Ioudaioi?* Our thesis would change the slant somewhat. Jesus is saying that salvation comes from the land of Judah and Jerusalem, and not from Samaria, and from its people there. Elsewhere in the Gospel, John is referring to people who live in Judah/Jerusalem, either the people or the Jerusalem authorities, and who by living there are given a special destiny as being in God's own Zion. These Judeans go up to Galilee, and go there to see what Jesus has to offer (6:41,52). They should, because as Judeans they have a special right to know who Jesus is.

When the Samaritan woman calls Jesus a Jew [John 4:9], she is not of course referring to Jesus living in Judah/Jerusalem. She is referring to his believing that the sacrifice pleasing to God is to be offered in Jerusalem. Jesus implicitly says that he is a Jew by saying "We speak what we know". Brown is surely right that the "we" [John 4:22] refers to Jesus speaking as a member of the Jewish religion.[51] This is quite legitimate as a meaning of *hoi Ioudaioi* when Jesus is speaking to those who are not members of the Jewish religion, or they are speaking to him. That same meaning is on the lips of Pilate as he retorts to Jesus "Am I a Jew?" [John 8:35]. This meaning of "Jew" would obviously be legitimate throughout the Roman Empire, as a member of that religion whose geographical and theological centre is in Jerusalem and in the Temple.

But when Jesus is speaking himself, or the evangelist is narrating in the Fourth Gospel, I suggest that *hoi Ioudaioi* means those with the privilege of living in the Jerusalem/Judah area, with its corresponding responsibility. In that sense, Jesus is not one of *hoi Ioudaioi* because he comes from "Galilee of the Gentiles". They have the responsibility of making sure that the Torah goes forth from Zion, and the Word of the Lord from Jerusalem. Such a subtle change of meaning within the Fourth Gospel is by no means impossible granted that, as we have seen, the terms *yehudah* and *yehudiy* had a complexity of meaning prior to the New Testament.

This proposed meaning, what we may call *theological/geographical*, explains why nearly all the references in John to *hoi Ioudaioi* are patient of a geographical meaning. Jesus went up to Jerusalem, to call the Judeans to fulfil their destiny, to be the agents of the Word of God under his, Jesus', leadership as the Light of the World. And that is the meaning of the dialogues with *hoi Ioudaioi* throughout the Fourth Gospel, and particularly in John 7-12. Far from being anti-Semitic, therefore, *hoi Ioudaioi* in John is used to make the last appeal to the Judeans before their Temple was destroyed and their geographical focus lost.[52]

This theory of the meaning of *hoi Ioudaioi* in John links up with what we have already seen of N.T. Wright's view of the mission and the ministry of Jesus as he sees it in the Synoptic Gospels. We saw in chapter 7 how Wright viewed Jesus' message as a challenge above all regarding those institutions most valuable to the Judeans, those in the theological and geographical centre of Judaism; Temple, Sabbath, Circumcision, Purity.[53] We quote Wright again. "As in Jeremiah's day, the Temple had become the focal point of the hope of national liberation, and hence was regarded as a guarantee of security against the pagans."[54] Jesus challenged this false sense of security among the Judeans, both the authorities and the people themselves. They were relying on things which were soon to pass away, especially their Temple.

What, then, were *hoi Ioudaioi* to rely upon, to fulfil their role of making sure that the word of the Lord went forth from

Zion? That is precisely what Jesus tells *hoi Ioudaioi* particularly in Chapters 5-12 of the Fourth Gospel.

Jesus' appeal to *hoi Ioudaioi*

Hoi Ioudaioi therefore are not the "symbolic representation of lack of faith" as Bultmann would claim. Nor are they the projection of the Johannine Community's frustration at being thrown out of the synagogue towards the end of the first century AD. They are the Jerusalem and Judean Jews to whom the historical Jesus made appeal to fulfil their destiny, and as a whole did not respond to that appeal. *Hoi Ioudaioi* as a group ended up shouting "crucify him, crucify him" [John 19:12-16].

As James D.G. Dunn says perceptively, "John's language is more the language of *intra*-Jewish polemic than of *anti*-Jewish polemic". Furthermore, we would freely admit with Dunn that, by the close of the first century AD, the emerging Christianity was increasingly alienating itself from a Judaism moving towards its post-Jamnia self-identification. As he says:

> Rather, it would be closer to historical reality to think of the situation presupposed in John's Gospel as reflecting the approaching breakdown of "ecumenical relations" between the two main bodies within post-Second Temple Judaism, the late phase of a forthright dialogue that was coming close to failure and not to be fully resumed until the Jewish-Christian dialogue of the twentieth century.[55]

That John's Gospel reflected the historical situation at the time when it was written need not be denied. Indeed, it would be strange if it did not. John is appealing to his contemporary fellow-Jews to follow Jesus the Light of the World. Again, Dunn, "John still hoped to persuade the doubters and waverers to stand with the believers, still mostly fellow Jews, in Messiah Jesus."[56] What we would deny is that, in order to make this appeal, John was creating a fictional story about what happened during the lifetime of the historical Jesus. Rather, he was describing what actually happened, even if in dramatic form, during the last days in Jerusalem of the life of the historical Jesus, of how Jesus' own people rejected his claims and his call to them to fulfil their destiny.

That was nothing new in Jewish history for God's own people not to listen; nor indeed in the history of the Catholic church, and of other Christian denominations, as generations of mission preachers will testify. Jesus said to *hoi Ioudaioi* "You are from your father the devil, and you choose to do your father's desires" [John 8:44]. That is because they were plotting to kill him; just as, John says, the devil entered into the heart of Judas Iscariot to betray Jesus [John 13:2]. But Jesus was following in a good prophetic tradition. Amos called the women of Samaria "cows of Bashan" [Amos 4:1]. Ezekiel likened the two kingdoms of God's people Israel and Judah to two whores thrusting their lewd bodies at the idolatrous nations [Ezekiel 23]. Jeremiah called Judah the unfaithful and wild vine [Jeremiah 2:21]. Jesus, and John in reporting what Jesus said, was no more anti-Semitic than Amos, Jeremiah or Ezekiel. Likewise, the Synoptic tradition has Jesus likening his own rejection to that of the prophets before him [Luke 11:49]; and indeed the Parable of the Wicked Husbandmen, as we have seen above.[57] All that we know concerning the historical Jesus is consistent with him speaking roughly to God's people, but all in the authentic prophetical tradition.

We would not deny, of course, that historical circumstances intensified John's dramatic presentation of his account of the conflict between Jesus and the *Ioudaioi*. There could hardly be any doubt that Christians, whether Jewish or Gentile, were more clearly defined *over against* Rabbinic Judaism after the destruction of the Temple in 70 AD, and that for its part, Judaism further defined its position over against Christianity. All this no doubt affected the Fourth Gospel's mode of address in a developing situation of polemic. Our contention in this chapter has been simply that the Fourth Gospel writer did not invent words and deeds of Jesus in order to score points in this polemic.

But, when Jesus' hour comes, his disciples are not much better either. At these moments also, the disciples manifest their incomprehension: Peter, 13:6, 10:36-38, Thomas and Philip (14:5-10). No one really understands who Jesus is. As Caron puts it superbly:

> Johannine misunderstanding [*Le "malentendu Johannique"*] is therefore not something fortuitous. On the contrary, it gives over the *inevitable* reaction of the human being before the extraordinary revelation which Jesus brings; it reveals essentially the human incapacity to grasp the profound mystery of the person of Jesus. As we have already affirmed many times over, it is this "incapacity" which leads to the elevation of Jesus on the cross. [cf. 12:31-32][58]

That even applies to those such as the disciples who have made an act of faith earlier in Jesus, in Chapter 6, the Second Passover. Caron here has grasped the essence of John's idea about revelation before the crucifixion and death of Jesus. Some have faith, but even that faith is limited, and awaits its full achievement after the Resurrection, with Thomas' "My Lord and My God" [John 20:28]. The disciples show incomprehension. And, on the other hand, some of *hoi Ioudaioi* it is said were going away from the chief priests and believing in Jesus [John 12:11]. We find also that there were *hoi Ioudaioi* with Mary, weeping 11:33. And, as we have already noted, Nicodemus makes a spirited defence of Jesus [John 7:51-53], and eventually after Jesus' death provides a tomb for his burial [John 19:39].

Hope of salvation for all

Thus Jesus was left with the Jewish authorities plotting his death, with *hoi Ioudaioi* eventually shouting for his crucifixion, and with a group of uncomprehending disciples. What happened can only be understood after the Resurrection. As the Fourth Evangelist puts into the mouth of Jesus, addressing *hoi Ioudaioi*:

> So Jesus said, "When you have lifted up the Son of Man, then you will realise that I am he, and that I do nothing

289

on my own, but I speak these things as the Father instructed. [John 8:28]

For Caron, this comprises two affirmations:

- The responsibility of *hoi Ioudaioi* for the raising up, i.e. the crucifixion of Jesus.
- The knowledge of the true identity of Jesus which follows from this action, as I AM.[59]

Caron therefore sees salvation as well as judgement in Jesus' dialogues with *hoi Ioudaioi:*

> Paradoxical as it may seem, there is a judgement here in view of salvation (*zum Heil*), the judgement which Jesus pronounces concerning the "Jews" in the narrative is an integral part of his mission of salvation. Once the salvific project of God is achieved in the exaltation of Jesus, it belongs from then on for humanity to accept or to refuse this ultimate manifestation of the love of the Father. In this sense, there will be a "second chance" for the Jews. *Pace* R. Fortna for whom "The Jews" "stand outside salvation."[60]

After the Resurrection, the Acts of the Apostles presents this not even as a "second chance" but as in a sense the first real chance of faith for Jesus' own people. Peter addresses *hoi Ioudaioi:*

> Men of Judea and all who live in Jerusalem [Acts 2:14], let this be known to you, and listen to what I say [Acts 2:23]. This man, handed over to you according to the definite plan and foreknowledge of God, you crucified and killed by the hands of those outside the law [Acts 2:24]. But God raised him up, having freed him from death, because it was impossible for him to be held in its power. [Acts 2:23-24]

We quote the Second Vatican Council:

> Although the Jewish authorities with their followers pressed for the death of Christ, [John 19:6] still those

things which were perpetrated during his passion cannot be ascribed indiscriminately to all the Jews living at the time nor to the Jews of today. Although the church is the new people of God, the Jews should not be represented as rejected by God or accursed, as if that follows from Holy Scripture. All should therefore take care that in holding religious instruction and preaching the word of God, they teach nothing which is not in keeping with the truth of the gospel and the spirit of Christ.

Moreover, the church, which condemns all persecutions against any people, mindful of its common inheritance with the Jews and motivated not by political considerations but by the religious charity of the gospel, deplores feelings of hatred, persecutions and demonstrations of anti-Semitism directed against the Jews at whatever time and by whomsoever.[61]

The author of the Fourth Gospel would totally agree with those sentiments. Regarding the Jewish authorities who arrested Jesus and handed him over to Pilate, there is no need to doubt their good intentions. Jesus himself warned his disciples "They will put you out of the synagogues. Indeed, an hour is coming when those who kill you will think that by doing so they are offering worship to God" [John 16:2]. Jesus is referring to a time when his followers will be cast out of the synagogues, which the Evangelist sees as fulfilled in his own day.[62] But these words rebound on Jesus' own historical situation. The Jerusalem authorities genuinely thought that Jesus was blaspheming in claiming equality with God. They, like Paul himself later, equally genuinely believed that they were doing God's work in putting the blasphemer to death.

For Jesus himself, it was obvious beforehand that, if he did clearly proclaim his divinity in the Temple courtyard, his own death would follow. This more than adequately would explain his foreboding expressed eloquently in the Synoptic Gospels regarding his final going up to Jerusalem. "From that time on, Jesus began to show his disciples that he must go to Jerusalem and undergo great suffering at the hands of the elders and chief priests and scribes, and be killed, and on the third day be raised" [Matthew 16:21]. It was not suicide, but was rather the awareness of inevitable death.[63] In the same way, a soldier in the first wave of an attack will know that his chances of survival are less than ten percent. He will most likely die for the success of the whole enterprise. He does not will to die, he hopes against hope to survive. But as a realist, he knows that he will most likely die.

So in the same way, Jesus knew that he would be arrested, tried and put to death. In this, he hardly needed supernatural knowledge of his fate. But he knew that his death was to bring about the new Temple of which he spoke; and this made his apparent cry of despair on the cross, "My God, my God, why have you forsaken me?" [Psalm 22:1] contain an implicit hope, which is expressed by the very last verses of that selfsame Psalm: "I will tell of your name to my brothers and sisters; in the midst of the congregation I will praise you" [Psalm 22:22].

hoi Ioudaioi: conclusion

We may therefore conclude with a summary of our findings from the investigation in this chapter and in the previous chapter.

The Fourth Gospel is reliable historically in recounting that:

- The Jewish authorities handed over Jesus to Pilate for his crucifixion.
- They did this because they considered him a blasphemer, and so worthy of death.
- They thought him a blasphemer because he claimed to be equal with God.
- Matters came to a head when Jesus came to Jerusalem for what was for him a final Passover, and summoned *hoi Iudaioi*, that is those who lived in Jerusalem and Judea, to fulfil their destiny by accepting him as divine Son of God.

For the author of the Fourth Gospel, the tragedy was that *hoi Ioudaioi* rejected that destiny, and handed over Jesus to Pilate. But, for him also, that offer of Jesus was still open after his Resurrection, to his own people.

NOTES – CHAPTER 15

1   Bieringer, R. *et al*, ed., entitle their recent symposium 2001, *Anti-Judaism and the Fourth Gospel*, London Westminster, John Knox Press. This acknowledges the difficulty of using the term "anti-Semitic" of a work, the Fourth Gospel, which recent scholarship has so affirmed is itself fundamentally Jewish.

2   Evans, A.E. and Hagner, D.A., ed. *Anti-Semitism and Early Christianity, Issues of Polemic and Faith*, Fortress Press, 1993, 126.

3   Casey, M., *Is John's Gospel True?* Routledge, London and New York, 1996, 229.

4   Bieringer, op.cit. 119.

5   Bieringer, op.cit. 120.

6   Ibid.

7   Bieringer, op.cit. 122.

8   Cf. pp. 175-6. CJH, 28.

9   RNT, 273.

10   Cf. pp. 121-3.

11   Cf. p. 140 for all the relevant texts in Mark.

12   Cf. pp. 114-8.

13   Cf. p. 116.

14   Cf. p. 116.

15   Cf. pp. 144-7.

16   Cf. p. 141.

17   Bruce, 1983, 6.

18   *hupéretés* an under rower; hence, generally, a servant, attendant minister; of a magistrate's attendant, Matthew 5:25; of officers of the Synagogue or Sanhedrin, Matthew 26:58…etc. AS 461.

19   Blomberg, C.L., *The Historical Reliability of John's Gospel*, Leicester, Inter Varsity Press, 136. Blomberg argues to the historical credibility of John 7:14-36.

20   Schnackenburg, II, 159.

21   Cf. p. 246.

22   Cf. p. 247.

23   Brown, I, 429. MJII, 831.

24 Cf. p. 116.

25 Cf. p. 115.

26 Cf. chapter 8.

27 Blomberg, op.cit. 164 XXX 10:22-42 states: "Jesus' teaching during Hanukkah aptly satisfies the double similarity and dissimilarity crierion."

28 JUIF.

29 Brown, I, LXXI.

30 JUIF, 23. *Pour la très grande majorité des commentateurs d'aujourd'hui comme d'hier, cette expression désigne les* autorités juives *(hostile à Jésus).*

31 JUIF, 23.

32 JUIF, 31.

33 JUIF, 32.

34 JUIF, 34, n.47.

35 UFG, 133-4.

36 JUIF, 35. *Selon Bultmann, le "dualisme cosmologique de la Gnose s'est transformé chez Jean en un "dualism de décision". (Entscheidung Dualismus).*

37 JUIF, 38.

38 JUIF, 39.

39 JUIF, 39.

40 JUIF, 41.

41 JUIF, 45. *C'est d'abord et avant tout ce rôle narratif qui va définir ou identifier les Juifs johanniques.*

42 JUIF, 42.

43 Issued together with *Encyclopaedia Britannica* Multimedia Edition, CD98, Chicago, Ilinois. 1997.

44 LVT, 298.

45 Cf. LVT *ad loc* for more references in each of the categories.

46 NJBC, **23:105**, 394. Perhaps Zorell is not quite accurate in describing *yᵉhudah* here as a 'member of the post-Exilic community' in Nehemiah 4:10 (=4.4.in MT). In any case, the usual word for "Judean" the person is *yᵉhudiy.*

47 Has *'ish yᵉhudiy,* "man of Judah" also a geographical as well as a religious meaning? Perhaps *'ish yᵉhudiy* also refers to the Diaspora Jews, cf. NJBC, **22:36**, 356. "People will come from all the earth to Jerusalem because God is there. The Jews who are establishing a Jewish presence in the Diaspora have a special role to play in this."

48 Cf. NJBC, **2:72**, 42.

49 ODCC, 377.

50 Brown, I, 172.

51 Brown, I, 172, correctly says that Bultmann, p.1396 in taking the "we" to be the Christians as opposed to both Samaritans and Jews, "does not take seriously the historical setting given to the episode".

52 Cf. p. 128.

53 Ibid.

54　JVG, 420.

55　Bieringer ed., 2001, 53.

56　Bieringer ed., 2001, 52.

57　Cf. p. 130f, 262-3.

58　JUIF, 212.

59　JUIF, 190.

60　JUIF, 118. *En ce sens, il y aura une seconde chance pour les "Juifs".* 118, n.115. *Pace* R. Fortna *pour qui les "Juifs" "stand outside salvation".*

61　Tanner, II, *970-*1 No.4, Decree on non-Christian Religions *Nostra Aetate.*

62　Moloney, 434, correctly, "The Johannine community has experienced expulsion from the synagogue, however local that conflict and expulsion may have been (cf. Introduction). There is no need to link this expulsion with the *birkat ha-minim.*"

63　The scholastics had the adage "Everything which is in the intellect is not in the will." A soldier leading an attack does not *want* to die, and so it is not suicide. But he *knows* that most likely he will be killed, and accepts that inevitability.

CHAPTER 16

THE RESURRECTION: AN HISTORICAL EVENT

> We submit that the tomb of Jesus was discovered empty on the first day of the week following Jesus' death, and that he appeared bodily to his apostles and to a chosen number of his followers to prove to them and to us that he was truly risen and that his claims to be God while on earth were finally vindicated.

"It is the Lord"

"It is the Lord!" [John 21:7] encapsulates not only the surprise and the wonder but also the relief of the disciples on recognising Jesus as risen from the dead, *and recognising him as Lord.* It was to become the touchstone of Christian faith. As Paul said to the Corinthian Christians in AD 57, "If Christ has not been raised, your faith is futile" [1 Corinthians 15:17].

Ignatius of Antioch expresses the early tradition of the Church, writing as he does c.110 AD, not long after the Gospels were written,[1] and on his way to martyrdom:

> For my own part, I know and believe that he [Jesus] was in actual human flesh, even after his resurrection. When he appeared to Peter and his companions, he said to them, "Take hold of me; touch me, and see that I am no bodiless phantom". And they touched him then and there, and believed, for they had had contact with the flesh-and-blood reality of him. That was how they came by their contempt for death, and proved themselves superior to it. Moreover, he ate and drank with them after he was risen, like any natural man, though even then he and the Father were spiritually one.[2]

The testimony of Ignatius is amazingly explicit and "physical", right at the beginning of the Christian era, less than one hundred years after the death and resurrection of Christ. It may well be that his target is "a Judaizing heresy with Docetic elements,"[3] against whom he wrote in his letters, and whom he perhaps feared might have a disintegrating influence on the Christian's firm belief in the Resurrection of the body of Jesus. Ignatius is most likely referring to Luke 24, where Jesus appears to his stupefied disciples and says:

> "Look at my hands and my feet; see that it is I myself. Touch me and see; for a ghost does not have flesh and bones as you see that I have." And when he had said this, he showed them his hands and his feet. While in their joy they were disbelieving and still wondering, he said to them, "Have you anything here to eat?" They gave him a piece of broiled fish, and he took it and ate in their presence. [Luke 24:39-42]

Unless he depended on early traditions of the Resurrection no longer available to us, Ignatius would also have had in mind the account in the Fourth Gospel, where the disciples see the risen Jesus on the shore actually cooking breakfast [John 21:9], and he invites them to bring them the fish they have caught, for him to cook [John 21:12-13]. Above all, there is the famous incident where Jesus appears through closed doors, and Doubting Thomas is invited by the Lord to "Put your finger here and see my hands. Reach out your hand and put it in my side. Do not doubt but believe"[4] [John 20:27].

Jesus actually died

He died on the cross on the first Good Friday, and he was buried in a sealed tomb.

It goes without saying that the early Questers of the late eighteenth and early nineteenth century did not accept that Jesus had actually risen from the dead. It was against all their Enlightenment principles. For Reimarus, after the death of Jesus, the disciples "did not take kindly to the idea of returning to their old haunts; on their journeyings the companions of the Messiah had forgotten how to work... So they stole the body of Jesus and hid it, and proclaimed to all the world that He would soon return."[5] Reimarus' account is hardly original. Eighteen centuries previously, according to the account of the discovery of the empty tomb in Matthew 28:11-15, the guards had told that same story, to the authorities disturbed by the disappearance of the body of the prophet they had crucified only three days previously.

Paulus, the prince of rationalists, had a more intriguing and imaginative explanation for the Resurrection, true to his principles of taking the Gospels at their word as historical descriptions, but explaining them rationally.[6] For him, Jesus never actually died. In fact, "the lance thrust [John 19:32], which we are to think of rather as a mere surface wound, serves the purpose of a phlebotomy."[7] Awoken by the earthquake which moved the stone to open the mouth of the grave, Jesus emerged and disguised himself as a gardener, deceiving Mary Magdalene [John 20:15], and appeared to his astonished disciples alive in Jerusalem.

> In this way Jesus lived with them for forty days, spending part of that time with them in Galilee. In consequence of the ill-treatment which He had undergone, He was not capable of continuous exertion. He lived quietly and gathered strength for the brief moments in which He appeared among His own followers and taught them. When He felt his end drawing near He returned to Jerusalem. On the Mount of Olive, in the early sunlight, He assembled His followers for the last time. He lifted up His hands to bless them, and with hands still raised in benediction He moved away from them. A cloud interposes itself between them and Him, so that their eyes cannot follow Him. As he disappeared there stood before them, clothed in white; the two dignified figures whom the three disciples who were present at the transfiguration had taken for Moses and Elias, but who were really among the secret adherents of Jesus in Jerusalem. These men exhorted them not to stand waiting there but to be up and doing.

> Where Jesus really died they never knew, and so they came to describe His departure as an ascension.[8]

This far back from the events, of course, it is impossible to verify medically that Jesus actually died, or, against Reimarus, that the disciples did not steal the body. To prove either case, we would either have to have some evidence that Jesus was still alive after the Resurrection, presumably dying some time afterwards; or we would have to find the body of Jesus and then prove that it had been stolen and removed. Neither evidence is forthcoming, or, two thousand years later, likely to be. All we can say is that, firstly, regarding the death of Jesus, Paul communicates the solemn testimony of all Christian tradition that Jesus did actually die and was buried [1 Corinthians 15:3-4]. Granted the fact of his crucifixion preceded by his scourging, it is hardly difficult to believe that he did. We have also the testimony of the soldier at the crucifixion that Jesus was actually dead [John 19:33]. It is surely significant that no one either in Jewish or Roman tradition ever questioned that Jesus died.

There is at first sight at least some biblical evidence of the explanation that the disciples stole the body of Jesus. According to Matthew's account, this was the story told by officialdom to explain the Resurrection:

> While they were going, some of the guard went into the city and told the chief priests everything that had happened. After the priests had assembled with the elders, they devised a plan to give a large sum of money to the soldiers, telling them, "You must say, 'His disciples came by night and stole him away while we were asleep.' If this comes to the governor's ears, we will satisfy him and keep you out of trouble." So they took the money and did as they were directed. And this story is still told among the Jews to this day. [Matthew 28:11-15]

As with so much of the Gospels, this appears to be a straight account of what actually happened, especially that final "And this story is still told among the Jews to this day." Certainly, it could be true. St Matthew's Gospel was written at the latest towards the close of the first century, and quite possibly earlier. Such information would certainly have been to hand only two generations after the death of Jesus.[9] It is certainly credible that this was the story told to counter the Christian account of the Resurrection.[10] The critical view that it was an apologetic fiction is purely gratuitous.

But even if we ignore for the moment Matthew's account that Jesus' body was stolen, the fact of the death and burial of Jesus can be stated surely as a "critical minimum". If the body had been stolen or Jesus had not really died, how was the faith of Christians so unanimous that Jesus had actually died and risen again? Would not doubts have entered in from some who actually knew the facts? Could such a secret, that Jesus had not really died, or that his body had been stolen, have been concealed for long? We can take it as reasonably verified, therefore, that at least what Paul said in 1 Corinthians 15:3-4 is correct, that Jesus genuinely died and was buried.

But we could say even more as a "critical minimum", even if New Testament scholars are not completely unanimous. There is a substantial number of scholars who accept the historical reliability of the story that Jesus' tomb was found empty on that first Easter morning.

The tomb was found empty on the first Easter morning

The discovery by the women that the stone had been rolled away from the tomb of Jesus, and that the body of Jesus was no longer there, is in all four accounts (Mark 16:1-8, Matthew 28:1-8, Luke 24:1-12, John 20:1-10), though there are variations in detail. Particularly significant is the fact that Mark's Gospel, if we accept that it ended at 16:8 and that there was no "lost ending" which we do not have, has the account of the discovery of the empty tomb, even if there is no account of the appearance of the risen Jesus except in 16:9-20, which is generally viewed as not originally part of the canonical Gospel.[11]

It is a valid conclusion of modern scholarship that complete harmonisation of the accounts of the discovery of the empty tomb is impossible. For instance. even the most ingenious of historical reconcilers will find it difficult to account for the fact that Mark's single "young man in a white robe seated on the right hand side" of the tomb (Mark 16:5) has suddenly acquired a partner in Luke's version of the same incident, where "two men in dazzling clothes stood beside them" (Luke 24:4). Not only was the experience itself of seeing the tomb empty or seeing the risen Jesus a traumatic one, making recounting of that experience most difficult; but it also seems clear that interpretative details were added in the telling of the Resurrection stories during the thirty years and more between the event and the compiling of the four Gospels. The reader will note that we have never tried to demonstrate in any part of this book any more than the *substantial* historicity of any part of the Gospels, not its *absolute* historicity.

Can we therefore validate as authentic an essential core of the story of the discovery of the empty tomb, even if we assume that some of the details of that story in the four evangelists cannot be verified? The core of the common tradition would be simply that early on the Sunday morning after the Friday of Jesus' burial, a woman Mary Magdalene (according to John 20:1), or possibly several women (Mark 16:1 has "Mary Magdalene, and Mary the mother of James, and Salome") came to the tomb where Jesus was buried, found the stone rolled away, and the body of Jesus gone.[12] Whence came this tradition?[13]

Some scholars link the story of the empty tomb with the practice common in the first century of building tombs to venerate famous prophets. This forms the background to Jesus' words in Luke 11:47, "You build the tombs of the prophets whom your ancestors killed". It is therefore possible from very early on, perhaps even by Paul's day, that the tomb of Jesus was venerated by Christians visiting Jerusalem.

But can we explain the genesis of the story of the empty tomb in this way? Schillebeeckx does, claiming that "The initial story of the women's going to Jesus' tomb on Easter morning is an aetiological cult-legend, which is to say that this story is intended to shed light on the (at least) annual visit of the Jerusalem church to the tomb in order to honour the risen One there and to listen to the tale still recognisable

301

in the pre-Marcan tradition behind Mark 16:1-8." For Schillebeeckx, we can go back no further than this to discover any event underlying the story.[14]

Léon-Dufour's position is similar to that of Schillebeeckx, namely that "What we have here is a community imagining itself in immediate proximity to the tomb, and the narrative must be read in that sense. This is the meaning of the surprising interest in the location. It is not a question of demonstrating the reality of the resurrection by the fact that the body is not there." In fact, Léon-Dufour's position is even more sceptical than Schillebeeckx's, because "it is not necessary to suppose that there really was an annual gathering at the tomb of Christ – it is difficult to prove the existence of such a pilgrimage. We only have to think of Sunday worship, with the purpose of calling to mind how God, in Jesus Christ, conquered Sheol and death. The open tomb is the place where the victory of God over death is apprehended."[15]

J. Kremer[16] and G.O. Collins[17] however, argue strongly that the story in Mark 16:1-8, which they see as the earliest narrative of the empty tomb discovery, is based upon an event, whatever dramatic expansions have been added by Mark himself, or later by Luke and Matthew in their version. The early Christians venerated not just the tomb of Jesus, therefore, but *the tomb of Jesus which was discovered empty on that first Easter Day*. As O'Collins argues convincingly:

> Crucial to any evaluation of the historical reliability of the empty tomb tradition is the place of a woman or women in the story. Surprisingly women enjoy a witness function in both the passion and resurrection narratives (Mark 15:40, 47; 16:1). By seeing where Jesus was laid, they could testify both to the fact of his burial and the location of his grave. Subsequently they discover that grave to be empty. If this discovery story were simply a legend created by early Christians, it remains difficult to explain why women find a place in the story. In Jewish society they did not count as valid witnesses. For legend-makers the natural thing would have been to have pictured Peter and other (male) disciples as having found the

tomb empty. But in the oldest tradition the disciples have nothing to do with Jesus's crucifixion, burial and the discovery of the empty tomb. The role of women in the story provides a sound argument for its historical reliability.

It can also be argued that at least in Jerusalem itself the preaching of Christ's resurrection would not have lasted five minutes, if friend or foe could have produced his body from the tomb outside the city. This would have effectively silenced the apostolic proclamation that God had raised Jesus from the dead. Finally, Jewish polemic against the resurrection supposed that the tomb was known and was empty. Various counter-explanations were offered: the disciples had stolen the body; a gardener had removed it. But the opponents agreed with the Christians on the basic fact that the body was gone.[18]

Brown argues similarly, that Fuller's contention that the empty tomb story arose as an explanation for the statement by Paul that Jesus was "raised on the third day" [1 Corinthians 15:4] also collapses for the same reason, as to why women should be narrated as the witnesses.[19] Brown concludes, "In summary, the Christian claim that the women found the tomb empty has not really been proved to be of late origin; rather such a claim may have been presupposed as far back as we can trace the tradition of the proclamation that Jesus had been raised."[20]

For the same reason, O'Collins contends, we cannot invoke St Paul as in any way presenting a counter-tradition to the narration of the discovery of the empty tomb. St Paul testifies to the death, burial, and resurrection of Jesus:

For I handed on to you as of first importance what I in turn had received: that Christ died for our sins in accordance with the scriptures, and that he was buried, and that he was raised on the third day in accordance with the scriptures, and that he appeared to Cephas, then to the twelve. [1 Corinthians 15:3-5]

How could Paul as a Jew believe that Jesus had truly risen from the dead if he had thought that his body was still there?

303

As O'Collins states, "His (Paul's) account of the risen body would be ruled out, if Jesus' corpse had still been in the grave. He maintains a reversal of death and entombment, a *transformation* of our mortal bodies, not the (creation and) *substitution* of brand-new risen bodies. For Paul to assert that God has raised Jesus from the dead necessarily implies a passage from the tomb – however difficult it may be to imagine such."[21]

So, the story that women found the tomb of Jesus empty on that first Easter morning should be acceptable as a critical minimum. But what does the discovery of the empty tomb prove?

The empty tomb as proof of Resurrection?

In itself, the discovery of an empty tomb or an empty grave proves little. One might say that it is negative evidence. According to Matthew 28:11-15, the authorities were quite prepared to accept that the body of Jesus was no longer there on Easter morning. But according to Matthew, they spread the story around that the body had been stolen.

A way in which this question is frequently framed is "If the bones of Jesus of Nazareth were discovered in Jerusalem today, would your faith remain the same in the Resurrection?"[22] For L. Evely, the answer would be that for him, his faith would be no different whatsoever if the corpse of Jesus were still in the tomb.[23] Similarly, Léon-Dufour considers that it is mistaken for the historian, qua historian, to try to ascertain where the body of Jesus went:

> Can the historian go a step further and state that the body of Jesus was taken out of the universe, or, within the perspective of faith, 'taken on' by the risen Christ? No, for a reply to this question is not his affair. The historical fact is that the body of Jesus was not there; nothing can be said about where it was, nor about its sudden 'disappearance'. Whatever hypothesis is envisaged to take account of the historical fact, the historian must

stand back and deny any competence to state what became of the body; he can say neither that it was lifted up in to heaven, nor that it was to be found in the tomb. These two interpretations are an attempt to give, to questions left unanswered by historical study, answers based on philosophical or dogmatic assumptions, whereas at the present stage of our inquiry, we are attempting only to establish the reality of historical facts.[24]

Thus, clearly for Léon-Dufour, the discovery of the empty tomb proves nothing historically one way or the other:

To attempt to prove faith in the resurrection. To reason as follows: 'He is risen, because he is not here'. The first Christians did not establish any intrinsic link between the empty tomb and faith in the living Christ; they reflected upon their faith and recalled that the tomb had been found empty. The empty tomb is not even a secondary basis for faith in the resurrection.[25]

On the contrary, however, the Catechism of the Catholic Church does call the Resurrection "an historical event" (CCC 643). We cannot consider this question fully until we discuss the nature of the Resurrection appearances of the risen Lord. The crucial question at this point is; is what happened to the corpse of Jesus important? Obviously, for those such as Evely and Léon-Dufour, Jesus could have died on Good Friday afternoon, been buried in the tomb, and corrupted there, or his corpse could have been moved. But Jesus would still have risen from the dead. In such a case, therefore, the tradition that the tomb of Jesus was found empty is reliable. But, one might say, in God's providence, this story was allowed as a necessary instrument to create faith in the first-century Christians, because they would not have believed that Jesus was risen from the dead unless they had actually thought that his body was no longer there. For us, it might be argued, with our superior scientific knowledge, we do not need such a story of an empty tomb, except as a symbol of the Resurrection.

In actual fact, the matter of our bodies changes regularly. Can we therefore make a distinction between our bodies and the matter of our bodies? Could one say that the matter of the body, the corpse, of Jesus, stayed in the tomb, while his actual body went up to heaven?

Some like Lampe have argued that in order for Jesus' incarnation to be like ours, he had to share not only in a death but also in a resurrection like ours. Our bodies corrupt in the tomb, while we wait for the General Resurrection. Why should not Jesus undergo the same experience?[26]

Firstly, the distinction between our bodies and the matter of our bodies just makes no sense. While the matter of our bodies changes, there is no such being as "my body" without some matter; just as there is no such thing as "my car" without its parts, even if over ten years it changes many of its parts. Our bodies share in the destructibility and changeability of material reality. Therefore, it is unintelligible (one hesitates to say "nonsense") to suppose that the "body" of Jesus went up to heaven without at least some of its "matter" being involved. And if some of its matter was involved, then why not all of it?

O'Collins sees in all attempts to eliminate the importance of the empty tomb as a crypto-Platonism, the denigration of matter in favour of the spiritual, which Platonism, O'Collins asserts, "may be hardier than we suspect"[27]:

> Acknowledgement of the empty tomb guards us from the constant temptation to let our interpretation of Christ become docetic. Too easily we can play down the bodily reality of the risen Christ, portray the resurrection as some kind of liberation of a 'spiritual' Christ and treat the physical world as illusory and incapable (or at least unworthy) of salvation. It is hardly a coincidence that Rudolf Bultmann's demythologised view of the resurrection both omits the empty tomb and goes hand in hand with an existentialist theology which fails to do justice to man's physical and social nature.

> For a proper appreciation and appraisal of the empty tomb it is important to hold two complementary affirmations before our attention. This doctrine asserts something about God as Redeemer, as well as something

about our material world. On the one hand, God intends to save the whole man and the world. He begins to transform the world and redeem human history by raising up Jesus' dead body. On the other hand, the world is neither an illusion from which we must awake nor an evil which will prove irredeemable. God shows this by beginning his work of re-creation in favour of Jesus's crucified body. The past can be recovered as raw material for the future kingdom. As we shall argue there is an identity-in-transformation between the earthly and the risen Jesus.[28]

O'Collins makes a crucial point here concerning the transformation of our bodies in the Resurrection of Christ. The Resurrection of the Body means that the whole of reality, material and spiritual, has been taken up in Christ. Therefore the whole Christ had to rise, which means that there could be nothing left there in the tomb. Hence, the absence of the corpse of Jesus was necessary for there to be a true Resurrection of Jesus; and therefore we would not have faith in his Resurrection if his tomb had contained his corpse.

In response to Lampe, Christian faith affirms not only the full humanity but the full divinity of Christ. He is thus different to us because he is God the Son, as well as one with us as man. Upon our death, our bodies can return to the earth from which they came, and await the final Resurrection of the Body. They will rise only at the last day, according to traditional Christian theology, because Christ calls them to life [John 5:25]; "Very truly, I tell you, the hour is coming, and is now here, when the dead will hear the voice of the Son of God, and those who hear will live." In classical theology, it is said that Christ's resurrection is the cause of our resurrection, precisely because he is God become man.[29]

A final word on the empty tomb from the *Catechism of the Catholic Church* will be useful at this point:

CCC 640 "Why do you seek the living among the dead? He is not here, but has risen."[30] The first element we encounter in the framework of the Easter events is the empty tomb. In itself it is not a direct proof of Resurrection; the absence of Christ's body from the tomb could be explained otherwise.[31] Nonetheless the empty tomb was still an essential sign for all. Its discovery by the disciples was the first step toward recognising the very fact of the Resurrection. This was the case, first with the holy women, and then with Peter.[32] The disciple "whom Jesus loved" affirmed that when he entered the empty tomb and discovered "the linen cloths lying there," "he saw and believed."[33] This suggests that he realised from the empty tomb's condition that the absence of Jesus' body could not have been of human doing and that Jesus had not simply returned to earthly life as had been the case with Lazarus.[34]

The risen Jesus really appeared bodily

Post-Bultmannian criticism would claim that the appearances of the risen Jesus became more and more "physical" the more the primitive Christian community reflected upon its tradition. Thus the legend grew the more the community's faith itself developed. The methodology follows the "critically orthodox" chronology of:

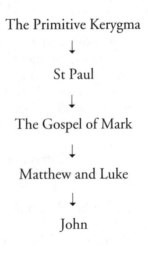

The Primitive Kerygma

↓

St Paul

↓

The Gospel of Mark

↓

Matthew and Luke

↓

John

Each of these stages, for some critical scholars,[35] would represent a process of the "physicalisation" of the Resurrection:

1. **The Primitive Kerygma**. Christ is risen! AD 40.

Using the method outlined above, some scholars would begin by trying to ascertain what the primitive kerygma stated concerning the Resurrection. In the speeches of Acts, there is no account of the discovery of the empty tomb, but a simple statement that "God raised this man Jesus to life, and all of us are witnesses to that" [Acts 2:32]. There is no explicit statement that Jesus appeared in bodily form to the disciples.

2. **St Paul**. An "Inward" Experience. AD 57.

1 Corinthians 15 is our first clear witness in written form to the Resurrection (AD 57), Paul says that "Christ died for our sins, in accordance with the scriptures, that he was buried." [1 Corinthians 15:4]; but, as we have seen, he does not mention that the tomb was found empty. Similarly, he mentions the fact that the risen Christ "appeared" to Cephas (Peter) and secondly to the Twelve, then to "more than five hundred of the brothers…" finally to Paul himself. The word which Paul uses throughout, with reference to the appearances to the others, and to himself, is *óphthé* [1 Corinthians 15:5,8].

The account of the appearance to Paul, as recounted in the Acts of the Apostles [9:1-9, 22:5-16, 26:10-18], does not mention that Paul had any bodily vision of Christ, only that he saw a light from heaven [Acts 9:4] and heard a voice speaking to him [Acts 9:4-6]. Was the appearance to the first witnesses of the Resurrection of this type, therefore, what we might call a non-pictorial religious experience, when one is particularly conscious of the presence of God? This would, of course, remove the "supernatural" in the accounts, of the discovery of the empty tomb with the angelic presence [Matthew 28:3], "His face was like lightning, his robe white as snow". More important still in this connection is that neither would we have the embarrassment of having to believe that Jesus came apparently through closed doors to see the disciples in the upper room [John 20:19], thereby seeming to compete with the best heroes of modern science fiction.

3. Mark's Gospel. The Empty Tomb Alone. AD 64.

Mark is quite perfunctory, particularly if we remove, as do most, 16:9-20 from the original Mark. All we have described is the discovery early on the first Easter morning of the tomb as empty, with the women running away "because they were frightened out of their wits; and they said nothing to a soul, for they were afraid." [Mk 16:8].

4. Matthew. The Empty Tomb Plus Appearances. AD 80.

Matthew has much more than Mark. He has an extended account of the discovery of the empty tomb [28:1-8], with the women this time actually being granted their own appearance by the risen Christ [28:9-10], and with a story of the Jews circulating a rumour [28:11-15] that his disciples had stolen Jesus' body. Matthew ends up with an appearance by the risen Christ to his disciples in Galilee [28:16-20].

5. Luke. A More "Physical" Jesus. AD 85.

Luke is even more realistic. After repeating the story of the discovery of the empty tomb with slight variations [Luke 24:1-8], he goes on to narrate that the women told the apostles [24:9-11] of this stupendous fact. The disciples did not believe them, but Peter came to the tomb "and saw the binding cloths but nothing else." [24:12]. In contrast with Matthew, Luke then has Jesus appearing to the disciples in the environs of Jerusalem rather than in Matthew's Galilee; on the road to Emmaus [24:13-35], in Jerusalem itself [24:36-43,44-49]; and finally in the outskirts of Bethany, from where Jesus ascends into heaven, and the Gospel comes to its triumphant conclusion [Luke 24:50-53].

Moreover, in Luke 24:30, Jesus, "When he was at the table with them, he took bread, blessed and broke it, and gave it to them". Then, in Luke 24:39, Jesus challenges them to

310

look at his hands and his feet, and to touch him, to show that he is not a ghost.

6. **John**. Still more "physical". Appearing through Closed Doors. AD 90-110.

Finally, with John, the progression is complete. Both Peter and the "other disciple" discover the tomb empty, after being told by Mary Magdalene [John 20:1-10], that "other disciple" beat Peter to the post because he was younger, and saw the empty tomb first. After the appearance to Mary Magdalene in the garden [20:11-18], there is, as with Luke, an appearance in Jerusalem, Jesus coming through closed doors to convince Thomas that he is truly risen, and inviting Thomas to touch his hands and his wounded side [20:27]. Then, in the final chapter, we have also a Galilean appearance of Jesus. Jesus being so "physical" as to be able to cook breakfast for them [John 21:9], and to have a long conversation with Peter [21:15-23].

We saw earlier, in chapter 2, how Heinrich Holtzmann used the theory of Marcan priority to form the basis of a liberal Protestant theology of the life of Jesus.[36] We can see here how convenient such a theory was for one who did not believe in the more physical aspects of the Resurrection appearances of Jesus. From a simple announcement in the primitive kerygma that Jesus is risen; from an inner experience of Paul on the Damascus Road; we travel up the road of increased physicality to the Fourth Gospel with Jesus cooking breakfast and appearing through closed doors. But is this type of subjectivist development coherent with the evidence?

Paul's experience is not necessarily normative

As so often in New Testament scholarship, one key is St Paul. Léon Dufour basically accepts the above paradigm of the Resurrection Appearances. He says "Finally, if the appearance to Paul is substantially identical to the appearances recounted

311

in the gospels, it follows that its essential substance is not always to be found in the images which are used to narrate it. An appearance cannot be defined by whether or not it is to a greater or lesser degree material, but by the initiative which brings it about and the mission which derives from it."[37] Thus, if we accept that the appearance (*óphthé*) to Paul is the basic paradigm, then must we see the description of the appearances in the Gospels as *theologoumena*: imaginative descriptions of an inner reality, the experience of the risen Christ. Léon Dufour insists that "One must avoid imagining the appearances as taking place in a 'marvellous' way."[38] But does that mean we must reduce the appearances to a spiritual experience? Even Paul was struck down on the road to Damascus by "a light from heaven which flashed around him" [Acts 9:3]. Was that light, and the strange voice from heaven, nothing "marvellous"?

Firstly, we must ask whether Paul considered that those to whom Christ appeared, who had met and known the historical Jesus had the same kind of "non-physical" experience that he had himself. Paul actually refers the appearance of Christ to him, his *óphthé*, as "Last of all, as to one untimely born (*tó ektrómati*) he appeared also to me" [1 Corinthians 15:8]. *Ektróma* (that word used only once, a *hapax legomena*, in the whole of the New Testament) means most clearly and obviously a "miscarriage"[39] therefore also "an untimely birth, an abortion."[40] But why does Paul use this particular image about the appearance of the risen Christ to him personally? Was it, as C.S.C. Williams thinks, that Paul "felt that he had entered on the 'new creation', being born again, in an untimely way (or was it that some converts called him 'the abortion'?)"[41]

However we interpret Paul calling himself an *Ektróma*, the fact is that he did consider himself in some way or other an anachronism among the apostles, in that they had known Jesus while on earth, whereas Paul had not. Thus we should be presumably careful in concluding that Paul must mean the same by the *óphthé* of Jesus as did the other apostles and chosen witnesses. There is no reason in principle why the original apostles and 500 witnesses of the resurrection [1 Corinthians 15:6] should not have had different types of experience compared with that of Paul. That is particularly the case if we remember that Paul's experience of the risen Christ would have taken place after the Ascension [Acts 1:9-11], when, according to the Gospels, the appearances of Christ came to an end, in preparation for Pentecost [Acts 2:1]. One possible interpretation of Paul's being "untimely born", his *Ektróma*, is in fact that the appearance of Jesus was to him after the generality of appearances had come to an end post-Ascension.

Now to come to the Gospels themselves. For a fuller answer than we can give in a single chapter such as this, we refer with confidence, as with chapter 7, to N.T. Wright, whose third volume in the series *Christian Origins and the Question of God* is entitled *The Resurrection of the Son of God*. Particularly relevant to our discussion here is his *Part Four. The Story of Easter*.[42] Here, we will simply present a reply to the objection which is another variant of the thesis which we have encountered throughout this book, namely that the primitive Christian community moved upwards in its faith in Jesus from belief in a Jewish prophet put to death by a cruel establishment to faith in a god risen from the dead. In this reply, we will relate to conclusions already affirmed elsewhere in this book.

The two document hypothesis is a shaky foundation

The theory of increasing physicalisation without historical basis depends upon a rigid application of the Two Document Hypothesis, which hypothesis is by no means certainly proven.

As we saw earlier,[43] the most frequently held opinion is that Mark's Gospel was first, followed by Matthew and Luke, who copied Mark with variations. The second Document in this Two Document Hypothesis was the hypothetical Q, which accounted for material in Matthew and Luke but not in Mark. The third element was contained in Matthew and Luke respectively, namely that content in Matthew not in Luke ('M') and that content in Luke not in Matthew ('L').[44]

Any standard New Testament Introduction will inform the reader, that, whereas the Two Document Hypothesis holds sway in New Testament scholarship, there are and always have been dissentient voices. Not only is the theory opposed root and branch by those who propose the priority of Matthew.[45] Also, there are many variations of the Two Document Hypothesis itself, such as those like B.H. Streeter, who "replaced the almost universally accepted two-source theory... with a four-document hypothesis which has been widely accepted in the English-speaking world... What distinguishes this hypothesis is... the ascription of the essential constituent parts of Luke's Gospel to a narrative source independent of Mark... the final result... is very materially to broaden the basis of evidence for the authentic teaching of Christ."[46]

Already, therefore, before we consider the contribution of Form Criticism to the study of the Synoptic Gospels, we have to take into account the possibility that authentic stories about Christ, notably concerning his Resurrection, may be independent of Q, Mark, Luke and Matthew, and possibly go back to the historical Jesus, if we stray with such as Streeter outside the rigid tram-lines of the Two Document Hypothesis.

Earlier traditions pre-date the written Gospels

As again we saw earlier, from Wrede onwards, and more specifically from Bultmann and Dibelius onwards,[47] New Testament criticism undertook the task of trying to identify traditions underlying the Gospel stories, and in particular oral traditions.

We saw that, at the beginning, this led to increased scepticism regarding the Synoptic Gospels. Holtzmann's straightforward Liberal Protestant faith, accepting the basic historicity of Mark, was shattered by Wrede. And Bultmann continued this process of increasing negativity regarding the historicity of the Gospels by his use of the Form-Critical Method. This meant, for instance, that it did not at all matter that a story was in Mark. For Bultmann, even if a Gospel story was in the earliest layer of the tradition which we have to hand, it could be and often was discarded as historically worthless. Thus Bultmann judges that Mark's story of the empty tomb [Mark 16:1-8] is a "tendentious secondary legend without historical value, the point of which is the empty tomb as the proof of the resurrection,"[48] that is despite the fact that, according to the orthodox Two Document Hypothesis, Mark's is the earliest account.

But what is sauce for the goose is sauce for the gander. If tradition must be separated from redaction in Matthew, Mark, Luke, and also Q, M, and L,[49] then equally it might well be possible that buried in Matthew and Luke are traditions earlier than those contained in Mark, even if Mark is accepted as the earliest account within the critical orthodoxy. Thus the Resurrection narratives might at least possibly be both early and authentic, even if in Matthew and Luke; or indeed, in John.

Yet again, how much can Jones swallow?

We have already demonstrated how the Form-Critical Method has been dogged by anti-supernaturalist presuppositions. Ultimately, we submit that Form and Redaction Criticism are inadequate in themselves in order to assess the historicity of the Resurrection narratives in the Gospels without judgements of credibility.

We have shown earlier how Bultmann's *Formgeschichliche Methode* is by no means pure science, but contains within its exercise historical scepticism. Bultmann was convinced that the historical Peter could not have recognised Jesus as Messiah during Jesus' lifetime, a conviction which, we maintain, is based upon philosophical presupposition rather than exegetical rigour.[50] We saw how Benoit's devastating analysis of Bultmann uncovered the layers of subjectivist presupposition in the use of the Form-Critical Method, particularly the idea that the primitive Christian community simply invented stories about Jesus to bolster its faith without concern that such stories were based upon the authentic words and deeds of Jesus.[51]

With this in mind, we would insist that the application of the Form-Critical Method without anti-supernaturalist presuppositions is the correct programme; but it is by no means easy to follow. Howard Marshall, indeed without such anti-supernaturalist bias, examines the Resurrection Appearance story in Luke 24:13-35, where Jesus meets two disciples on the Emmaus road and then breaks bread with them. Marshall says "It is difficult to assess the validity of attempts to differentiate tradition from Lucan redaction."[52] However, after opting for the Emmaus story coming out of a tradition, Marshall asks further "But if the story has a basis in tradition, does it have any claims to historicity? In the nature of the case, it is impossible to provide proof of its historicity, but at least it may be claimed that the objections raised to its historicity are weak."[53]

N.T. Wright agrees that "The resurrection stories are, in fact, very difficult to classify by the normal canons of form-criticism. They are dense and tight, and do not admit of easy hypotheses."[54] We are obviously moving towards the subject which we dealt with in chapter 4, where we attempted to forge a very basic and common sense philosophy of history. At the end of the day, examining the Resurrection Narratives, we will not find answers to their historicity in the mechanisms of literary, tradition or Form Criticism. We are back to the question of how much Jones can swallow. We have the Resurrection Story E for Emmaus. X tells me E happened. Do I believe X about E? Are judgements of historical credibility justified in this case?

All scholars come to this point eventually. Theissen and Merz give us their usual comprehensive and rigorous presentation of the question in "The Risen Jesus and its Interpretations."[55] They subject us to the full range of literary-critical questions and possible answers. But, in the latter section of that Chapter, it becomes clear that we cannot answer the question as to the nature of the Resurrection itself unless we adopt a philosophical and theological stance. If we are Bultmannian, the Resurrection story will be a myth.[56] If we follow Karl Barth, we see the Resurrection not as accessible to historical analysis, but nevertheless it really happened, though it is accessible only through divine revelation accepted in faith.[57] If we are followers of Wolfhart Pannenburg, we see the Resurrection as truly an historical event, verified through the "purposive process" of universal history understood as a totality.[58]

Finally, then, we must make a judgement of credibility, and leave form-critical analysis. Can we produce criteria which tip the scales towards the historicity of the Resurrection accounts, and against a Bultmannian subjectivist mythologisation?

Eye-witness tradition

We have argued more than once that the four Gospels in their final edition are all potentially based upon eye-witness testimony to the events of 31 AD. Indeed, granted the time-span, it would be surprising if some if not many eye-witnesses were still alive, at least for the early stages of the Synoptic Gospels,[59] if not for the final edition.

But can we argue that the accounts of the Resurrection in the four Gospels are reliable historically, and not a mythical presentation of existential faith? N.T. Wright is convinced that he can so argue, and give reasons, to me most convincing:

1. Wright claims that the Resurrection stories are told "straight", "*with virtually no embroidery from the biblical tradition.*"[60] Wright says that this is unlike the remainder of the Gospels "with a persistent build-up of scriptural quotation, allusion, reference and echo". Wright concludes that "these Lucan stories, though in themselves consummate works of art, are not in themselves works of midrash or exegesis".[61] Surely they would be, says Wright, if they were simply mythical constructs in Straussian mode.

2. The next feature observed by Wright is the *Absence of the Personal Hope* of the Resurrection in the stories. Apart from

the Gospels, Wright argues, any mention of the Resurrection leads to consideration of *our* Resurrection, as indeed in 1 Corinthians 15. But in the Gospel accounts of the Resurrection, there is no mention whatsoever of the future Resurrection of the Christian. "The stories are about something else altogether; the vindication of Jesus, the validation of his messianic claim, and the commissioning of his followers to act as his heralds, announcing to the world its new, surprising, but rightful Lord."[62] If the primitive community was so creative, Wright would argue, why did it not demonstrate to its pious readers that the Resurrection of Jesus meant their future hope of resurrection?

3.   The third feature observed by Wright is the *Strange Portrait of Jesus* in the stories. Wright argues that, if the stories of the Resurrection of Jesus were purely creative, then why for instance does not Jesus rise like a star, as Daniel 12:2-3 says the just will? Instead, says Wright, "Jesus is almost routinely depicted in these stories as having a human body with properties that are, to say the least, unusual. The same Lucan text that tells us that Jesus ate broiled fish, and invited his followers to touch him and see that he was real, also tells us that Jesus appeared and disappeared at will, that at one of these appearances two close friends and colleagues did not recognise him, and that in the end he was taken up into heaven..."[63] Wright is presenting here a prime case of double discontinuity.[64] Neither in the Old Testament nor in the documents of Rabbinic Judaism, not in the documents of the early church, do we find any vision or revelation of God presented in such an apparently bizarre way, or indeed as truly a *mysterium tremendum*. The accounts are, therefore, Wright submits, historically credible.

Wright produces in the subsequent pages many more examples of the unique *genre* of the Resurrection narratives, which should lead us to accept them as genuine. There is not adequate space here for us to assess all those arguments. But the three above are to me persuasive, if taken together with Wright's conclusion, which claims historical coherence[65] as the criterion validating the authenticity of the Resurrection Appearances of Jesus:

> Throughout it all we have seen the obvious but important point, that those who held the complex but remarkably consistent early Christian view gave as their reason that Jesus of Nazareth had himself been raised from the dead. And we have now seen what they meant by this: that on the third day after his execution by the Romans, his tomb was empty, and he was found to be alive, appearing on various occasions and in various places both to his followers and to some who, up to that point, had not been his followers or had not believed, convincing them that he was neither a ghost nor a hallucination but that he was truly and bodily raised from the dead. This belief about Jesus provides a historically complete, thorough and satisfying reason for the rise and development of the belief that he was Israel's Messiah and the world's true lord. It explains the early Christian conviction that the long-awaited new age had been inaugurated, opening new tasks and possibilities. Above all, it explains the belief that the hope for the world in general and for Jesus' followers in particular consisted not in going on and on for ever, not in an endless cycle of death and rebirth as in Stoicism, not in a blessed disembodied immortal existence, but in a newly embodied life, a transformed physicality. And we have now seen that the central stories upon which this belief is based, though they have been skilfully shaped and edited by the four evangelists, retain simple and very early features, features which resist the idea that they were made up decades later, but which serve very well to explain the developments from Paul onwards.[66]

Wright's argument from historical coherence and of sufficient reason takes us very close to the argument we find in the *Catechism of the Catholic Church*:

> CCC. 44. Even when faced with the reality of the risen Jesus the disciples are still doubtful, so impossible did the thing seem: they thought they were seeing a ghost. "In their joy they were still disbelieving and still wondering."

[Luke 24:38-41]. Thomas will also experience the test of doubt and St Matthew relates that during the risen Lord's last appearance in Galilee "some doubted" [Cf. Jn 20:24-27, Mt 28:17]. Therefore the hypothesis that the Resurrection was produced by the apostles' faith (or credulity) will not hold up. On the contrary their faith in the Resurrection was born, under the action of divine grace, from their direct experience of the reality of the risen Jesus.

As we demonstrated above, regarding the tradition of the discovery of the empty tomb, if Jesus' body had been discovered, a Jew would not have believed in his Resurrection. For the Jew, there was no immortality of the soul without the resurrection of the body [Cf. 2 Maccabees 7:14].[67] How, then, we may ask further, could a group of Jewish followers of Jesus believe in his Resurrection if they had not at least believed that he had appeared to them in some physical form? We can argue therefore also that the tradition of Jesus' appearances to his disciples must have been an early tradition.

In the early Jerusalem days of the church, Christians had to demonstrate that the Resurrection of Jesus was in keeping with the scriptures. Jesus had died a common criminal, unjustly [Acts 2:22-36, 3:11-26] and did not the Torah say "anyone hung on a tree is under God's curse"? [Deuteronomy 21:23] But the Resurrection proved that Jesus was not cursed by God; rather he was now at God's right hand as Lord and Christ.

With the church growing among the Gentiles in the second half of the first century, there was a need to emphasise further the bodily nature of the Resurrection, as we see Ignatius of Antioch does, writing at the close of the first century and the beginning of the second.[68] We know of the prevalence of Docetism[69] from 1 John 5:14, the denial that Jesus Christ had really taken on human flesh, but was a kind of Greek god come to earth. Against this, it was most necessary to emphasise the physical nature of the Resurrection appearances. The need became even greater in Ignatius' own time, the apostle's having died or being close to death, and the need evident to hand on the authentic tradition. That is why we have always insisted that those who wrote the Gospels did not invent stories, but while interpreting all that they said in the light of the Resurrection, handed on what Jesus actually said and did. This is most of all important regarding the accounts of the Resurrection which, as we have already said, were blurred as to detail, but contained the essential fact of Jesus' appearance to them in visible human form.[70]

The appearances in John: proof of divinity

These accounts in John take place in Chapters 20 and 21. There is a widely held view that Chapter 21 is by a later redactor.[71] However, such a hypothetical redactor of Chapter 21 could quite conceivably have had contact with eye-witness tradition.

With Wright, we hold to the substantial historicity of these accounts, allowing for post-Easter interpretation on the part of the evangelist himself (e.g. 21:11, possibly the number of fish caught 153[72]). This is in keeping with the evangelist's purpose, as we have demonstrated earlier, to show that the Word has become flesh precisely *in history*[73] It was precisely the evangelist's purpose to hand on a substantially accurate account for future generations [21:24].[74] In keeping with what we have seen earlier regarding the Resurrection accounts in general, John's details may well have been blurred. But, the very vividness of the experience: seeing the empty tomb [20:5]; hearing Mary Magdalene's account of meeting the Lord [20:19]; the Lord meeting them in the Upper Room and saying "Peace be with you" [20:20]; Jesus appearing through closed doors [20:26]; meeting Jesus on the shore and having breakfast with him [21:9-14]; the dialogue between Jesus and Peter when Jesus says to him "Do you love me?" [21:16]; John's own disclaimer that Jesus had said that he was to remain alive until he came [21:22]; all this leads us to conclude that the evangelist is recounting what he really saw and heard.

Regarding the long dialogues and discourses of Jesus in the Fourth Gospel, we could admit a large amount of reconstruction and skill on the part of the evangelist, who wrote the speeches in his own literary style; but even there we argued with Schnackenburg[75] that the statements were those of the historical Jesus, even if in reported speech rather than the direct *ipsissima verba*. When Vatican II's DV19 spoke of the process of synthesis, selection and explication in the formation of the four Gospels, it is not implied in that text that the Council Fathers thought that the evangelists actually invented sayings and deeds of Jesus. Similarly, regarding the Resurrection appearances, we may well have accounts put into different contexts or geographical situations.[76] But regarding the events themselves, here we have a case of direct testimony by the Evangelist. Either he is creating fiction; for what purpose? Or, much more likely, he is truly testifying to what he saw and heard, as he himself makes claim [John 1:14].[77] That it was fifty years since he saw and heard those things of which he wrote matters little.[78] If they truly happened as he said, and if he was there as we contend, he would hardly have forgotten what happened in that Upper Room in Jerusalem and on the shores of Galilee. The account in Chapters 20-21 reads like a sober account of amazing happenings.

But who can believe it? Could one accept the truth of these events purely as historical facts, without any faith other than what we have described as historical faith, namely X told me Y happened, and I believe X?[79] Initially, in terms of our three events concerning the resurrection of Jesus, it would seem that 1. requires complete faith; 2. does not require faith at all; and 3. requires at least conditional faith[80]:

1. **The Resurrection itself.** Clearly, only a full believer could accept that Jesus, after dying and being buried in the tomb, rose from the dead to sit at the right hand of his Father in heaven.

2. **The discovery of the empty tomb.** An impartial observer could hold that for some reason or other the tomb was found empty. That observer might think that the body had been stolen, or that Jesus had not really died; or simply that the discovery of the tomb of Jesus empty on that first Easter

morning is one of those many events which happened in history for which there is no certain explanation.

3. **The Resurrection Appearances**. At least conditional faith is necessary to accept that the Resurrection Appearances occurred in any way close to how the Fourth Gospel describes them. An atheist might hold that the disciples *thought* they saw Jesus risen from the dead, but that they were under an illusion. To accept that the disciples genuinely saw the Lord in those appearances implies at least that the person is moving towards faith.

This leads us to our final chapter. Granted all these amazing historical events, how legitimate is it to proceed to an act of faith identical with that of doubting Thomas, in saying "My Lord and my God"? [John 20:28]. Seeing is not sufficient without faith. The homily of Pope Gregory the Great (540-604)[81] puts the whole relationship of resurrection faith and seeing, in a nutshell:

> His [Thomas'] scepticism was more advantageous to us than the faith of the disciples who believed. Inasmuch as he came to believe by actually touching we can lay aside all doubt, for our faith is made whole. So this doubting disciple, who actually touched, became a witness to the reality of the resurrection.

> Thomas touched him and cried out: 'My Lord and my God.' Jesus said to him: 'Because you have seen me, Thomas, you have believed.' The apostle Paul said: 'Only faith can guarantee the blessings that we hope for, or prove the existence of the realities that remain at present unseen.' It is abundantly clear that faith provides the proof for those things that cannot be seen; visible things do not require faith, they command recognition. Inasmuch as Thomas saw and touched, why was it said to him: 'Because you have seen me, you have believed.' What he saw was one thing; what he believed, another. A mortal man could not have seen God. Thomas saw a man but by his words, 'My Lord and my God', he

323

acknowledged his divinity. It was by seeing that he believed for he recognised the reality of the man and cried out that he was God, although he could not see God.[82]

If we accept the historicity of the Resurrection as described in the Gospels, therefore, how does this lead us to faith here and now in the divinity of Christ? That is the subject, the Big Question, of our final chapter.

NOTES – CHAPTER 16

1 ODCC, 689. "Nothing is known of his life beyond his journey to martyrdom from Antioch to Rome under a guard of ten soldiers." But the authenticity of his seven letters, to Ephesus, Magnesia, Tralles, Rome, Philadelphia, Smyrna and to St Polycarp, after a "learned defence" by Lightfoot, has "won general acceptance".

2 Ignatius of Antioch, *Letter to Smyrna*, Nos. 1-4, 1. Translation in *The Divine Office, The Liturgy of the Hours According to the Roman Rite*. Vol. I, London, Collins, 1974, 466-7.

3 ODCC, 688-9.

4 "Thomas was offered exactly what he sought. John does not say that he accepted the opportunity; rather he hints (v.29) that the resurrection body, though it could pass through closed doors, could also be handled; it was physically 'real'". Barrett, 572.

5 QHJ, 21.

6 For Paulus' equally intriguing account of "what really happened" at the transfiguration, cf. 6.1., QHJ, 52-3.

7 QHJ, 54.

8 QHJ, 55.

9 NJBC, **42:4,** 631.

10 PCB, 798, 695i.

11 NJBC, **41:109,** 629.

12 CCC, 640.

13 CCC, 641.

14 JEC, 336.

15 Léon-Dufour, X., *Resurrection and the Message of Easter*, London, Geoffrey Chapman, 1974, 113.

16 Kremer, J., Zur Diskussion über "das Leere Grub" in Phanis, ed., Resurrexit. Actes du Symposium Internatonale su la Résurrection de Jesus, Libreria Editrice Vaticana, 1974, 137-8.

17 EJ, 38-45.

18 EJ, 42-43.

19 Brown, II, 976-7.

20 Brown, II, 978.

21 EJ, 44.

22 Students at a well-known London catechetical college were asked, "If the bones of Jesus of Nazareth were discovered in Jerusalem, would your faith remain the same?" The answer was clearly expected, "It would remain the same, even if the bones of Jesus were discovered there." Redford, ed., 2002, 19.

23 Evely, L., *The Gospels without Myth*, New York, 1971.

24 Léon-Dufour, op.cit. 211-2.

25 Léon-Dufour, op.cit. 251.

26 EJ, 91.

27 EJ, 94.

28 EJ, 95.

29 Aquinas states that Christ's Resurrection is the cause of the resurrection both of our bodies, III.q.56, a.1, and of our souls, III.q.56, a.2. Aquinas argues that the resurrection of Christ is the cause of our resurrection *per virtutem Verbi uniti*. III, q.56, a.1, ad.1.

30 CCC, Note 492. Lk 24:5-6.

31 CCC, Note 493. Cf. Jn 20:13; Mt 28:11-15.

32 CCC, Note 494. Cf. Lk 24:3, 12, 22-23.

33 CCC, Note 495. Jn 20:2, 6, 8.

34 CCC, Note 496. Cf. Jn 11:44; 20:5-7.

35 HJCG, 478 quotes Bultmann, "The church had to surmount the scandal of the cross and did it in the Easter faith. How this act of decision took place in detail, how the Easter faith arose in individual disciples, has been obscured in the tradition by legend and is not of basic importance (*Theology* 1*, 45)."

36 Cf. pp. 47-8.

37 Léon Dufour, op.cit. 79.

38 Léon Dufour, op.cit. 246.

39 VGT, 200. Moulton and Milligan quote from a Cairo manuscript AD 362, "where a complaint is made with reference to certain persons to Taesis who was pregnant they occasioned by their violence the miscarriage of her child."

40 AS, 142.

41 PCB, 963, 841c. Murphy-O'Connor agrees. "Possibly a term of abuse used by Paul's opponents, who mocked his physical appearance (2 Corinthians 10:10) and denied his apostleship." NJBC, **49:66**, 812.

42 RSG, 587-738.

43 Cf. pp. 47, 139.

44 Cf. NJBC, art. *The Synoptic Problem*, by Frans Neirynck. **40**, 587-595.

45 Cf. p. 53, Orchard, Longstaff, ed.1978, 51.

46 NTHIP, 327.

47 Cf. p. 49ff.

48 HJCG, 484. Bultmann, HST *287.

49 Cf. p. 51f.

50 HST, 257 *-8*. Cf. p. 56.

51 Cf. pp. 53-6. ET, 52.

52 Marshall, I. Howard, *The Gospel of Luke: a Commentary on the Greek Text*, Exeter, Paternoster Press, 1978, 890.

53 Ibid, 891.

54 RSG, 596.

55 HJCG, 474-511.

56 HJCG, 505-506.

57 HJCG, 506.

58 HJCG, 507.

59 Cf. NJBC, art. *The Synoptic Problem*, by Frans Neirynck. **40**, 587-595. Also cf. Introductions to Matthew, Mark and Luke to see the proposed stages whereby those books were compiled.

60 RSG, 600.

61 RSG, 601.

62 RSG, 604.

63 RSG, 604.

64 Cf. p. 115.

65 Cf. pp. 111, 125-6.

66 RSG, 681-2.

67 When he was near death, he said, "One cannot but choose to die at the hands of mortals and to cherish the hope God gives of being raised again by him. But for you there will be no resurrection to life!" Cf. NJBC, **26:73**, 444. "Thus the author states the theology of martyrdom and the resurrection of the just."

68 Cf. p. 296.

69 ODCC, 413.

70 "The absence of neutral witnesses is no automatic reason for rejecting testimony" EJ, 67.

71 For a thorough argumentation insisting on a separate redaction for John 21, cf. Zumstein in CHJ, 215-9. For a spirited defence of the view that John 21 is integral to the original work, cf. Hoskyns, 561-2.

72 Brown, II, 1074. "The idea that the writer may have had a hidden, symbolic purpose in citing the exact numeral 153 has led to an enormous amount of speculation: "everything from gematria to geometrical progression" (Marrow), but nothing dispelling Augustine's contention that the number is 'a great mystery'."

73 Cf. p. 191.

74 That our position is substantial rather than absolute historicity, cf. pp. 192-3.

75 Schnackenburg, I, 24.

76 Some scholars argue for and some against either Jerusalem and/or

Galilee appearances. But this depends on the reconstruction of events from the Synoptic material. EJ, 36-8. If John the Son of Zebedee is at least possibly in some sense or other the author of the Fourth Gospel as is our opinion, and thus John 20 and 21 were written by an eye-witness, then there might well have been both Jerusalem and Galilee appearances.

77 Cf. Jackson, H.M. Ancient Self-Referential Connections and their Implications for the Authorship and Integrity of the Gospel of John. *Journal of Theological Studies*, 50 (1999), 1-34.

78 Cf. pp. 159-60. We accepted for the purposes of hypothesis the critically agreed dating of 110 AD for the Fourth Gospel. However, we noted J.A.T. Robinson's objections to a late dating, and agreed that the evidence is hardly compelling against his view. Robinson, 1976, 273-4. Robinson has at least demonstrated a *terminus post quem* of before 70 AD.

79 Cf. 93-6, 100.

80 Cf. p. 98.

81 ODCC, 594.

82 Hom. 26,7-9. Translation in *The Divine Office: The Liturgy of the Hours According to the Roman Rite*. London, Collins, 1974. 94* Feast of St Thomas the Apostle, 3 July, Office of Readings.

CHAPTER 17

THAT YOU MAY BELIEVE

> We have used the principles of historical criticism together with "conditional faith" to demonstrate that the historical Jesus claimed to be God the Son during his life on earth, and vindicated that claim by his miracles, and above all by his bodily Resurrection. We submit in this final chapter that we now have sufficient historical grounds to make an act of faith, while willingly conceding that faith is a gift of God.

Jesus was not bad or mad, he was God

Right at the beginning of this investigation, we quoted the view of O'Collins, with reference to the old apologetic argument to the effect that Jesus claimed to be God, therefore he had to be either bad, mad or God. This, as O'Collins insists, depends on the answer to the question "Can we verify that Jesus, at least by implication, claimed an authority and identity that were truly divine?"[1]

We have attempted to go further than demonstrating that Jesus only by implication claimed to be divine. We have attempted, by a necessarily long and complex argument, to demonstrate that historically, Jesus did say something very close to "Before Abraham was, I am" [John 8:58], and "I and the Father are one" [John 10:30]. We have attempted to demonstrate that in this, the Fourth Gospel is reliable, and that Jesus in the Gospel of John was making what amounts to the only unambiguous claim in the four Gospels to full divinity on the lips of Jesus.

Our title: *Bad, Mad or God?* is not a gimmick. It expresses in the simplest form our entire argument. A key point of that argument is our contention that the four Gospels, and in particular John, are historically reliable in insisting that Jesus was put to death because his Jewish contemporaries thought he was blaspheming; namely, they thought that he was bad, or possibly mad.

We have also demonstrated that, far from Jesus being either bad or mad, as his opponents claimed in his own day (John 10:20: "Many of them said, "He has a demon, and he is mad; why listen to him?") he demonstrated that he was God the Son. We have argued to the factual nature of the Miracles of the Walking on the Water and of the Multiplication of the Loaves. Particularly in the Walking on the Water, Jesus appeared to his disciples as the God YHWH,[2] a fact which they realised more fully after the Resurrection, when they saw the full meaning of his words "Fear not, I AM" [John 6:20]. Above all, in the previous chapter, we have shown how the fact of Jesus' Resurrection led justifiably to his disciples accepting that he truly was the Word Incarnate.

Jesus was neither bad nor mad, therefore, but he was what he claimed to be, God the Son. It is now time to work out the implications of such an affirmation in terms of personal faith.

BMG, valid historically

Most recently, Stephen T. Davis has revisited the argument "Was Jesus Bad, Mad or God?" (which he abbreviates to BMG), and tested out its logic.[3]

He perceives that the BMG argument stands or falls most decisively on (1). Did Jesus actually claim to be God? If he did, then it does seem that either he was what he claimed to be, or he was bad or mad. As Davis says, "What is clear, and I think is quite beyond dispute, is that a literalistic and ahistorical reading of the Gospels, and especially the Fourth Gospel, strongly supports premise (1)."[4] Davis therefore rejects those such as J.A.T. Robinson, whose views we have also rejected earlier,[5] who attempt to argue that Jesus' *egó eimi* claims in the Fourth Gospel do not imply full divinity.

Davis does not attempt, as we have done, to demonstrate that Jesus actually claimed divinity in the full sense of the incarnation. For that, he would have had to argue, as we have done, that to affirm the full claims of Jesus to be God the Son in the Fourth Gospel, is indeed not "literalistic and ahistorical" at all, but can be concluded positively after a long and thorough investigation of the Fourth Gospel using all the legitimate methods of critical scholarship.

Yet he does affirm that the historical Jesus claimed to be God, but "implicitly". In this, he uses those very texts which we have seen J.A.T. Robinson employing to demonstrate that the Fourth Gospel, in putting the *ego eimi* absolute statements on the lips of Jesus, is only making explicit what was implicit in the Synoptic view.[6] John's Christology is therefore not contrary to that presented in the Synoptics, as we have continually argued, particularly in chapter 8, where we have demonstrated the authenticity and the high Christology of Mark 14:64, the Trial of Jesus, where Jesus is eventually condemned for blasphemy. Davis notes in particular that, in the Synoptic presentation of the teaching of Jesus, he "spoke with 'authority', not citing sources or precedents of famous rabbis."[7]

Davis argues that the historical Jesus implicitly claimed to be God, and that this provides good grounds for the early Christians worshipping Jesus;[8] for which worship,[9] we have good first or at least early second-century evidence.

Of course, we would want to go further and argue strongly, as we have done, that the historical Jesus explicitly claimed to be God, as evidenced in the Fourth Gospel. But what is interesting is, first, that Davis refuses to see any contradiction between the Synoptics and John in Jesus claiming to be God, except that in the Synoptics his claims are only implicit; and secondly that even if we only accept that Jesus implicitly claimed to be God, the BMG argument is still valid.

Davis insists "I am definitely not suggesting that the BMG argument is the only or even the best argument Christians can give for the divinity of Jesus."[10] Our argument, however, is that it must be the best argument *from the historical dimension* (while of course admitting that there are many other dimensions of apologetics than the historical, e.g. the philosophical[11]), since it is based upon Jesus *own self-understanding and self-proclamation*. Indeed, we might say negatively that, whatever other arguments might be given for the full divinity of Jesus in the Incarnational sense, there will always remain a defect in the rational foundations for belief in Jesus' full divinity if we cannot demonstrate that he himself had an adequate self-understanding of his own full divinity, at least by his adult life. This we argued at the very beginning of this enquiry.[12]

Thus, while applauding the progress made in historical Jesus research in the last decade of the twentieth century onwards, from N.T. Wright's *Jesus and the Victory of God* onwards, we believe that this investigation is important, because it has gone on that extra mile, to vindicate the Fourth Gospel account of the ministry, death, and Resurrection of Christ, Jesus making his final appeal to *hoi Iudaioi* in the Temple couryard to fulfil their destiny by following him as the Light of the Word, the *egó eimi* of Jewish tradition. If we wish to argue the doctrine of the Incarnation from the foundational Christian documents, that Jesus had conscious-ness of his own full divinity, and yet of his own dependence on God the Father as the only-begotten son [*monogenes theos*, John 1:18], John's Gospel not only gives us our best lines, it gives us our only sure lines.

Only the Fourth Gospel has the foundation of all those elements of genuinely Incarnational doctrine which we saw expounded in chapter 13, that foundation reaching its climax in the Christological Councils of the fourth and fifth centuries.[13] Only the Fourth Gospel records the claims of Jesus to be God the Son, and the vindication of those claims in the miracles, the death and Resurrection of Jesus. So, ultimately, we would contend, only the Fourth Gospel can give us a fully effective apologetic for the Incarnation, a fully effective use of the BMG argument. Thus its historicity, as we have argued in this book, is an essential component of that argument, demonstrating the first point of BMG.

Nevertheless, arguing convincingly that Jesus implicitly made claims to divinity in the Synoptic Gospels has given invaluable support for the *historical credibility* (using the criterion of historical coherence)[14] of the Johannine picture of the Jesus who said "Before Abraham was, I AM". Far from the picture being of a Jewish prophet in the Synoptic presentation who in the Fourth Gospel becomes a Gentile God; on the contrary what we have in truth is a historical

Jesus who made implicit claims to divinity in the Synoptic Gospels, and made those claims explicit in his final days as recounted in the Fourth Gospel. And, furthermore, we have argued that this movement from implicit to explicit claim is not just the theological imagination of the author of John, but rather based upon the sequence of events in the life of the historical Jesus, which began with the Messianic Secret, and ended with the explicit affirmation of divinity in John 7-10, as Jesus entered his last days on earth.[15]

BMG, valid logically

Being convinced that the historical Jesus implicitly claimed divinity, Davis attempts to demonstrate that logically, from that premise, the BMG argument is valid:

> It will facilitate matters if I lay out the argument in what I take to be its logical form:
>
> 1. Jesus claimed, either explicitly or implicitly, to be divine.
> 2. Jesus was either right or wrong in claiming to be divine.
> 3. If Jesus was wrong in claiming to be divine, Jesus was either mad or bad.
> 4. Jesus was not bad.
> 5. Jesus was not mad.
> 6. Therefore, Jesus was not wrong in claiming to be divine.
> 7. Therefore, Jesus was right in claiming to be divine.
> 8. Therefore, Jesus was divine.[16]

He demonstrates that this "Jesus bad, mad or God" argument is basically valid; with however clarifications and nuances. For instance, he claims that everyone seems to accept that Jesus was neither bad, nor was he mad.[17] "Virtually everyone who reads the Gospels – whether committed to Christianity or not – comes away with the conviction that Jesus was a wise and good man."[18]

But Davis also sees that the question as to whether Jesus actually made the claim to be God is not the only possible objection to the BMG argument. He quotes Donald MacKinnon, to the effect that, if a person claims to be God, "it presupposes that we know what it is like to be God."[19] If so, we cannot use the BMG argument validly. This, at first sight, is a curious objection. The BMG argument is used to demonstrate that Jesus was, and is, God incarnate. Therefore, that argument proceeds from the presumption that we do know something about what is stated in the conclusion of that argument, that is that the historical Jesus was God. In that case, we claim to know at least something about "what it is like to be God", even if not very much. Furthermore, it seems to me, the BMG argument is still valid even if that presumption is false. That is simply acknowledging the distinction between saying that an argument is logical and therefore valid, and saying that an argument can lead us to the truth. An illustration will suffice. We may say:

All cats are green
Felix is a cat
Therefore, Felix is green

The conclusion is nonsense, but the logic is flawless. The conclusion is nonsense because it is simply not true that all cats are green. Thus, it seems to me, Davis has argued impeccably that the BMG argument is logically valid, even if we are atheists. What he has not argued effectively is that Jesus was in fact God, since that depends upon the veracity of a statement at least that God exists, in order for Jesus to be identical in being with him.

We may indeed argue that BMG is a valid argument logically speaking. Let x be "What orthodox monotheists think that they mean by God." We could then use the BMG argument quite validly. The argument then would go:

Jesus claimed to be x.
If Jesus was either bad or mad, he could not have been x.
Jesus was either bad, mad or x.

He was not bad or mad.
Therefore, he was *x*.

However – and this is where McKinnon's point is valid – there is a legitimate question as to what we mean when we say the word "God", and therefore in what sense, if in any sense, we know what it is to be like God. A philosopher in the Logical Positivist [20] tradition would claim that the statement "God exists" is meaningless. But that philosopher would claim also that any statement which is not empirically verifiable (like "that is a cat", seeing a furry black feline), or tautological (when the subject is implied in the predicate, like 2 x 2=4), is also meaningless. Thus moral arguments like "it is wrong to kill" would also by that same token be meaningless, as well as saying "God exists".

Logical Positivism, after a short period of popularity after the Second World War, is no longer in favour among philosophers, even if it could be said to survive in a general antipathy to metaphysics, particularly in Anglo-Saxon thinking. Logical Positivism is founded on a self-destructive proposition. If we say "all statements which are not empirical or tautological are meaningless", then that very statement "all statements which are not empirical or tautological are meaningless", is itself meaningless, because it is neither empirically verifiable nor tautological. Some kind of meta-physics is necessary in order to do any philosophy,[21] or indeed any science.[22] That means that we presume that we can know something of what we mean when we make metaphysical statements like "God exists".

God is not a myth

MacKinnon draws attention to the fact that the BMG argument depends upon the belief of the person using the argument that God does in fact exist, and that there is some conformity between our idea of God and the idea of God which Jesus had when he made the claim two thousand years ago to be God.

334

Jesus thought that he knew what he meant when he claimed to be God. Those who heard him in his own day thought that they knew what he meant when he claimed to be God; as with believers in our own day. We mean "the omnipotent creator of all things made". No doubt there are mysterious implications in the concept of "God"; but that does not prevent us being able to say that we think we know what we mean when we say "God". There are mysterious implications in the statement "I am a human being", but that does not prevent us thinking that we know what we mean when we say, "I am a human being".

What would an atheist make of the BMG argument? Presumably, an atheist would say that, because God does not exist, it was futile for Jesus to claim to be a non-existent deity, still less to prove it. Presumably, also, an atheist would say that he or she would not necessarily conclude that Jesus was either bad or mad, in claiming to be God. Rather, Jesus had the naïve belief of a pre-scientific age that an unseen God made and ruled the world; and furthermore that he was himself to be identified in some way or other with that deity. His belief in being himself that deity was bolstered by the fact that he seemed able to perform miracles, and persuade others that he was at least some kind of superior prophet. But Jesus need not have been either bad or mad to have such a belief, only, for the atheist, deluded.

An extreme position is held by the Anglican academic priest Don Cupitt, in whose opinion all statements about God have only a mythical content. They do not refer to any objective being which we call "God". They are only statements about ethical values. Cupitt's position differs in no way in intellectual content from that of an atheist:

> The view that religious belief consists in holding that a number of picturesque supernatural propositions are descriptively true is encouraged by the continuing grip on people's minds of a decadent and mystifying dogmatic theology. In effect I am arguing that for the sake of clarity it should be discarded entirely, and replaced by the practice of religion – ethics and spirituality – and the

philosophy of religion. Then religion can become itself again, with a clear intellectual conscience at last.[23]

Cupitt therefore could say "Jesus was not bad, nor was he mad. He claimed to be God. In a sense, he *was* God. But his understanding of God was mythical first century". Cupitt therefore could say that Jesus' view of himself was subject to post-Enlightenment de-mythologisation.

Theoretically, Cupitt could come to the same positive conclusions about the historical Jesus that we have arrived at in this book. He could conclude that the historical Jesus actually said "Before Abraham was, I AM" [John 8:58]. Cupitt could then have proceeded to demythologise Jesus' view of himself *as* God; although no doubt Cupitt would not have accepted the validity of the demonstration of that claim by miracles and bodily resurrection. That presumably he would have to explain as Jesus and his disciples *thinking mistakenly* that he had healed the sick and raised the dead by miraculous powers, and that he had risen bodily from the grave.

In fact, Cupitt does not hold such a view, but has a much more reduced view of the historical Jesus' self-consciousness.[24] He treads the well-worn anti-supernaturalist path regarding the historical Jesus, the line straight from Reimarus through Strauss to Bultmann via Schweitzer. My only contention is that having adopted a mythical view of God, Cupitt *could* have concluded that Jesus saw himself as God, but then Jesus' view of himself as God could be demythologised in Cupitt's terms.

This is only to indicate that the investigation is not closed just when we have demonstrated however convincingly from the historical view that Jesus claimed to be God, and that he vindicated that claim by his miracles and by his bodily resurrection. The act of faith requires some understanding of what we mean by "God" and in whom we have faith.

Earlier, we outlined three beliefs which are necessary pre-conditions in order to conclude that Jesus was and is God Incarnate[25]:

• belief in the existence of God,

- belief in the possibility that God can reveal himself to the human race through direct intervention in history.
- belief that this man Jesus of Nazareth might possibly be the Son of God as Christian faith claims him to be.

This is what Kereszty, as we have seen, calls "conditional faith", faith at least in the possibility of God working in this particular event.

How do we know that God exists?

There is no space here for me to fully discuss the various proofs for God's existence, nor am I a professional philosopher with full competence to do so. There already exist excellent books on this subject,[26] except that I would say that I still accept the validity of St Thomas Aquinas' *Five Ways*. I still think that the argument from movement to a Prime Mover is valid, as is the argument from Cause to a Prime Cause, and the argument from Contingent to Necessary Being. The finite world in which we live, I would submit, does demand the existence of an Infinite Being we call God. We take for an example the argument from Prime Mover:

> Everything therefore which is moved, must be moved by something else. If therefore that by which it is moved is itself moved, then it follows that that which acts as the mover is also itself moved by something else; and that again by something else. But here we cannot proceed to infinity; because in this case there would be no first mover, and, in consequence, neither would there be anything else moving, because secondary movements do not move unless moved by a primary mover, just as a stick does not move unless it is moved by a moving hand. Therefore it is necessary to proceed to some Prime Mover, which is itself not moved by anything; and this everyone understands as God.[27]

The old objection 'Who made God?' misses the point of this argument, which demonstrates that something needs to exist *which was not made*. What is also true is that everything in our experience *is* made. Thus we must look outside of our immediate experience to a SOMETHING which is the Prime Mover, or the First Cause, which we call 'God'. The real question which Aquinas answers is how anything can come to be out of nothing.

The distinguished scientist Denis Alexander in his book *Rebuilding the Matrix: Science and Faith in the twenty-first century*, attempts to combine in a more synthetic fashion the Five Ways of Aquinas, arguing cogently for the necessity of a *superior intelligence* as a necessary cause of an intelligent being such as the human person, what he calls an "anthropic argument":

> At the least such anthropic arguments are an embarrassment to atheism. Atheism provides no explanation for why the universe, as Hawking puts it 'should bother to exist'. As Sartre was fond of pointing out, the fundamental philosophical question is why something exists rather than nothing. And our finely tuned universe is not just any old 'something', but contains within it a planet full of people who postulate theories about cosmology and the meaning of the universe, who write poetry, fall in love, build socially complex societies, and who believe in justice, freedom, ethics and the reality of good and evil. Atheism provides no insights into why such an odd entity should exist. Nor for why the physical parameters of the universe should be so precisely correct as to make the existence of such an entity possible. If atheism is true, then it can be argued that the emergence of conscious life and personhood within this vast and largely if not completely, impersonal universe remains a total enigma. For scientists who look for explanations for things. this is not a very satisfactory position to adopt.[28]

For Alexander, this forms the equivalent at least of a kind of scientific proof for the existence of God:

Clearly the idea of an all-powerful God, who chose to create a universe with particular properties such that conscious life would be possible, was not a theory postulated in quite the same way as a scientific theory. On the other hand, the style of reasoning which suggests that the properties of the universe are indeed consistent with such an idea is quite similar to the form of reasoning with which scientists are rather familiar. The data pointing to a series of remarkably finely tuned constants which have promoted the emergence of conscious life sit more comfortably with the idea of a God with plans and purposes for the universe than they do with the atheistic presupposition that 'it just happened'.[29]

For the *Catechism of the Catholic Church*, such "proofs" act as predispositions to accept God's revelation in Christ:

> CCC 31 Created in God's image and called to know and love him, the person who seeks God discovers certain ways of coming to know him. These are also called proofs for the existence of God, not in the sense of proofs in the natural sciences, but rather in the sense of "converging and convincing arguments," which allow us to attain certainty about the truth.

> These "ways" of approaching God from creation have a twofold point of departure: the physical world, and the human person.

> CCC 34 The world, and man, attest that they contain within themselves neither their first principle nor their final end, but rather that they participate in Being itself, which alone is without origin or end. Thus, in different ways, man can come to know that there exists a reality which is the first cause and final end of all things, a reality "that everyone calls 'God'."

Nevertheless, the Catholic Church in its official teaching does not canonise any particular proof, but leaves that open to discussion among philosophers and theologians. Rather, it quotes the First Vatican Council:

36 "Our holy mother, the Church, holds and teaches that God, the first principle and last end of all things, can be known with certainty from the created world by the natural light of human reason."[30] Without this capacity, man would not be able to welcome God's revelation. Man has this capacity because he is created "in the image of God."

Vatican I does not assert that we can *prove* the existence of God. But neither does it assert that it is a matter of *faith*. Rather, the Council states that we can *know* that God exists from our reason. In this, it is dependent on Paul's letter to the Romans, where he asserts that the Gentiles, even if they did not have the privilege of God's revelation, should have known that he existed:

> For what can be known about God is plain to them, because God has shown it to them. Ever since the creation of the world his eternal power and divine nature, invisible though they are, have been understood and seen through the things he has made. So they are without excuse [Romans 1:19-20].

There may be some for whom any kind of rational proof for God's existence is either unnecessary or alien to their way of thinking. But they surely must think that there is some reason to believe, even if such a reason cannot be clearly expounded. That is a kind of "knowledge", as when a person falls in love but cannot explain why he or she loves someone else. The Hebrew word for knowledge, *yada'* does not mean merely intellectual knowledge, but a personal union, even sexual intercourse, as Genesis 4:25: "Adam knew his wife again, and she bore a son." Our knowledge of God's existence and infinite power is itself mysterious; but it is none the less rational.

Belief in the possibility that God can reveal himself

Having become convinced of the existence of God, it is hardly incredible that such an omnipotent, all-knowing being should not be able to make himself known in some way or other to his creatures who are themselves gifted with an intellect. The only way that God can reveal himself is somehow through human language, through messages to us. This brings us to the question of religious language.

Contrary to Cupitt, God in traditional terms is not a mythical expression for human values, although that God is the ultimate source and end of human values. Rather, the God of monotheism truly exists as the invisible omnipotent Mind, the creator and conserver of everything that exists, and without whom nothing could exist.

We reject Cupitt's view that the idea of God is a myth. Cupitt never discusses the scholastic concept of analogy. Rather, he seems to accept without question Bultmann's programme of demythologisation.

For Bultmann, any "supernatural" language must be myth.[31] This is the basis of his programme of demythologising (*Entmythologizierung*). We can never say, therefore, that God is present directly in this or that specific action, whether miracle or, above all, in the Resurrection.[32] This refers both to events with a supernatural dynamism and to any statements about God. He seems to be unaware, or perhaps has already rejected, the classical idea of analogy; that we can speak of God by analogy with creatures. The consequence is that it is difficult to see how Bultmann's position differs from that of an agnostic, unless he can tell us how in some way or other we may be able to know God. Then, of course, the problem is that, if he can tell us, his own view itself moves into self-destruct mode, since he is disobeying his own principles by telling us something objective about God.

There is one sense in which traditional theology would agree with Bultmann. In scholastic theology, God is certainly not an object such as a tree, a human being, or even a thought of the imagination. A transcendent God is greater than any object of our thought. It is true what Maimonides stated,[33] that we can only know what God is not. But this would always be balanced in a scholastic presentation by emphasising that there is an analogy between creatures and the creator. The *Catechism of the Catholic Church* attempts to express this balance concerning our human knowledge of God:

Since our knowledge of God is limited, our language about him is equally so. We can name God only by taking creatures as our starting point, and in accordance with our limited human ways of knowing and thinking.

All creatures bear a certain resemblance to God, most especially man, created in the image and likeness of God. The manifold perfections of creatures – their truth, their goodness, their beauty – all reflect the infinite perfection of God. Consequently we can name God by taking his creatures' perfections as our starting point, "for from the greatness and beauty of created things comes a corresponding perception of their Creator."

God transcends all creatures. We must therefore continually purify our language of everything in it that is limited, image-bound or imperfect, if we are not to confuse our image of God – "the inexpressible, the incomprehensible, the invisible, the ungraspable" – with our human representations. Our human words always fall short of the mystery of God.

Admittedly, in speaking about God like this, our language is using human modes of expression; nevertheless it really does attain to God himself, though unable to express him in his infinite simplicity. Likewise, we must recall that "between Creator and creature no similitude can be expressed without implying an even greater dissimilitude;" and that "concerning God, we cannot grasp what he is, but only what he is not, and how other beings stand in relation to him."[34] [CCC 40-43]

Traditional theology would therefore go a long way with Bultmann, and thus with Cupitt. But the real difference appears to be that there is no acceptance on Bultmann's part that comparison with creatures gives us true, though always severely limited, knowledge of God.

Belief that this man might possibly be the Son of God

Traditional Christianity has always claimed that God can, and indeed has, revealed himself in history, in the life, death, and resurrection of Jesus of Nazareth. This belief has been radically challenged by post-Enlightenment philosophy.

Lessing, in the name of the Enlightenment's Enthronement of Reason, threw down the initial eighteenth-century challenge to traditional Christianity by affirming that the accidental truths of reason can never become the proof of necessary truths of revelation.[35] In promotion of this philosophy, as we saw at the outset of this investigation[36] Lessing published the anonymous Wolfenbüttel Fragments in 1778, which their author Reimarus, by then deceased, had been too terrified to publish. Thus was launched the Quest of the Historical Jesus.

But contrary to Lessing, any statement of the truth is universal and eternal. It is eternally true that I had a cup of coffee at 10.30 this morning. Thus if Jesus once manifested that he was truly the only-begotten son of God, he manifested himself eternally and for always that he was and is such. In this way, Nineham's objection, in his postscript to *The Myth of God Incarnate* symposium, that any description of the life of the historical Jesus must be too limited to make a faith commitment[37] is also answered. We do not need to know every act of the historical Jesus if once he has demonstrated his divinity. We can draw certain reasonable conclusions as to Jesus' activity from knowledge of his divinity, e.g. Jesus' sinlessness which would be entailed by his divinity. If, on the other hand, we had concrete and positive knowledge that Jesus did sin, that would destroy our belief in his divinity. Otherwise, granted the positive signs which would lead us to say that he was the Son of God, and lacking any evidence that he did in fact sin, then we could reasonably conclude that he did not.

Either way, it is quite legitimate to proceed from a limited yet significant knowledge about a person to a conclusion concerning that person's identity, even as in Jesus' case his divine identity. Historicity therefore, contrary to Lessing, is not a bar to revelation either on God's part or on ours; any more than it was a barrier to the Fourth Gospel witnesses who "saw his glory", or to the blind man who worshipped Jesus as the Son of God.

Rather, the problem regarding revelation for Lessing and for the whole of the post-Enlightenment critical tradition, is that for a rationalist, God cannot reveal himself *precisely because God is limited to the closed world of secondary cause.* For the Deist or Pantheist God cannot act without secondary cause. We saw earlier how this was explicitly stated by Strauss as his major principle of exegesis, prior to any examination of the text.[38]

This is the importance of miracle. A correct understanding of a miracle sees how it is the "ordinary" way, if one may put it thus, that God breaks this chain of secondary causality, by providing a sign saying "I, God, am specially acting here."[39] The miracle is a divine intervention by God indicating his special act. But how does the miracle do this? After a detailed discussion of the subject, Latourelle offers the following definition of a miracle, which immediately indicates its importance for revelation:

> A miracle is a religious wonder that expresses, in the cosmic order (human beings and the universe), a special and utterly free intervention of the God of power and love, who thereby gives human beings a sign of the uninterrupted presence of his word of salvation in the world.[40]

In emphasising that the miracle is a "religious wonder", Latourelle is immediately flagging up its revelatory significance. It is not a magical act, but truly a religious act, confronting us with God's transcendence in act, but also *in history.* That is why Latourelle insists that the miracle is an act in the "cosmic order", i.e. in the order of reality, and not in Kantian terms simply in terms of one's subjective experience. God is confronting us objectively, in reality, in history itself, by his transcendence and cosmic power.

Miracle and natural causality

In Catholic theology, there has been a long debate concerning the relationship between miracle and natural causality, which in a sense preceded and parallels the post-Enlightenment critical discussion. As Latourelle recounts, post-scholastic Catholic theology was strongly influenced by Aquinas' definition of the miracle: "An event is miraculous when it transcends the entire order of created nature (*fit praeter ordinem totius naturae creatae*). God alone is capable of producing such an event."[41]

For Latourelle, this led after Aquinas to an over-emphasis upon a miracle being outside or even against the law of nature.[42] Hence the definition of miracle by the twentieth-century Thomist Garrigou-Lagrange, that a miracle "was an event in the world, produced by God and falling outside the ordinary course of nature in its entirety."[43] Garrigou-Lagrange, Latourelle argues, made the task of the post-Enlightenment apologete become impossible:

> Once it adopted this incomplete definition of miracle, apologetics found itself ill equipped to confront the scientific rationalism of the eighteenth, nineteenth, and twentieth centuries. Philosophers and scientists were claiming: Our ignorance of the laws of nature is such that we will never be able to say with complete certainty that a fact for which science has no explanation really transcends the powers of all created nature. By what right can one pass from the lack of a scientific explanation to a metaphysical explanation asserted as necessary and calling for a direct intervention of divine causality? If one limits oneself to miracles as "wonders" and conceives of them as facts of the physical order that are beyond the effective powers of all creatures, and does not bring in the semiological or intentional aspect of these phenomena, the answer to rationalism will never be satisfactory, because it reduces a religious problem to a problem solely of efficient causality. For a miracle, viewed in what is most specific to it, is a gracious command issued by God.[44]

Latourelle in reaction quotes with approval Maurice Blondel, (1861-1949)[45] who in his theology of miracles emphasises that "they are not simply physical marvels belonging exclusively to the realm of the senses or science or philosophy, but are at the same time signs addressed to the whole person, signs belonging to the spiritual order and having a moral and religious character..."[46]

But Latourelle is careful not to minimise the cosmic dimension of the miracle. Otherwise the miracle becomes merely a subjective sign, without any objective referent in the physical order. We are back then in the Kantian trap. What Latourelle insists upon is that the miracle is not in fact "contrary to nature", even though it arouses wonder, but is truly "above nature".[47] This leads to a less rigid understanding of what natural law is, and conversely what through a miracle might transcend that natural law. We human beings see something wonderful happening, associated with a religious context. We conclude that this is God acting in a special and direct way, without necessarily giving a full account in terms of the breaking of physical laws.

This brings us back to our earlier discussion about miracle in chapter 12, where we quoted Malevez's third hypothetical objection to the miracle:[48] that we will never know enough about the physical laws governing the universe in order to know when they are transcended by a miracle. Malevez answers this by emphasising the fact that to estimate that there has been a miracle must be an *empirical judgement*. He argues that it is legitimate to use the laws of probability and to discount the opposite.[49] We used these same laws of probability to demonstrate that it was reasonable to conclude the divinity of Christ from the constant stream of his miracles, especially the more "transcendent" of his miracles such as the walking on the water, the feeding of the multitude, and the raising of Lazarus, not to say the resurrection appearances of Jesus himself; plus all the other signs which went with those miracles. We do not need to be a laboratory physician to recognise the wonders of God in Jesus, just a human being open to the truth.

This hermeneutical shift proposed by Latourelle is highly significant for Christian apologetics. The argument becomes more complex, but more holistic. In a fascinating article in the London *Daily Telegraph*, the scientist Denis Alexander takes us in the same direction, pointing towards a new understanding both of science and of the theology of miracles.

First, Alexander takes the old objections to miracles, as expressed by the eighteenth-century empiricist philosopher David Hume, to task. In response to the Enlightenment view that miracles are just impossible, Alexander replies:

> First, if you start with the dogma that "miracles are impossible", then clearly they are impossible. This is a statement, not an argument.
>
> Second, our understanding of the "laws of nature" has changed considerably since the eighteenth century, when nature was seen as "obeying" scientific laws in the way that we obey traffic regulations. In contrast, today's notions of a scientific law is more like a handy summary of highly reproducible results, constructed by the scientific community.
>
> Third, Hume's approach looks closed-minded. Scientists are supposed to be open to the evidence, wherever it leads, rather than pretending they already know the answer. Hume's stance suggests that, even if the evidence for something is overwhelming, you still shouldn't believe it. That jars.[50]

Alexander goes on to note that "science is good at investigating and explaining reproducible phenomena, but ill-equipped to answer questions about unique events (such as what really happened at the Battle of Hastings). That is the province of historians and lawyers". Clearly, the phenomena which we have been investigating in this book come into the category of unique events performed by a unique person: Jesus walking on the water, multiplying loaves and fishes, appearing after his death to his amazed disciples through closed doors. We have argued strongly throughout this book that these events can and should be defined as "historical" in the sense that they really happened. But they do not fit into any particular scientific category, precisely because of their uniqueness.

Alexander then demands a new understanding of the relationship between miracles and faith, which both confirms Latourelle's approach and leads us on to consider more deeply this relationship:

> Christians today do not (generally) believe in God because they believe in miracles but rather believe in miracles because they first believe in God. Just as good theories in science make novel data coherent, so does a theistic framework render miracles both coherent and plausible.[51]

Alexander's point is well made. But it reverses the argument if we compare this with the pre-Vatican II apologetic, *à la* Garigou-Lagrange. The old argument would say that it was *because* Jesus performed miracles and made divine claims, *therefore* he was truly what he claimed to be God the Son. But do we have to believe rather that Jesus Christ is God the Son *before* we can accept his miracles? We can possibly agree with Bultmann that valid argumentation can be circular,[52] but only provided that the arguments themselves have validity. Our complaint with Bultmann has not been so much that his argument is circular, but that the arguments by which the circle is described are question-begging; that his scepticism is gratuitous, and that he does not allow the possibility of the historicity of the Gospels to be seriously considered. This we have taken great pains to correct in this volume.

Perhaps, indeed, it would be better to describe our argumentation as spiralling rather than linear; a continual turning back to validate further and more strongly principles already validated. Thus the existence of a gracious and revealing God is confirmed more strongly than by philosophical arguments for his existence, if that God can be reasonably shown to have revealed himself in his Son, the Word become flesh.

It is difficult to see how, if God decided to assume a human nature at any time in history, he could persuade the world of his divine nature without actions such as miracles to demonstrate his own divine power above and beyond secondary causes. This is precisely what Jesus says in John's Gospel when he speaks of his "works" (*erga*), as we have discussed earlier, particularly with reference to John 5:18.[53] Those works are the sign of Jesus' divine nature, since he acts as God himself. Yet of course, the miraculous dimension of Jesus' ministry cannot validate his claims, without his sinlessness and his teaching. But this is only, according to John's Gospel, the way precisely his contemporaries came to recognise Jesus as God the Son.

Miracles and faith in John (*Semeia*)

Throughout this book,[54] we have only been trying to do what John first intended to do in his Gospel. This becomes clearest of all when we think of John's statement of his purpose in writing the Fourth Gospel [John 20:31]: "But these are written so that you may come to believe that Jesus is the Messiah, the Son of God, and that through believing you may have life in his name" This was just after Jesus had said to the no longer doubting Thomas "Blessed are those who have not seen and yet have believed".

Perhaps Bultmann's greatest misinterpretation of John consists in his refusal to consider the first eye-witnesses as being in any way privileged. Thus of John 1:14, "We beheld his glory (*etheasametha tén doxan autou*). Bultmann says:

> The *etheasametha* is not spoken by a limited number of "eye-witnesses", any more than *theórein* 6:40; 12:45 and *horan* 14:9 are limited to "eye-witnesses". But because there were once believing eye-witnesses, it is spoken by all believers; in the same way the Evangelist desires to pass on the *theasthai* through his Gospel.[55]

In focussing on *theórein* and *horan*, two Johannine verbs for "see", Bultmann admittedly has identified two words complex in their meaning in the Fourth Gospel. 6:40, which Bultmann quotes "This is indeed the will of my Father, that all who see the Son and believe in him may have eternal life; and I will raise them up on the last day." obviously does not refer necessarily to physical sight at all, but could refer to the perception by faith of all Christians. As Brown says, *theórein* here "seems to represent the deepest and most perceptive sight."[56] Likewise, in 12:45, "And whoever sees (*theorón*) me sees (*theórei*) him who sent me." Bultmann's third reference, 14:9, "Whoever has seen (*heórakós*) me has seen (*heóraken*) the Father" most likely refers to the spiritual seeing of all Christians.

But Bultmann strangely ignores the complexity of the usage of these verbs in John.[57] There are instances where *theórein* refers obviously to witnessing Jesus' miracles, for example "When he was in Jerusalem during the Passover festival, many believed in his name because they saw the signs that he was doing"[58] [John 2:23]. This obviously refers to physical eye-witness seeing. Even more obviously 16:16, as Brown translates it, "There is just a little while before you lose sight of me [*theórein*=physical sight] and again a little while before you see me [*horan,* i.e. with the eyes of faith after the resurrection]."[59] In that instance, John uses *theórein* for physical sight and *horan* for the vision of faith. The Fourth Gospel therefore uses these words for "seeing" in fundamentally different ways of meaning *depending on the context.*

Now what is the context of *etheasametha tén doxan autou*? "To see the glory" is a biblical expression with its roots in the Old Testament. It refers to a physical seeing, as again Brown makes clear. Brown defines seeing the glory in the Old Testament as "a *visible* manifestation of His majesty in *acts of power*". [Exodus 16:7-10].[60] That same use is in John 11:40 where Martha sees the miracle of Lazarus coming out of the tomb. There is a final glory which awaits the Christian to be with Jesus after death [John 17:24]. But that glory was visible on earth to the chosen witnesses, just as glimpses of that glory were seen even before Christ in the Old Testament.

Thus, as Brown says, when John 1:14 speaks of "seeing his glory", he is referring to eye-witness vision of the historical Jesus, to those who also had faith, but nevertheless also were privileged with eye-witness sight:

Since Jesus is the incarnate Word of God, he is an embodiment of divine glory (1:14). The two elements of *kabod* are present in him. He represents the visible divine presence exercising itself in mighty acts. More than the Synoptics, John insists that this *doxa* was visible during the ministry and not only after the resurrection. It is true that John does not describe the Transfiguration which for the Synoptics is really the only manifestation of glory during the public ministry (Luke 9:32). Yet John does stress that the divine *doxa* shone through Jesus' miraculous signs (2:11, 11:40, 17:4).

The whole NT agrees that the resurrected Jesus was the vehicle of *doxa* because the resurrection was the mighty act of God par excellence. Since John conceives of passion, death and resurrection as the one "hour", John sees the theme of glory throughout the whole hour. In fact, the hour is the time for the Son of Man to be glorified [12:23, 28, 13:32, 17:1]. Jesus prays in the midst of the hour: "So now glorify me, Father, in your presence with that glory which I had with you before the world existed" [17:5].[61]

This understanding is closed to Bultmann, because, as we saw earlier, he is unable to see the direct action of God in history, being still limited to the straightjacket of secondary causality as heir to the Enlightenment.[62] Bultmann must avoid any recognition of the value of the miraculous in his *theologia negativa*. But in this case, as so often in John, it is just running away from the obvious. As Brown says regarding Bultmann's interpretation of *sémeia*, "Part of Bultmann's motive in extending the meaning beyond signs is that he does not want to interpret John to mean that miraculous signs can lead people to faith – miracles are crutches for the infirm, and one should believe on the word of Jesus."[63]

But this, as we have demonstrated, leads Bultmann seriously to misinterpret the Fourth Gospel in a key area; a misunderstanding which arises from the theological blinkers of post-Enlightenment criticism. Rather our Christian faith is essentially historical, in that we trust the testimony of those who "saw the glory", the miraculous signs which Jesus performed during his life, above all his death and resurrection, and witnessed his appearance as truly the Word become flesh. They saw the glory while he "pitched his tent among us". We believe because they saw the glory *of the historical Jesus.*

Miracles, faith and revelation

For Christian tradition, therefore, faith, what we would call after Kereszty "conditional faith", as expressed in Hebrews 11:6 ("And without faith it is impossible to please God, for whoever would approach him must believe that he exists and that he rewards those who seek him") has a totally rational basis. But how can this faith proceed together with reason to at least possibly embrace the revelation given by God through his Son Jesus Christ? We have been discussing the BMG argument as perceptively analysed by Davis. But even if we have resolved at least to our own satisfaction the question as to who we think God is for Jesus to claim to be, we could not rest secure with the proof negatively that he was neither bad nor mad alone. We would need some more positive demonstration that Jesus was God the Son. This for Christian tradition was by means of his miracles, and most of all by his bodily resurrection. But even then, how and why could such faith be justified?

Faith cannot just be the conclusion of a syllogism. A simple illustration will suffice. It is generally acknowledged that one of the greatest heavyweight boxers of all time was Mohammed Ali. Time and time again on the media, before and after a fight, he would repeat "I am the greatest". Knocking out opponent after opponent in the ring was sufficient to demonstrate that his statement was verified. No faith in the boxing ability of Mohammed Ali would be required. The conclusion would be "I am the greatest. Q.E.D."

But if a person says "I am God", the statement is mysterious, and the proof of it is not final without faith. It remains to discover what that person means when he or she says "I am God", and that involves faith in whom that God is, *and in what and to whom God is revealing himself.* Thus we are told in the Fourth Gospel that the man born blind, after acknowledging that Jesus was the source of his cure, was challenged by Jesus to make an act of faith in him as Son of Man. "He said, "Lord, I believe." And he worshipped him" [John 9:38]. The blind man could come to the conclusion that Jesus was someone special from the fact that he had been cured of his blindness. But to make the act of faith in Jesus the Son of God, he had to respond to the personal invitation of Jesus.

But what, precisely, *is faith*, and what is the process by which we come to faith in Jesus as the Son of God become man for our salvation?

The certitude of faith

For the orthodox Christian, the certitude of faith is based upon the authority of God who reveals, and ultimately upon nothing less. The role of historical evidence in the act of faith is to provide *criteria of credibility.*

There is a supreme paradox in the Roman Catholic theology of faith, which is still not, and perhaps never will be, entirely resolved. Throughout this book, I have attempted to demonstrate historical facts about Jesus because of my faith that in Jesus the Word has truly and objectively become flesh. That is a traditional Roman Catholic theological emphasis, an emphasis upon incarnational reality. Yet, at the same time, Catholic theology maintains that faith itself does not depend upon reasons given for it, however convincing, but upon God himself who reveals, and on whom alone faith puts its confidence. To state this as strongly as possible, I quote an old textbook of Catholic theology, written twenty years before the Second Vatican Council, which makes this point more powerfully, even extremely, than I have ever seen it expressed before or since:

The certitude of faith is supreme because the believer's assurance rests upon a ground more secure than all human science, upon the infallible authority, of God. "If we receive the testimony of man," says St John, "the testimony of God is greater" infinitely, unspeakably greater, since God is very Truth. But, as in regard to the freedom of the act of faith so also in regard to its certitude, a difficulty often arises from a misconception of the precise motive of faith. It is sometimes urged that since no chain is stronger than its weakest link, therefore the assent of faith can enjoy no greater certitude than the assent given to any of the preambles of faith, which are its foundation. Metaphors are misleading here. Even the word "foundation" may lend itself to misunderstanding. The preambles of faith are the foundation of faith in the sense that they are a necessary prerequisite. But they are not its foundation in the sense of supplying the security of the edifice. The metaphor of the chain is no less fallacious. There is no continuous "chain" of reasoning that leads from the first argument which proves the existence of God to the truth, for example, that in one God there are three Persons. If the act of faith were the logical conclusion of such a chain, then evidently that conclusion could have no greater weight than is warranted by the series of arguments that lead to it. But the act of faith is not an inference from preceding arguments. The series of truths which we have called the preambles of faith leads logically to the judgement of credibility, but no further.[64]

Mgr. Smith has made a strong statement here; but it is only an expansion and development of what the First Vatican Council stated in its Dogmatic Constitution on the Catholic Faith in 1870:

> Since human beings are totally dependent on God as their creator and lord, and created reason is completely subject to uncreated truth, we are obliged to yield to God the revealer full submission of intellect and will by faith. This faith, which is the beginning of human salvation, the catholic church professes to be a supernatural

virtue, by means of which, with the grace of God inspiring and assisting us, we believe to be true what he has revealed, not because we perceive its intrinsic truth by the natural light of reason, but because of the authority of God himself, who makes the revelation and can neither deceive nor be deceived.[65]

What role then could historical reasoning, or indeed any other kind of reasoning, have in the act of faith? Does not this paragraph make the act of faith entirely gratuitous, truly a Kirkegaardian leap in the dark? Again, Smith gives us the key. The preparations for the act of faith are only in effect *criteria of credibility*. It is not dissimilar to the process whereby a person may fall in love. No love can continue without *trust* between the individuals concerned. When that trust is thrown into doubt, then one party has to prove the credibility of his or her love to the other. But the love itself is not based upon credibility of trust itself, but is simply love, which has its own reasons. There are many people who may be trusted, but with whom one is not in love.

But how are these criteria of credibility related to the act of faith? We may summarise this process as follows:

- The historical investigation of the sources leads to the conviction that those sources are reliable.
- Those historically reliable sources contain accounts of divine revelation, concerning which the reader may have moral certainty.
- The reader is now stimulated by these investigations and by the inner working of the Holy Spirit to make an act of faith in the God revealing himself as the Father of Jesus Christ.

Tenuit ac tenet: historical faith

In judging historical questions in relation to faith and revelation, we may attain the certainty of historical conviction as a preamble to genuine faith.

With this conditional faith operative, which we have insisted is in no way "unscientific", we now submit to the reader that we have demonstrated in the preceding investigation that the Gospel of John is substantially historically reliable in reporting that Jesus claimed to be God the Son, that he performed miracles which validated that claim, that he was handed over to death because his opponents thought he was blaspheming, and that he rose again from the dead bodily as a final vindication of his divinity and as a promise of the gift of the Spirit to his followers.

If these conclusions are correct – although like any "historical fact" they require an act of *historical faith* ("X told me that Y happened, and I believe X"[66]) – they are truly conclusions *about the historical Jesus*, and not only about the "Christ of faith". This, we now propose, is the first stage in an act of faith in Jesus. It is an act of conviction in the reasonable certainty of an historical fact, and is not in itself an act of religious faith.

This seems clearly to be the teaching of the Second Vatican Council. In *Dei Verbum,* the article on the apostolicity of the Gospels, Article 18, and the article on historicity, Article 19, contain the key phrase 'maintained and continues to maintain' (*tenuit ac tenet*) regarding the church's position on the apostolicity and historical reality of the Gospels. We can set out the sentences in parallel:

Article 18	Article 19
…The Church has always and everywhere maintained, and continues to maintain (*tenuit ac tenet*) the apostolic origin of the four Gospels	Holy Mother Church has firmly and with absolute constancy maintained and continues to maintain (*tenuit ac tenet*) that the four Gospels, whose historicity she unhesitatingly affirms...

Why did the Council Fathers use the phrase 'always maintained and maintains' (*tenuit ac tenet*) regarding both the apostolicity and the historicity of the Gospels? Is not the historicity and apostolicity part of the faith of the church? Would not therefore 'believed and still believes' (*credidit ac credit*) be a better expression of the church's position on this matter?

The Doctrinal Commission which originally drafted *tenuit ac tenet* was asked precisely this question during the debates on this article from 30 September until 6 October 1964. Some bishops would have preferred a statement of pure faith at this point. The answer given by the doctrinal commission was that *tenuit ac tenet* was used in both cases in preference to *credidit ac credit*, because certainty regarding both apostolicity and historicity was based not upon faith alone, but upon *faith and reason*.[67]

In this way, the Council Fathers were committing themselves, and indeed the whole church, to the need for continuing historical investigation of the Gospels. They were convinced that both in the past and in the present (and so implicitly also in the future) a solid and reliable investigation of the four Gospels using a correct methodology would serve only to confirm the apostolicity and historicity of those documents. There could be no more confident statement in historical investigation itself, as well as in the credibility of Christian faith.

Our investigations have confirmed this confident assertion. We began in Part II by arguing that the Fourth Gospel possibly at least is based upon eye-witness sources of the historical Jesus. We then argued in Part III that, along with the other three canonical Gospels, it gives us genuine information about the historical Jesus. By the use of criteria developed in historical Jesus research, we confirmed the "critical minimum" in the Synoptics and in John concerning Jesus; that he preached the kingdom of God: that he performed miracles wonders and signs; that he was put to death by crucifixion; and that his tomb was discovered empty on the first Easter morning.

But, we affirmed with N.T. Wright that we can go much further than the critical minimum. We argued that, in the

Synoptic Gospels, Jesus made claims for himself which led his opponents to accuse him of blasphemy. We demonstrated that these claims of Jesus, which were at least close to claims for divinity, e.g. especially Mark 14:62, are from the historical Jesus, and serve to authenticate the more explicit claims which Jesus makes in the Fourth Gospel account, especially 8:58 ("Before Abraham was, I am") and John 10:30 ("I and the Father are one").

This conclusion includes of course hundreds, even thousands, of exegetical decisions which *could be otherwise*. This takes us back to the original Enlightenment objection that a sure decision of faith in divine revelation cannot be based upon contingent historical fact, or upon a collectivity of historical facts which are always disputable. In the present book the reader will have noted that my exegetical decisions have, in the nature of the case, not always attained a high level of certainty. The clearest example of this is the question of authorship by John the Son of Zebedee. My own personal belief, outlined in chapter 4, is that John the Son of Zebedee wrote the Fourth Gospel, and that he was the problematic "Beloved Disciple". But I have freely admitted that the question is too complex to give a certain answer, and have settled for the claim that at least he *could have been the author*, leaving open the *clear possibility* that the author was an eye-witness of the events written about in the Fourth Gospel. That is very much an exegetical decision, even though it is I would argue most reasonable. Many, if not all, exegetical decisions have been of that contingency.

We have reached *reasonable historical certainty*. The investigation has been cumulative, a build-up of evidence. But how do we move from historical conviction regarding the sources to faith in God's revelation in Jesus, which is what the Fourth Gospel challenges us to do?

Moral certainty of the fact of revelation

Standard Catholic theology would refer to the conclusions of a reasoning process outlined above as attaining *moral certainty of the fact of revelation*. The certainty which comes from deciding that Jesus is truly the revelation of God, a certainty which we see the man born blind and disciples such as Thomas attaining in the Fourth Gospel, is a practical certainty for everyday living; the same practical certainty which makes us certain that this job is for us, or this spouse is for us. Every day in our lives we make hundreds of practical decisions, based upon reasonable but not absolute certainties. It is this kind of certainty which the Vatican Council defined in 1870 as being the level of conviction which says that God *has spoken in Jesus*. It is that kind of reasoning which led the man born blind to say in response to his inquisitors regarding Jesus, "he is a prophet" [John 9:17].

The First Vatican Council, having as we have seen earlier, insisted upon the supernatural quality of the act of faith, then goes on to insist equally strongly that reason is operative in demonstrating the fact of revelation, giving us what scholastic theologians called the moral certainty of the fact of revelation. We claim the reader's indulgence in quoting this important statement in full a second time:

> Nevertheless, in order that the submission of our faith should be in accordance with reason, it was God's will that there should be linked to the internal assistance of the holy Spirit outward indications of his revelation, that is to say divine facts (*facta divina*), and first and foremost miracles and prophecies, which clearly demonstrating as they do the omnipotence and infinite knowledge of God, are the most certain signs of revelation and are suited to the understanding of all.[68]

This moral certainty, however, is not limited to miracles and prophecies, even if they are "first and foremost" (*praesertim*) certain signs of revelation and suited to the understanding of all. What presents itself as the ultimate reason for moral certainty of revelation in Jesus is the total presence of Jesus himself, which we quote again in conclusion of our discussion, just as we quoted it in our introduction:

> 4. After God had spoken in many and various ways by the prophets, "in these last days he has spoken to us by a

Son" (Heb 1, 1-2). He sent his Son, the eternal Word who enlightens all humankind, to live among them and to tell them about the inner life of God (see Jn 1:1-18). Thus it is that Jesus Christ, the Word made flesh, sent as a human being among humans, "speaks the words of God" (Jn 3,34) and accomplishes the work of salvation which the Father gave him to do (see Jn 5,36; 17,4). To see Jesus is to see also his Father (see Jn 14,9). This is why Jesus completes the work of revelation and confirms it by divine testimony. He did this by the total reality of his presence and self-manifestation (*tota suipsius presentia ac manifestatione*) – by his words and works, his symbolic acts and miracles, but above all by his death and his glorious resurrection from the dead, crowned by his sending the Spirit of truth. His message is that God is with us, to deliver us from the darkness of sin and death, and to raise us up to eternal life.[69]

The grammar of assent

In his *Grammar of Assent,* Newman confronts the post-Enlightenment objection to faith that it cannot be justified by the logical reasons given for it. Newman replies that human reason itself does not work that way. The assent which affects our everyday lives is for Newman not merely "notional" but "real" assent. For Newman, faith is an example supremely of "real assent". That is to say, it is not just an assent to an abstract proposition, but "it is directed towards things, represented by the impressions which they have left on the imagination. These images, when assented to, have an influence both on the individual and on society, which mere notions cannot exert."[70]

Faith, therefore, we might say, is rather a driving force than an formula, even a formula such as "Jesus is God". For Newman, this same act of faith is also the result of inference from facts; such facts, as for example, we have been using and assessing in the present work. "We are in a world of facts", Newman says, "and we use them, for there is nothing else to use".[71] In assessing these facts, and drawing concrete inferences from them, for Newman we further need what he calls the "Illative Sense", which he defines as the "power of judging and concluding, when in its perfection."[72]

So, for Newman, in order to carry out successfully the very investigation into Gospel truth which we have just completed, we need this "sixth sense" which goes beyond the strict logic of the inferential argument, and finds the dynamic truth of faith, that Real Assent of which he speaks. "Such a living organon", he says, "is a personal gift, and not a mere method or calculus."[73] We need this Illative Sense, therefore, just as much in Jesus research as the detective needs it in criminal investigation, or the housewife as she smells out a bargain in the Saturday morning market.

For Newman, this Illative Sense works on the "convergence of probabilities", a number of facts coming together. Thus, for him, it would not be miracles on their own, or Christ's life on its own, which would lead to faith, but rather the whole complex of Jesus' life, death, and Resurrection taken together in their full impact. Thus he would be quite prepared from this to infer the human perfection and sinlessness of Christ, even though the Gospels do not and cannot record every deed and thought of Jesus. After a decision based upon the convergence of probabilities, together with the quasi-Illative Sense of faith, that Jesus is the Word of God, inferences from this could be made which go beyond pure logic, but which are driven by the force of the gift of faith itself, which Smith as we saw insisted was not confined to the evidence alone, leading to "real assent."[74]

Newman's account is surely close also to the way in which the first Christians, as recounted in the New Testament, actually came to faith. It was a combination of the powerful persuasive images of the miracles and authoritative teaching of Jesus, plus a personal encounter with him. Kereszty's concept of "conditional faith" is also operative here.[75] Yet surely those same first Christians were also convinced that their assent was not irrational. On the contrary, they considered faith the most rational act they had ever performed. And, as we have tried to argue throughout this book, they had the "confluence of probabilities" on their side. It was not a leap into the dark. Rather, as John Coventry said perceptively, it was more a "leap into the light".

It is that same Illative Sense which guides the mind towards the sifting of evidence, and which sense is at the same time guided by incipient faith. It is not dependent on every single exegetical decision; yet it is dependent on the collectivity moving in the direction of the recognition of revelation being present in the life, teaching, death, and Resurrection of the historical Jesus. We have constantly asserted that it is not illegitimate for faith to be present throughout this investigation, providing direction and the principle unifying the whole process.

This assembly of facts leading to a conclusion which is at first unproven is again common in all areas of human science, e.g. in the work of a detective. There is no reason at all why it should not also be valid in the field of the investigation of the historical Jesus. I hope that one real advantage of this methodology is that often exegetical decisions about the Fourth Gospel have been left in isolation. But if we put a number of reasonable historical decisions together, then they do mount up to an argument from historical coherence.

Newman's approach also gives guidance on the question about how proofs in religious questions actually work. Why the old apologetic failed eventually to convince was that human beings do not normally work in entirely logical order, even if their decisions are sometimes, even often, logical. Thus the order of the act of faith does not actually (or we might say *existentially*) necessarily move from belief that Jesus performed miracles to faith in him as Son of God, being first convinced of the essential historicity of the four Gospels. The actual process might work in a much more complex way; first, the enquirer being drawn by the amazing personality of Jesus, then by the possibility that he might be someone special from God; then, the person would be drawn more to believe in God, a belief which before was not strong, not again necessarily by proofs for God's existence, but rather because of Jesus as a person. And this whole process might be encouraged, not first and foremost by an objective historical study of the Gospels, but by a vibrant and challenging Christian community. It might be only after a person becomes an already convinced Christian that more in-depth study of the historicity of the four Gospels, and further discussion as to the existence and the nature of God is required as part of growth towards Christian maturity.

Even more important to understand is that, in Newman's philosophical matrix, in his *Grammar of Assent*, the level of what we might call "pure faith", i.e. acceptance of God's revelation not because of the reasons for credibility but on the pure authority of God who reveals, *is also working throughout the investigation.* That instinct of faith is more than merely Kereszty's conditional faith. It is faith itself, drawing us to the revealing God beyond the reasons for credibility, but not contrary to them. This links Smith's concept of faith[76], clearly one based upon the First Vatican Council[77], with the whole investigation. The act of faith does not necessarily, even usually, come at the conclusion of a demonstration. It is actively there often from the beginning. The reason why a believer comes to believe is because belief is there already. The argumentation, the reasons given, are simply part of the process of such a faith really there becoming more explicit, yet at the same time as part of a rational process.

This leads us to the final question.

Is the investigation fixed?

To anticipate one objection to this book, many will say that *I want it to be true* that Jesus is in fact what Christian confession makes him out to be, the eternal divine Son of God. Can one's approach, and one's conclusions, be "objective" and "scientific" therefore?

We have already discussed the question of objectivity in historical enquiry.[78] Using the analogy of the courtroom, which we suggested was a better model for historical investigation than the science laboratory,[79] we maintained that bias in favour of a given cause was not necessarily a bar to the discovery of objective truth; indeed that in a courtroom the passionate defence of a given cause is sometimes the only way of the truth being heard and conquering. But I would suggest now that not only is passion permissible in an historical investigation of a matter as important as the historical Jesus; my own passion for this enquiry has actually improved the objective quality of my work.

Moreover, in passionately believing in my cause, I am only following the good historical Jesus Enlightenment tradition. Way back in chapter 2, we quoted Schweizter: "For hate as well as love can write a Life of Jesus, and the greatest of them are written with hate – that of Reimarus, the Wolfenbüttel Fragmentist, and that of David Friedrich Strauss." Yet Scheitzer goes on to say "And their hate sharpened their historical insight. They advanced the study of the subject more than all the others put together."[80] An emotion can drive a person to a more intensive study than would be that person's normal inclination.

When I first read Schweitzer's *Quest of the Historical Jesus* back in 1967, I was fascinated by it not only because I immediately realised that this was the greatest intellectual challenge, yes, even threat, to the Christian faith in the modern era. It seemed to me that, as I read Schweitzer's *Quest*, I could feel the Titanic of Christendom running into successive icebergs as it entered the freezing waters of the modern era. It fascinated me because I could feel some of that burning hatred, that wish to dethrone Christ from his supernatural pedestal, of which Schweitzer speaks, coming from such as Reimarus and Strauss. I could feel it more strongly, precisely because, however imperfect a Christian I am, I matched it with an equally if not more powerful emotion of my own, a passionate belief in and love for God himself become man in Jesus for our salvation. I wanted just as badly to keep Christ on that supernatural pedestal, at the right hand of God, as well as admitting freely and happily that he was at the same time a "marginal Jew". The historical Jesus quest for me was not only an intellectual challenge. It was an emotional and above all a spiritual challenge as well, even a quest for spiritual survival.

My hope is that it has sharpened my historical insight. I

could sense the sadness of Strauss as well as his honesty, as Hodgson says the sadness of the "alienated theologian."[81] Strauss writes of the joy of the early Christians, for him without doubt the regret of *le temps perdu.* "How richly fraught with blessing and elevation, with encouragement and consolation, were the thoughts which the early Church derived from this view of the Christ!" [82] Would I have the equivalent honesty of Strauss, to go wherever he thought truth led him, away from joy to sadness? Strauss' passion was not only as Schweitzer said "hatred" for the supernatural enthroned Christ, but also passion for the truth, even if, in the Christian view, it was a misguided passion.

A police inspector visits a woman when she is alone in her house, to tell her that he suspects her husband of murder. The woman's first instinct is that the police inspector is prejudiced against her husband. She is not only distressed. She loathes that police inspector even for suspecting that her husband could do such a terrible thing. But as the evidence unfolds, she realises that it is in fact more than possible that her husband did commit that murder. Even though her emotions told her that her husband could not have committed that murder, in the end she has to come to terms with the evidence and admit the hard truth. And also in the end, the very love she had for her husband made her search more honestly for the truth, even the truth she did not want to know.

I have always *wanted* it to be true that Jesus was and is the Son of God become man. But I hope that I would have the honesty to conclude that it was not true, if such is the case. My conviction is that, although I was inclined to accept orthodox Christianity, I have in this book tested the historical Jesus in John's Gospel rigorously, and that the Gospel has come through that test every time.

There is a strange story in the book of Genesis, about Jacob fighting a duel with God all night. We will not discuss its historicity! Perhaps this is an image of the critical mind in the face of religion:

> Jacob was left alone; and a man wrestled with him until daybreak. When the man saw that he did not prevail

against Jacob, he struck him on the hip socket; and Jacob's hip was put out of joint as he wrestled with him. Then he said, "Let me go, for the day is breaking." But Jacob said, "I will not let you go, unless you bless me." So he said to him, "What is your name?" And he said, "Jacob." Then the man said, "You shall no longer be called Jacob, but Israel, for you have striven with God and with humans, and have prevailed. "Then Jacob asked him, "Please tell me your name." But he said, "Why is it that you ask my name?" And there he blessed him. So Jacob called the place Peniel, saying, "For I have seen God face to face, and yet my life is preserved." [Genesis 32:24-30]

Throughout this book, we have been wrestling with the historical Jesus. Perhaps many have lost their spiritual peace in this particular intellectual struggle, striving with God and with humans. But it is my conviction that there is a blessing to be obtained, if the historical Jesus question is honestly faced and followed through with the correct methodology; even if, in the process of the investigation, there is the pain of the testing of one's faith, even possibly a spiritual wounding. The blessing results from coming face to face with Jesus himself, who reveals himself as YHWH God bestriding the sea, just as he revealed himself two thousand years ago on the sea of Galilee saying "I AM, be not afraid", as the historical Jesus. If that miracle, and indeed the miracle of the whole life, death and resurrection of Jesus, is a scandal for our post-Enlightenment world, a rock of stumbling, then it can also be a cornerstone for the renewal and recovery of genuine Christian faith in the twenty-first century.

1 Cf. p. 18-9. INC, 130-131.
2 Cf. p. 229.
3 Davis, 221-245.
4 Davis, 228. Although why should a reading be «literalistic and ahistorical» if it comes to the conclusion that the historical Jesus actually claimed to be God, as demonstrated by a sound hermeneutic?
5 Cf. p. 240ff.
6 PJ, 388-389.
7 Davis, 241.
8 "The prevalence and centrality of the worship of Jesus in early christianity from an early date has frequently been underestimated…" Davis, 234.
9 JSD, 234. Cf. HJCG, 79.
10 Davis, 224.
11 For a combined theological, philosophical, and biblical apologetic for the Incarnation, cf. INC.
12 Cf. pp. 30-4.
13 Cf. p. 241.
14 Cf. pp. 111, 116f.
15 We have accepted S.R. Driver's simple, but nevertheless completely convincing, explanation of the Messianic Secret as a requirement of the earlier part of Jesus ministry, but no longer necessary or indeed possible in the latter stages of that ministry. HDB, IV, 586. This renders redundant Wrede's scepticism, cf. pp. 49, 149.
16 Davis, 224.
17 "But Peter Kreeft argues convincingly that Jesus shows none of the character traits usually associated with those who have delusions of grandeur or 'divinity complexes'. Such people are easily recognised by their egotism, narcissism, inflexibility, predictable behaviour, and inability to relate understandingly and lovingly to others." Davis, 226.
18 *Ibid.*
19 Davis, 222. Davis heard Donald MacKinnon express this objection to the BMG argument at a lecture at the Cambridge Divinity School, 1978.
20 ODCC, 1112. The famous exponent of Logical Positivism was A.J. Ayer, *Language, Truth, and Logic,* 1936.
21 CMM, 135.
22 In outlining a basic philosophy of historical investigation, cf. pp. 85-6, we have claimed that the three presumptions of any scientific enquiry, (a) the existence of ourselves, (b) the existence of a world external to ourselves, i.e. a "real world", and (c) the existence of an order of nature whereby things in the real world generally operate according to predictable laws, which we call laws of "cause and effect", are not in

themselves scientifically demonstrable. They are therefore, to that degree "metaphysical" but are not for that reason invalid.

23 Cupitt, D., *The Sea of Faith: Christianity in Change*, BBC, London, 1984, 270.
24 Cupitt, D., *The Debate About Christ*, London, SCM, 1979, 137.
25 Cf. p. 99.
26 Davies, B., *Thinking About God*, London, Chapman, 1985.
27 T. Aquinas, *Summa Theologiae*, I., q.2, a.3.
28 RM, 422.
29 RM, 424.
30 Tanner, II, 806.
31 "Accordingly the resurrection narrative does not refer us to the historical event of an actual corporeal resurrection but proclaims the meaning of the historical event of the cross." DFT 90.
32 EF, 81-2. We have argued earlier, p. 92, that even scholars such as G.E. Ladd whose Christological orthodoxy is not in doubt yet will not call historical those events which lie outside the closed system of natural causality.
33 ODCC, 859.
34 St Thomas Aquinas, *Summa Contra Gentiles* I, 30.
35 ODCC, 817.
36 Cf. p. 41.
37 MGI, 188.
38 Cf. p. 42f. LJCE, 88.
39 The problem I have with John Meier's philosophy of miracle relates immediately to what I see as the limitation of his definition of "history" and "historical". Cf. p. 94. Cf. MJ2, 510.
40 MJTM, 276. This is very close, if not indeed identical, to what Denis Alexander understands as the biblical understanding of miracle: "an unusual or extraordinary event brought about by God within a significant historical-religious context". *The Daily Telegraph*, 21.12.2001, 18.
41 MJTM, 270. MJTM, 354, n25. *Vera miracula sola virtute divina fieri possunt, quia solus Deus potest mutare naturae ordinem, quod pertinent ad rationem miraculi.* S.T. 3, 43,2.
42 MJTM, 272.
43 MJTM, 272. MJTM, 355, n39 R.Garrigou-Lagrange, *De Revelatione per Ecclesiam catholicam proposita*, (Rome, 1950). 2:40: *Factum a Deo productum in mundo, praeter ordinem agendi totius naturae creatae.* Cf. above, our discussion on the validation of the miracle of the walking on the water, cf. pp. 224ff.
44 MJTM, 272.
45 ODCC, 180-1.
46 MJTM, 273. MJTM, 356, n.43, Letter of M. Blondel to J. Bricout, in *Revue du clergé français,* April 15, 1904, 405.
47 MJTM, 278.

48 Cf. p. 226.
49 CMM, 137-8. Ibid.
50 *The Daily Telegraph,* 21.11.01, 18.
51 Ibid.
52 HST, *5.
53 Barrett, 75.
54 Cf. especially chapter 10, *St John's Gospel as Apologia.*
55 Bultmann, 70.
56 Brown, I, 502.
57 This complexity once more is well set out and analysed in Brown, I, Appendix I, 501-2.
58 Brown's conclusion, that it is difficult to see any use of *sémeion* in John as not referring to a miracle. Brown I, 528.
59 Brown, I, 502.
60 Brown, I, 503.
61 Brown, I, 503-4.
62 Cf. p. 53f.
63 Brown, II, 1058.
64 Smith, G.D. ed., *The Teaching of the Catholic Church: a Summary of Catholic Doctrine,* London, Burns Oates and Washbourne, 1952, 22.
65 Tanner, II, *807.
66 Cf. p. 93-6.
67 V2AP, 308 Cf. 317, n.42. *Acta Apostolis Sedis,* Vatican II, vol. IV, 722-723.
68 Tanner, II, *807, Vatican I, Dogmatic Constitution on the Catholic Faith, Chapter III, *de Fide.*
69 DV4. Tanner II, 972-3.
70 GA, 57.
71 GA, 263.
72 GA, 268.
73 GA, 240.
74 Cf. Pailin, D.A., *The Way to Faith: An Examination of Newman's Grammar of Assent as a Response to the Search for Certainty in Faith,* Library of Ecumenical Studies, London, Epworth Press, 1969.
75 Cf. p. 98.
76 Cf. pp. 354-5.
77 Tanner, II, *807.
78 Cf. pp. 99-100.
79 Cf. pp. 88, 90-1. RM 2001, 450.
80 QHJ, 4-5.
81 LJCE, xv.
82 LJCE, 759.

COMMENTARIES ON
ST JOHN'S GOSPEL

The following are the commentaries on John which I have used in writing this book. Endnote references to commentaries on St John's Gospel mention only the author's surname, the volume if more than one, and the page number (Brown, I, 233).

Barrett, C.K., *The Gospel According to St John. An Introduction with Commentary and Notes on the Greek Text.* 2nd edition, London, SPCK, 1978.

Brodie, *The Gospel According to John: A Literary and Theological Commentary.* Oxford University Press, 1993.

Brown, R.E., *The Gospel According to John.* Two volumes, London, Chapman, 1971.

Bultmann R., *The Gospel of John,* Transl. G.R. Beasley-Murray *et al,* Oxford, Basil Blackwell, 1971.

Bruce, F.F., *The Gospel of John: Introduction, Exposition, and Notes.* Michigan, Eerdmans, 1983.

Carson, D.A., *The Gospel According to John,* Leicester, Inter-Varsity Press, Eerdmans, Michigan, 1991.

Haenchen, E., *Johannes Evangelium: Ein Kommentar.* Tübingen, J.C.B. Mohr, 1980.

Hoskyns, E.C., ed. Davey, F.N., *The Fourth Gospel.* London, Faber and Faber, 1947.

Hunter, A.M., *According to John.* London, SCM, 1968.

Lightfoot, R.H., *St Johns Gospel: A Commentary.* Oxford University Press, 1956.

Moloney, F., *The Gospel of John.* Collegville, Minnesota, The Liturgical Press, 1998.

Mullins, M., *The Gospel of John: A Commentary.* Dublin, Columba, 2003.

Schnackenburg, R., *The Gospel According to John,* Volume I, Transl. Kevin Smyth, London, Burns and Oates, New York, Herder and Herder, 1968. Volume II, Transl. Cecily Hastings, *et al.,* London, Burns and Oates, 1980.

Westcott, B.F., *The Gospel According to John.* Originally published 1880. New edition, London, James Clark, 1958.

ABBREVIATIONS

ALGT — Mounce, W.D. *The Analytical Lexicon to the Greek New Testament.* Grand Rapids, Zondervan, 1993.

APO — Dulles, A. *Apologetics and the Biblical Christ.* London, Collins, 1963.

AS — Abbott-Smith, *A Manual Greek Lexicon of the New Testament.* Edinburgh, T and T. Clark, 3rd edition 1937.

BI — Megivern, J.J. *Bible Interpretation. Official Catholic Teachings.* Consortium Books, North Carolina, McGrath.

CBQ — Catholic Biblical Quarterly.

CCC — *Catechism of the Catholic Church.* London, Geoffrey Chapman, 1994.

CJH — Kaestli, J.D. Poffet, J.M, and Zumstein, J. *La Communauté Johannique et son Histoire. La Trajectoire de L'Évangile de Jean aux Deux Premiers Siècles.* Labor et Fides, Geneva, 1990.

CM — Dunn, J.D.G. *Christology in the Making.* London and Philadelphia, SCM, 1980.

COD — Allen, R.E. ed. *The Concise Oxford Dictionary of Current English,* 8th edition. Oxford University Press, 1990.

Davis — Davis, Stephen T. Kendall, D. and O'Collins, G. ed. *The Incarnation. An Interdisciplinary Symposium on the Incarnation of the Son of God.* Oxford University Press, 2002.

DFT — Latourelle, R. and Fisichella, R. *Dictionary of Fundamental Theology.* English Language Edition, ed. R. Latourelle, Slough, St Pauls, 1994.

DV — *Dogmatic Constitution of the Second Vatican Council on Divine Revelation Dei Verbum ("The Word of God").* The version used in this book is in Tanner, II, 971-981 (for Tanner, cf. below.)

EBT — Bauer, J. ed. *Encyclopaedia of Biblical Theology.* London, Sheed and Ward, 1970.

ECD — Kelly, J.N.D. *Early Christian Doctrines.* London, Adam and Charles Black, 1968.

EF — Bultmann, R. *Existence and Faith. Shorter Writings of Rudolf Bultmann.* Ed. and Int. Schubert Ogden. London, Collins, 1961.

EJ — O'Collins, G. *The Easter Jesus.* London, Darton, Longman and Todd, 1973.

ENTM — Finegan, J. *Encountering New Testament Manuscripts.* London, SPCK, 1975.

ET — Benoit, P. *Exégèse et Théologie.* Les Éditions du Cerf, Paris, 1961.

FG — Funk, R. and Hoover, R.W. and the "Jesus Seminar". *The Five Gospels. The Search for the Authentic Words of Jesus.* Scribner, New York, 1993.

FU — Bultmann, R. *Faith and Understanding.* Ed. Robert Funk and transl. Louise Pettibone Smith, New York: Harper and Row, 1969. This is a translation of most of the articles contained in *Glauben und Verstehen,* Vol. 1.

GEAT   Kraus, H.J. *Geschichte der Historisch-Kritischen Erforschung des Alten Testaments.* 2nd edition, Neukirchener Verlag, 1969. GA Newman, J.H. *An Essay in Aid of a Grammar of Assent.* New edition, edited and introduced by C.F.Harold, New York, Longmans, Green and Company, 1947.

GEL   Bauer, W. *A Greek-English Lexicon of the New Testament and Other Early Christian Literature.* Transl. W.FR. Arndt and F.W. Gingrich. 2nd edition, 1958. Chicago Univ. Press, 1979.

HDB   Hastings, J. *A Dictionary of the Bible.* 5 vols. Edinburgh, T. and T. Clark, 1900.

HJCG   Theissen G. and Merz. A. *The Historical Jesus: A Comprehensive Guide* by London, SCM, 1998.

HST   Bultmann, R. *The History of the Synoptic Tradition.* Translated John Marsh. Revised Edition 1968.

HTFG   Dodd, C.H. *Historical Tradition in the Fourth Gospel.* Cambridge University Press, 1965.

IAM   Ball, D.M. *'I am' in John's Gospel: Literary Function, Background and Theological Implications.* JSNTS, 124, Sheffield Academic Press, 1996.

IB   Laymon, C.M. ed. *Interpreters' One Volume Commentary on the Bible.* London, Collins, 1972.

IFG   Dodd, C.H. *The Interpretation of the Fourth Gospel,* Cambridge University Press, 1953.

IJ   Ashton, J. ed. *The Interpretation of John.* Edinburgh, T. and T. Clark, 1986.

INC   O'Collins, G. *Incarnation.* New Century Theology, London, Continuum, 2002.

INT   Brown, R.E. *An Introduction to the New Testament.* London, Doubleday, 1997. [INT Brown]. Klijn, *An Introduction to the New Testament.* Transl. M. van der Vathorst-Smit. Leiden, Brill, 1967 (INT Klijn).
        Kümmel, W.G. *Introduction to the New Testament,* London, SCM, 1966.

ITQ   Irish Theological Quarterly.

JCM   Bultmann, R. *Jesus Christ and Mythology.* New York, Charles Scribner's Sons, 1958.

JEC   Schillebeeckx, E. *Jesus: An Experiment in Christology.* Transl. H. Hoskins. London, Collins, 1979.

JPGG   Casey, M. *From Jewish Prophet to Gentile God; The Origins and Development of New Testament Christology.* London and New York, Routledge, 1991.

JQ   Hengel, M. *The Johannine Question.* Transl. John Bowden. London, SCM, 1989.

JR   Dunn, J.D.G. *Jesus Remembered. Christianity in the Making, Vol.1.* Eerdmans, Grand Rapids, 2003.

JSD   Dreyfus, F. *Jésus savait-il était Dieu?* Paris, Cerf, 1984.

JTS   *Journal of Theological Studies.*

JUIF   Caron, G. *Qui son les "Juifs" de l'évangile de Jean?* Recherches 35, Quebec, Bellarmine, 1997.

JVG   Wright, N.T. *Christian Origins and the Question of God. Volume II, Jesus and the Victory of God.* London, S.P.C.K., 1996.

JW   Bultmann R. *Jesus and the Word.* Transl. Louise Smith and Erminie Lantero. London, Collins, Fontana Books, 1958.

LJCE   Hodgson, Peter C. ed. *David Friedrich Strauss. The Life of Jesus Critically Examined.* London, SCM, 1973.

LVT   Zorell, F. *Lexicon Hebraicum et Aramaicum Veteris Testamenti.* Roma, Pontificium Institutum Biblicum, 1968.

MGI   Hick, J. *The Myth of God Incarnate.* London, SCM, 1977.

MJ1   Meier, J.P. *Rethinking the Historical Jesus.Volume One: The Roots of the Problem and the Person.* New York, Doubleday, 1991.

MJ2   Meier, J.P. *Volume Two: Mentor, Message, and Miracles.* New York, Doubleday, 1994. (JMJ2).

MJTM   Latourelle, R. *The Miracles of Jesus and the Theology of Miracles.* Transl. O'Connell M.J. New York, Paulist Press, 1988.

MLM   Bockmuehl, Markus, *This Jesus: Martyr, Lord, Messiah.* Edinburgh, T and T Clark, 1994.

ND   Neuner, J, and Dupuis, J. *The Christian Faith in the Doctrinal Documents of the Catholic Church.* London, Collins, 1983.

NJBC   Brown, E. Fitzmyer, J.A. Murphy, R.E. ed. *The New Jerome Biblical Commentary.* London, Geoffrey Chapman, 1989. (The system of numbering of this commentary we adopt in this book will be the article number, followed by a colon and the paragraph number of that particular article (all bolded), followed finally by the unbolded page number, e.g. NJBC, **42:75**, 653).

NRSV   *The New Revised Standard Version Bible; Catholic Edition.* Copyright (c) 1993 and 1989. Division of the Christian Education of the National Council of the Churches of Christ in the United States of America." Electronic edition, *Catechism and Scripture Disk for Windows,* London, Chapman.

NT   Novum Testamentum.

NTA   Hennecke, E. *New Testament Apocrypha.* Transl. R. Mc L.Wilson, Vol I, London, SCM, 1963. Vol II London, SCM, 1965.

NTH   Bruce, F.F. *New Testament History.* London, Oliphants, 1969.

NTHIP   Kümmel, W.G. *The New Testament: The History of the Investigation of its Problems.* Transl. S. Mclean Gilmour and Howard C. Kee. London, SCM, 1973.

NTI   Wickenhauser, *New Testament Introduction.* New York, Herder and Herder, 1958.

OC   Moule, C.F.D. *The Origins of Christology.* Cambridge University Press, 1977.

ODCC   Cross, F.L. & Livingstone, E.A. ed. *The Oxford Dictionary of the Christian Church.* Oxford University Press, 1974.

PCB   Black, M. and Rowley, H.H. *Peake's Commentary on the Bible.* Revised Edition London, Nelson, 962.

PJ   Robinson, J.A.T. *The Priority of John.* London, SCM, 1985.

QHJ   Schweitzer, A. *The Quest of the Historical Jesus.* A Critical Study of its Progress from Reimarus to Wrede. Transl. W. Montgomery. London, A. and C. Black, 3rd edition, 1954.

RGG   Religion in Geschichte und Gegenwart.

RL   Barker, M. *The Risen Lord: The Historical Jesus is the Christ of Faith.* London, SPCK, 1996.

RM   Alexander, D. *Rebuilding the Matrix: Science and Faith in the 21st Century.* Oxford, Lion, 2001.

RNT   Robinson, J.A.T. *Redating the New Testament.* London, SCM, 1976.

RSG   Wright, N.T. *The Resurrection of the Son of God. Vol.3, Christian Origins and the Question of God.* London, SPCK, 2003.

SHJ   McArthur, Harvey K. ed. *In Search of the Historical Jesus.* London, SPCK, 1969.

Tanner   Tanner, N. P. ed. *Decrees of the Ecumenical Councils.* II Vols. London & Washington, DC, Sheed & Ward and Georgetown University Press, 1990.

Taylor   Taylor, V. *The Gospel According to St Mark: The Greek Text, with Introduction, Notes and Indexes.* 2nd edition London, MacMillan, 1966.

TGI   Green, M. ed. *The Truth of God Incarnate.* London, Hodder and Stoughton, 1977.

TJC   Hahn, F. *The Titles of Jesus in Christology. Their History in Early Christianity.* London, Lutterworth Press, 1969.

TROC   Trocmé, É. *The Formation of the Gospel According to Mark.* Transl. Pamela Gaughan. London, SPCK, 1963.

UFG   Ashton, J. *Understanding the Fourth Gospel.* Oxford, Clarendon Press, 1991.

V2AP   of R. Latourelle, ed. *Vatican II Assessment and Perspectives, Twenty-Five Years After (1962-1987),* Volume One, New York, Paulist Press,Mahwah, 1988.

VGT   Moulton, J.H. and Milligan G. *The Vocabulary of the Greek Testament. Illustrated from the Papyri and Other Non-Literary Sources.* Michigan, Eerdmans, 1930.

YHWH   A transliteration of the divine name, often now designated *Jahweh.* In the Hebrew Bible, the consonants – *yhwh* appear with the vowel pointing of *Adonai,* Lord, because the Jews would not pronounce the divine name.

\\   If a Synoptic Gospel, e.g. Matthew, has instances of the same narrative in the other two Synoptists, i.e. Mark and Luke, then we will follow the convention to abbreviate by backslash lines \\, indicating synoptic parallels, e.g. Matthew 26:26-29\\.= Matthew 26:26-29, Mark 14:22-25, Luke 22:19-20.

INDEX OF AUTHORS AND SUBJECTS

SCRIPTURAL INDEX
OLD TESTAMENT

NEW TESTAMENT

383